UNDERSTANDING
LEARNING
DISABILITIES

Understanding Learning Disabilities

SECOND EDITION

Tanis H. Bryan
University of Illinois, Chicago Circle

James H. Bryan
Northwestern University

 Alfred Publishing Co., Inc.
Sherman Oaks, California 91413

Alfred Publishing Co., Inc.
15335 Morrison Street,
Sherman Oaks, California 91403

Library of Congress Cataloging in Publication Data
Bryan, Tanis H.
Understanding Learning Disabilities, second edition

Bibliography: p.
Includes index.
1. Learning disabilities. 2. Minimal brain dysfunction
in children. I. Bryan, James H., joint author. II. Title.
LC40704.B79 1978   371.9'28   77-25987
ISBN 0-88284-056-8

Preface to the Second Edition

Because this is the second edition, some comments should be made concerning the differences between the two editions. In this edition, we have retained much of the research orientation. We have updated the content and have also added information. Sections of the book dealing with intelligence, remediation, language development, information processing, reading, and current legislation were updated, expanded, and rewritten. The chapters concerned with the history and theoretical models of learning disabilities, the brain, and diagnosis are mostly unchanged. Because of numerous requests, we have also written a test manual covering the materials presented in this edition.

Finally, no book is written or rewritten without help from others. We are particularly grateful for the efforts of Roslyn Wheeler and Judy Felcan. Time and support were provided by the Illinois Department of Developmental Disabilities, for which we continue to be thankful. And we are grateful for Gerald Mahoney's thorough review of the manuscript. Lastly our thanks to those teachers and students who used the first edition, for providing us with feedback and the encouragement to do this revision.

TANIS H. BRYAN
JAMES H. BRYAN

Preface to the First Edition

Many parents find they have one, and all teachers at one time or another have at least one—namely a child who experiences great difficulty surviving our educational system and meeting the peer group's requirements for achievement. Through research, theories of assessment and intervention have evolved; and through public and private pressure, corrective programs have been developed in the past few years to help such children.

In writing this book, we have attempted to integrate what we have learned from clinical and research studies, but have been biased towards emphasizing the products of research. It is our belief that systematically gathered information is better than casually collected data, and therefore we have stressed research. Indeed, in making judgments about "truth," we have been cautious about relying on clinical data, not because we know that such data are wrong, but rather because we do not know whether the observations on which the data are based are correct.

The reader will note that the learning-disabled have been defined in a variety of ways. They are the brain-damaged, the poor reader, the poor speller, and the poor mathematician. In other words, the learning disabled are a melange of children with a variety of academic problems. Clearly, these children are not really alike in all important elements, but they all fall within the scope of the learning disability specialist. How they will be grouped, viewed, and otherwise treated in the future remains to be seen. More information is needed on the similarities and differences which exist among children labeled as learning disabled.

We have been critical of the field. It is a field of imperfect knowledge, imperfect programs and imperfect progress. Yet, so are all fields studied. We trust our criticism will not dim the enthusiasms of students, but rather will provide them with freedom from dogmas and inspire them to improve conditions.

Finally, no book is written without help from others. We are particularly grateful for the efforts of Jean E. Slater and Roslyn Wheeler, who served as right-hand women in tasks which required both hands. Time and support were provided by the Illinois State Pediatric Institute, for which we are quite grateful. Lastly, our thanks to those reviewers who offered valuable suggestions concerning the organization, style, and substance of the text.

TANIS H. BRYAN
JAMES H. BRYAN

Contents

I | OVERVIEW: THE DEVELOPMENT OF THE FIELD

The first three chapters of this book comprise an introduction to the field of learning disabilities and to the professionals who work in it, a brief history of its development, and also some definitions of its population. The first chapter examines the growth of the field, its organizations and professionals. It also discusses the laws, proposed regulations, and the funding which are germane to learning-disabled children. The second chapter briefly describes the work of the pioneers in this field and the various perspectives gained from their efforts. Finally, Chapter 3 presents the field's attempts to define the population of children to which it should address itself and also considers the ways in which investigators have attempted to classify children into increasingly refined groups.

Our presentation of this material rests upon several basic beliefs. It is important for the student to realize that as a professional dealing with learning-disabled children, his activities will be affected by a variety of influences and pressures. Professional groups can be important in determining just how and when the individual special educator will serve, since they often affect the enactment of laws and the establishment of regulations and ethical standards of conduct. Their lobbying efforts may determine who will educate the learning-disabled child, and what methods and funds will be used. Moreover, the special educator's audience is greater than the individual child: it includes parents, teachers, and other professionals. To be able to counsel these groups regarding the legitimacy of their demands, as well as any legal constraints involved, the special educator must keep up-to-date on contemporary social and legal events within the field. As is true of most modern professions, the burden of work does not justify ignorance of new developments.

While our historic overview of the development of this field is brief, such brevity should not minimize history's role in affecting contemporary practices. The particular practices and perspectives of the pioneers have been passed down to the current specialists and have had an important impact upon virtually all activities of the special educator. What the pioneers did and why they did it affect, to this day, the research, diagnoses, and remedial activities designed to help the learning-disabled child. Understanding the work of the early pioneers enables one to comprehend the myths, facts, and efforts of today's learning disability specialists.

In Chapter 3 we present definitions and classifications pertaining to the learning-disabled child. These important initial definitions attempt to identify those children who will be the objects of study and aid, as well as those who will not be. Definitions channel ones's efforts toward a particular population of children. In effect, they carve out the professional's "turf," excluding some professional groups from the claim of expertise and limiting one's own colleagues to a relatively narrow and well-defined assemblage.

These first chapters are intended to make you appreciate the issues confronting the field and the research and the drama that have gone into establishing this discipline. Most importantly, we hope you will increase your understanding of these children we hope to save from stereotypical thinking and hasty judgment.

1 | Introduction

This is a book about children who have problems learning in school. It is concerned with how we define such children, what we believe we know about their problems, the characteristics we associate with these problems, and the diagnostic and remedial procedures developed to help these children.

Who is the child with learning disabilities? The current working definition of this child is that developed by the National Advisory Committee on Handicapped Children. The definition is:

> Children with special learning disabilities exhibit a disorder in one or more of the basic psychological processes involved in understanding or in using spoken or written language. These may be manifested in disorders of listening, thinking, talking, reading, writing, spelling, or arithmetic. They include conditions which have been referred to as perceptual handicaps, brain injury, minimal brain dysfunction, dyslexia, developmental aphasia, etc. They do not include learning problems which are due primarily to visual, hearing, or motor handicaps, to mental retardation, emotional disturbance, or to environmental disadvantage (Clements, 1966).

The definition is not precise, because it includes many different types of problems. It is difficult for any diagnostician to be even reasonably certain of judgments concerning a child with learning problems. By what criteria does one define a disorder of listening, thinking, talking, or reading? Just what is a perceptual handicap? How might one recognize such a symptom? And how can one ever demonstrate the absence of an emotional disturbance when it is so difficult to diagnose its presence? And should a child be excluded from professional help because he is a member of a cultural minority? While there has been continuing dissatisfaction with the definition of learning disability, apparently, like the weather, no one seems to be able to do much about it. Extensive efforts by professionals, stimulated by pressure from legislators who were developing the Education for All Handicapped Children Act of 1975, resulted in so much disagreement they finally agreed the definition of 1969 should remain the standard definition. They also agreed that more research is needed to further delineate the characteristics of learning-disabled children (NaLDAP, 1976).

Problems of definition aside, there are many children failing to learn who are not blind, deaf, or dumb. A new profession devoted to serving the needs of these children has blossomed during the last dozen years. It has now reached the point where it advocates its own technology, jargon, institutional support, and fee structure. It has, to a considerable extent, achieved these initial hopes. The newness of the profession does not imply that the problems it confronts are new problems. Rather, it is the importance of these problems to our society and the perspectives by which their origins and solutions are viewed which have changed dramatically. Although views of the causes of learning problems were once very narrow and similar to beliefs in witches and demons as causes of deviant behavior, research and education have had a profound effect on our understanding of the learning-disabled child. The views of children with learning problems today are not associated with a few "eggheads" or disgruntled parents, but are presented by spokesmen, learning disability specialists, who have received specialized training and the status associated with that training.

FORCES OF CHANGE

What factors precipitated the development of this new field? One can only speculate as to their nature, but three forces seem to be particularly relevant. The first is the rapid advance of technology in the United States; the second is the advance made in educational technology during and after World War II; the third is recent medical advances.

Since 1947 one's survival in the modern world has become increasingly dependent upon his ability to understand technological advances. Learning how to use new home appliances or how to analyze a computerized billing or bank statement can present problems to the illiterate or poorly educated. The requirements for existing jobs have become increasingly tied to educational achievements, even though it is likely that many of the functions of the job do not require advanced training. The college diploma, whether relevant or not, has become a prerequisite for many jobs. Perhaps for this reason alone, the percentage of Americans 25 years or older who have completed four years of high school more than doubled during the decade of the sixties and jumped to 52.5 percent of the population. Likewise, the percentage of this age group who completed four years of college more than doubled, rising from 4 percent to 10.7 percent. A child failing to acquire academic skills can no longer be viewed with equanimity by a middle-class parent. The future of a child within this society who cannot read is very dim. Difficulties in school are serious ones indeed for the concerned parent. How can a child who is unable to read complete high school or receive a college degree and compete in the job market? Such parental and national concern for literacy is evidently much more intense within the United States than in other countries of the world. Downing (1972) reports that children in Finland and France may also have difficulty in learning, but this is of no great concern in these nations. Apparently, the American family is particularly worried about school failure, and well they should be, given this highly technical society.

Educational technology and changes in educational perspectives are additional likely sources for nourishment to the field of learning disabilities. *educational technological advances* As a result of the national crisis in World War II, new techniques were developed for teaching complex skills to soldiers and basic skills to illiterates so they could become soldiers. Since the war, the results of many workers, such as Grace Fernald, B. F. Skinner, and A. A. Lumsdaine, to name a few, filtered down to the educational system in the forms of individualized and programmed instruction and behavior modification. The emphasis within these views was upon the principles of learning and task analysis, not the personality of the child. These developments have permitted us to view individuals in more discrete and specific categories regarding their ability to meet the demands of the learning task. No longer can global judgments of children as lazy, stupid, or bad suffice. On the contrary, the field of learning disabilities has been free to develop lists of specific behavioral and learning characteristics viewed as relevant to school failure.

Finally, advances in medical technology have resulted in the appearance *medical technological advances* of increased numbers, and perhaps types, of developmental disabilities. Infants who once might not have survived gestation, or who suffered anoxia, low birth weight, birth injury, or condemning maternal infections like rubella, are now more likely to suffer developmental and learning risk" children, as they are more likely to suffer developmental and learning problems than infants who did not suffer these traumas (Graham, Ernhart, Thurston, and Craft, 1962; Werner, Honzik, and Smith, 1964).

In addition, and perhaps because of advances in medical technology, researchers within the learning disabilities area began to view failure to learn in terms of physical malfunctioning rather than familial retardation or emotional disturbances, labels associated with considerable stigma within our society (Nunnally, 1961). The discovery that failure to learn could be caused by brain damage rather than genetic deficiencies or some failure of the parents to help their child grow emotionally and socially has relieved many concerned parents. Until these developments they were reluctant to publicly express their fears; and they were hesitant to press schools and legislatures for assistance.

MEETING THE CHALLENGE

What effect might these social forces have had upon the field of learning disabilities? Clearly, there are different variables by which one can measure the development of a field. One measure is the number of professionals still needed. The number of college students pursuing learning disabilities as a career is such that the number of professionals in one major organization, the Council for Exceptional Children, more than doubled in two years (D.C.L.D. *Newsletter,* 1973). At least twenty-nine states now have certification requirements which specify the courses and hours which must be completed by future learning disability teachers. There appears to be growing concern for a tightening of the standards governing the conduct and training of the learning disability specialist (D.C.L.D. *Newsletter,* 1973).

Another reflection of professional growth is the estimate of the number of children who require learning disability programs and the cost of such programs. Illinois, for example, estimated that $18,330,400 in nonfederal funds was to be spent on learning disability programs and that an additional $9 million was needed. In 1971 these figures of nonfederal spending for learning disabilities in Illinois increased to $15.5 million to be expended and an additional $22 million needed to provide adequate and appropriate services. It was estimated that within Illinois 9,900 children would be served in 1970, but that an additional 15,000 should but would not receive such help. By 1971 these figures increased to 12,500 children to be served and an additional 17,500 who should but would not receive aid.

More recently the federal government has been increasing its assistance. One source, Title IV, G of the Model Demonstration Program for Children with Specific Learning Disabilities, has programmed more than $3 million for fiscal year 1974–75 and has increased the figure to $5 million for fiscal year 1975–76. In January, 1977, the Bureau of the Educationally Handicapped was funding thirty-eight Child Service Demonstration Centers (Kukic, 1976).

Dr. Edward Sontag of the Program Development Branch of the Bureau of Educationally Handicapped reported that congressional appropriations for Child Service Demonstration Centers has been increased by 80 percent for the fiscal year 1977, from $5 to $9 million (NaLDAP Centerfold, 1976). The Education for All Handicapped Children Act of 1975 specifies the proportion of funds to be provided to the states by the federal government for providing special education and related services to handicapped children. The allocations are specified as 5 percent for the fiscal year ending September 1978; 10 percent, 1979; 20 percent, 1980; 30 percent, 1981; and 40 percent, 1982. Congress is thus authorized to spend $100 million for fiscal year 1976; $200 million for 1977; and so on. Of this approximately one-sixth will be allocated to provide services for children with learning disabilities (learning-disabled children represent 2 percent of the 12 percent of children who can be labeled as handicapped). Although we recognize the distinction between what is allocated and what is actually appropriated, this kind of federally based concern and legislation is a good indicator of the escalating interest and concern for learning disabilities research and remediation.

It is estimated that as much as 28 percent of the elementary school population within the United States suffers from a learning disability (Clements, 1966; Bruinincks, Glaman, and Clark, 1971). One research study, however, reported that 41 percent of the kindergarten and first-grade children within their school district were categorized by teachers as exhibiting characteristics associated with learning disabilities and in need of the services of trained personnel (Rubin and Balow, 1971).

The problem of learning disabilities has drawn increased attention from federal and state legislatures. Federal and state agencies have played two major roles. The first has been encouraging, by funding and legislation, universities and state departments of public education to establish teacher training programs and intervention programs for children with learning disabilities. The second has been establishing laws specific to the provision of services to children. Thus, the legal profession has become involved in problems of labeling and placement of children in special education settings.

State and national agencies became active in defining the field of learning disabilities in the mid-sixties. The National Society for Crippled Children and Adults, in part supported by the National Institutes for Health, organized three task forces to study the status of the field. Task Force I (Clements, 1966) reported on definitions and terminology used to describe learning-disabled children; Task Force II defined educational, medical, and health-related services relevant to these children; Task Force III (Chalfant and Scheffelin, 1969) focused on related research data. These three short publications encapsulated the directions, interests, and problems in the field.

In 1966 Congress passed legislation which created Title VI of the Elementary and Secondary Education Act. This established programs of funding grants to state departments of education and funds for the establishment of the Bureau of Education for the Handicapped.

In 1969 Senator Ralph Yarborough, chairman of the Committee on Labor and Welfare, reported that between 500,000 and 1.5 million children were in need of learning disability intervention programs and that only 18 percent of these children were estimated to be receiving this help. Yarborough introduced a bill, passed by the 91st Congress, entitled the Children with Learning Disabilities Act. This act mandated the federal government to facilitate the development of the field of learning disabilities as a separate entity within special education. The act led to the authorization of experiments, surveys, demonstrations, and professional training for education personnel either teaching or preparing to teach learning-disabled children. Model centers to develop special educational treatments and make these treatments available to other programs for learning-disabled children were authorized.

The most recent encompassing federal legislation to provide services to handicapped children is the Education for All Handicapped Children Act of 1975 (Public Law 94–142). While this act has its roots in federal laws developed since the late 1950s, PL 94–142 is a major effort to provide adequate and appropriate special education and related services to all handicapped children. This law specifies procedures to be followed in providing a free public education to handicapped children. The law defines special education as specially designed instruction to meet the unique needs of handicapped children. An individualized education program is defined as a written statement for each handicapped child developed by appropriately prepared persons. This statement is to include annual goals, including short-term instructional objectives, a description of the specific educational services to be provided, the projected date for initiation and anticipated duration of such services, and the appropriate objective criteria and evaluation procedures for determining, on at least an annual basis, whether instructional objectives are being achieved. The state educational agency is required to submit a plan for providing services, a plan which is to be available to the general public before it is submitted. The local educational agency is to: maintain records of the individualized education programs; establish procedural safeguards which assure education for children in least restrictive environments (the state must justify removal of handicapped children from the regular educational environment); the state must specify that assessment procedures and materials will not be racially or culturally discriminatory and will be administered in the child's native language; and no state can use only one procedure to determine the appropriate educational program for a child. Public hearings and consultation with handicapped persons, as well as their parents and teachers, must also be provided by state educational agencies. Parents or guardians of handicapped children may examine all relevant records, and must be given written prior notice if the education agency is going to alter the child's placement.

Parents or guardians have the right to complain and receive an impartial due process hearing conducted by persons not involved in the education or care of the child. If still unhappy, parents may appeal to the state educational agency, which is charged to conduct an impartial review of the problem. At this hearing, parties may be accompanied by a lawyer and by special education professionals. Both sides have the right to present evidence, confront, cross-examine, and compel the attendance of witnesses, and to have a written or electronic verbatim record of the hearing. If there is still unhappiness, the aggrieved can appeal the problem to the state court or district court of the United States.

When states are found not to be in compliance with PL 94–142, the commissioner of education can stop federal payments to the noncompliant school district. During this time, the child can either remain in the current educational placement or be placed in a public school program, according to the parents' wishes.

The states have met the challenge of learning disabilities in a variety of ways and with varying speeds. Legislatures in some states (e.g., New York) define the type of child to receive help and demand that public schools render appropriate services; others (e.g., Maryland) provide the funds and allow the departments of public education to make these funds available to those school problems which they deem particularly urgent. In recent years twelve states have proposed legislation which refers specifically to learning disabilities. Four states, Connecticut, Florida, Hawaii, and

Massachusetts, used the term *learning disabilities* in their legislation. Nevada used the term *perceptual impairments,* Pennsylvania used *brain damage,* while California and Colorado adopted the term *educationally handicapped* (Kass, Hall, and Simches, 1969). Whatever the predilection of the state, more than two-thirds had legislated services directly or indirectly to learning-disabled children by 1976.

The School Code of Illinois as amended may be exemplary of trends in legislation for handicapped children. This act specifies that school districts must screen, identify, and locate all handicapped 3- and 4-year-old children, make appropriate in-depth studies of these children, make plans to deliver noncategorical services, and involve parents and community agencies in such efforts. The act incorporates the lowering of the age for which services are to be provided, specifies what schools must do to establish these programs, indicates the date by which school districts must be in compliance, and explicates the standards which must be used for hiring teachers in order to get state reimbursement. As part of the Education for All Handicapped Children Act of 1975, incentive grants are being offered to the states to increase the number of programs available for children ages 3 to 5 years. In addition to money generated by counting the same preschoolers under the larger formula in PL 94–142, states will receive an additional $300 for each child ages 3 to 5 (pending appropriation).

State certification requirements for teachers of learning-disabled children vary from state to state. Some have stringent criteria. Minnesota requires teachers to have twenty-four hours of college credit in learning disability courses. Twenty-nine states now have explicit certification requirements for the learning disability teacher (D.C.L.D. *Newsletter,* 1973). Other states have not established requirements, either because of indifference or because of a noncategorical approach to learning problems (e.g., Massachusetts).

The passage of laws does not guarantee conformity or success. There have been a number of landmark court cases in which aggrieved parents, unhappy with the decision or procedures by which their children have been labeled and placed in special education programs, have brought their problems before the judiciary system. Since 1967, the courts have been increasingly active in intervening in the affairs of school districts. In 1967, Judge Skelly Wright, in the Hobson vs. Hanson case, ruled that the method used by school personnel in Washington, D.C., to test ability and achievement for the purpose of class placement was illegal. The result of this decision was that the school district was ordered to eliminate this tracking system of school placement on the basis that it created de facto segregation. We know that similar cases have been or are continuing to be heard in both California and Massachusetts.

Complaints revolve primarily around the issues of labeling, of diagnosis, of placement, and of the parents' opportunity to be heard in the decision-making process (Cruickshank, 1972). A new twist is being added in a number of cases. Parents are suing for damages because their child did not receive an appropriate education; that is, the child failed to achieve to the level the parents believed he should have achieved. In one case a child was labeled as having a learning disability in the first grade, received special help from a learning disability teacher for one year, and was then discharged from the remedial program. When the child reached junior high school, she started receiving failing grades in her academic courses. The parents argued that the school failed to adequately remediate the child's problem and dismissed the child from the remedial program prematurely.

One can only agree with Cruickshank's belief that for the judicial system to have to specify for educators what is good and bad is an "awful indictment of educational leadership at the local level" (1972, p. 387).

Indictments are usually followed by action, and this particular one is no exception. The federal government has recently taken a very active and intrusive role in influencing the professional activity of the learning disability specialist. The freedom of professional services and activities will be considerably reduced if these proposed regulations are adopted. Indeed, such a combination of already existing laws and these proposed regulations will define exactly what special education is, how many need it, and how to go about doing it. No doubt good intentions exist on both sides; nonetheless, the federal takeover of special education means considerable federal control. Just how much and what kind of control may result, and has already resulted, will be discussed when we consider diagnosis.

The manner in which school districts respond and the degree to which they can respond will be a critical issue in special education and learning disabilities in the coming years.

Public concern about handicapped children is sufficiently aroused to have supported such publications as *The Rights Handbook* and *How to Organize an Effective Parent Group and Move Bureaucracies.** State and nationally defined rights of parents and children as well as the school districts' responsibility for the evaluation and placement of children is outlined in the first publication. The second publication contains information that will help parents educate themselves on how to lobby, form groups, change laws, raise money, and make headlines—even how to develop their own private special education school or class.

Partly in response to such public concern, the Council for Exceptional Children, a national organization serving parents and professionals involved with handicapped children, in 1973 formed an organized lobbying mechanism which has been titled Political Action Network (PAN). Using a pyramid structure to disseminate information about public policy and governmental actions germane to the handicapped, PAN reflects a nationwide organization which permits the mobilization of enormous numbers of persons to react to critical issues at critical moments in special education. Indeed, the greatest public response to an education issue was received by the White House, and urged President Ford to sign the Education

---

*Both publications are available from the Co-ordinating Council for Handicapped Children, Room 1075, 407 South Dearborn, Chicago, Illinois 60605.

for All Handicapped Children Act of 1975. Much of this response was a result of the efforts of PAN (Ziemer, 1977).

The field of learning disabilities is firmly entrenched in the laws, if not yet the customs, of this country. It is unfortunate that the already overburdened judicial system is required to define and enforce the provision of services to children. But their involvement, along with that of the legislature, virtually guarantees the maintenance and growth of services to children. In all likelihood, our judges, lawyers, parents, and school administrators have benevolent aims, which may far exceed the capacities of the learning disability specialist to deliver; the goals have outstripped the available technology.

REFERENCES

Bruinincks, R., Glaman, G., and Clark, C. "Prevalence of learning disabilities: Findings, issues, and recommendations." Research Report, June, #20, Department of Health, Education, and Welfare, 1971.

Chalfant, J. and Scheffelin, M. "Central processing dysfunctions in children: A review of research." NINDS Monograph No. 9. Bethesda, Md.: U.S. Department of Health, Education, and Welfare, 1969 (Task Force III).

Clements, S. D. "Minimal brain dysfunction in children." NINDS Monograph No. 3, Public Health Service Bulletin #1415. Washington, D.C.: U.S. Department of Health, Education, and Welfare, 1966.

Division for Children with Learning Disabilities Newsletter, 1973, *iii,* No. 1.

Downing, J. "A cross-national investigation of cultural and linguistic mismatch in fourteen countries." Paper prepared for the World Federation for Mental Health Conference, Tucson, Arizona, November, 1972.

Graham, F. K., Ernhart, C. B., Thurston, D., and Craft, M. "Development three years after perinatal anoxia and other potentially damaging newborn experiences." Psychological Monographs, 1962, 76 (No. 3).

Kukic, S. J. The Washington Scene. *Division for Children with Learning Disabilities Newsletter,* 1976, 4.

NaLDAP *Centerfold,* November, 1976.

Nunnally, J. C. *Popular Conceptions of Mental Health, Their Development and Change.* New York: Holt, Rinehart & Winston, 1961.

Rubin, R. and Balow, B. "Learning and behavior disorders: A longitudinal study." *Exceptional Children,* 1971, 38, 293–299.

Werner, E. E., Honzik, M. P., and Smith, R. S. "Prediction of intelligence and achievement at ten years from twenty months pediatric and psychologic examinations." *Child Development,* 1968, 39, 1063–1075.

Ziemer, C. W. "PAN: Working to make the reality equal to the promise." *Illinois Council of Exceptional Children Quarterly,* 1977, 26, 13–17.

2 | Historical Background and Theoretical Models

To understand this developing profession and its methods of assessment and remediation, one must examine its history. The more recent influences upon the development of the field of learning disabilities stemmed from two parallel sources. One was Kurt Goldstein, a German physician. His ideas influenced pioneers Alfred Strauss and Heinz Werner. They in turn founded a whole school of American professionals, among them Laura Lehtinen and William Cruickshank. The second source was the founder of Gestalt psychology, Max Wertheimer. His ideas influenced Wolfgang Kohler and Kurt Koffka, who developed a view of human behavior which was adopted by Goldstein, among others, and strongly influenced the direction in which the field of learning disabilities developed. Goldstein and Wertheimer shared a mutual interest in relating brain activity to behavior and, what is particularly important to the student of learning disabilities, to learning processes.

PIONEER RESEARCH

In the beginning (middle 1800s), notions of phrenology dominated perspectives of the causality of normal and abnormal behavior. Phrenologists believed that one could achieve considerable predictive and explanatory precision by studying and mapping the bone structure of a person's skull. The phrenologist's ability to feel bumps would unlock the secret of man's complexity to science. Needless to say, this venture was not spectacularly successful. But it was not a total failure either, since it set up a perspective that could be and was challenged.

Broca and Wernicke

Broca's aphasia

A particularly important antagonist to the phrenologists was the physician Paul Broca. He rejected the bump-feeling method of diagnosis, but retained the position that specific parts of the brain were related to specific human processes. Of particular importance was that Broca had two patients who had lost the ability to talk during their middle years. Broca labeled this symptom *aphemia*. Alas for the two patients, but to the advantage of science, the two men died during Broca's lifetime. Broca performed autopsies on the two brains and reported both had suffered atrophy of a section of the brain, the third frontal convolution in the left side of the frontal hemisphere. Ultimately, this finding became part of contemporary jargon; the loss of the ability to speak is called *Broca's aphasia* or *expressive aphasia*. More important, for the first time there had been an empirical demonstration that there was a relationship between damage to a particular section of the brain and an observable symptom in man.

During the same period (1860–1880) more than one investigator rejected the phrenologists' perspective and devoted their efforts to the study of the relationship of brain structures to motor behaviors. Fritsch and Hitzig (1870) mapped the motor cortex of dogs through the use of galvanic currents, cut out parts of the brain in an ablation procedure and demonstrated alterations in the dogs' motor movements. Monk (1881) performed ablation experiments with dogs and monkeys focusing upon the brain locale for the visual system. Monk was successful in demonstrating that blindness, partial or total, could be induced through physical assaults upon the occipital lobe of the cortex. Ablation of one side of the occipital lobe would produce partial blindness so that the visual field of both eyes was limited (homonymous hemianopsia), whereas ablation of both sides was necessary to produce total blindness.

Monk

By 1874 so much progress had been made in the study of the relationship of parts of the brain and aphasia, loss of the power of speech, that one investigator, Karl Wernicke, declared that "everything was known that was necessary for the understanding of aphasia" (Schuell, Jenkins, and Jimenez-Pabon, 1965). This statement may carry the errors associated with overenthusiasm; nonetheless, it is safe to say these scientists made discoveries which still stand as truths today.

Wernicke

Optimism was not Wernicke's chief contribution to science. That was, instead, his refinement and extension of Broca's position on aphasia. Wernicke believed that Broca's aphasia was one type of loss of speech, a loss in the motor ability to produce words. He demonstrated another type of aphasia, the inability to understand the speech of others. This was not a defect in hearing, nor stupidity, but rather that speech which was formerly comprehensible could no longer be understood. The loss of the comprehension of speech became known as *Wernicke's aphasia* or *receptive aphasia*. Wernicke asserted that the location of brain damage which would result in the loss of speech comprehension was the temporal lobe of the cerebral cortex. He also hypothesized that there are neural connections between the temporal lobe, Wernicke's area, and the frontal lobe, Broca's area. In essence, there is a connection between the front and left sides of the brain. Damage to this connection would result in another type of aphasia, now called *conduction aphasia*. Symptoms typically include neologisms, nonspecific vocabulary, and jargon. Wernicke was apparently correct and his observations refined our knowledge of speech disorders.

The pioneering efforts of these scientists influenced investigations of the causes and treatments of aphasia and made significant contributions to our understanding of this malady (Geschwind, 1968). They also influenced perspectives and techniques employed by the learning disability practitioner. Hundreds of thousands of children are being exposed to diagnostic procedures which involve analyses of *receptive, expressive,* and *integrative* processes irrespective of whether the child has speech, writing, or arithmetic learning problems. The model originated by Karl Wernicke for the analysis of aphasia was adopted by modern psychoeducational specialists and applied to the study of virtually all types of learning problems not associated with obvious emotional turmoil. Even those investigators who turned away from the hope that brain dysfunction could be correlated with learning problems in young children apply this process of analyzing skills within this trichotomous classification scheme.

The major assumption implicit in the efforts of Broca and Wernicke was that specific centers localized within the cerebral cortex governed particular activities. In spite of the multitude of important contributions made by these men, their assumptions did not go unchallenged.

Jackson and Head

John Hughlings Jackson (1864) was a great clinician who criticized localization theory. His argument was that words were not speech; therefore, ablation or destruction of brain centers which destroyed words did not necessarily mean the brain area responsible for speech was affected. The search for the spot responsible for speech was seen as futile because speech is not saying individual words. Speech was controlled by the whole brain rather than a segment of cortex. Jackson anticipated modern linguistics by his emphasis on the sentence as a major unit for the communication of ideas.

Jackson viewed the human brain as the most advanced model on the evolutionary continuum. Various brain processes increase in complexity, specialization, and integration as one ascends the phylogenetic scale. The most numerous interconnections among parts of the brain are found at the highest level of brain development. Man's brain is not simply a collection of locales, each independent of the other, but parts of the brain are intimately linked. Jackson reasoned that any defect, whether it affected speaking, reading, writing, or conceptual tasks, would not be identified by localizing a single cortical point. Many segments of the brain in various ways and to varying degrees would be involved. Destruction or damage to any one part of the brain would reduce a man's skills on a general level. Later we will see how this work affected another pioneer in this field, Kurt Goldstein.

Sir Henry Head, a student of Jackson, devoted his life to fulfilling Jackson's notion that empirical data on aphasic subjects should be collected. The "Golden Rule," voiced a great deal today, was to assess what a person could and could not do but to avoid attaching labels to the person. Above all, he was an empiricist who vigorously followed this golden rule, demanding that careful observations, not quick categorization, direct the investigator. Head undertook an extensive clinical research program. He produced two volumes which reported his clinical observations of aphasics and standardized tests of aphasia. He tested and later retested twenty-six World War I veterans who had suffered some type of brain damage which resulted in aphasic conditions.

By modern day psychometric standards, Head's test is woefully inadequate. Nonetheless, a systematic observational technique had been generated. Spurious clinical observations and inferences would be replaced by more reliable techniques. On the basis of his observations Head devised a classification scheme for aphasic symptoms which included four categories. These categories were *verbal defects,* difficulty forming words; *syntactical defects,* saying words with an incorrect emphasis or joining words inappropriately; *nominal defects,* difficulty understanding the meaning of words; and *semantic defects,* difficulty stringing words together in a logical way.

This categorical system did not prove to be viable because there was too much overlap among the categories. Aphasics did not suffer one or another of these defects, but demonstrated symptoms from more than one category. As is frequently the case, pure types were hard to find.

Head's radical contributions did not end with the development of a test of aphasia, a category system or extensive data collection. It extended to one more issue, one very much with us today. This is the nature of intelligence and the relationship between intelligence and language. Contrary to his contemporaries, such as Paul Pierre Marie, Head believed that aphasics did not suffer generalized intellectual impairment. They were not stupid because they suffered brain damage; they were unable to demonstrate their intellectual capacities because of their language difficulties. Clearly, the direction of therapeutic intervention would be, and still is, very much affected by which side of this controversy a clinician, school administrator, or politician takes.

The work of two investigators, Theodore Weisenburg, a neurologist, and Katherine McBride, a psychologist, should be included in a review of "ancient history." Weisenburg and McBride made two contributions, one substantive and the second methodological. Substantively, they developed a classification scheme wherein aphasia was divided into four categories: *predominantly expressive,* problems in speaking and writing; *predominantly receptive,* problems in understanding the speech of others; *expressive-receptive,* all types of language performance is affected; and *amnesic,* difficulty evoking words. This classification system was used in the pioneering work of Helmer R. Myklebust to describe aphasia in young children. On the methodological side, these investigators were the first to compare in a systematic rather than intuitive way the performances of aphasics with nonaphasic subjects. The development of a standardized test for abnormality now had a control or comparison group incorporated.

Goldstein

Last, but certainly not least, is the very important work of Kurt Goldstein, a German physician who treated brain-injured soldiers in World War I. Goldstein was a significant worker within Gestalt psychology. In this framework, it was believed that patients did not suffer separate losses of functions as a result of brain damage induced by war wounds. Goldstein described their problems as reflecting a de-differentiation, a systematic reduction of all abilities. Particular abilities were not affected; whole systems were affected. He viewed aphasia as reflecting brain damage, never mind that the damage might be undetectable, in which a disintegration of the nervous system resulted in a wide variety of symptoms. One symptom was difficulty in discriminating between foreground and background, a major tenet of Gestalt psychology. The experimental tests of this ability are typically visual in nature, such as discriminating one important feature in a visual display from the background in which it is shown. Goldstein felt that aphasic patients have such problems; but he employed the terms *foreground* and *background* not only to refer to visual processes, but to other processes as well. He used the terms in a metaphorical, not literal, sense. It was Goldstein's view that brain-damaged subjects had difficulty separating the important from the unimportant, the necessary from the trivial. The implication of this analysis was that brain-damaged patients suffered *perceptual impairments*. Goldstein speculated that brain-damaged patients suffered decreased receptivity and increased reaction time because of a disintegration of the nervous system. This resulted in an abnormal spread and duration of stimulus influences within a person. Essentially he argued that whatever stimuli were affecting the individual would affect him for too long and in too many ways. Today this is known as *perseveration.* In addition, these patients were described as being abnormally affected by external stimuli. Today this is known as *distractibility.*

It should be noted that within this frame of reference it was, and still is, suggested that brain-injured people pay too much attention to stimuli, perseverate, and yet are highly distractible. Until we know which stimuli, at what intensity, and in which sequence evoke which response we are faced with an impossible contradiction.

Goldstein went on to describe brain-damaged patients as exhibiting emotionally disabling reactions. The brain-damaged were viewed as lacking in initiative and rigid in their responses. They failed to have either the energy or the creativity to engage in new action and were presumed tied to a fixed pattern of responses in order to govern their daily existence. A shift in these fixed patterns or environmental arrangements resulted in their undergoing a catastrophic reaction, of great anxiety and behavioral disorganization. The patient's daily activity, rigidity, and lack of initiative were construed as reflecting, in part, an attempt to avoid a catastrophic reaction which would result from excessive stimulus input. Goldstein thus introduced concepts of psychic processes into the study of brain damage.

Because of Hitler's rise to power, two of Goldstein's contemporaries, Heinz Werner and Alfred Strauss, migrated to the United States in 1937. They spread Goldstein's views to colleagues and students in America and this resulted in the development of the field of learning disabilities. A specific and direct outcome of the substance of Goldstein's viewpoint is that area of learning disabilities known as "perceptual handicaps."

RECENT RESEARCH

In covering the period from the 1850s to about 1925 we focused upon those individuals whose work germinated critical substantive topics for the field of learning disabilities. Broca and Wernicke stimulated interest in brain localizations and the relationship of the brain to language; John Hughlings Jackson greatly influenced the bases of modern linguistics and clinical practices; Sir Henry Head designed a systematic analysis of aphasia; and from Kurt Goldstein emanated the foundations for the study of perceptual handicaps. All were giants in their time and still appear to be so today. Some ideas were correct, some incorrect; some were not carried far enough. But all were sufficiently provocative and explicit to challenge the status quo of their generation, to stimulate new ideas and new data, and to inspire their students and colleagues, who carried their work forward. It is hard to overestimate their contributions and easy to trace their influences on learning disabilities today.

Strauss and Werner

Alfred Strauss and Heinz Werner, located at Wayne County Training School near Detroit, Michigan, collaborated in studies of brain damage in mentally retarded children. By focusing upon children rather than adults, upon the intellectually incompetent rather than the competent, they brought about a courtship, if not a marriage, of the fields of neurology and education. The implication of their work was that learning might be inhibited by brain damage as well as character flaws or emotional turmoil. Educators were thus alerted to those cues which might be associated with brain damage in children, cues like hyperactivity and distractibility. In time, children who could be described as hyperactive, distractible, or disinhibited were labeled as suffering from the "Strauss syndrome." The views of Strauss and Werner, and later collaborators Laura Lehtinen and Newell Kephart, all under the influence of Kurt Goldstein, were to be widely disseminated in two volumes, both entitled *Psychopathology and Education of the Brain-injured Child.* Through these vehicles, probably the most influential books written in the field of learning disabilities, they argued that dull, or mentally retarded, children who exhibited hyperactivity, distractibility, and disinhibition, and those characteristics associated with brain-damaged adults as described by Goldstein, also suffered brain damage. Strauss and Lehtinen (1947) and Strauss and Kephart (1955) argued that children with learning problems may have suffered brain damage and that learning problems could therefore be organic rather than just genetic. In addition, children with brain damage will demonstrate a variety of behavioral symptoms.

As time passed, this view was perverted by many to the position that any child who exhibited these symptoms was likely to be suffering from some brain defect. Hence, competent but active, bright but distractible, and adequate but disinhibited children came to be viewed as brain damaged. This position is far removed from that originally advocated by Strauss, Lehtinen, and Kephart.

The Wayne county group was revolutionary in a variety of ways. They introduced the idea of comparable problems across developmental spans. Children, as well as adults, who suffered an insult to the brain could be hyperactive, distractible, and disinhibited. Because of this group's concern with individual differences among children of similar intellectual abilities, they greatly facilitated the concern with the development of methods of remediation tailored to meet the educational requirements of a learning problem. The assumption that school competence was highly predictable on the basis of general intelligence was now challenged, and questions were raised as to how one might tailor a specific educational program to meet the needs of the particular child. Further refinements were introduced into category systems used to place a handicapped child. Intelligence alone as a categorical system would no longer suffice. New programs and new institutions were born designed to be particularly suitable to the needs of brain-damaged children. If a child is unable to read, what are his perceptual skills? If a child is distractible, what is the effect of rearranging the furniture? If a child is hyperactive, what is his response to motor activities designed to be educational in and of themselves? The broad category of intelligence was replaced with a new perspective as to etiology (origin of causes) and remediation. The recommendations were not taken lightly. Sharp discriminations as to educational techniques with normal and learning-disabled children were initiated, and educators are, to this day, greatly influenced by them.

Orton

During approximately the same period, 1925 to 1948, the work of Samuel T. Orton, professor of psychiatry at the University of Iowa, played a very influential role in laying the foundation for the field of learning disabilities. Orton studied language problems, laterality of motor skills, and brain dominance in children. He described the problems of children with *strephosymbolia* in reading, speech, and writing. Orton observed that children with these problems had difficulty remembering the order of letters and sounds. He theorized that these disturbances were related to specific brain locations, reasoning that one side of the brain was dominant, while the other side was dormant and useless. His particular theories of brain processes have not stood the test of advances in knowledge, but Orton's procedures for remediating children's severe learning problems were brilliant, effective, and used in a variety of teaching methods today.

Orton's (1937) method of teaching can be described as a slow-motion phonics approach. We shall see later that this method has been demonstrated more effective than other methods in teaching reading to normal and deficit children, irrespective of the "type" of child (Bateman, 1964). Orton also developed an approach in which discriminations were made as to the defective styles of children. For instance, a child who cannot write may have difficulty because of very slow motor movement, or be unable to form the letters properly. This close examination of the separate movements needed to perform a given task is known as "task analysis" (Johnson, 1967).

In addition to devising effective remedial methods for teaching children with severe reading, writing, and speech problems, Orton made a number of other significant contributions. He related reading problems to language deficits. This set the stage for a viewpoint of learning-disabled children quite distinct from that of Strauss, Lehtinen, and Kephart. The emphasis was upon language and not upon perception skills. A society was created and named after him. This organization, the Orton Society, is active today, holds conferences, and publishes *The Bulletin of the Orton Society*,* and generally supports all efforts to improve research and study of language problems.

Fernald

Meanwhile on the West Coast at the University of California at Los Angeles, Grace Fernald developed a remedial clinic for a wide range of children. Fernald developed a remedial reading approach which could be used with

*Copies of the bulletin may be obtained from the Orton Society, Suite 115, 8415 Bellona Lane, Towson, MD. 21204.

severely retarded children or children with normal intelligence who were experiencing reading problems. The Fernald method is discussed further in Chapter 12.

The field of learning disabilities is a young one and the professionals trained by professors and colleagues associated with the Wayne County Training School, the Orton group, or the Fernald clinic are very active today. People like William Cruickshank, Newell Kephart, Samuel Kirk, Helmer Myklebust, and Laura Lehtinen—all influenced to some extent by the efforts of Strauss, Orton, and Fernald—were the professionals who defined and shaped the field of learning disabilities as we know it. These second-generation pioneers are our contemporaries.

DISABILITY MODELS

Whatever differences in theories and practices have separated these first- and second-generation learning disability pioneers, one similarity existed. They all generally held a perspective of man which was analogous with the *medical model*. Because of this perspective, the discipline of learning disabilities, until the very recent past, can be characterized as one holding a medical model of man.

The development of a discipline, such as that of teaching the learning disabled, is structured around the acceptance of a basic core of concepts and assumptions. Persons trained in this discipline use these concepts and assumptions as a frame of reference by which to view the world (Mercer, 1968). Measures, tools, and vocabulary develop around this common core of concepts, which the practitioners then use to solve the problems of their discipline. Practitioners come to believe and accept these concepts as self-evident.

There have been two dominant models which have served to guide the development and perspectives prevalent within the field of learning disabilities. One is the disease model of medicine; the second is the statistical or psychometric model. These models have been so influential in shaping the field of learning disabilities that they warrant some discussion.

Medical Model *(disease model)*

While there are many different medical models within the field of medicine (London, 1972), the disease model has shown great influence upon clinical practices of psychologists and educators. The disease model provides the practitioner with an approach which focuses upon the person with the problem, rather than upon the social milieu of that person, in searching for the source of the difficulty. The assumption is made that if the problem can be removed from that person he will be immune to it, irrespective of the social context in which it might occur.

Historically, the medical disease model developed as a conceptual tool to interpret the nature of biological disease processes in order to cure persons afflicted with disease. Historically and legally, physicians are concerned with the elimination of abnormal functioning. The physician's emphasis is upon the study, detection, and cure of such abnormalities. In the medical model perspective, normal becomes defined as that which has no "abnormal" signs. The patient is viewed in terms of a bipolar continuum in which placement at one end represents normal and at the other end represents being abnormal. Emphasis in this perspective is placed upon the identification and cure of abnormal characteristics, not upon the identification and facilitation of normal functions. Persons are labeled by what is wrong with them, and not what is right. In addition, the medical disease model focuses upon biological explanations for problems, and biological functions deemed important are those intrinsic to the patient. Pathology now becomes an integral part of a person. Social and cultural factors which may be related to etiology are ignored in this framework; organic malfunctioning is primary. The disease model regards its methods and findings as transcending social or cultural systems (Mercer, 1968). By and large, this is a heuristic model for physicians dealing with physical disturbances. Considerable question has been raised about this model when it has been extended from physical problems about which there is general consensus to other problems for which a physiological basis is unknown and technically beyond our ability to know.

Virtually all of the assumptions underlying the medical disease model have been challenged. Justified or not, these are some of the objections to this model. There is little evidence relevant to the biological foundations of many personality and educational problems. While a virus produces syphilis, does a virus produce reading difficulties, hyperactivity, or suicide? Is it reasonable to assume that the causes of problems transcend situations so that they can survive in the context of many varying social contexts? And, even if there is a physical base to whatever ails the student, patient, or client, does the disease model yield cures for these ailments? Finally, if a disease is "cured," how immune is the patient from further behavior problems if he is returned to the same social system?

Concern with the application of the medical model to psychological and educational problems is not limited to the fear that this perspective will lead the technician astray. Concern extends to the fear that this perspective may create more problems than it cures (Scheff, 1966). This fear is based upon two factors, the conservative strategy correlated with the medical model and the stigma often associated with diagnostic labeling.

The medical disease model induces in its practitioners a concern about the elimination of abnormality. The safest strategy is to assume that a client or patient is somehow and somewhere pathological. If a practitioner is to commit an error of diagnosis, it is best to commit a safe one, to diagnose the presence of illness which is not there rather than to diagnose the presence of health when there might be pathology. If the diagnostic error is on the safe side, all a patient may lose is a little time and a lot of money. On the other hand, if the practitioner commits a diagnostic error and concludes the patient is healthy when he is ill, the cost to the patient may be his life. Hence, the medical model tends to be associated with a conservative strategy, one that dictates the diagnosis of illness unless proven conclusively otherwise.

This particular strategy is reasonable when one is dealing with a physical illness. But is this strategy reasonable when applied to school, social, and emotional problems? The answer to this question is critically dependent upon the laws and stigma surrounding the particular problem. To be labeled as mentally ill by a physician will frequently and with appalling rapidity result in a citizen's loss of freedom and civil rights (Scheff, 1966). To be labeled learning disabled will mandate a school system to institute an appropriate educational program, often in a self-contained classroom. This will considerably alter the nature of an important aspect of a child's life. An adoption of the conservative strategy is based upon a diagnosis which in itself is based upon rather primitive guesswork; yet it can have significant life consequences for the labeled individual. In addition, the degree to which the label is associated with stigma, as is the case with diagnosis of mental illness (Goffman, 1961; Nunnally, 1961) and mental retardation (Christoplos and Renz, 1969; Jones, 1972) is the degree to which the conservative strategy may produce long-lasting, damaging effects for the patient.

Most of the initial conceptions of learning-disabled children have been based upon the disease model of medicine. Early workers in this field have perceived the locus of a child's problem within the child, and the cure for the child's ailment rested in changing the child. Children were described as having symptom complexes parallel to those observed in brain-injured adults. Children having school problems were seen as hyperactive, like the brain-injured adult; to experience perceptual problems, like the brain-injured adult; to perseverate, like the brain-injured adult; to show emotional lability, like the brain-injured adult. The search was on to locate the site and dynamics of the brain damage experienced by the child. The search has proved to be a failure, as there has been little success in finding that children with learning disabilities are brain damaged (Myklebust, Boshes, Olson, and Cole, 1969; Owen, Adams, Forrest, Stolz, and Fisher, 1971). It may well be that brain-injured children have learning disabilities, but that is considerably different from the assumption that children with learning disabilities have suffered an assault to the brain. As the empirical evidence yielded disappointing results in the search for damage, many professionals began to believe it foolish to invest so much time, energy, and resources arguing about which part of the brain might be damaged or underdeveloped. No doubt the search for brain-behavior correlates will continue, as it should, but the efforts will be concentrated within medical research centers rather than educational sites. The medical disease model will no longer be the only perspective in town.

Statistical or Psychometric Model

A second model, developed as a response by those disenchanted with the medical model, is the statistical model, in which the definition of normal is based upon the statistical concept of the normal curve. Whether one is normal or abnormal depends upon where a person's score falls on the distribution of scores from a population. Both ends of the curve are abnormal, as such scores occur infrequently. The score that falls toward the middle or mean of the distribution is not abnormal, because it occurs most often. Transposing the score to a person means that an abnormal person is one who stands out, has visibility due to being different. The normal person is one who cannot be differentiated from most members of that population, a person who is in effect invisible. The statistical model is presumed to be nonevaluative. An abnormal score means an infrequently occurring score. To make the inference that a person who obtains an abnormal score is, therefore, abnormal relative to his peers is based upon an arbitrary criterion. But tests are given to determine the status of some function or trait of importance to the person or to society, to describe and define socially valued characteristics. Evaluations of abnormality become impossible to avoid. Thus, it is bad to have a low IQ score and good to have a high one, even though both scores are equally deviant from the average IQ score. While descriptive statistics operate in a moral vacuum, individuals cannot.

Mercer (1968) has suggested that these two models, the statistical and medical, have become fused into the "clinical perspective." Practitioners who apply the clinical definition to troubled persons use the statistical model to define the existence of a problem and the medical model to diagnose and understand the dynamics of the problem. Children who obtain a score which is infrequent and which reflects a state or trait deemed undesirable are than investigated as if the score were symptomatic of some underlying physiological malfunction. The transposition of a low, undesirable score into a sign of pathology carries with it all the implications of the disease model of medicine. This occurs in the absence of any evidence that this sign has any important relationship to that person's biological functioning.

The importance of this perspective is that it has channeled the allocation of our resources into limited types of research programs congruent to the model. Data are lacking with respect to the learning disabilities field, but there is little reason to assume that it will differ in significant respects from the field of mental retardation. In the field of mental retardation, more than 50 percent of the retarded are described as having types of mental retardation which have no known biological involvements. Research funds, however, have been almost exclusively channeled into the study of organic factors in mental retardation. Thus, 99 percent of the resources have been directed toward the study of the biology of mental retardation, while funds have been very limited for the study of the emotional and social factors affecting the diagnosis of mental retardation (Mercer, 1973).

The remediation of the learning-disabled child might be facilitated by a diagnostic-remedial scheme emphasizing task analysis, social factors affecting the child and his labelers, and the emotional or motivational states of the child. But an adherence to the medical model in learning disabilities is likely to be less than optimal in advancing the current status of knowledge about these children.

Disenchantment with both the medical and psychometric models has resulted in the increasing popularity of what might be termed the "educational model." As proponents of the medical model have failed to yet relate central nervous system dysfunctioning to learning disability, and the psychometricians have failed to provide educational plans based on psychometric data, school districts across the nation seem to be going "pragmatic." That is, school districts are increasingly defining children as learning disabled if the children manifest any signs whatever of underachievement in academic subjects areas, whether or not the individual has potential for learning. One can sympathize with the school districts trying to make sense out of, and to act upon, the definitions of learning disabilities.

It seems that school districts have taken an adaptive route: they have simply labeled children failing to meet the demands of their school curricula as in need of help, ergo, learning disabled. While such an approach is likely to provide much-needed services to a variety of children, there are problems with it, both theoretical and practical. While educational institutions are not in business to promote science, it should be noted that this categorizing of children who fail for a variety of reasons under one conceptual umbrella is quite likely to retard our ability to understand the characteristics, processes, and problems associated with learning-disabled children. Certainly the professional learning disability specialist should resist the grouping together of such heterogeneous children. Practically, such use of the learning disability label has produced negative political repercussions from professionals in other fields (e.g., remedial reading teachers) who may justifiably claim an expertise in the rendering of services to such children, but who will be excluded from such services by virtue of such crude labeling.

As we describe the knowledge and practices related to the field of learning disabilities in subsequent chapters, the reader will surely become sensitive to the impact these models have had upon this field. These models are important, as they determine the approach we take and attempts we make to understand the child failing in school. Since their applications have such significant and enduring effects upon the immediate and future lives of the children we are trying to help, the importance of these models must be recognized.

REFERENCES

Bateman, B. "Learning disabilities—Yesterday, today, and tomorrow." *Exceptional Children,* 1964, 31, 167–177

Christoplos, F. and Renz, P. "A critical examination of special education programs." *Journal of Special Education,* 1969, 3, 317–379.

Geschwind, N. "Neurological foundations of language." In H. R. Myklebust (ed.), *Progress in Learning Disabilities, Vol. I.* New York: Grune & Stratton, 1968.

Goffman, E. *Asylums.* New York: Anchor Books, Doubleday & Co., 1961.

Johnson, D. J. "Educational principles for children with learning disabilities." *Rehabilitation Literature,* 1967, 28, 317–322.

Jones, R. "Labels and stigma in special education." *Exceptional Children,* 1972, 38, 553–564.

London, P. "The end of ideology in behavior modification." *American Psychologist,* 1972, 27, 913–920.

Myklebust, M. R., Boshes, B., Olson, D., and Cole, "Minimal brain damage in children." Final Report. U.S.P.H.S. Contract 108–65–142. Evanston, Ill.: Northwestern University Publications, June, 1969.

Orton, S. *Reading, Writing and Speech Problems in Children.* New York: W. W. Norton, 1937.

Owen, R. W., Adams, P. A., Forrest, T., Stolz, L. M., and Fisher, S. "Learning disorders in children: Sibling studies." *Monographs of the Society for Research in Child Development,* 1971, 36, No. 144.

Scheff, T. J. *Being Mentally Ill: A Sociological Theory.* Chicago: Aldine, 1966.

Schuell, H., Jenkins, J., and Jimenez-Pabon, E. *Aphasia in Adults.* New York: Harper and Row, 1965.

Strauss, A. and Kephart, N. *Psychopathology and Education of the Brain-injured Child.* New York: Grune & Stratton, 1955.

Strauss, A. and Lehtinen, L. *Psychopathology and Education of the Brain-injured Child.* New York: Grune & Stratton, 1947.

3 | Definitions and Classification Systems

As a new discipline is developed its practitioners devise terminology and classification systems to facilitate communication among those concerned with that field. The terminology and typologies are used to describe persons and procedures which appear to share common characteristics relevant to the goals of the labeler. For instance, the verbal skills of persons who score high on tests of intelligence may be of concern, whereas their height, weight, and eye color would not be. Classifications based upon the shared characteristics of a large population lead to the development and use of labels to categorize these characteristics, which, in turn, permits practitioners to make predictions and provisions for those so labeled. Sometimes a special language fosters better communication, but sometimes it obscures and confuses.

ESTABLISHING STANDARDS

A variety of labels have been generated to describe learning disabilities. A number of diagnostic classification systems have been devised and employed but remain untested. However, an overview of the labels used to describe learning disabilities leads one to conclude that virtually any child with any problem falls within the domain of the learning disability specialist. Any combination of characteristics, particularly socially undesirable ones, have been included as part of some syndrome. These laundry lists of socially maladaptive traits reflect both a wide variety in the types of difficulties included and great differences in the severity of the problems. Categories of dysfunction in learning disabilities thus range from severe organic deficits (e.g., choreiform syndrome, aphasoid syndrome, association deficit, cerebral dys-synchronization syndrome) to perceptual and behavioral problems (e.g., hyperkinetic impulse disorder, perceptual motor handicaps, attention disorder)(Clements, 1966). There is apparent consensus that such problems have been observed in some children, but that not all children will exhibit all or even many symptoms. One might assume that everyone is talking about the same behaviors when the identical terms are used or talking about different behaviors when different words are used, but studies to objectively define terms or investigate the reliability and validity of the nomenclature are rarely conducted.

An example of the types of problems we run into when we fail to have well-defined terminology and typologies can be seen in estimates of the incidence of learning disabilities. Estimates are required in order to know how many teachers to train and employ and how many facilities and resources will be needed. This is a critical administrative problem which must be solved well in advance of the appearance of problem children at the school door. But the estimate of incidence of learning problems is related to the definition which is used, and has varied from 1 percent to 41 percent of the school population. This very wide range exists because estimators have used different samples, defining criteria, instrumentation, and methods (Bruinincks, Glaman, and Clark, 1971, p. 5).

The difficulties in establishing consensually agreed upon definitions of learning disabilities stem from the application of varied theoretical and philosophical approaches to normal and atypical children. Some taxonomies have been developed from a perspective which emphasizes etiology and organically related problems (Johnson and Myklebust, 1967). Others have developed from a psychometric or psychological theoretical construct (Bateman, 1964; Kirk and Kirk, 1972). Some taxonomies have been the products of program development or the translations of what is known about controlling children's symptomatic behavior into their educational objectives (Cruickshank, Bentzen, Ratzeburg, and Tannhauser, 1961; Hewett, Taylor, and Artuso, 1969; Hewett, 1970). Others, which have nothing directly to do with learning disabilities, are nonetheless very much a part of the field. These represent systems to describe a theoretical viewpoint of child development and an educational program devised on the basis of this construct (Barsch, 1967; Doman, Spitz, Zucman, Delacato, and Doman, 1967). As Keogh has suggested, the psychoanalytic psychologist focuses on psychodynamic and personality functions, the general psychologist on perceptual functions, and the cognitive psychologist on intellect and cognitive style. "Disturbance, like beauty, may be in the eye of the beholder" (Keogh, 1971, p. 545).

Each of these taxonomies has resulted in educational programs, although claims regarding the success of these methods have not been adequately tested. The few which have been put to the test have not yielded encouraging results as to the soundness of the typology or the educational methods which stemmed from them. In spite of such shortcomings, professionals have struggled to improve their services to children experiencing school difficulties.

DEFINITIONS OF LEARNING DISABILITIES

Several definitions specific to learning disabilities have been used to delineate the boundaries of school services. There are many dangers involved in labeling children, because labels have been found to carry stigma while carrying little implication for remedial treatments (Rosenthal and Jacobsen, 1968; Seaver, 1973; Scheff, 1966). However small or great the dangers involved in labeling children as learning disabled, it is necessary, indeed critical, to set limits to the population to be studied and assisted. With limited resources, limited numbers of children can receive assistance. Attempts to define learning disabilities reflect attempts to devise a categorization system which aids in the development and the implementation of therapeutic efforts. Although children have stubborn ways of avoiding a clean fit into even the most narrowly limited categorization system, legislators still provide funds and legislation to protect children who need additional assistance and give direction to the kinds of children to be favored by remedial services. Additionally, such systems are intended to assist professionals to make sense out of their dealings with a heterogeneous group of children by narrowing interest to particular rather than to all children.

Task Force I, 1966

Several definitions of learning disabilities have evolved since 1962 (Kass, 1969). The most critical evolutionary change was the shift from a definition of cerebral malfunctioning as "minimal cerebral dysfunction" to a definition which made no reference to organic etiology. Nevertheless, both definitions perpetuated the assumption that the locus of damage or dysfunction was internal to the child. The first formal definition, government agency sponsored, was advanced by Task Force I cosponsored by the National Society for Crippled Children and Adults and the National Institutes of Neurological Diseases and Blindness of the National Institutes of Health (Clements, 1966). This definition linked learning problems and minimal cerebral dysfunction, and described a group of children who shared the common characteristic of minimal, often physiologically undetectable, brain damage. This definition read:

> The term "minimal brain dysfunction syndrome" refers in this paper to children of near average, average, or above average general intelligence with certain learning or behavioral disabilities ranging from mild to severe, which are associated with deviations of function of the central nervous system. These de-

viations may manifest themselves by various combinations of impairment in perceptions, conceptualization, language, memory, and control of attention, impulse, or motor function (1966, pp. 9–10).

Specialists were unhappy with this definition because it imposed on them the burden of detecting brain dysfunction. While gross damage may be relatively easy to detect, minimal dysfunction is not. The implication of organic distress presented the diagnostician with grave difficulties. The problem is that the educational diagnostician is limited to evaluation of intellectual and social behavior. The stronger the direct evidence for brain damage, such as seizures or paralysis, the less likely the diagnostic conclusion is to be "minimal" damage. The less direct the medical evidence, the more the reliance upon social and academic performance, and the more likely the diagnosis of "minimal brain dysfunction." By definition, the linkage of brain damage with learning disabilities through direct evidence becomes an impossibility.

The dilemma was resolved by the generation of another definition which makes no reference to organic etiology. The specification of central nervous system damage and the inference of the presence of minimal cerebral dysfunction were eliminated. In their stead was a reliance upon psychological variables as the criteria to distinguish learning-disabled children.

Children with Specific Learning Disabilities Act, 1969; the Discrepancy Definition

The National Advisory Committee to the Bureau of Education for the Handicapped, Office of Education, recommended the following definition, which subsequently was used for federal legislation concerning the funding of services for learning-disabled children. The 1969 Children with Specific Learning Disabilities Act defined this group:

> Children with special learning disabilities exhibit a disorder in one or more of the basic psychological processes involved in understanding or using spoken or written language. These may be manifested in disorders of listening, thinking, talking, reading, writing, spelling, or arithmetic. They include conditions which have been referred to as perceptual handicaps, brain injury, minimal brain dysfunction, dyslexia, developmental aphasia, etc. They do not include learning problems which are due primarily to visual, hearing, or motor handicaps, to mental retardation, emotional disturbance, or to environmental disadvantage (Children with Specific Learning Disabilities Act of 1969, PL 91–230, The Elementary and Secondary Amendments of 1969).

The development of the Education for All Handicapped Children Act of 1975 (PL 94–142) triggered organized efforts by professionals and legislators to include a new, improved definition of learning disabilities. There were many voices of dissatisfaction and many suggestions made for change.

Some complaints focused on the ambiguity of the 1969 definition (Hammill, 1974); others on the exclusion clause which eliminates children from minority subgroups and children with other handicapping conditions (Kirk, 1974). The main problem in changing the definition was succinctly expressed by Congressman Lehman: "No one really knows what a learning disability is" (Cong. Rec. daily ed. at H 6655, July 29, 1975). The result of these definitional efforts is that there remains little agreement on those conditions defining a specific learning disability. There are no hard research data collected on a sufficiently large sample to state with certainty which are the common characteristics of all learning-disabled children. The only point of agreement among professionals is that a major discrepancy exists between such a child's expected achievement and his actual ability which is not the result of other known and generally accepted handicapping conditions or circumstances (Federal Register, 1976, p. 52404).

Thus it came to pass that the 1969 definition of learning disabilities was incorporated into PL 94–142. But the proposed rules and regulations which may govern the labeling of children with learning disabilities expanded upon the idea of a discrepancy between achievement and ability, and also the areas in which the discrepancy should occur in order for a child to be defined as learning disabled. Specifically, the child must not be achieving commensurate with his or her age and ability levels in one or more of eight areas, when provided with learning experiences appropriate for the child's age and ability levels. In addition, the child must exhibit a discrepancy between achievement and intellectual ability in one or more of these areas: oral expression, reading comprehension, written expression, basic reading skills, listening comprehension, mathematics, calculation, mathematics reasoning, and spelling (Federal Register, 1976, p. 52407).

While the proposed regulations considered providing educational definitions of the myriad of terms associated with learning disabilities (e.g., dyslexia, minimal brain dysfunction), the Office of Education decided to leave such terms undefined for the present.

This definition removed the burden from the professional to establish the presence of minimal brain dysfunction as a prerequisite for initiating remedial efforts for children with learning problems. No doubt it also lessened the stigma or anxiety of parents and their children so diagnosed. Essentially, children who evidenced some difficulty with the development or use of language and related skills were to be perceived as reflecting something other than emotional or intellectual deficits. In effect, children who showed these language-related problems, if they were not otherwise socially or intellectually impaired, were to be within the purview of the learning disability specialists.

There are, however, several problems associated with discrepancy definitions of learning disability. First is the concept of potential. When one argues that a child has potential, does he mean for mastering the particular content being taught at that moment, for mastering substantive materials in related areas of concern, or for always being able to master any material?

Second, how is potential assessed? Potential is typically assessed by a child's performance on some kind of intelligence test. But performance on intelligence tests is quite variable for individual children and such performances are affected by the atmosphere of testing, the nature of the tester, the child's motivation, and other external and basically irrelevant factors (Masland, 1969).

Moreover, while intelligence test scores are reasonably stable for many children, some children show wide variations from year to year (Honzik, Macfarlane, and Allen, 1948). Since 9 percent of the children will show variations of IQ scores of 30 points or more from one testing to another, how is one to know which particular score reflects the "true self"? Because of these and other factors, intelligence test scores are not particularly powerful predictors of school performance, although perhaps they are the best predictors currently available. Given the variations in motives and interpersonal relationships which might facilitate or inhibit a high score on an intelligence test, aside from simple "pure intellectual abilities" (whatever that might mean), a prediction of potential school achievement on the basis of such scores becomes particularly hazardous. Any estimates of actual intelligence, not to mention potential ability, are open to frequent serious errors and such errors have repercussions for both the research and diagnostic-remedial efforts within the field of learning disabilities. Moreover, even assuming a reliable estimate of potential and achievement discrepancies, how can educational programs be generated from such test scores (Torgeson, 1975)?

Advances in knowledge are often the result of narrowing the population studied, devising ideas or theories concerning the population, and generating applicable remedial techniques. The 1969 definition and the 1976 rules and regulations provide the means to limit the learning disabilities population to specifiable characteristics. Of course, definition is still broad and ambiguous; many terms remain undefined; we are still dependent on inadequate assessment techniques to determine the existence of a severe discrepancy; and many children are omitted from the definition. Hopefully, national recognition of this definition problem along with both the needs for research and the specifications for assessment should result in improvements in the methods by which children are defined as learning disabled. In the meantime, investigators have developed means to further limit the populations to be defined by using their own perspectives and theoretical interests. These definitions span the range from exclusions of other types of handicaps to inclusions of children with certain psychometrically defined characteristics.

Psychoneurological Learning Disabilities

Two important contributors to the field of learning disabilities are Doris Johnson and Helmer Myklebust (1967). They advanced a definition of learning disabilities based on their research of psychoneurological problems; and they incorporated an emphasis upon neurological dysfunctions. As a result of their specific concentration in these areas, however, their definition does not account for children who are retarded or have problems resulting from or compounded by socioeconomic conditions. This means that the child's achievement and behavior have been disturbed as a result of some dysfunction within the brain which results in altered processes, but not a generalized incapacity to learn (1967, p. 8). This definition incorporates the philosophy that the brain and behavior are significantly intertwined in a way which can be specified by careful diagnostic evaluation and corrected by appropriate teaching techniques. By this view, the learning disability represents a shift in brain processing of information which affects a child's achievement, but not his potential to achieve.

Maturational Lag

Another definition specifies normal potential in light of academic failure, but incorporates the idea that this reflects a maturational lag (Bender, 1938). A "maturational lag" refers to a time lag in the development of certain skills relative to others (deHirsch, Jansky, and Langford, 1966). The concept of the brain and its relationship to behavior is again included, but rather than believing that this is a result of a shift in the way the brain works, it is suggested that parts of the brain mature at different rates. If one part is slower in development than others, the result will be a strange array of skills and deficits as observed in learning-disabled children.

Definition by Exclusion

Learning disabilities have also been defined on the basis of the exclusion of other possible problems (Lerner, 1971). If a child is not deaf, blind, severely retarded, or very poor, yet is having learning problems, he must have a learning disability. This definition reflects the first stage in the diagnostic evaluation whereby other explanations and associated treatments are excluded. It permits further delineation of the responsibilities for intervention by professional groups into the affairs of children and schools. But school problems may be associated with a variety of situational conditions and children may share few characteristics aside from the "symptom" of school difficulty. This definition allows a most heterogeneous array of children to be grouped as similar although they are likely to be no more similar to one another than to any same-aged peer.

CHARACTERISTICS OF CHILDREN WITH LEARNING DISABILITIES

As previously mentioned, Task Force I (1966) was concerned with the development of a consensually agreed upon definition of learning disabilities, then called *minimal cerebral dysfunction*. In addition, this group set about

trying to describe the symptoms and signs by which such children could
be identified. The problems in so doing were admittedly great. Systematically
gathered information as to which signs and symptoms were associated with
each other and with particular types of children were not, and are still
not, available. Some of the terms being used, such as poor school achievement, are so general or vague that they have virtually no value. In other
cases, there are many terms which describe the same behavior or many
behaviors covered by one term (e.g., excessive motor behavior and hyperactivity). In an attempt to categorize all of the symptoms cited in the literature, preliminary categories of signs and symptoms were established. These
are included with accompanying examples (Clements, 1966, pp. 11–13).

  a. Test performance indicators
    1. Poor geometric figure drawing
    2. Poor performance on group tests
    3. Scatter on the subtests of the WISC
  b. Impairments of perception and concept-formation
    1. Impaired discrimination of size
    2. Impaired discrimination of right-left and up-down
    3. Impaired judgment of distance
  c. Specific neurologic indicators
    1. Many "soft," equivocal, or borderline findings
    2. High incidence of left and mixed laterality
    3. Hyperkineses (hypokineses)
  d. Disorders of speech and comprehension
    1. Impaired discrimination of auditory stimuli
    2. Slow language development
    3. Mild hearing loss
  e. Disorders of motor function
    1. Frequent delayed motor milestones
    2. General clumsiness or awkwardness
    3. Frequent tics and grimaces
  f. Academic achievement and adjustment
    1. Reading disabilities
    2. Spelling disabilities
    3. Poor printing, writing, or drawing ability
  g. Disorders of thinking process
    1. Poor ability for abstract reasoning
    2. Difficulties in concept-formation
    3. Poor short-term and long-term memory
  h. Physical characteristics
    1. Excessive drooling in the young child
    2. Food habits often peculiar
    3. Easy fatigability
  i. Emotional characteristics
    1. Reckless and uninhibited
    2. Poor emotional and impulse control

      3. Low tolerance for frustration
   j. Sleep characteristics
      1. Body or head rocking before falling into sleep
      2. Sleep abnormally light or deep
      3. Excessive movement during sleep
   k. Relationship capacities
      1. Poor group relationships
      2. Socially bold and aggressive
      3. Frequently poor judgment in social and interpersonal situations
   l. Variations of physical development
      1. Frequent lags in developmental milestones (e.g., language)
      2. Physically immature
      3. Physical development normal or advanced for age
  m. Characteristics of social behavior
      1. Social competence below average for age and measured intelligence
      2. Behavior often inappropriate for situation and consequences apparently not foreseen
      3. Possibly antisocial behavior
  n. Variation of personality
      1. Overly gullible and easily led by peers and older youngsters
      2. Frequent rage reactions and tantrums when crossed
      3. Excessive variation in mood and responsiveness from day to day and even hour to hour
  o. Disorders of attention and concentration
      1. Short attention span for age
      2. Motor or verbal perseveration
      3. Impaired ability to make decisions, particularly from many choices

Obviously, not all children with learning disabilities will experience all, many, or even several of these problems, and if they experience them, evaluations will vary according to the child's age and the predilections of the labelers. Moreover, it is highly unlikely that any of these characteristics are specific only to the learning-disabled child, however defined. At any rate, certain of these characteristics are more frequently cited than others in labeling children learning disabled. These characteristics appear to have been generated through clinical observation, a notoriously weak procedure for obtaining precise measures, rather than through systematic measurement of a large and well-defined sample of children. It appears that most people assume the presence of some or all of these characteristics, along with school difficulties, to be associated with the learning disabled. It is important to note that the inappropriateness of other explanations for the behavior in question, explanations such as mental retardation or emotional disturbance, is assumed when weighing the significance of these characteristics. The ten characteristics most frequently mentioned are:

   1. Hyperactivity (motor behavior which is not demanded by the situation or the task involved and which is disruptive to the group or to the expectations of observers).

2. Perceptual-motor impairments (difficulty in coordinating a visual or auditory stimulus with a motoric act, such as copying letters of the alphabet).
3. Emotional lability (emotional outbursts which are not reasonably expected by observers on the basis of knowledge concerning the situation or the immediate past history of the child).
4. General coordination deficits (clumsiness).
5. Disorders of attention such as: *distractibility,* behavior which reflects the child's interest in things other than those on which he should be concentrating; *perseveration,* behavior which reflects the child's inability to change the focus of his attention even when the reason for his interest has changed.
6. Impulsivity (behavior which appears to reflect little thinking concerning its consequences).
7. Disorders of memory or thinking (difficulty in recalling material which should have been learned, or difficulty in understanding abstract concepts).
8. Specific learning disabilities (inability to learn or remember reading, writing, arithmetic, or spelling).
9. Difficulty in comprehending or remembering spoken language, deficits in articulation of speech or in expressing self verbally, using appropriate grammar and vocabulary.
10. Equivocal neurological signs (neurological signs which are not clearly associated with particular neurological problems but which are not clearly within the normal range of functioning).

TAXONOMIES OF LEARNING DISABILITIES

Initial models constructed to describe learning-disabled children were nested in the notion that these children had minimal cerebral dysfunction. Within this structure, there were two primary, but divergent, paths of model building. One focused upon the language development of the disabled child, while the second concentrated upon perceptual and motor development. These emphases led to ever finer observations, more discrete categories of behaviors, and new terms to describe the phenomena. Within these structures diagnostic labels became equivalent to shorthand communications among proponents of these models. It has often been the case that the utility of the scheme was unknown, or known but limited; nonetheless, the system has been absorbed by our profession.

We now review examples of taxonomies of learning disabilities in children. Systems based upon remedial techniques are discussed elsewhere in this text. In this section we are concerned with attempts to classify types of learning problems. The examples offered do not exhaust the efforts which have been made to describe learning-disabled children, but represent primary models. The systems which are reviewed include the psychoneurological model (Johnson and Myklebust, 1967); the psychometric model (Kirk and Kirk, 1972); an attentional deficit syndrome perspective (Dykman, Walls, Suzuki, Ackerman, and Peters, 1970); varieties of the perceptual-motor construct (Kephart, 1963; Barsch, 1967; Cratty, 1969) and a behavioristic paradigm (Hewett, 1970).

Psychoneurological

In the case of early models based upon language deficits, an analogy was made between adult and childhood aphasia. Aphasia in adults represents the loss of the ability to speak and is usually the result of a cerebrovascular accident (a stroke) or injury to the brain. Aphasia in children, however, is the absence of the development of language. The dynamics of brain injury were considered analogous insofar as it was believed that particular parts of the brain were malfunctioning and that malfunction was reflected in the language behavior of both child and adult.

One of the most influential theorists in the field of learning disabilities has been Helmer Myklebust. His descriptions of children experiencing language development delays or disturbances reflected one model used to describe adult speech deficits (Schuell, Jenkins, and Jimenez-Pabon, 1965). Myklebust, adopting the Weisenburg and McBride classification system used to describe adult aphasics, categorized children on the basis of whether they had difficulty in processing language inputs, or producing language, or a combination of both. Children, like adults, could be classified as having language problems which were predominantly receptive, predominantly expressive, mixed aphasia, and central aphasia. Children who were classified as having *receptive aphasia* evidenced difficulty in comprehending spoken language. These children failed to respond appropriately to the spoken words of others. Such children could hear, they responded to sounds, but the meaningfulness of the sounds escaped them. Examples given by Myklebust included the lack of responsiveness to a door bell or telephone, and difficulty executing simple commands. *Expressive aphasia* described children who could understand and respond appropriately to others' speech, but were unable themselves to express an idea, make requests, and otherwise engage in age-appropriate language behaviors.

There are different forms of expressive aphasia. Some children may be unable to recall a particular word, some may be unable to use grammar properly, and others may have difficulty voluntarily executing the motor pattern involved in speech even though no paralysis of any kind is present. *Receptive aphasia* is considered a more severe problem than expressive aphasia because it has reciprocal effects on expression. A child unable to connect meaning with sounds is going to have difficulty figuring out how to express feelings, events, and ideas. *Mixed aphasia* was used to describe children who demonstrated problems in both comprehension and expression of language. When the language deficit interferes with a child's ability to

TABLE 3-1: Stimulus characteristics of language-disabled children

Stimulus	Dimension		
	Receptive	Expressive	Mixed
Visual	Reading	Writing	Reading and writing
Auditory	Comprehending spoken language	Talking	Talking and understanding
Combined	Severe language problems	Talking and writing	

use language for cognitive processes, such as thinking to oneself or dealing with abstract concepts, the child is said to have *central aphasia*. Language problems were thus viewed as reflecting difficulties coping with stimuli or with the adequate production of responses.

In addition to the dimension receptive-expressive, Myklebust added another. He suggested that the nature of the stimulus was critical to the required response. Stimuli were catalogued as either auditory or visual. Hence, receptive aphasia could be further categorized on the basis of whether the problem was more or less related to dealing with auditory stimuli, such as understanding someone's speech, or visual, such as comprehending the written word. As in the case of mixed receptive and expressive problems, children could have difficulty with auditory and/or visual stimuli. Table 3-1 outlines this classification system with examples of the types of problems evidenced.

The 1954 Myklebust model was the product of a study of preschool-aged children who were failing to develop language. The purpose was to delineate how such children could be separated into primary diagnostic categories of aphasia, deafness, mental retardation, and emotional disturbance. Each of these categories were subject to diagnosis on the basis of developmental and behavioral data, but the category of childhood aphasia was most notable as a definition by exclusion. If the child was not deaf, retarded, or emotionally disturbed, the lack of language development was assumed to be the result of brain damage. The model of childhood aphasia was subsequently expanded by Johnson and Myklebust (1967) to describe children who were failing to achieve academically. This latter model carried forward the hypothesis regarding the assumed relationship of the brain processing of information as a cause for the failure of some children to learn to read, write, spell, and do arithmetic. The terminology used to describe these academic deficits incorporated the brain-deficit emphasis plus the auditory/visual and receptive/expressive dichotomies. The category of childhood aphasia became "psychoneurological learning disorders" and the role of the diagnostician was to specify the exact nature of this disorder.

Failure to learn to read in spite of adequate intelligence and instruction was labeled *dyslexia,* a term which carries the implication of an organic cause for the failure. This term had been used since the 1800s, but almost exclusively by members of the medical profession. *Auditory dyslexia* suggested the child had difficulty because of inability to adequately process information heard. *Visual dyslexia* referred to a failure resulting from difficulty in comprehending stimuli presented visually. In school talk, difficulty learning to read by a phonics approach would be indicative of a possible auditory dyslexia, while difficulty when taught by a whole-word approach might indicate visual dyslexia. *Receptive dyslexia* would be indicated if the child had difficulty comprehending what he read (word caller) and *expressive dyslexia* if the problem were related to writing.

Not all problems could be interpreted as the result of language deficits. Some appeared to be related to motor movements of the child. When a child had difficulty learning to ride a bicycle, manipulate a pencil, use scissors, or tie shoelaces, in the absence of any paralysis, the child was described as *apraxic.* Praxic problems were associated with poor eye-hand coordination, difficulty carrying on purposeful movement and inability to make use of objects (Waugh and Bush, 1972). The delineation of the breakdown in learning was further refined, or expanded, to analyze the ability to execute the specific skills each learning task required. For instance, a written language problem, *dysgraphia,* could be a function of difficulty manipulating writing utensils, inability to master syntactic principles of English or inability to remember what was to be written. The expansion integrated a number of other symptoms, or behavioral characteristics, associated with dyslexia. The "dyslexia syndrome" involved more than difficulty learning to read, as such children were observed to also have difficulty developing concepts about space and their position in space, concepts of time, and memory deficits. This translates to problems learning left from right; how to tell time; reversals in letters, words and numbers; and resulting difficulty in developing the necessary associations between sounds heard and letters seen.

There are certain inadequacies in this taxonomy. One problem is to what degree any complex set of stimuli can be classified as purely auditory or visual. Reading, for instance, is defined by Johnson and Myklebust as a "visual symbol system superimposed on auditory language" (1967, p. 148). If it is not possible to separate the stimuli, implied by the use of the term *predominantly,* to what degree can and must one aspect predominate over another for a child to be viewed as failing because of a breakdown in that system? Most children cannot be easily labeled as having exclusively receptive or expressive problems. And most stimuli cannot be easily categorized as exclusively auditory or visual. To the degree that people, processes, and tasks cannot be so classified, the taxonomy breaks down.

Irrespective of the limitations of this classification system, Johnson and Myklebust made important contributions to perspectives of language and school difficulties. They specified dimensions of language which may be critical to remediate school-related problems as well as how to implement such remediation. They brought diagnosis out of the clinic and into the classroom, and moved therapy away from affect and familial relations to innovative intellectual training of both children and learning disability teachers.

Attentional Deficits

According to Dykman, Ackerman, Clements, and Peters, children with learning disabilities "or the medical equivalent, minimal brain dysfunction" (p. 56) share a common syndrome characterized by a deficit in attention. Attention is defined as consisting of four components: alertness, stimulus selection, focusing, and vigilance. Difficulties children display in language, perception, or motor skills are interpreted as reflections of attentional problems, in particular those aspects of attention which require a child to get ready to do something *(becoming alert)* and concentrate on the relevant information for the appropriate length of time *(focusing)*. It is believed that attention is physiologically controlled by the reticular activating system, a diffuse network of fibers which begins in the spinal cord, enlarges in the brain stem, and connects with many other parts of the brain. Dykman et al. reason that if the reticular activating system controls attentional skills, a deficit in attention reflects malfunctioning in the reticular system. These authors have contributed some excellent laboratory research studies of learning-disabled and normal children, using a number of physiological and behavioral measures in their attempt to test their ideas concerning this etiology of learning disabilities. The differences so far reported between subject groups do not yet constitute a typology of learning disabilities, but the resulting group differences shed light on the direction this type of research may lead us in specifying behavioral and physiological correlates of learning disabilities.

Dykman and his colleagues have conducted a number of impressive experiments concerning the attentional deficit hypothesis. For example, in a study of impulsivity (1971), they found that children 6 to 12 years of age diagnosed as having minimal brain dysfunction were slower than comparison children to match appropriate motor movements (pressing one of two telegraph keys) to appropriate signals (green or white light flashes). The two groups of children did not differ in the number of incorrect responses, simply the speed with which they responded. A question remained, however, as to whether this difference in response is a function of some deficit in motor abilities or in attention. The same children were subsequently tested on a tone discrimination task in which they had to indicate which of two tones was higher or lower in pitch. A difference between the performance of the two groups was found, with the minimal brain dysfunction group committing more errors of judgment. Apparently, many of these errors were the result of this group's failure to remember one tone for the thirty-second period prior to the onset of the second tone. Finally, each child was given a differentiation task in which he was required to pull a cord attached to a coin dispenser to the appropriate tone stimulus. This response was reinforced for one tone, but not the other. Thus, there was an attempt to condition the child to pull the cord to the tone stimulus associated with reward more frequently than to the one associated with no reward. Prior to and during this task, physiological measures of the child's skin resistance, heart rate, and muscle action potentials were obtained. While these two groups of children were equally alert prior to the experimental task, it was the nondamaged children who maintained their physiological arousal during the task, not the minimally brain-damaged ones. Additionally, the latter group failed to show conditioning. The authors interpreted their results as indicating that minimally brain-damaged children suffer an "inability to persist in attentive efforts, the vigilance aspect of attention" (p. 62).

In a second series of experiments employing children who were experiencing school achievement difficulties, Dykman et al. (1971) replicated and extended their previous findings. Again, learning-disabled children committed more errors on a discrimination task, took longer to initiate and terminate a motor response, and demonstrated less electrical brain activity associated with initiating actions than did the control subjects.

The results of a number of studies suggest that learning-disabled children are less attentive than their nondisabled peers. Kawabe (1976) reviewed the literature pertaining to attentiveness of learning-disabled children and reported that they are more likely to be distracted by irrelevant features of the material with which they are working than their nondisabled counterparts. It is not so much then that such children are likely to be distracted by extraneous events in the environment, but rather they are likely to be distracted by irrelevent features within the task. Kawabe also cites the results of several experiments which indicate that learning-disabled children who are also hyperactive are especially likely to be unable to maintain vigilance on a task and also are likely to respond to improper cues as if they were appropriate ones.

Similar findings are reported by Whalen and Henker (1976) in their review of research on hyperactive children. They report that such children have difficulty in sustaining attention on a task when it has been structured and imposed by someone else. While Kawabe, Whalen, and Henker focused primarily on the results of laboratory-based experiments of attention, there are data from naturalistic classroom observation studies that also implicate the importance of attentional deficits of the learning-disabled child. Several investigators have reported that learning-disabled children spend less time in on-task classroom behavior than their nondisabled peers. It has been repeatedly found that learning-disabled children simply pay less time attending to assigned classroom tasks and activities than do their nondisabled peers (Bryan, 1974: Bryan and Wheeler, 1972; Forness and Estveldt, 1971). While the results of these studies do not link attention deficits to brain processes as hypothesized by Dykman and his colleagues, they do indicate that such deficits may well characterize many of the children labeled learning disabled.

There does seem to be support, then, for the position that learning disabilities are associated with deficits in maintaining attention to the environment. The characteristics which would appear likely to discriminate learning-disabled children from their nondisabled counterparts would be their adequacy in responding to instructions, their ability to persist on a task, the number of errors committed in the task, and the speed with which the child can initiate a motor movement. The outcroppings of these problems within the school would be the child's inability to comprehend and/or follow instructions, to memorize material and to determine what is or is not relevant to reinforcements within his environment. The work of Dykman and his colleagues seems particularly important. They have proposed an elaborate theory concerning attention deficits and are carefully and systematically gathering information relevant to it. Moreover, it is increasingly apparent that learning-disabled children do have attentional problems, and both careful theory construction and empirical tests of such theories are needed. Dykman and his colleagues have provided the field with such a theory and the empirical facts related to it.

Perceptual-motor Development

Other researchers have addressed themselves to the motor development of children and have categorized their observations along quite different dimensions. Three such theorists are Newell Kephart, Raymond Barsch, and Bryant Cratty. While various theorists may use different terminology when discussing their observations, it should be noted that when discussing perceptual and motor skills, the behaviors being described are essentially the same: namely, the execution of motor movements by developing children. The major difference between these theorists may not be in what they observe but in their interpretation of these observations.

Kephart Newell Kephart (1960, 1963, 1967) suggests that children come to school unable to deal with symbolic materials because they have not assimilated critical experiences related to time, space, and movement. In this paradigm, cognitive development is intimately connected with muscular activity. Kephart makes distinctions between muscular activity which represents the primary acquisition of a skill and muscular activity which represents a learned pattern. Using the example of learning to walk, Kephart describes how walking itself is the end goal for an infant in the developmental period following crawling. Once the basic locomotor pattern is established, the child is in a position to use walking for a purpose, that is, to move from one spot to another. The shift in the acquisition of motor patterns to the utilization of motor patterns represents a giant step in the infant's development.

In Kephart's typology four motor patterns are thought to be particularly significant. One pattern is *balance and maintenance of posture*. This demands the child to maintain himself physically in space. Ability to maintain posture under varying conditions permits the infant freedom within his environment; failure sorely limits exploratory behavior. The second pattern is *locomotion,* which includes moving the body through space; walking, skipping, and running. The third category is *contact* or *motor activities,* which describes the child's manipulation of objects. As the child learns to reach, grasp, and release objects, he develops form perception and figure-ground relationships. *Receipt* and *propulsion* is the fourth basic motor pattern. This is typified by continuous movements which incorporate familiarity of movements of objects simultaneous with body movements. The example offered is throwing and batting a ball. At this point the child must be able to integrate extensive information regarding the nature of the physical environment, his relationship to this environment and the effects of the movements of himself and objects within that environment. When a child has this type of information integrated into his repertory of knowledge regarding himself and his environment, he can begin to explore the stationary, perceptual world. Ocular and tactile motor control result in *perceptual-motor match*, a stabilization of the child's world as he knows it motorically, visually, and through the integration of both of these channels. These patterns of motor activity are the components of the *motor-spatial system.*

But Kephart believes that the child must also develop the *motor-temporal system,* the integration of one's movements within the parameters of time. Higher learning is considered critically dependent upon the management of information within the time spectrum. The degree to which a child has difficulty executing simultaneous movements *(synchrony),* anticipating or committing acts in certain orders *(sequence),* or executing a sequence of acts with appropriate time intervals *(rhythm)* is the degree to which he is likely to experience difficulties in academic achievement.

Kephart's classification scheme was extended to diagnosis and remediation techniques used with learning-disabled children. Children are assessed (and thus categorized) and treated on the basis of: balance and posture, body image, perceptual-motor match, ocular control, and form perception. Specific techniques are discussed in Chapter 12. To summarize, Kephart believed that difficulties observed in children's school performance are fundamentally related to defects in the development of basic motor activities. Without adequate development of the motor-temporal and motor-spatial systems, children are particularly vulnerable to learning problems in school.

Kephart's classification system and the associated diagnostic and remedial procedures emphasize motor movements and ignore language-related skills. While Kephart recommends the inclusion of language-related evaluative and therapeutic exercises, these tasks are of limited importance in his general approach.

The strength of Kephart's program rests not in teaching verbal or strictly academic subjects, but in the concrete programming advice it provides for teachers to assist children in extra-academic problems. Methods and materials are provided to improve skills which are not verbal or academic in the strict sense, but are skills which the child must master before he can perform academic tasks. For instance, Kephart suggests a program of progressive relaxation for the hyperactive child in which the child is taught to control his own movements. Or, noting the difficulties in sequentializing materials when reading, a problem noted in research studies of learning-disabled children, Kephart suggests how teachers might assist children to overcome this type of difficulty. One method he suggests is by using patterns to give the child an experience which will require him to progress from one stimulus demand to another. An exercise he found useful required only poker chips as materials. The teacher would lay out several chips in a line, alternating colors from red to blue. The teacher would then help the child learn to read the line of chips (Kephart, 1971, p. 306). As such, the Kephart approach provides potentially valuable activities for difficult-to-solve problems.

Barsch   Raymond Barsch developed a theory concerned with the maturation of movement outside the learning disabilities field which has been adopted by learning disability specialists (Lerner, 1971). The curriculum derived from the theory has been incorporated into many classrooms for learning-disabled children across the country. Barsch's theory, "movigenics," is a conceptualization of child development, particularly of a child's motor development.

There are ten ideas which form the foundation of "movigenics," as follows:

1. Movement efficiency is the key to life. To help a child learn to move adequately is a major goal of instruction.
2. Movement efficiency is required for man's survival. "The more efficient the movement of the individual—social, economic, academic, and physiological—the greater his survival chances." . . . "Learning is movement" (Gearheart, 1972, p. 39).
3. Movement occurs in an energy surround (Lerner, 1971, p. 100). As a person moves he must select from his environment information that helps him to survive (Gearheart, 1973, p. 39).
4. The percepto-cognitive system is the means by which man acquires information. Information is obtained through six channels: sight, hearing, touch, feeling, smell, and taste—the "sensitivity system" (Barsch, 1967). To learn well requires an efficient percepto-cognitive system.
5. The terrain of movement is space. Movement and, therefore, learning occur in space. Man must learn to control his movement in physical and cognitive space.
6. Developmental momentum thrusts the learner toward maturity. According to Barsch, maturity ("developmental momentum") continues till age 50 or so and then there is a slow descent.
7. Movement efficiency is developed in a climate of stress. Man exists

in a constant state of stress with more or less discomfort depending upon the efficiency of his percepto-cognitive system. Stress is seen as a necessary part of man's life, with distinctions made in degree and type experienced.

8. Human efficiency requires feedback. Man's "feedback system" permits him to know if he is performing effectively. The better the feedback system, the better the learning.

9. "Development of movement efficiency occurs in segments of sequential expansion" (Gearheart, 1973, p. 40). Development patterns move from simple to complex so that constant movements results in increasing complexity. A slowdown of any of the continuous segments affects the entire organism.

10. "Movement efficiency is symbolically communicated through the visual-spatial phenomenon called language" (Gearheart, p. 48). The ultimate criterion of movement is language.

Barsch developed certain curriculum guidelines for teachers which permit them to evaluate a child's performance on movement patterns and the degree to which the child is "performing in an increasingly complex manner in processing information through these channels from various distances in space and regardless of directionality of movement" (Gearheart, 1973, p. 40).

Barsch has had a great deal of experience working with physically and neurologically handicapped children as well as with learning-disabled children (Gearheart, 1973). This approach and accompanying viewpoint of children and education appear more applicable to young children and those who are more handicapped physiologically than to the learning-disabled school-age child.

Cratty An outstanding example of how a perceptual-motor approach to classification and remediation can be used with children with learning disabilities has been developed by Bryant Cratty (1969). Like Kephart's, the strength of this program is its guidance for behaviors described as problematic for learning-disabled children which are not specifically academic in nature. Cratty declares that the first kind of learning is motoric, that this is critically related to learning through the visual modality and that there are relationships between motor output and children's skills within the classroom. More specifically, he suggests that motor movement is the means by which we express intellect. One such example is the need for a child to be able to write down answers to a test or thoughts on some subjects. The translation, or expression, of learning and of intelligence is made through the motor mode of writing. Another specifically related example is that children are evaluated in school on tests which are timed. Not only must the child be able to perform the required motor task to demonstrate adequate learning, but must be able to do so in a limited time span. Speed of response is a factor which has been demonstrated to differentiate learning-disabled from academically successful children (Dykman et al., 1971). Thus, integrating motor skill learning with movements under timed conditions is an important adjunct to a learning disability paradigm. Cratty integrated the attentional problem noted in learning-disabled children to motor movements, suggesting that attention can be controlled by appropriate levels of motoric arousal, which is best achieved through moderate levels of physical exercise. Furthermore, Cratty suggests that using physical exercise and a games approach may alleviate motivational problems experienced by learning-disabled children. There is a side benefit, as children who are adept at playing games, particularly boys, are more likely to be valued by peers.

Cratty acknowledges the difficulty of expecting generalizations to remain valid from one type of learning to another. It cannot be guaranteed that teaching gross or fine motor movements to children will result in improved academic performance by learning-disabled children. While the empirical data are lacking, the observation is made that generalization of types of learning across situations will not occur automatically but needs to be taught. For these reasons, particularly the approaches offered to assist children in pre-academic skills of arousal and attention, and the realization that generalization of learning will not be automatic, it is believed that Cratty's program may offer a valuable approach to defining learning disabilities and to subsequent programming of intervention.

A Behavioristic Model

Frank Hewett's model reflects a marriage of the theory of child development and the technology of behavior modification applied to the needs of special education. Johnson and Myklebust (1967) based their taxonomy on the basis of medical model. Children's auditory and visual processing capacities and these sensory processes' interventions with each other provided the vantage point from which one might conceptualize the learning-disabled child. Hewett, relying upon our knowledge of child development and the responses necessary for the child to function adequately in school, has proposed a sequence of the development of skills and responses necessary for continuing educational mastery. The model thus presents a number of developmental stages through which diagnosis and treatment might be made. The first stage that must be reached by the child in order to learn is that development which enables the child to *attend*. Attention is defined as "the ability to focus on relevant cues in the environment" (1970, p. 48). The child's attention is assessed by means of rating scales; the behaviors which are thought to be critical by this assessment are as follows:

1. The child's focusing upon tasks presented by school authorities.
2. The child's preference for attending to external events rather than internal ones (e.g., lack of day dreaming).

3. The absence of repetitive behavior which interferes with learning (e.g., self-stimulation, rituals, or compulsive behaviors).
4. The absence of bizarre or "immature" beliefs.
5. The child's focusing upon the teacher at appropriate times.
6. The child's demonstration reflecting profits from instructions (e.g., retains and employs the instructional material given).

The second capacity that must be evident to produce learning is the *response,* obviously not entirely independent of attentional abilities. Hewett writes, "Noticing something starts the learning process; the child must next do something, that is, make a response, in order to learn" (p. 49). The behaviors of note within this response category include ratings of:

1. The child's failure to make a response
2. The child's showing repetitive errors under conditions where change of response should occur.
3. The child's range of interest, his willingness to try new or different tasks.
4. The child's willingness to interact with teacher or peers within a learning context.
5. The child's willingness to respond in different settings, e.g., the regular classroom, special education classrooms.

The third development necessary to produce learning within the classroom is the child's capacity to understand *order.* A "child must follow directions and develop order in his attending and responding" (p. 50). This means that the child, once he pays attention and is ready to respond, must learn that behaviors, such as bicycle riding or reading, represent sequential acts in which one thing is done before another. Hewett suggests the importance of the following observations in assessing the child's understanding of order:

1. Does the child follow instructions?
2. Is the child uncontrolled in learning? Is he impulsive?
3. Does the child disrupt the group?
4. Does the child finish his learning tasks?

The fourth prerequisite to learning consists of *exploratory* activities. Hewett writes, "Multisensory exploration provides the child with raw material, the basic facts which he needs in learning" (p. 51). Ratings are obtained with regard to:

1. Children's exploratory activity of their environments.
2. Children's dependency on others for choices of interests or activities.
3. Children's deficiency in learning because of motor, physical, sensory, perceptual, or intellectual difficulties.

According to Hewett, once the child masters the first four levels of this hierarchy, he will also be a member of a group. During the period of the first four levels, the child is "given, shown, and told" by others. At the fifth level, the child must orient himself to others, becoming sensitive to the means by which he may gain social praise and avoid social censure. Thus, *social* responses are thought critical in the development of adequate academic performance. Two items on which the child is rated are:

1. Does the child gain approval from others?
2. Is the child overly dependent on attention or praise from others? Will he only work with constant supervision and attention?

The sixth level within the learning hierarchy is that of *mastery*. This level of development is assessed by means of the child's attainment of the traditional academic and adjustment skills. Reading, writing, and arithmetic are part of the mastery level, but so are learning to tell time, avoiding dangerous situations, and self-care habits. Thus observations are made as to the child's functioning in:

1. Self-care behaviors.
2. Intellectual tasks, relative to his capacity.

Finally, the seventh level refers to *achievement* functions. "This is the enrichment level where self-motivation in learning is developed and where pursuit of intellectual and adaptive skills in depth is important" (p. 54). At this level, the child learns for the joy of learning, participates in class activities beyond the point of just following directions to do what one is told. Now the child becomes a participant in learning by such acts as "asking questions, volunteering for extra work, and researches out additional facts" (p. 54).

Hewett, incorporating a behavior modification paradigm into this sequence, also defines and assesses reinforcements for the child. Reward refers to "a positive consequence which tends to maintain or increase the strength or frequency of behavior associated with accomplishing tasks related to the achievement of educational goals on the developmental sequence" (p. 65). The child needs some kind of reward for the work in school to be worth doing. A smile from the teacher or a gold star pasted on a completed work sheet may provide such a reward. Children who have experienced failure are less likely to experience such rewards. Hewett thus includes an estimate of the child's responsiveness to reinforcements in his analysis of the child's developmental stage. These are rated according to an estimate of their occurrence as "always, sometimes, or rarely."

1. Child not rewarded by tangible rewards (e.g., food, money, tokens) in learning.

2. Child not rewarded by social attention in learning tasks.
3. Child not rewarded by finishing learning tasks.
4. Child not rewarded by multisensory experiences in learning.
5. Child not rewarded by gaining approval and avoiding disapproval for learning.
6. Child not rewarded by doing learning tasks correctly.
7. Child not rewarded by acquiring knowledge and skill.

Assessments of the child, according to the classification scheme proposed by Hewett, rely primarily upon rating scales completed by parents, teachers, or others familiar with the child. Hewett, however, has added further requirements for the evaluator, which appear particularly useful and needed. First, multiple observations or ratings of the child should be made. That is, rather than assuming that any rating reflects a stable trait or condition of the child or his world, it is imperative that the diagnostician make additional assessments after certain elapsed times. Changes of important functions to learning are recognized as possible, and adequate diagnosis demands that the evaluator monitor the possibility of such alterations. Second, the diagnostician is obliged to specify the instructional implications of his findings. Whatever Hewett's intent, this particular imperative is likely to greatly diminish the number of vacuous statements offered by the diagnostician, those statements which sound impressive but which fail to help the practicing teacher. Both of these requirements are surely likely to improve the services rendered to the disabled child, his teachers, and his parents.

This model was employed in the development of an education program, labeled an engineered classroom for educationally handicapped children (California's term for learning-disabled and emotionally disturbed children). The Santa Monica Project was an experiment to obtain data to assess the efficacy of this educational design. The program was presumed to have several distinguishing and important features. One was that the children in various activities were separated spatially in accordance with their developmental levels as conceived within the model. Second was the systematic use and monitoring of social and material rewards contingent upon children's behaviors. Finally, an attempt was made to train children to be reinforced by symbolic rewards, such as grades, rather than by tangible goods. Children were assigned to one of six classrooms. One classroom was exposed to the educational innovations of the engineered program for one school year, while a second classroom was in a non-Hewett type of educational instruction for one school year. Two classrooms began with the control type of educational program and switched to the engineered classroom at midyear. The remaining two classrooms started the year with the Hewett plan and switched to the control program at midyear. Classes used for the control condition were permitted to have features of the engineered classroom with the exception of the use of tangible rewards for appropriate classroom behaviors. The behavior studied to assess the efficacy of the experimental design was the time spent by a student maintaining eye contact with the task or assignment given him by the teacher, that is, the child's attention. If eye contact was irrelevant to the task or the observer could not see the child's eyes, body and head orientation were assessed as indicative of task attention. Two observers coded behaviors of children in each of the six classes for the project's year duration. In addition, achievement tests in spelling, reading, and arithmetic were administered to all of the participating children at the initial screening, at midyear, and at the end of the school year.

The results of the Santa Monica Project indicated that the engineered classroom (when compared to the control classroom) resulted in significant improvement in arithmetic fundamentals and increasing task attention. The results were not significant for spelling and reading. The significant effects were explained as the result of the procedures followed during the arithmetic lessons in the experimental program. Students had to put things in their places, follow directions, have all work corrected each fifteen minutes, and count their daily check marks. It was observed that in the engineered program the students were able to work more independently and persistently than the comparable group of children in the non-Hewett program, where teachers were observed to spend relatively more time controlling student behavior. Hewett fails to provide clues as to the failure of the engineered classroom to have effects on reading and spelling achievement. At least for the learning of arithmetic, the engineered program was effective. Whether it was effective because of the systematic use of tangible rewards, the differential use of space within the classroom, or the teacher's or children's enthusiasm for a novel educational experience was not determined.

The second major finding in this study is related to the role of tangible rewards. It was found that most students within the Hewett program did not need to be given tangible rewards to continue work efforts once these efforts or habits had been established. Most children were ready for other types of rewards by the end of the first semester and many were evidently ready to respond to symbolic rewards (e.g., approval, grades) after several weeks. The progression of rewards took students from the receipt of tangible rewards to check marks, to privilege time, and finally to graphing check marks somewhat similar to receipt of traditional grades.

The benefit of an engineered classroom is that it incorporates a theoretical viewpoint from child psychology and special education. It integrates what is known about normal development into programming for children who deviate from expectations. Furthermore, various approaches to treatment are defined as acceptable and integrated into theoretical and practical ideas and procedures. Theory was thus translated into an educational design which both clinicians and teachers can implement. It smiles upon, and uses to its advantage, an experimental approach to evaluate the theory and the educational design.

There are some caveats regarding this model of which the student should be aware. The model has not been adequately tested, the Santa Monica

Project being a multidimensional one. The adequacy of Hewett's theorizing is not yet known; causes and effects have not yet been determined. Additionally, in terms of diagnostic assessments, it is not known that the items used to rate children tap those functions which they are presumed to test or whether the items are measuring other aspects of development. The items do not appear to correspond to their assessment functions in terms of their content and there are no data presented to indicate either their reliability or validity.

Caveats aside, Hewett did take an important social problem, developed a model which attempted to integrate psychology and special education, translated this model into an educational program, and then, most importantly, has begun to test the validity of the model on the basis of empirical results. No doubt, data will prove him wrong on some points, correct on others. But as long as there is a continuing attempt to test empirically the model and its educational implications, corrections will be made.

This chapter covered a great deal of material and ideas developed by persons in their attempts to provide organization and structure to conceptualization and treatments of children evidencing learning difficulties. It is notable that the field has advanced from the 1969 collection of terms used to describe the characteristics of the learning-disabled children to the development of more sophisticated medical, psychological, and educational models to incorporate in a meaningful and useful way the problems noted in this most heterogeneous group of children.

REFERENCES

Barsch, R. H. *Achieving Perceptual Motor Efficiency.* Seattle, Wash.: Special Child Publication, 1967.

Bender, L. "A visual motor Gestalt test and its clinical use." *American Orthopsychiatry Assoc. Res. Monograph,* 1938, No. 3.

Bryan, T. "An observational analysis of classroom behaviors of children with learning disabilities." *Journal of Learning Disabilities,* 1974d, 7, 26–34.

Bryan, T. and Wheeler, R. "Perception of learning disabled children: The eye of the observer." *Journal of Learning Disabilities,* 1972, 5, 484–488.

Clements, S. D. "Minimal brain dysfunction in children." NINDS Monograph No. 3, Public Health Service Bulletin #1415. Washington, D.C.: U.S. Department of Health, Education, and Welfare, 1966.

Cruickshank, W. M., Bentzen, F. A., Ratzeburg, F. H., and Tannhauser, M. T. *A Teaching Method for Brain-injured and Hyperactive Children.* Syracuse: Syracuse University Press, 1961.

Cratty, B. *Perceptual-Motor Behavior and Educational Processes.* Springfield, Ill.: Charles C. Thomas, 1969

de Hirsch, K., Jansky, J., and Langford, Q. *Predicting Reading Failure.* New York: Harper and Row, 1966

Doman, R. J., Spitz, E. B., Zucman, E., Delecato, C. H., and Doman, G. "Children with severe brain injuries: Neurological organization in terms of mobility." In E. C. Frierson and W. B. Barke (eds.), *Educating Children with Learning Disabilities.* New York: Appleton-Century-Crofts, 1967.

Dykman, R. A., Ackerman, P. T., Clements, S. D., and Peters, J. E. "Specific learning disabilities: An attentional deficit syndrome." In H. R. Myklebust (ed.), *Progress in Learning Disabilities, Vol. II.* New York: Grune & Stratton, 1971, pp. 56–93.

Dykman, R. A., Walls, R., Suzuki, T., Ackerman, P., and Peters, J. E. "Children with learning disabilities: Conditioning, differentiation, and the effect of distraction." *American Journal of Orthopsychiatry,* 1970, 40, 766–781.

Federal Register, 41, No. 230, November 1976.

Forness, S. R. and Estveldt, K. C. "Classroom observation of learning and behavior problem children." Graduate School of Education, University of California, L.A., 1971.

Gearheart, B. R. *Learning Disabilities: Educational Strategies.* Saint Louis: C. V. Mosby Co., 1973.

Hammill, D. "Learning Disabilities: A problem in definition." *Division for Children with Learning Disabilities Newsletter,* 1974, 4, 28–31.

Hewett, F. *The Emotionally Disturbed Child in the Classroom.* Boston: Allyn & Bacon, 1970.

Hewett, F., Taylor, F. D., and Artuso, A. A. "The Santa Monica Project: Evaluation of an engineered classroom design with emotionally disturbed children." *Exceptional Children,* 1969, 35, 523–529.

Honzik, M. P., Macfarlane, J. W., and Allen, L. "The stability of mental test performance between two and eighteen years." *Journal of Experimental Education,* 1948, 17, 309–324.

Johnson, D. J. and Myklebust, H. *Learning Disabilities: Educational Principles and Practices.* New York: Grune & Stratton, 1967.

Kass, C. E. "Introduction to Learning Disabilities." *Seminars in Psychiatry,* 1969, 1, 240–244.

Kawabe, K. K. "Attentional deficits in learning-disabled children." *Division for Children with Learning Disabilities Newsletter,* 1976, 2, 35–41.

Keogh, B. K. "A compensatory model for psychoeducational evaluation of children with learning disorders." *Journal of Learning Disabilities,* 1971, 4, 544–548.

Kephart, N. C. *Learning Disability: An Educational Adventure.* West Lafayette, Ind.: Kappa Delta Pi Press, 1967.

Kephart, N. C. *The Brain-Injured Child in the Classroom.* Chicago: National Society for Crippled Children and Adults, 1964.

Kephart, N. C. *The Slow Learner in the Classroom.* Columbus, Ohio: Merrill, 1971.

Kirk, S. "Introduction to State of the Art: Where are we in Learning Disabilities?" Association for Children with Learning Disabilities and California Association for Neurologically Handicapped Children Publications, Los Angeles, 1974.

Kirk, S. and Kirk, W. P. *Psycholinguistic Learning Disabilities: Diagnosis and Remediation.* Urbana: University of Illinois Press, 1972.

Lerner, J. W. *Children with Learning Disabilities.* Boston: Houghton Mifflin, 1971.

Masland, R. L. "Children with minimal brain dysfunction–A national problem." In L. Tarnopol (ed.), *Learning Disabilities.* Springfield, Ill.: Charles C. Thomas, 1969.

Schuell, H., Jenkins, J., and Jimenez-Pabon, E. *Aphasia in Adults.* New York: Harper and Row, 1965.

Seaver, W. B. "Effects of naturally induced teacher expectancies." *Journal of Personality and Social Psychology,* 1973, 28, 333–342.

Torgesen, J. "Problems and prospects in the Study of Learning Disabilities." In Mavis Heathering (ed.), *Review of Child Development Research.* Chicago: University of Chicago Press, 1975. Vol. 5.

Waugh, K. W. and Busch, W. J. *Diagnosing Learning Disorders.* Columbus, Ohio: Charles Merrill, 1971.

Whalen, C. K., and Henker, B. "Psychostimulants and children: A review and analysis." *Psychological Bulletin,* 1976, 83, 1113–1130.

II | PSYCHOLOGICAL AND PHYSIOLOGICAL CHARACTERISTICS

We have described some of the historical and contemporary events affecting the growth, the perspectives, and the concerns of the field of learning disabilities. In the six chapters following, we consider the general question: What do we know about learning-disabled children? The chapters cover such diverse topics as the brain, intelligence, studies of the behavior of learning-disabled children, the complex subject of information processing, language development and disorders, and finally investigations concerning the learning of reading and mathematics.

We have focused upon these topics because they are involved in many clinical guesses about the learning-disabled child. Theories about information processing, intelligence, brain dysfunction, language, and reading failures comprise the major constructs by which the special educator views such children. Most professionals in the field of learning disabilities will focus on one or more of these topics in their attempts to solve the teaching problems they face each day. Obviously studying brain activity reflects the historical influences of the early pioneers, while evaluating reading and arithmetic progress is characteristic of the more contemporary influences of the psychometric model. But whatever the paternity of the hypothesis, all of these topics have received considerable attention, if not excessive investigation, by the specialists in learning disabilities.

The following chapters are based upon systematic research. As we stated in the preface, clinical observations are often fruitful sources for interesting ideas. But it is our belief that systematically gathered information, garnered in accordance with modern scientific research methodology, is the *best* source of knowledge. Certainly, it is true that most research findings describe the behavior of the "average" child, and that the complexity and uniqueness of the individual participating child is overlooked. It is also true, however, that clinical observations which detect the unique features of a child are not very useful to those involved with other, also unique, children. Moreover, we believe that research findings, while sometimes leading to errors when applied to the individual child, are likely to lead to fewer errors than unbridled clinical guesses.

Thus, the following chapters are based on the findings of research and are indebted to the work and dedication of many investigators. Additionally, we believe that while the number of studies about particular behaviors might be small, there is a corpus of research knowledge that special educators should be aware of, if only to impose some limitations upon their clinical imaginations.

We have also presented information, when appropriate, concerning the normal development of the behavior being studied. In order to understand the deviations, one must of course have some understanding of normal development. We have also drawn liberally from the contributions made by those in fields other than learning disabilities, as workers in other areas of the social sciences may have information of value to the special educator.

Additionally, the reporting in this section is diverse and sometimes complex. Since the definitions of learning disabilities vary, the particular kinds of children employed as subjects in research may also vary. An ambiguous or evershifting definition leads to the inclusion of subjects with ambiguous and perhaps ultimately irrelevant problems. Thus in reviewing research, we have included studies involving not only children who couldn't read, but also those which investigated the brain-damaged, the impulsive, and the mentally retarded. We have been cavalier about the limits imposed by the definitions of learning-disabled children and have included whatever studies seemed useful or important for understanding the behavior and characteristics of these children. Such reporting may be complex, but it is the most honest way to present the data necessary to develop an informed, realistic view of current research methods.

Lastly, the material and findings presented are often diverse. One study shows this, another that, and finally a third neither. Perhaps some show sex differences, others show age differences, yet others show differences which can be accounted for in still other ways. But the human is a complex apparatus, so it can hardly be surprising that research findings reflect such complexity. Indeed, many sciences develop a technology of such complexity that only a select few, after years of training, can even understand its jargon. You will no doubt be reassured that this is not yet the case with the field of learning disabilities. But research knowledge is being accumulated and it is of course essential for the newcomer to the field to be familiar with it.

4 | The Brain and Learning Disabilities

Theories and vocabulary, as well as diagnostic and remedial practices, both past and present, have reflected assumptions about the relationship between the brain and the behavior of the learning-disabled child. The historical link between brain dysfunction and the field of learning disabilities outlined in Chapter 2 makes this bias understandable. What is important is the influence of these assumptions upon current diagnostic procedures. To understand these diagnostic procedures requires some familiarity with current ideas regarding the relationship of the brain to behavior. For this reason, a description of the brain and the theories which have sought to describe the relationship of brain dysfunction to the etiology of learning problems is included in this chapter. Several hypothetical explanations for learning disabilities can be traced to theories regarding the cerebral cortex.

HISTORICAL LINK

There have been three sources of information linking the brain and learning disabilities. One has been experimental studies of lower animals (Geschwind, 1968; Dykman et al., 1970, 1971). The second has been studies of adults afflicted with war wounds or other forms of cerebral trauma, such as stroke (Strauss and Lehtinen, 1947; Luria, 1961; Schuell, Jenkins, and Jimenez-Pabon, 1965). The third source has involved experimentation with epileptics undergoing brain surgery (Penfield and Rasmussen, 1950). The study of samples of animals and adults has its limitations in furthering our knowledge of the etiology of learning disabilities in children. Children are not likely to experience the state of "cathood" or "rathood," stroke or war wounds, or brain surgery. Knowledge about the relationship of the brain and learning problems is technologically limited to analogies rather than being based upon direct observation and experimentation.

Trauma experienced by adults usually affects large portions of the brain. It is thus difficult to pinpoint specific locales which might be relevant to problems of learning. Epileptics who undergo brain surgery have typically experienced longstanding severe brain damage before this radical operation is performed. The chronicity of the disease, the effects of brain surgery, and electrical stimulation involved in exploring the brain may well obscure the relevant features of the brain and learning which specialists might wish to explain. In addition, the loss of a function may have different causes and effects than the lack of development of the same function (Hebb, 1949). For example, are the same places, processes, and effects upon persons observed when one individual has lost the ability to speak and the other has never developed this skill?

Many professionals believe it is an exercise in futility to be concerned with the brain, as it may not be related to the occurrence of learning disabilities. It is often suggested that the technology of brain research has not yet advanced to the state where it can provide evidence that brain damage, dysfunction, maldevelopment, or delayed development are implicated in learning-disabled children. Even when there is strong medical and neurological evidence to support the possibility that a child has some kind of neurological malfunction, the brain locale cannot be specified with any assuredness. While there has been a good deal of speculation about neurological signs in learning-disabled children, there has not been a corresponding abundance of empirical attempts to study the signs and symptoms associated with a brain-damage hypothesis of learning disabilities. It is argued that unless there is evidence that medical intervention is necessary, learning problems are the domain of the educator.

It is also argued that if a teacher has knowledge that a child with learning disabilities is suspected of having neurological involvement, the teacher will demonstrate less motivation in her efforts to remediate the educational difficulty. This argument can be reduced to concern about public relations or the political effects of knowledge. Better teaching performances might be obtained from the teacher if the teacher is uninformed or misinformed concerning the child's neurological integrity. Presumably, the good results accompanying these good intentions serve to justify the suppression of information. The concern for the manipulation of teacher motivation leads ultimately to the suggestion that teachers should be kept in a state of ignorance for the good of the brain-damaged child.

It is probably true that speculations regarding brain processes and learning disabilities have led to few successful educational programs. It is not true such speculations are worthless. Studies of the effects of assaults upon the brain have led to interesting theorizing. These in turn have produced empirical efforts bound to increase our sophistication concerning learning-disabled children. These studies have given rise to ideas about the brain and language, the brain and information processing, the role of sensory modalities, and the relationship of modalities to each other as these affect the reception, storage, and use of information. As will subsequently be discussed, Dykman's fertile theory of attentional deficits of learning-disabled children, Geschwind's ideas of the manner in which brain locales and pathways can result in dyslexia, Kirk and Kirk's work based on the Osgood model of information processing, and Johnson and Myklebust's typology and remediation of learning problems have been the products of these studies on cats, rats, and the wounded adult.

The theoretical position which emphasizes the relationship of the brain to learning disabilities is based upon the control of human behavior by the brain. It is believed that inadequate behavior and learning might reflect inadequate brain control or functioning. Presumably, knowledge as to the discrete brain processes or locale responsible for this inadequacy should facilitate appropriate educational programming. The theoretical emphasis upon brain processes and their relationship to learning and behavior is reflected in the diagnosis of learning disabilities. Behaviors observed on various tests are used to infer the adequacy or inadequacy of various brain areas and processes. Because of this emphasis on the brain to interpret test data, some discussion of relevant structures and functions of the brain are included.

ANATOMY OF THE BRAIN

The spinal cord and the brain are the two major components of the central nervous system (see Figure 4-1). The spinal cord serves as one important center for the integration of motor activities. The brain is comprised of three major parts: the brain stem, the cerebellum, and the cerebrum (cerebral cortex). The major functions of the brain stem involve the integration of several visceral functions (e.g., control of heart and respiratory rates) and control of a variety of motor reflexes. The cerebellum coordinates the efferent, voluntary muscle system and plays a role in controlling balance and coordinated muscle movements. The cerebrum plays a dominant role in the nervous system, as it is concerned with conscious functions or those behaviors which distinguish man from lower animals. Major theories related to learning disabilities have focused on the functions of the brain stem (Dykman et al., 1970) and the cerebral cortex (Geschwind, 1968).

Brain Stem

The brain stem is composed of four regions which have discrete functions. These are the medulla oblongata, pons, midbrain and diencephalon. The medulla, a continuation of the spinal cord, has nuclei (cell bodies) and

FIGURE 4-1: The central nervous system

Central nervous system

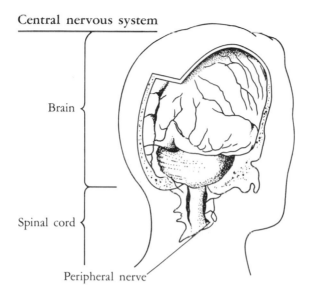

Brain

Spinal cord

Peripheral nerve

tracts (axons) which have functions in controlling respiration and the cardiovascular system. The pons is associated with sensory input and output flow to the face, and is located at the upper limit of the medulla. The midbrain has a huge pair of tracts which carry messages down from the cerebral hemispheres and it has the sensory tracts which start in the spinal cord and go to the brain stem. The midbrain is associated with wakefulness or the conscious state of the entire brain. Some theorists attribute attentional deficits in learning-disabled children to breakdowns in the midbrain (Dykman et al., 1971). The diencephalon, the upper portion of the brain stem, is a major center for the passage and integration of sensory information (see Figure 4-2).

Cerebral Cortex

The cerebral cortex is divided into right and left hemispheres which are connected by the corpus callosum. This is a large tract of fibers which connects the two sides and keeps them at least reasonably well informed as to their mutual activities and interests (Mountcastle, 1962). The surface of the cerebral cortex has many convolutions, an economical spatial arrangement for cramming many cells into a relatively small area. The convolutions have been labeled as *gyri* (ridges), *sulci* (valleys), and *deep sulci* (fissures). Maps of the brain have been drawn to mirror these ridges and valleys.

FIGURE 4-2: The three connections between the cerebellum and the brain stem

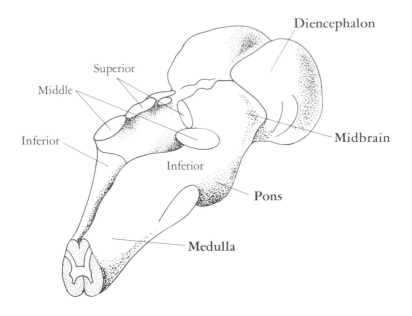

Some of the gyri and sulci have been linked to behavioral functions. In other cases, the functional role of the area in affecting behavior is not known (see Figure 4-3).

The organization of activities in the cortex differs for various behaviors. Certain functions, such as vision and audition, are controlled by both the left and right sides of the cortex. Motor movements, such as of the arms and legs, are coordinated by both sides, but in a contralateral fashion; the left side of the brain controls the right side of the body, while the right side controls the left side of the body. There are some skills that are not represented in these fashions, but are controlled largely by one hemisphere. For example, across cultures there is a great preponderance of right-handedness and left-hemisphere dominance for language. About 93 percent of the adult population is right-handed and about 96 percent has left-hemisphere dominance for speech and language functions (Curtis et al., 1972). The right hemisphere is purportedly more in control of making complex visual discriminations and processing of nonverbal and perceptual information, such as music and mathematical symbols, than the left hemisphere (Milner, 1962).

While the dominance of the left hemisphere for language skills in adults has been well demonstrated, there is some question about the equipotentiality of both sides of the brain to develop language processing skills in children. For many years, the development of one hemisphere's dominance over the other was considered critical in a child's ultimate language

FIGURE 4-3: Left and right sides of the cerebral cortex

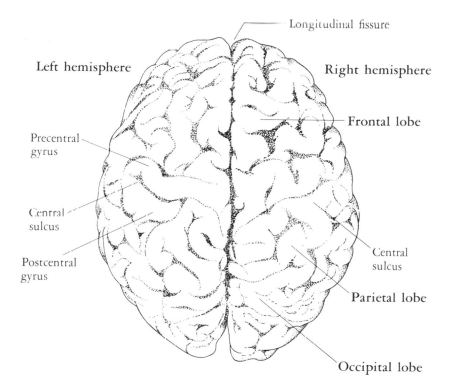

ADAPTED FROM: DeArmond, Fusco, and Dewey, *A Photographic Atlas Structure of the Human Brain*. New York, Oxford University Press, 1974.

and academic development. For example, Orton's (1937) work was based on the notion of the necessity for one side of the brain to achieve dominance over the other, with the accompanying hypothesis that failure to learn to speak or read reflected a lack of cortical dominance. Tests of hand, arm, and eye usage were part of the clinical battery to assess brain damage or inadequate neurological maturation. For many years, parents would try to train a left-handed child to use his right hand, as it was believed harmful to the child's language development to be a "lefty." More recently, however, Lenneberg (1967) has stated that damage to the dominant left hemisphere in a child 11 years or younger will not have enduring damaging effects upon the child's ability to use language, because the right hemisphere will have the capability of compensating for the damage. At this point, we are not so concerned about right- or left-hemisphere dominance as we are in some signs of neurological integrity and maturity. Rather than being concerned as to whether the child uses his right or left hand, of more critical importance is the child's consistency or preferences for one over the other.

It should be noted that for many years it was assumed only the cerebral cortex was involved in the learning process. While most of the foregoing discussion is focused on the role of the cerebral cortex in governing behavior, remember that other parts of the nervous system between the spinal column and the cortex are involved in learning. The brain is organized vertically as well as horizontally (Thompson, 1967).

The cerebral cortex has been divided into four major regions. These are the frontal, temporal, parietal, and occipital lobes. There are major landmarks used to set some of the boundaries for individual lobes. For instance, the lateral sulcus is the landmark to separate the frontal from the temporal lobes, while the central sulcus separates the frontal from the parietal lobe.

Frontal Lobe

Different areas of the frontal lobe are related to emotional control, coordination of complex motor movements, and the ability to speak. The anterior section of the frontal lobe, shown in Figure 4-4, has many connections with other parts of the brain and the brain stem. This prefrontal region is considered involved in controlling virtually all of man's behaviors referred to as abstract thinking, mature judgment, tactfulness (Gatz, 1966), and to "maintain the integrity of personality and intellect" (Schuell et al., 1965, p. 69). Experiments on the frontal lobe of monkeys have indicated that damage to this area will result in changes in short-term memory, will reduce the rapidity with which new tasks are learned and affect extensive hyperactivity (Thompson, 1967). Knowledge about the role of the prefrontal area in humans has come also from prefrontal lobotomies for persons suffering severe chronic pain or exhibiting uncontrollable and unacceptable behaviors. In these surgical procedures, the frontal lobe fiber connections to and from other cortical and subcortical areas are disconnected (Curtis et al., 1972). The results of such treatments are personality, intellectual, and emotional changes in patients, so that patients may suffer considerable impairment and become less sensitive to the possible consequences of their behavior.

The motor strip lies anterior to the central sulcus. It is organized in homunculus fashion so that one end is responsible for the control of toe movements, while the other end is related to swallowing, with the remaining motor movements organized in an orderly fashion along the strip (Curtis et al., 1972). Anterior to the motor strip is the premotor strip, which is believed responsible for an elaboration of motor movements more complex than those controlled by the motor strip. Experiments using lower animals have indicated that damage to the premotor area results in spasticity (abnormal, involuntary contractions of muscles), whereas damage to the motor strip results in flaccid paralysis (softness and weakness of muscles) (Gatz, 1966). When human beings suffer cerebral lesions in this area, the damage

FIGURE 4-4: The cerebral cortex (side view)

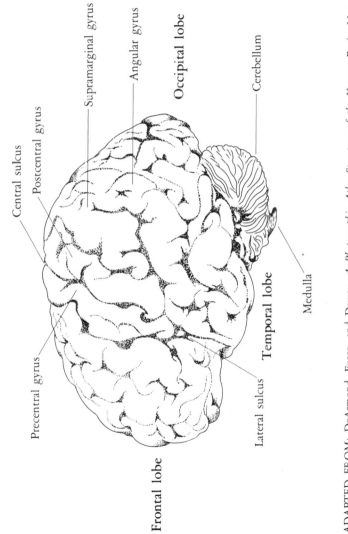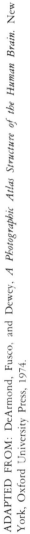

Central sulcus

Postcentral gyrus

Supramarginal gyrus

Angular gyrus

Occipital lobe

Cerebellum

Precentral gyrus

Frontal lobe

Lateral sulcus

Temporal lobe

Medulla

ADAPTED FROM: DeArmond, Fusco, and Dewey, *A Photographic Atlas Structure of the Human Brain*. New York, Oxford University Press, 1974.

usually affects both the motor and premotor areas, resulting in paralysis with spasticity (Gatz, 1966). In some epileptic attacks, the person may suffer massive discharges in all parts of the motor cortex which result in tonic spasms (muscles contract in steady and uniform manner) and clonic movements (muscles contract and relax alternately).

Directly below the motor strip is Broca's area and anterior to it is the supplementary motor cortex. These are two of three cortical areas related to the production and control of speech. Broca's area is in the posterior part of the inferior frontal gyrus near the motor area which controls tongue and larynx movements (Gatz, 1966, p. 112). As mentioned earlier, Broca was the surgeon who noted the association between the loss of the ability to speak in two patients and subsequent autopsy revelations of damage to this cortical area. Brain surgery on epileptic patients (Penfield and Roberts, 1959; Penfield and Rasmussen, 1950) has corroborated Broca's observations. Damage to Broca's area, in the dominant hemisphere, results in expressive or motor aphasia: a person who has no paralysis of the tongue or other body parts connected with speaking, who knows what he wants to say, but cannot speak or who produces garbled speech (Gatz, 1966). Penfield and his associates have revealed the supplementary motor cortex also to be related to speech, but evidently excision of the supplementary motor cortex does not have the drastic and long-lasting negative effects on speech as damage to Broca's area. Aphasia, loss of the ability to speak, is more likely to result from damage to Broca's area and is more likely to be long-lasting than when damage is in the supplementary motor area.

Temporal Lobe

One particular function can be specifically and uniquely related to the temporal lobe. The primary auditory cortex is located at the "posterior and dorsal margin of the temporal lobe buried on the inner slope of the lateral fissure" (Curtis et al., 1972, p. 3). Reception, comprehension, and interpretation of sound is a specific function of this area. When a brain lesion affects the primary auditory cortex, the result is sensory aphasia, an inability to understand the meaning of spoken language. The person's ability to hear remains intact, but the ability to interpret what is heard is impaired. This is noted when the damage occurs to the dominant, usually the left, hemisphere, but the same effect is not noted when the damage occurs in the right or nondominant hemisphere. Sensory aphasia is also known as receptive aphasia and as Wernicke's aphasia, after the surgeon who first noted the difficulty certain persons had in interpreting spoken language. The deficit in comprehension of language usually has a reciprocal effect upon the person's ability to speak in a meaningful manner.

The functions of the remainder of the temporal lobe are not as well known. Curtis et al. (1972, p. 516) have summarized the results of Penfield and his colleagues' work on the temporal lobe. They report that stimulation of the temporal lobe results in auditory sensations (tinnitus–ringing tone, buzz, or knock), vestibular sensations (vergigo dizziness), alterations in perception (auditory or visual illusions or hallucinations of previous experiences), fear, hallucinations in the auditory or olfactory spheres, arrest of speech, repetitive motor movements (e.g., rubbing ear), complex emotional behavior, and confusion in association with defects in memory (e.g., confusion plus amnesia).

When it has been necessary to perform a bilateral temporal lobectomy, usually done to relieve severe, chronic epileptic seizures, the individual is reported to suffer impairment in the ability to form new associations and remember newly occurring events, although events which occurred in the distant past remain recallable.

Parietal Lobe

The parietal lobe is separated from the frontal lobe by the central sulcus and from the temporal lobe by the lateral fissure. The separation from the occipital lobe posteriorly does not have such well-defined landmarks. The parietal lobe is the primary receptive cortex for both impulses from sensory receptors in the skin and for the higher integration of language, reading, and writing.

The organization of sensory reception is such that specific areas along the postcentral gyrus receive projections from specific parts of the body. The parietal lobe functions so as to allow us to be aware of body movements and the position of the body in space, and to be able to make discriminations of size, shape, and texture. The specifics of these sensations are evaluated in neurological examinations and a number have been specifically linked to learning-disabled children. These include evaluation of the following.

1. Position sense–perception of movement and direction of movement.
2. Tactile localization–the ability to accurately localize the specific portion of the body which is being stimulated.
3. Two-point discrimination–the ability to perceive that a double stimulus with a small space of separation has touched a particular part of the body.
4. Stereognosis–the ability to distinguish and recognize objects based on feeling but not seeing them.
5. Graphesthesia–the ability to recognize which numbers or letters have been traced on the finger, hand, face, or leg.
6. Weight discrimination–the ability to discriminate among relative amounts of pressure.
7. Perception of simultaneous stimuli–the individual recognizes that both sides of the body have been simultaneously stimulated.
8. Perception of texture–the ability to perceive the patterns of things felt (Curtis et al., 1972, p. 498).

Ablation, or damage to areas in the parietal lobe, will affect these various functions. Thus, a person who suffers damage to some part of the postcentral gyrus may be able to feel pain when stuck with a pin but be unable to tell the location of the pinprick. Destruction of one side of this area of the brain may result in loss of awareness of the actions of the contralateral side of the body. Persons have been observed to forget to put on one sleeve of a shirt, evidently unaware of that side of the body.

Several problems associated with learning-disabled children, labeled minimal cerebral dysfunction, have been linked theoretically to the parietal lobe. The critical parietal areas referred to in descriptions of these syndromes are the supramarginal and angular gyri of the dominant left hemisphere. One problem is Gerstmann's syndrome. The symptoms include *dysgraphia,* an inability to write in the absence of paralysis; *dyscalculia,* a deficit in the ability to manipulate mathematical symbols; *left-right confusion,* difficulty learning directions; and tactile *agnosia,* errors in finger recognition in spite of intact sensory reception. These have been associated with *dyslexia* (serious difficulties in learning to read) and *apraxia* (difficulty in performing skilled motor movements on command), again in the absence of paralysis or losses of sensations. Two things should be noted. The first is that the syndrome is somewhat of a mirage insofar as these symptons do not always occur together, sometimes appearing in isolation or in varying combinations (Benton, 1959). Second, these particular symptoms are problems noted in child suffering from severe rather than mild problems in reading.

Problems of body image are often presumed to be associated with learning disabilities. While definitions of body image are often not presented or are so vague as to be of little value, it is known that damage in the nondominant parietal lobe may produce a lack of awareness of the left side of the body, a lack of awareness of partial paralysis, and disturbances in perception (e.g., neglect of the left visual field, inability to interpret drawings or pick out objects from a complex figure) (Curtis et al., 1972).

Occipital Lobe

The occipital lobe is the cortical area responsible for vision. Specific visual skills can be matched to specific areas in the occipital lobe. When there is destruction of both sides of the occipital cortex, blindness results. Damage to discrete areas has predictable differential effects. Depending upon the site of the damage, a person might only lose peripheral vision or show blindness to only particular areas of the visual field. It is believed that damage which occurs in the visual association area, that area surrounding the primary visual cortex, may affect visual recognition and reading. The problem is that the damage is seldom limited to just these association areas and the surrounding areas might also play a role in affecting these visual deficiencies (Curtis et al., 1972).

Association Areas

The parietal, temporal, and occipital lobes are primary sensory receptors for the various modalities of audition, vision, tactile, and kinesthetic perception. What arrives at the cortex is just the raw data, however. These must be elaborated and analyzed in order for comprehension and subsequent appropriate responses to occur. The elaboration of the various sensations is believed to be the business of association areas which surround the primary reception zones. Communication between the modalities is the domain of the association areas. The elaboration and interpretation of the message is believed to occur in and among association areas. Thus, for the hand to know what the eye is doing requires messages passed between the appropriate parietal and occipital association areas. It has been theorized that one major difference between man and lower animals is the development of these association areas (Geschwind, 1968).

THE BRAIN AND LEARNING DISABILITIES

Relatively discrete areas of the brain have been demonstrated to be responsible for specific behaviors by man. A number of these are particularly relevant to the understanding of learning disabilities. Those systems in the brain related to speech and language production and to perceptual skills are most closely tied to certain conceptualizations of children with learning problems.

Penfield and colleagues (1950, 1959) electrically stimulated the brain cortex and identified three areas as involved in the production of speech and language. They have postulated that speech and language are the responsibility of the centrencephalic system. This is a central system which includes the three speech centers in the cortex, two in the frontal lobe, and one in the temporal lobe, plus connections with the descending pathway to the spinal column. Fibers project from the cortex to the midbrain, brain stem, and spinal cord and carry messages to and from each other at various levels. Damage to any of these areas in the adult has debilitating effects upon that person's ability to use speech and language. According to Lenneberg (see Table 4-1), the child's language development until 30 months of age involves his entire brain, with left-hemisphere dominance for language beginning to show towards the end of this period. Between ages 3 and 10, language functions are assumed by the left hemisphere along with polarization of other behaviors to either the left or right side. It is still possible, however, to reverse this polarization if the child experiences some trauma. That is, before ages 10 or 11, damage to the left hemisphere which results in language problems can be compensated for by the right hemisphere. It apparently is not easily accomplished, but is possible. By the mid-teens, language is definitely localized in the left hemisphere and traumas to this area are not compensated for by the right hemisphere.

TABLE 4-1: Language and brain development

Age	Usual language development	Effects of acquired, lateralized lesions	Physical maturation of central nervous system	Lateralization of function	Equipotentiality of hemispheres	Explanation
Months 0 to 3	Emergence of cooing.	No effect on onset of language in half of all cases; other half has delayed onset but normal development.	About 60 to 70 percent of developmental course accomplished.	None: symptoms and prognosis identical for either hemisphere.	Perfect equipotentiality.	Neuroanatomical and physiological prerequisites become established.
4 to 20	From babbling to words.					
21 to 36	Acquisition of language.	All language accomplishments disappear; language is reacquired with repetition of all stages.	Rate of maturation slowed down.	Hand preference emerges.	Right hemisphere can easily adopt sole responsibility for language.	Language appears to involve entire brain; little cortical specialization with regard to language through left hemisphere beginning to become dominant toward end of this period.
Years 3 to 10	Some grammatical refinement; expansion of vocabulary.	Emergence of aphasic symptoms; all disorders recover without residual language deficits (except in reading or writing). During recovery period two processes ac-	Very slow completion of maturational processes.	Cerebral dominance established between 3 to 5 years, but evidence that right hemisphere may often still be involved in speech and language functions. About one	In cases where language is already predominantly localized in left hemisphere and aphasia ensues with left lesion, it is possible to reestablish language presum-	A process of physiological organization takes place in which functional lateralization of language to left is prominent. "Physiological redundancy" is gradually

TABLE 4-1: Language and brain development (continued)

Age	Usual language development	Effects of acquired, lateralized lesions	Physical maturation of central nervous system	Lateralization of function	Equipotentiality of hemispheres	Explanation
	tive: diminishing aphasic interference and further acquisition of language.			quarter of early childhood aphasias due to right hemisphere lesions.	ably by reactivating language functions in right hemisphere.	reduced and polarization of activities between right and left hemisphere is established. As long as maturational processes have not stopped, reorganization is still possible.
11 to 14	Foreign accents emerge.	Some aphasic symptoms become irreversible (particularly when acquired lesion was traumatic).	An asymptote is reached on almost all parameters. Exceptions are myelination and EEG spectrum.	Apparently firmly established, but definitive statistics not available.	Marked signs of reduction in equipotentiality.	Language markedly lateralized and internal organization established irreversibly for life. Language-free parts of brain cannot take over except where lateralization had been blocked by pathology during childhood.
Mid-teens to senium	Acquisition of second language becomes increasingly difficult.	Symptoms present after 3 to 5 months post insult are irreversible.	None.	In about 97 percent of the entire population language is definitely lateralized to the left.	None for language.	

SOURCE: Lenneberg, V. E. *Biological Foundations of Language.* New York: Wiley, 1967.

On the basis of clinical observations, children have been described as having different types of aphasia, expressive and receptive. When a child has difficulty in understanding what is said, he has a receptive language problem. Expressive problems relate to the child's ability to produce spoken language. There can be a breakdown in this speaking process at various points. The child may have an expressive problem which is related to transmitting a message. If the child has deficits in controlling motor movements associated with speaking, in the absence of any kind of paralysis or weak muscles, the child has an expressive deficit. This particular kind of expressive problem is referred to as *dysarthria* or *apraxia.* The child might have an expressive language problem which is related to the conceptualization component of language production. In this type of expressive problem, the child might have difficulty in remembering the right words, using appropriate words to express his ideas, connecting the words with proper syntax, putting words together to formulate a sentence, or connecting words with their symbolic meanings.

The bases upon which we associate such behaviors in children to specific brain sites are hypothetical and are founded primarily upon sources of information largely unrelated to children. More recently, Lenneberg has provided some evidence, derived from studies of children, to support the notion that specific language deficits can be linked to particular areas in the brain. Lenneberg (1967) has reported two types of difficulty which result in dysarthria (i.e., a problem of articulation). Children who have suffered damage to or experience abnormal growths in the area which immediately surrounds the thalamus often show problems of articulation. Lenneberg's findings lend support to the notion that when a child has difficulty in the acquisition of language skills some brain area may be directly involved. It also lends support to Penfield and his colleagues' inclusion of the midbrain as part of the speech system.

Still at the hypothetical level, the work of Norman Geschwind, a neurologist, is quite relevant to the theories of learning disabilities. Two of Geschwind's theses are particularly salient. In one case, Geschwind links the developmental sequence of the neurological process of myelination to successive stages of psychomotor and language development. Myelination refers to the process whereby an outer sheath develops to cover and protect nerves. The nervous system is not completely developed when the infant is born and the areas of the brain which myelinate last are vulnerable to insult for a longer period. The order in which parts of the nervous system myelinate reflects the development of man's brain across centuries. The older parts of the brain from a phylogenetic view myelinate first. The areas are those concerned with sensory and motor functions and the limbic system, a system controlling experiences of pain and pleasure and survival of the organism. The sensory areas which show early myelination include the auditory, visual, and somesthetic cortex, which have connections with their adjacent association areas, but not directly with each other.

The second areas to myelinate are the association areas. These areas surround the sensory areas, but allow, through long interconnecting fibers, various sensory areas to communicate with each other.

The last areas to myelinate are in the parietal lobe, the angular gyrus, and a spot where the temporal, parietal, and occipital lobes meet (see Figure 4-4). These particular areas are described by Geschwind as critical to language and, consequently, to language problems. The angular gyrus and the occipital-parietal-temporal lobe junction are presumed responsible for man's ability to make cross-modal associations, that is, to transfer information from one modality, such as vision, to another modality, such as audition. In man, unlike other animals, cross-modal associations can be made directly through the association areas without going through the more primitive limbic system. This is the anatomical basis for labeling, and Geschwind suggests that damage to this area may be one explanation for learning disabilities, particularly dyslexia. His hypothesis is that since this area myelinates last and boys mature more slowly at this stage of development than girls, the overrepresentation of boys in learning disability samples indicates that boys are more likely to have suffered some damage to this area of the brain. Boys are seen as susceptible to damage to slowly myelinating brain centers longer than girls.

Geschwind's thesis regarding the critical nature of certain areas in the parietal lobe, particularly the angular gyrus, or the association areas which connect fibers from the occipital, parietal, and temporal lobes, has been expanded into an area of study referred to as cross-modal associations or cross-modal integration. This is a body of research which focuses on the means whereby messages are communicated and integrated between the various sensory modalities. Geschwind notes that man differs from monkeys in his ability to transfer information from one major sensory input system, such as the visual cortex, to another major system, such as the auditory cortex, without going through midbrain transmissions. The angular gyrus is of particular importance, because its strategic position and connecting fibers allow it to integrate information from all sensory and motor areas. Translating a thought into a motor act is likely to involve this area. One theory to explain learning disabilities is that these pathways or areas are dysfunctional. The child's inability to achieve in a variety of areas may be indicative of varying degrees of dysfunction. Damage to these pathways may affect relatively easy tasks, such as learning names, as well as complex ones, such as learning to read and write. There is some support for Geschwind's hypothesis concerning the importance of the angular gyrus in learning disabilities. Birch and Belmont (1964) studied the ability of retarded readers to make auditory, visual, and tactile associations. Children with reading problems were less competent than comparison children in making these associations. While the study did contain some methodological flaws, the results are consistent with ideas regarding the functions of the angular gyrus and the hypothesis is quite provocative.

Dykman and his colleagues (1970, 1971) have developed a theory of learning disabilities in which the core problem is defined as an attentional deficit. The corresponding neurological structure implicated in this theory is the midbrain, particularly the reticular formation within the midbrain. This subcortical area is deemed responsible for maintaining a state of consciousness and awareness. A disturbance in the midbrain area affects the individual's ability to pay attention. This includes his ability to stay alert, to maintain vigilance, and to focus on important stimuli in any given situation. Learning-disabled children are viewed as having an organically based deficit, localized in the midbrain, which affects their ability to maintain states of attention. The reticular activating system in the midbrain is described as follows.

> The reticular formation is a diffuse network of polysynaptic fibers which begins in the spinal cord and enlarges greatly in the brain stem. Some of its fibers pass directly through the thalamus to the cortex while others go indirectly. . . . The reticular formation receives fibers from the cerebellum, the spinal cord, and the higher brain structures. The limbic structures are important in memory, emotions, and drive states. Electrical stimulation of the reticular formation alters respiration, vasomotor tone, muscle tonus, cortical neural activity, subcortical neural activity, and receptivity of certain sensory neurons. It also produces certain phasic movements similar to those seen in states of motor restlessness. These effects are mediated by fibers which descend from the cortex to the reticular formation (descending system) and by fibers which ascend from the reticular formation to the cortex (ascending system). If the reticular formation is damaged or cut off (e.g., by anesthetization), sensory messages reach the cortex but there is no awareness of stimulation of perception (Dykman, Walls, Suzuki, Ackerman, and Peters, 1970, p. 777).

The hypothesis that learning-disabled children have an attentional deficit which reflects midbrain dysfunction is based upon extensive laboratory research studies of reaction time, impulsivity, and the conditioning of learning-disabled children. The results have indicated that children with learning disabilities, defined as children with limited reading skills and excessive motor activity, demonstrate slower patterns in reaction times, different electroencephalographic responses (that is, different brain wave activity), and decreased physiological reactivity when compared to nondisabled children. These are behaviors which have been linked to reticular system activities. Dykman offers additional evidence to support this theory. In one case, evidence is drawn from the effects of drugs upon learning-disabled children. Stimulant drugs are believed to increase children's attentiveness, but have no effect on their performance on intelligence tests. The reticular activating system is thus indirectly implicated. More circumstantial evidence is derived from test score patterns on the Wechsler Intelligence Scale for Children. Learning-disabled children reportedly do particularly poorly on subtests which are supposed to tap attention (e.g., memory for a sequence of numbers).

The signs indicating midbrain dysfunction, such as hyperactivity and poor performance on certain tests, attenuate with age. Children younger than 10 years who are experiencing learning problems are more likely to evidence these signs of "neural ineffectiveness" than children older than 10 years. This decrease in differences between adequate and inadequate learners suggests that the initial problem is one of developmental immaturity, or developmental lag, rather than permanent dysfunction. Geschwind points to cortical areas responsible for naming and for carrying information to and from cortical and subcortical areas.

Dykman and colleagues have concentrated on the role of the reticular system in the midbrain in inhibiting and arousing behavior as the central explanation for the wide variety of learning problems. It is interesting to note that both theorists have drawn upon the theories and related research of Luria (1961, 1966), a man whose work has been particularly concerned with the development of self-control through the use of verbal mediation.

It should be noted that the discussion of verbal mediation represents an expansion of usual notions of the role of speech and language. We traditionally think of and define language in terms of communication and academic achievement. Now we are expanding upon the role of language to direct our thoughts and subsequent behaviors. Research studies which have been concerned with verbal mediation typically investigate the changes in learning which occur when children are instructed to use some kind of verbal mediation when learning or executing the task. These studies direct the child to view materials in a certain fashion and to rehearse what is viewed in order to remember it. It has been demonstrated that such rehearsal facilitates learning (Bandura, 1969; Flavell, Beach, and Chinsky, 1966) and hypothesized that instruction to learning-disabled children on how to use verbal mediators will facilitate their achievement. While Bryan (1972) failed to find that rehearsal aided learning-disabled children, Palkes, Stewart, and Kahana (1968) and Palkes, Stewart, and Freedman (1971) did find that such instructions facilitated performance of hyperactive children. As yet, little is known concerning the training of self-control, attention, or discriminations through alterations of verbal mediations, but interest in this important question is increasing. Studies of different types of mediators for learning different types of materials at varying ages and for varying types of learning problems should provide us with very useful knowledge to translate into educational practices.

The theories and research discussed thus far have been addressed to the role of the brain in causing learning disabilities and to areas of the brain which may be involved in cases of academic and behavioral difficulties. It should be noted, however, that within recent years, questions have been raised as to the value of such research in aiding the learning-disabled child. For example, Kirk and Kirk (1972) focus upon overt behavior, not brain waves, and upon psychological tests, not neurological examinations, as the most productive means toward understanding and aiding the learning-disabled child.

The position of Kirk and Kirk has had tremendous influence in shifting perspectives of learning problems from the neurologist's to the psychologist's office. But, the views of Kirk and Kirk can be construed as consonant with the ideas expressed by both Dykman and colleagues and by Geschwind. The Kirks' approach is based upon the Osgood model of communication. In essence, this model schematizes communications according to *receptive, expressive,* and *organizational* processes which take place through *sensory* channels of audition and vision and are expressed through speaking and movement. These processes can occur at a *representational* level, which requires some verbal mediation, or at an *automatic* level, which involves complex motor actions but not verbal mediation.

The Illinois Test of Psycholinguistic Abilities (ITPA) has been developed with the goal of reflecting these sensory, expressive, and integrative processes, using tests of children's auditory, visual, and motor skills. The ITPA has been constructed to permit assessment of a child's skills in processing information receptively, that which is seen and heard; and the child's ability to respond expressively, either through speech, pointing, manipulation of objects, or mimicry of well-known acts (e.g., lighting a cigarette). The organization process is believed to occur as the child must be able to make associations between what is seen and heard and the appropriate spoken and motor responses. The two levels at which communicative behavior is tested are the automatic level and the representational level. The automatic level tests highly integrative, but less voluntary, types of patterns, such as the ability to repeat a sequence just heard or reproduce a pattern just seen. The representational level requires the child to use some type of mediational process to complete the task, and by this the authors refer to behaviors which "require the more complex mediating process of utilizing symbols which carry the meaning" (1972, p. 22). The test is constructed to permit the profiling of a child's performance so that his assets and deficits can be seen relative to himself and to same-age peers.

The Kirk model is fundamentally based upon a psychological approach to learning disabilities, substituting educational for neurological perspectives. However, parallels between the neurological approach as developed by Geschwind or Dykman and the psycholinguistic model presented by Kirk and Kirk should be noted.

One can translate low scores on subtests of the ITPA which measure receptive and expressive language processes into indicators of Broca's or Wernicke's aphasia. Kirk and Kirk, like Geschwind, are dealing with the ability to deal receptively and expressively with information and include the need to integrate sensory information from different modalities into their respective models. Aspects of the ITPA which deal with automatic responses, such as learning a pattern or rote learning, seem very much in agreement with Dykman's descriptions of the role of the reticular activating system in controlling attention. The inclusion of symbolic mediators integrates into this schema Luria's work on verbal mediation and self-control of behavior. While very different perspectives are taken by these researchers, it appears that each model provides some means of explaining sensory-expressive processing of information plus the role of language to integrate this information.

With this introduction to the brain and a few perspectives on how the brain may influence a child's ability to learn, it is hoped that greater sensitivity will be developed to the rationales which are the basis for procedures often involved in the diagnosis of a child's academic or behavioral problems.

REFERENCES

Bandura, A. *Principles of Behavior Modification.* New York: Holt, Rinehart & Winston, 1969.

Benton, A. *Right-Left Discrimination and Finger Localization.* New York: Hoeber-Harper, 1959.

Birch, H. G. and Belmont, L. "Auditory-visual integration, intelligence, and reading ability in school children." *Perceptual and Motor Skills,* 1965, 20, 295–305.

Bryan, T. "The effect of forced mediation upon short-term memory of children with learning disabilities." *Journal of Learning Disabilities,* 1972, 5, 605–609.

Curtis, B. A., Jacobson, S., and Marcus, E. M. *An Introduction to the Neurosciences.* Philadelphia: W. B. Saunders Co., 1972.

Dykman, R. A., Ackerman, P. T., Clements, S. D., and Peters, J. E. "Specific learning disabilities: An attentional deficit syndrome." In H. R. Myklebust (ed.), *Progress in Learning Disabilities, Vol. II.* New York: Grune & Stratton, 1971, 56–93.

Dykman, R. A., Walls, R., Suzuki, T., Ackerman, P., and Peters, J. E. "Children with learning disabilities: Conditioning, differentiation, and the effect of distraction." *American Journal of Orthopsychiatry,* 1970, 40, 766–781.

Flavell, J. H., Beach, D. R., and Chinsky, J. M. "Spontaneous verbal rehearsal in a memory task as a function of age." *Child Development,* 1966, 37, 283–299.

Gatz, A. J. *Manter's Essentials of Clinical Neuroanatomy and Neurophysiology.* Philadelphia: F. A. Davis Co., 1966.

Geschwind, N. "Neurological foundations of language." In H. R. Myklebust (ed.), *Progress in Learning Disabilities, Vol. I.* New York: Grune & Stratton, 1968.

Hebb, D. O. *The Organization of Behavior.* New York: John Wiley & Sons, 1949.

Kirk, S. A. and Kirk, W. P. *Psycholinguistic Learning Disabilities: Diagnosis and Remediation.* Urbana: University of Illinois Press, 1972.

Lenneberg, E. *Biological Foundations of Language.* New York: John Wiley & Sons, 1967.

Luria, A. *The Role of Speech in the Regulation of Normal and Abnormal Behavior.* London: Pergamon, 1961.

Luria, A. *Higher Cortical Functions in Man.* New York: Basic Books, Inc., 1966.

Milner, B. "Laterality effects in audition." In U. B. Mountcastle (ed.), *Interhemispheric Relations and Cerebral Dominance.* Baltimore: Johns Hopkins, 1962, 179.

Mountcastle, V. B. (ed.), *Interhemispheric Relations and Cerebral Dominance.* Baltimore: Johns Hopkins, 1962.

Orton, S. *Reading, Writing and Speech Problems in Children.* New York: W. W. Norton, 1937.

Palkes, H., Stewart, M., and Freedman, J. "Improvement in maze performance of hyperactive boys as a function of verbal-training procedures." *Journal of Special Education,* 1971, 5, 337–342.

Palkes, H., Stewart, M., and Kahana, B. "Porteus maze performance of hyperactive boys after training in self-directed verbal commands." *Child Development*, 1968, 39, 817–826.

Penfield, W. and Rasmussen, T. *The Cerebral Cortex of Man.* New York: Macmillan, 1950.

Penfield, W. and Roberts, L. *Speech and Brain Mechanisms.* Princeton, N.J.: Princeton University Press, 1959.

Schuell, H., Jenkins, J., and Jimenez-Pabon, E. *Aphasia in Adults.* New York: Harper and Row, 1965.

Strauss, A. and Kephart, N. *Psychopathology and Education of the Brain-injured Child.* New York: Grune & Stratton, 1955.

Thompson, R. F. *Foundations of Physiological Psychology.* New York: Harper and Row, 1967.

5 | Intelligence

"What does it mean to be dumb? You can't count or nothing and dress up in dirty clothes." (from a six-year-old boy)

For many years psychologists and educators have been arguing, research-ing, and publishing, and have been maintained in some economic bounty by the nature and measurement of intelligence. Very recently, controversy about intelligence and the tests which are presumed to measure it have spread from professionals who deal with such material and the parents affected by these professionals to legislators and concerned citizens. The administration, uses, and interpretations of intelligence tests have become a matter of national concern. Should intelligence tests be given to minority children? If so, which tests and by whom? Should test results be open to public scrutiny, and become part of the child's permanent school record? And what do the results of testing mean, anyway? These questions have been posed by persons concerned about the uses and abuses of intelligence tests. The answers to these questions have varied, but the consensus is that the professional tester must not be an island unto himself, and that the practice and procedures involved in intelligence testing must be under the control, at least to some extent, of nonprofessionals. Public Law 94–142 makes this point quite explicit.

There has always been controversy among professionals concerning the nature and assessment of intelligence. But public concern over the methods used in assessment have probably never been so great. Why is there so much public involvement now?

No doubt many factors have caused the critical eyebrows of the public to be raised. Intelligence testing has long been a handmaiden to practical affairs; so it was inevitable that the public would become involved. After all, there is hardly a man, woman, or child recently schooled in the United States who has not been administered some standardized test of intellectual abilities, capacities, or skills. In addition, the public's awareness of several factors concerning intelligence test usage has been sharpened during the last few decades.

First, it has been increasingly recognized that intelligence test scores are not constant. The same person may receive scores which vary considerably from one test administration to another. Since this is frequently the case, is it wise to use test scores for identification and school placement of individuals?

Second, through the work of sociologist Howard Becker (1963) and psychologist Robert Rosenthal (1966; Rosenthal and Jacobson, 1968) considerable interest has been generated concerning the role of the diagnostician or labeler in affecting judgments of children. To understand the diagnostic process one must focus not only on the individual who is being diagnosed but also upon the forces that may affect the diagnostician. It is even suggested that the label may cause the disease, that the individual once diagnosed as deviant may come to act the part and fulfill the prophecy.

Finally, some have argued that the controversy about intelligence is a reflection of an underlying change in our basic values. L. J. Cronbach, a distinguished professor of psychology, has written, "the controversy over tests was a symptom of the shift of forces. The world view entrenched before World War II is now under attack, and an alternative scheme that cherishes pluralism, affiliations with local communities, and fulfillment rather than 'perfection' is taking shape . . . it is this struggle for the minds of men, and not concerns for specifics such as mental tests, that has generated the recent controversies" (1975, p. 12).

To better understand intelligence tests, we now turn to a discussion of the history of this movement, which is followed by a description of the most commonly used intelligence tests.

HISTORY

Concern for differences among the intellectual capacities of individuals is a comparatively recent development. While the Greeks used terms to mean "reason," they were more preoccupied with differentiating man from beast than man from man (Tuddenham, 1962). Reflections on separating and distinguishing man from lower animals persisted until the late 1800s. Consideration of how people differ from other people has been occurring only for the past 200 years.

Early Influences

Several events in the 1700s played an important role in subsequent test development and the accompanying controversies. One event was the work generated in the Wundt laboratories in Leipzig, Germany. It was found that an individual's reaction time was affected by many apparently trivial events. The intensity of the stimulus, the instructions given to the subject, and the sensory modality concerned were found to affect a subject's quickness to respond to a stimulus. Tuddenham writes, ". . . their discovery that small-appearing differences in experimental conditions could lead to large differences in results sensitized the intelligence testers of a later day to the necessity of providing for their instruments the most complete specification of test materials, instructions, and scoring standards" (1962, p. 473).

A second early influence upon the subsequent development of intelligence tests was the work of Mesmer in France. Mesmer's efforts to study and perhaps exploit his "animal magnetism" helped to focus interest upon hypnosis and abnormal psychology. While he failed to "mesmerize" the professional community with his demonstrations and explanations of hypnotic states, he did influence others to examine individual differences among men, and especially raised interest in the topic of abnormal conditions of behavior.

Perhaps the granddaddy of the testing movement was Francis Galton, a cousin of Charles Darwin. Galton, evidently influenced by his cousin, became interested in the role of genetics in causing differences among people. Indeed, Galton has been credited as the founder of eugenics (Tuddenham, 1962). Galton was an empiricist rather than an armchair philosopher. He began his study of individual differences in a laboratory at the South Kensington Museum. For a small fee of three cents, Galton would measure the head size, arm span, imagery, color vision, hearing acuity, and a multitude of other sensory and physical functions of volunteering subjects (Cronbach, 1960; Tuddenham, 1962). Galton not only tested about 10,000 paying customers, but he introduced a concept with became extremely important to theories about measuring intelligence. This concept was that man can be meaningfully measured in terms of a position relative to other men. Man's standing relative to others was thus perceived as providing meaningful data for both theory and practical affairs. To this day, intelligence test scores reflect individuals' rankings relative to others of comparable age.

The Next Phase

The term *mental testing* did not appear in an American journal until 1890. Even then the topic was not a popular area of research. Psychologists within the United States were primarily preoccupied with determining the structure of the average mind, not individual differences in how people used their minds. But one psychologist, J. M. Cattell, at Columbia University, was interested, and he worked on the measurement of individual intelligence in the manner developed by Galton. Cattell focused on measures of uncomplicated, basic processes of human behavior. Among his carefully garnered measures were tests of an individual's ability to detect sensations, quickness in responding to a stimulus, accuracy in estimating ten-second intervals, and speed in naming colors. His work generated considerable enthusiasm among his professional colleagues, thus launching psychological interest in individual differences and intelligence testing within the United States.

Then two subsequent studies greatly altered the course this interest took. In 1899, Stella Sharp found that the measures employed by Cattell failed to correlate with or predict intellectual performances which were more complex. In 1901 Wissler found that Cattell's measures failed to be related to college students' grades and that Cattell's tests were not correlated with one another. Whatever Cattell was measuring, the tests were not related to the same thing, and they were failing to assess ability important in practical achievement, such as school grades.

In fact, intelligence testing as we know it today was not generated so much by the theoretical concerns and laboratory findings of psychologists as it was by the work of physicians (Cronbach, 1960). The major figure involved was Alfred Binet, a French physician. Binet was an eminent scientist long before he became involved in the development of intelligence tests. His interests ranged from studies of the psychic life of insects to chess players, using methods which ranged from head measurements to inkblot tests. His intellectual range was vast; his reputation as a humanitarian and scientist was excellent. Like many of his contemporary French physicians and social scientists, Binet's curiosity turned toward the study of individual differences in general, and toward intellectual functioning in particular. Binet's view of intellectual functioning differed markedly from that of Galton and Cattell. According to Binet, intellectual functions were not reflected by simple sensory processes, but rather by performance of complex tasks. While Binet never defined the concept of intelligence, he stressed fairly complex mental operations in his discussions. Early in his career, Binet emphasized the role of memory and mental imagery; later he focused more upon the importance of attention and adaptation to the demands of novel environments. Still later he suggested that intelligence was tied to one's power to understand and to reason. When Binet urged a shift of attention away from simple sensory tests of hearing acuity and color vision toward the study of more complicated mental processes (Tuddenham, 1962), his suggestion was followed.

Binet's contributions were not limited to preaching. He devised the first test of intelligence, a test whose format and approach have not been radically changed to this day. His development of this test has had a profound impact upon scientists, practitioners, and the public.

The circumstances surrounding the development of the test are also important. In 1904 France's minister of public instructions created a commission to inquire into how public education could be improved for defective children. The commission decided to start special schools for these children, but their concerns about instituting such schools anticipated concerns expressed today. Tuddenham provides us with a quotation in which

Binet is quoted as saying: ". . . decided that no child suspected of retardation be eliminated from regular school and admitted to a special school without having undergone a pedagogical and medical examination attesting that his intellectual state render him unable to profit in the ordinary measure from the instruction given in regular schools" (1962, p. 482). In our current jargon, mainstreaming—retaining children in regular classrooms—was a major consideration of the commission. They were also concerned with how to measure the child's intellectual status. They were particularly worried about the problem of the biases of those persons who were making judgments about the intellectual status of children at that time. The commission fully recognized that school placements which were "special" were likely to carry special social stigmas. Tuddenham quotes Binet as writing: "It is necessary to guard against the judges who will compose them getting into the habit of leaving decisions to luck, based on subjective and hence uncontrollable impressions, which will be sometimes good, sometimes bad, and will give too large a part to the arbitrary, the capricious. . . . It will never be to one's credit to have attended a special school" (1962, p. 483). Binet clearly implied that the commission was concerned with both the elimination of tester's biases and the damaging consequences of misdiagnosis.

Binet and a coworker, Simon, then developed a test which could be useful to help detect those children in need of special services, but which would prevent children not in need from being the victims of arbitrary and capricious events. Their goals were more practical than theoretical, and their efforts were guided by two factors. First, they wished to help public education to better serve children. Second, their approach was empirical. In attempts to determine what measures were best, they sampled from a wide variety of measures ranging from palm readings and the size of the child's cranium to the child's ability to deal with complex problems (Cronbach, 1960). Palmistry did not pay off, but the problem-solving activities, memory tests, and reasoning tasks were found to be promising.

In sum, Binet and Simon developed a measure to predict schoolroom performance; they did not undertake to develop a measure of adjustment, general competence, social skills, or vocational success. Quite sensibly, many of the test items were devised to measure skills directly related to school activities; indeed some of the items were adaptations of French teachers' teaching materials. As a result, many items on the original and subsequent revisions of the scale assessed verbal skills. Competencies in other arenas of life outside the classroom were not included. Skillfulness in hunting, lovemaking, or survival in the streets of an urban slum were not issues. The mission dictated the method, and the method has had a pervasive, enduring influence upon intelligence testing to this day.

The intelligence test devised by Binet and Simon, and its subsequent revisions, had limited impact upon academic institutions in the United States. It was not long, however, until the scale was discovered by clinicians, educators, and social reformers. These persons picked up the baton and led the march of the intelligence testing movement in this country. Mental testing was adopted in institutions across the country which had programs for the mentally retarded, and by numerous state teachers colleges. The test was advertised by proponents within the United States as the royal road toward the resolution of virtually all the social problems confronting the country. Whether it was a result of the enthusiasm of its proponents, the popularity of its use, or other unknown factors, the test did become an acceptable object for study within prestigious universities in the country. Lewis Terman, a professor at Stanford University, became one of the most important American scientists to be involved with the test. It was Terman who produced the 1916 Stanford-Binet intelligence test, the prototype of a series of similarly titled tests periodically revised. Terman translated the test into English and made it suitable for use with American children. He carefully standardized it to account for the idiosyncrasies of United States culture.

The original Binet-Simon test and the Terman revision were constructed to yield a single score, an intelligence quotient which would allow educational decisions to be made about children free from the personal biases of the decision makers. Thus intelligence was summarized by a single score through a standardized, objective procedure.

The development of a group test of intelligence was another very important event in the testing movement, a development which sprang from a national crisis. During World War I the nation needed to develop an easily administered test to screen men entering the military services. Eminent psychologists devised group tests, the Army Alpha and Beta, which the armed services used in testing more than 1.75 million men. The successful development of group tests for adults led, unsurprisingly, to the development of group tests for children. Within thirty months of publication, about 4 million children were administered group intelligence tests (Cronbach, 1975).

Since the pioneering work of Binet, Simon, and Terman the history of the testing movement has been marked by concern for practical problems. These tests were developed in order to create more objective decision-making procedures to maximize the educational, and subsequently social, benefits for the child and adult. No matter how the test creators had originally construed intelligence, it was reduced to a single score which became, in the hazy and befuddled translations of lay persons and professionals alike, a single entity or thing. The score which had been designed for practical purposes became viewed as an attribute of the person tested. As the tests became popular they were administered to virtually all children and adults who had contact with public institutions. It is not surprising that anxiety about the tests would similarly increase (Cronbach, 1975). At present, at least one city has banned the use of intelligence tests (Bersoff, 1973) and public scrutiny of these tests is being evidenced across the country.

We now turn our attention to contemporary views of intelligence, how it is measured, and a consideration of the usefulness of these measurements.

PERSPECTIVES OF INTELLIGENCE

Definitions

There have been wide variations in definitions of intelligence from theorist to theorist since the early 1900s. Indeed, in a famous symposium held by distinguished psychologists in 1921 the number of definitions of intelligence matched the number of participating psychologists.

Binet's view of intelligence, as mentioned earlier, shifted during the course of his work. Binet eventually settled on the idea that intelligence was the power to reason and understand (Sattler, 1974; Tuddenham, 1962). Terman believed intelligence was reflected in one's ability to carry on abstract thinking. Goddard, another early pioneer and enthusiastic supporter of the intelligence testing movement, suggested that intelligence was a single underlying faculty or function of the brain, which was determined by the genetic compositions of the individual. This underlying faculty was assumed by Goddard to control most human conduct of social or personal significance (Tuddenham, 1962).

Wechsler, a recent prominent figure in the testing movement and the author of a very popular test, the Wechsler Intelligence Scale for Children (WISC), defined intelligence as ". . . the capacity of an individual to understand the world about him and his resourcefulness to cope with its challenges . . ." (1975, p. 139). Wechsler further argues that intelligence cannot be equated with intellectual ability or capacity, since it includes motives, persistence, awareness of one's goals as well as reasoning processes.

Tuddenham suggests that intelligence is ". . . not an entity, nor even a dimension in a person" (p. 517), but rather it is ". . . an evaluation of a behavior sequence from the point of view of its adaptation adequacy" (p. 517). Similarly, Cleary, Humphreys, Kendrick, and Wesman view intelligence as the ". . . entire repertoire of acquired skills, knowledge, learning sets, and generalization tendencies considered intellectual in nature that are available at any one period of time" (1975, p. 19). These recent definitions of intelligence make it very clear that whatever intelligence tests measure, it is certainly not the capacity of the individual as defined by Wechsler (1975) or Cleary et al. (1975).

It is thus seen that intelligence has been defined in a manner which ranges from general adaptiveness to cognitive skills, knowledge, and specific reasoning abilities. There is some consensus among professionals as to what constitutes intellectual operations. Most psychologists appear to exclude from the definition the consideration of temporary motivational, social, or situational factors which might affect behavior. The consensus appears to be closer to the perspective of Binet, Simon, and Terman than that proposed by Wechsler.

Controversies about the definition are not the only debates that surround the field of intelligence. The nature of intelligence, the role of heredity, and the meaning of intelligence test scores are others; we turn now to these disputes.

General vs. Specific Abilities

Questions about the nature of intelligence represent one of the most long-standing issues among those theorizing about intelligence. This dispute revolves around the debate of whether intelligence is (a) many different and separate abilities, (b) a single overriding capacity which underlies each individual ability, or (c) a single entity in combination with a few specific abilities. Goddard was perhaps the first to argue that a single underlying factor accounted for an individual's performance on many tasks. Goddard apparently believed that a single factor best described intelligence, while Spearman believed that a general factor plus a specific factor best accounted for the pattern of results based upon measures of intellect. Thurstone, however, argued that intelligence was composed of many separate elements, each reflecting an ability. In this vein, Guilford (1966) has proposed a model of intelligence which hypothesizes that some 120 factors serve to reflect intelligence.

The current trend is to conceptualize intelligence as a cluster of partially independent abilities or operations rather than as a general single factor (Reese and Lipsett, 1970). On the one hand it does seem reasonable to look at the relationships between various measures of intellectual operations, and group them according to whether they correlate or are associated with each other. This is essentially the approach taken in factor analysis. It frequently yields results which reflect the operation of specific abilities rather than one ability which underlies the individuals' performances on a variety of tasks.

On the other hand, the view that intelligence should be construed as reflecting a multitude of separate abilities does not appear to lead to better predictions of an individual's later performance than would the use of tests designed to assess general intelligence. Oftentimes the predictions are worse (McNemar, 1964). Tests designed to measure specific abilities do not yield results which help obtain practical goals. Additionally, many of the discovered specific abilities do not appear stable. By using other subjects and somewhat other test items, old factors are not confirmed, and new abilities are discovered (Tuddenham, 1962). It is perhaps for these reasons that tests of specific abilities have not been able to supplant tests which assess to a minor degree a variety of abilities. Tests measuring complex functions, rather than specific abilities, still remain the most popularly employed measurement devices for assessing intelligence.

Genes

Perhaps no other topic has produced such violent controversy within recent years as the impact of genes upon intellectual functioning. It is a reflection of our times that the hypothesis that genes may be important in intellectual functioning has become so controversial, because this hypothesis has been advanced from almost the publication of the Binet test in 1905.

A popular early conception of intelligence was that such abilities were primarily if not exclusively determined by the subject's genes. Indeed, during the early 1900s, such conceptions were so widespread and held by so many distinguished psychologists that discriminatory legislation was enacted concerning the immigration of various ethnic groups to the United States (Kamin, 1973). The theory that there is genetic influence upon intellectual functioning was then, as it occasionally is now, employed for purposes of ethnic and racial discrimination.

But this use was not the only unfortunate application of early theorizing. A second notion associated with the genetic hypothesis was that any attribute stemming from man's biological basis was not amenable to change through remediation techniques. It was assumed that genes set the limits of an individual's behavior, and when those limits were reached so was the man's fulfillment of his hopes and dreams. It was further assumed that intelligence tests measured this innate capacity (McNemar, 1964).

It is our belief that this notion concerning genes, limits, and tests is still prevalent among laymen, if not among professionals. There really seems to be little reason to assume that the biological foundations of man are not somehow involved in the operations of his intellectual functions. We agree with Cleary et al. (1975) that such a faith is warranted on the basis of a number of studies on lower animals which have demonstrated the importance of selective breeding on a variety of behaviors (Fuller and Thompson, 1960). Activity level, aggression, sexual behavior, specific learning ability, to name but a few, of lower animals, have all been shown to be affected by genes.

To express such faith in the importance of biology's effect on intelligence, however, does not necessarily mean agreement with the implications often drawn from this position. It is increasingly realized that the impact of genes upon behavior is determined by the specific environment in which the individual finds himself. While there is certainly no learning without genes, neither can there be genetic actions without an environment. And apparently the influence of genes changes across environmental settings. We do not yet know how to assess the environmental-genetic interaction upon man. Thus it is not yet possible to determine just what role each may play in affecting intellectual functioning. It should also be noted that genes do not set the limits of intellectual functioning, since shifts in the environment can cause shifts in performances. Insofar as we do not yet know just how and what environments may alter intellectual functioning, we cannot determine when any individual has reached this presumed hypothetical limit (Liverant, 1960; Zigler, 1968).

Finally, there is no reason to assume that genetic influences on intelligence follow racial or ethnic lines. Until we are able to determine just how environments interact with specific genes affecting intellectual abilities, any notions that races or ethnic groups differ intellectually because of genetic sources cannot be reasonably assumed.

Whatever the definitional and theoretical disputes among professional researchers, it is our undocumented conviction that the public believes intelligence has two properties. First, laymen believe that intelligence is the capacity to act in all those ways necessary to have a meaningful, acceptable, and enriching life, and to make all the decisions necessary for maintaining that life. Secondly, we believe that laymen also assume that intelligence is a fixed attribute that characterizes an individual, and which remains fairly stable from early infancy to old age. McCall, Hogarty, and Hurlburt (1972) nicely summarize this popular conception of intelligence. They write that many believe that intelligence is "an unchanging characteristic that governs nearly all of the individual's mental performance at every age" (1972, p. 728). Finally, many people believe that intelligence tests measure this capacity. These assumptions concerning the breadth, stability, and measurement of this "thing" called intelligence are now being challenged.

The remainder of this chapter will be devoted to a discussion of methods of administration of some of the popularly employed tests of intelligence and the research findings relevant to them.

TESTING INTELLIGENCE

To understand the uses and abuses of intelligence tests, it is necessary to remember the history of the intelligence test movement. Binet's original goal was to help provide special education for intellectually defective children. He was aware that providing such special services to children might well result in stigmatizing them, and he was eager to reduce faulty diagnostic practices resulting from teacher's or judge's biases. He hoped to reduce such biases by providing a measurement procedure which was objective, would yield reliable scores, and would also predict the likelihood that children would benefit from exposure to ordinary classroom experiences. Both Binet's original test development and its current offspring of intelligence tests are far removed from theories concerning intelligence.

Today we have several good instruments which can be used to assess present or near future academic performance or achievement. Many people, however, do not think of or use intelligence tests with these limited goals in mind. Intelligence test results are presumed to provide information which transcends that of supplying predictions concerning school grades.

But what do such tests tell us? Do they predict behaviors, and if so, which ones? Is the information drawn from such tests reflecting a stable phenomenon not subject to significant changes? Is this information useful for discriminating among children for diagnosis, special classroom assignment, tutoring, or psychotherapy? Can an analysis of an individual's responses to various parts of the examination be used to help describe the personality and personal difficulties of the test taker? How are the tests administered and of what do they consist? The remainder of the chapter is addressed to these questions concerning intelligence tests.

It is clearly beyond the scope of this book to discuss the nature and results of all of the many tests which are presumed to assess intellectual capacities. Instead we will focus upon two of the more frequently used instruments. Before we do so, however, we will discuss briefly the methods for evaluating the merits of a particular test.

Reliability

Any method of assessing differences among people must be evaluated in terms of its reliability and validity. *Reliability* "means the dependability of the assessment you are making" (London, 1975, p. 317). The question is whether the results that are obtained from the test are likely to be obtained again. There are several ways to determine the dependability of the measure.

One method is to ask the same questions of an individual at different times. This method, the *test-retest* method, is simply giving the subject the same test on two different occasions. If he repeatedly answers most questions the same way, the test will be judged reliable; i.e., dependable.

A second method of determining reliability is that in which you determine whether the test taker answers the question in the same way when the phrasing of the question is somewhat different. If the individual's answers are consistent, the test question will be judged reliable. This second method for determining reliability is often referred to as the *split-half,* or *alternative form,* method. If the results of tests are not reliable or dependable, then they cannot be used to make predictions concerning the test taker's future behavior.

It should be noted that reliability does not establish the truthfulness of the test; it says nothing about what you are measuring, but simply that whatever you are assessing you are obtaining dependable answers. As London points out, "all sane observers, using the naked eye alone, can agree that the earty is flat and the sun goes around it—the observation is perfectly *reliable,* and perfectly *untrue"* (p. 317). But reliability is not enough to establish the adequacy of a test. A test must also be *valid.* The evaluation of a test requires that the scores obtained are useful in predicting something other than how the individual will answer the same questions again.

Validity

Validity refers to the test's predictive powers, and there are various methods for establishing validity. One form of validity is called *criterion* or *predictive validity.* This form of validity refers to how well test results will predict something. Thus, one method of validating an intelligence test would be to determine if such tests predict subsequent performance in school, in learning tasks, or in creativity. The validity of the test is determined by how well the results can predict some behavior other than behavior on the same test.

The second type of validity is *construct validity*, which refers to the degree to which the test correlates with behaviors dictated by some theory. Validation requirements for construct validity are more rigorous than other kinds of validity checks. A single prediction will not suffice to establish construct validation. Rather a network of predictions between the test and the behaviors which the theory suggests as relevant must be demonstrated. "A test with high construct validity approaches the concept from many different angles which should be logically related to each other . . . and tries to see empirically if the logical relations are supported by the facts of behavior" (London, 1975, p. 321). "Construct validity is evaluated by a complex combination of logical and empirical operations in which the test and the theory underlying it are subjected to simultaneous scrutiny" (Cleary et al., 1975, p. 25).

Sechrest (1967) has proposed another type of validity which should be employed when evaluating a test. While his recommendation has not been generally accepted or applied, it is our belief that it is an important one. Sechrest has proposed that tests be evaluated as to their *incremental validity*. Given that a test has some form of validity, Schrest suggests that it also be evaluated as to whether it demonstrates "efficiency over the information otherwise easily and cheaply available" (p. 369). It really does not make sense to administer lengthy tests at high costs of time and money to determine an answer to a question that can be answered at considerably less cost.

There is yet another consideration concerning tests that must be addressed, and that concerns the use of tests for individual diagnosis. Teachers and parents involved with exceptional children are fundamentally concerned with aiding particular children to achieve particular goals. Interest is at the individual level rather than being concerned with the benefits that might be derived by groups of children. All currently available psychological tests, however valid, are not perfect. Some are better than others, but none can yield perfect measures. Whenever a test is given to a group of children, errors of measurement will be made. Sometimes the test score of a particular child will lead to the inference that that child has an attribute which in fact he does not. Hence, a child may be labeled as anxious, or hyperactive, or aggressive when, in fact, he is neither anxious, nor hyperactive, nor aggressive. Such pseudo high scores thus lead to an incorrect labeling of a child. These instances of false labeling are referred to as *false positives*. On the other hand, children's scores on any particular test may be inaccurately low. Hence such children may be viewed as not being anxious, hyperactive, or aggressive when in fact they are. These instances of misdiagnosis are referred to as *false negatives*.

All psychological tests will yield some false negatives and false positives. Thus professionals involved with the diagnosis and treatment of individuals are often faced with an important question, and their answer to it will have important implications for the children with whom they deal. That question is: How many false negatives and false positives are acceptable in a particular test? Tests simply must be viewed as to these false instances, and testers should be aware that reliance on one or even a multitude of tests will yield misdiagnoses. Just what standards concerning these instances should prevail in good clinical practice?

A study by Huelsman (1970) nicely illustrates these points. In the field of learning disabilities, there is a prevalent hypothesis that discrepancies of performance on particular subparts of intelligence tests can be used for individual diagnosis. There is some evidence that reading failures, as a group, can be discriminated from children without such difficulties on the basis of subtest discrepancies. But if one were to use this evidence as the basis of diagnosing individual children's reading capabilities, 39 percent of the reading failures and 38 percent of the reading achievers would be misdiagnosed! Whether such error rates in diagnosis would be acceptable to most clinicians is doubtful.

Finally, you shoud be aware that the publication of a test docs not guarantee that the test is reliable or valid. Meeting the minimal standards of reliability and validity as indicated by the book *Standards for Educational and Psychological Tests and Manuals,* published by the American Psychological Association, is voluntary on the part of the test constructor. Many tests are published which do not meet these standards and appear to be valuable only for producing a healthy income for its constructors. Before one puts faith in a test, one should investigate its dependability and accuracy.

Let us now turn to descriptions of some of the more popular tests of intelligence, and to those research findings relevant to them. We will first discuss some of those measures which are often employed in testing infants. Then we will attend those tests more frequently employed with the preschool and school-age youngster.

INFANT INTELLIGENCE TESTS

The development of infant intelligence tests has a long history. The first test of the mental abilities of infants was proposed by Gesell in 1925. Since Gesell's pioneering work, other scales, such as Cattell's *Mental Test for Infants and Young Children* and Bayley's *Scales of Infant Development,* have been offered. Cattell's test hit the market in 1940, while Bayley's initial version was first produced in 1936. Infant tests have been around for a while, and because of their availability, considerable research on and refinements of these tests have occurred. The assumption of a number of early theorists was that intelligence might be inherited, or at least it was something not easily influenced by environmental forces. If these assumptions were correct, then it would be possible to develop a measure of intellectual capacity of the infant.

One of the major desires is the development of methods to detect potential learning problems in preschool and kindergarten children. The employment of infant tests of intelligence for such purposes is predicated upon the assumption that detection and intervention at this stage of the child's development will prevent failure in the elementary school years. To detect and intervene requires a measure which will predict school failure at some future time. Discrepancies in the growth of critical areas, such as language and perceptual motor skills, are assumed to be predictive of subsequent failure in reading, writing, and arithmetic. The faith in early detection is a faith in our ability to detect inadequacies in very young children. The latter faith is based upon the notion that a child's development proceeds in a regular and predictable fashion, that delays in defined developmental areas are linked critically to skills needed by the child as he progresses, and that measures of these important developments can be devised for application with very young children.

A further assumption underlying the early detection movement is that intervention provided for children experiencing developmental delays will eliminate later problems. If problems are dealt with early, special services may not be required later. These assumptions have been based in large part upon longitudinal studies of high-risk infants in which traumas related to birth have been linked to conceptual and behavioral problems later exhibited by such children; post hoc analyses of parental descriptions of the developmental histories of their disabled children; and studies of language development in normal and language-deviant children.

The Nature of Infant Tests

Insofar as these tests are frequently used, the reader should be aware of the particular behaviors which are important in the evaluation of the child.

The Gesell scales were first reported in 1925 and have undergone a series of revisions. The scales give norms for critical ages beginning at age 4 weeks and terminating at age 36 months, spanning the first three years of a youngster's development. The behaviors which are assessed at each age level are divided into four categories: motor, adaptive, personal-social, and language (Bayley, 1970). There are several categories which do not appear to reflect the operation of mental function. For example, the category of motor behaviors includes assessment of body control, manual coordination, creeping, walking, and jumping while the personal-social items refer to such behaviors as feeding oneself, toileting, and dressing. According to Bayley (1970), the tested mental responses are those which fall into the categories of adaptive and language actions. Adaptive behaviors refer to the child looking at, reaching for, and manipulating an object such as a rattle or cube; his building of a tower from blocks or placing blocks into a form board. Language items include cooing, being alert, speaking, and understanding simple words.

The Cattell Infant Intelligence scale employs many of the language and adaptive category items from the Gesell scales. Test items are available for use with 2- to 30-month-old infants. At the older levels, items from the Stanford-Binet Intelligence test are intermingled with those drawn from the Gesell scales. Unlike the Gesell scales, which yields a developmental age score, the Cattell scales are scored to produce an intelligence quotient (mental age/chronological age × 100).

Bayley's Mental and Motor scales are suitable for use with children ranging in age from 1 to 30 months. Like the Cattell scales, this test has borrowed many items from previously published infants scales. Thus the Motor scale includes items of holding one's head up, creeping, standing, turning over, sitting, and manual skills like throwing a ball. The Mental scale consists of items referring to adaptive behaviors; for example, attending to visual stimuli, shaking a rattle, cooing, smiling, imitating, following instructions, and showing memory for an object no longer in view (Bayley, 1970). The Mental and Motor scales are scored separately to yield a Mental Development index and a Psychomotor Development index. The final form of the test was developed on the basis of over 1,200 children's responses. The care taken in developing this test and providing normative information concerning children's responses to the test items makes this test the best developed of the three infant tests discussed.

Accuracy of Infant Tests

The original hope of infant test developers was to devise an assessment procedure which could be employed with infants so that predictions concerning their later intellectual development could be made with some accuracy. This hope carried with it some assumptions. With respect to such aspirations and measures, Kagan has written, "Much of the research on infant mental development has been guided by two related—and essentially unproven—hypotheses. The first posits a hypothetical entity, called intelligence, which can be measured by noting the rate of development of those response systems that are emerging at the moment. . . . There are neither adequate data nor persuasive theory to support this axiom. . . . A second assumption guiding work with infants presumes that early cognitive structures are derivative of sensorimotor actions, a view usually attributed to Piaget. The significance of sensorimotor coordination for adaptive functions is readily acknowledged, but their necessary causal connections to cognitive development are, we believe, still open to debate" (1971, 177–178). Kagan directly challenges the utility of current concepts of infant intelligence and, by implication, the utility of tests which rest upon these concepts.

The traditional method for determining the validity of an infant intelligence test is to administer the test to a group of infants, wait several years, and then administer a test of intelligence (usually the Stanford-Binet) to the same group of children. The validity of the infant test is indexed by the degree to which scores on it are predictive of scores on the second test. But most reviewers of research on infant intelligence tests have generally concluded, with varying degrees of pessimism, that infant tests are of little use in predicting later intelligence test scores. Bayley (1970) has written, "The findings of these early studies of mental growth of infants have been repeated sufficiently often so that it is now well-established that test scores earned in the first year or two have relatively little predictive validity (in contrast to tests at school age or later), although they may have high validity as measures of the children's cognitive abilities at the time. . . . The lack of stability in the first three years cannot be attributed to poor reliability of the measuring instrument" (1970, p. 1174). In a somewhat more optimistic vein, McCall, Hogarty, and Hurlburt write, "it is something of an overstatement to say that there is 'no prediction' from the infancy period to childhood IQ. There are correlations that attain statistical significance between certain ages from some tests, but the size of the relationships is not particularly impressive and certainly not adequate for clinical application" (1972, p. 729).

By and large it is safe to say that there are no genuinely valid infant intelligence tests, if validity is meant to imply that a test given to an infant under 2 years of age will predict his scores on intelligence tests given years later. As early as 1939, Anderson failed to find correlations between scores obtained by the children on the Stanford-Binet Intelligence scale at age 5. In 1972, the picture had not appreciably changed. McCall, Hogarty, and Hurlburt (1972) summarized the results of nine separate studies which involved the repeated testing of children over a long period of time, and indicated that none reported consistent findings which would suggest that intelligence test scores correlated with those obtained from the same children some years later. Pease, Rosauer, and Wolins (1961) administered the Gesell and Cattell scales to infants at ages 3, 6, 9, and 12 months and found no correlation of the test scores with scores obtained in adjacent months. Likewise, Hindley (1960) failed to find that children's scores on the Griffiths Scale of Infant Development (another often used test) at 3, 6, 9, 12, and 18 months were correlated across ages on any of the five scales of this test.

These are but a few of the many studies which led to the conclusion that there is a lack of predictive validity in infant intelligence tests. The interested or disbelieving reader is referred to a more complete review by Bayley (1970), Lewis (1973), and McCall et al. (1972) for further demonstration. The evidence on this point has been well summarized by Lewis, who states, "Within a wide variety of standardized tests such as the Bayley and Gesell there is relatively little interage consistency in test performance during the first two years of life. Thus, children who are precocious at one age are not necessarily precocious at another. Moreover, early precociousness in the first two years seems to be unrelated to childhood performance on standard IQ tasks" (1973, p. 111).

It is now clear that summary scores on the various infant tests of intelligence are unlikely to be predictive of subsequent intellectual development. Why is this the case and is it always true?

First, it must be recognized that the procedures for the development of the Cattell and Gesell scales are, by today's standard, inadequate. In developing their scales, these pioneers simply used too few children upon which to base their norms (Bayley, 1970). However, the problem of the accuracy of these tests cannot be simply attributed to the low reliability of the scales. Bayley's scales have been demonstrated to have adequate dependability.

Types of Behaviors Measured

A second potential problem associated with the use of infant scales for predicting future test results lies in the types of behaviors measured. It is possible that many of the infant scales reflect both errors of commission and errors of omission. First, most of the items comprising such tests are addressed to sensory and motor skills, skills not assessed by childhood IQ tests such as the Stanford-Binet (SB) or the Wechsler Intelligence Scale for Children (WISC). The latter scales primarily tap linguistic or verbal skills. Bayley has suggested that the "lack of consistency over time in mental test scores reflects a series of changes in the nature of mental processes as they progress from simple sensori-motor adjustments to increasingly complex forms of adaptations, generalizations, abstractions, and their accompanying reasoning processes" (1970, p. 1177). On the face of it, it would be surprising if simple sensorimotor abilities were correlated with the verbal skills developed by the child as he matures. These tests do not measure the same abilities continuously across different ages.

There is another reason why scores on infant tests are not good predictors of subsequent scores on childhood intelligence tests. Some evidence suggests that perceptual and attentional factors may be an important basis for intellectual development (Kagan, 1969; Lewis and Goldberg, 1969; Maccoby, Dowling, Hagen, and Degerman, 1965). Specific items designed to assess these factors have not been included within the popularly employed infant tests. Hence, it would appear that the infant tests of intelligence might well be measuring the wrong behaviors, and not measuring the appropriate behaviors, at least if one's goal is to predict infants' subsequent IQ scores on the SB or the WISC.

It would be misleading to suggest that the baby should be thrown out with the dirty bath water. Not all aspects of the infant scales fail to be predictive, nor is the total score useless for all children. One particular feature of the infant scales that may be predictive of subsequent intelligence test scores is that pertaining to vocal behaviors and language development. McCall et al. (1972) reported a number of studies which suggest that there is some hope for the utilization of infant scales, but that there is some need to reexamine what leads to what and for whom.

In one study, infants who had been administered the Gesell scale at 6, 12, 18, or 24 months were subsequently administered Stanford-Binet at 3½, 6, or 10 years of age or the Weschler scale at a later time. It was found that items on the Gesell scale which involved vocalizations best predicted later IQ scores, and this was particularly true for female infants. The authors also referred to other investigations which suggest this relationship between vocalization and later IQ scores. In a study conducted in England, for example, the results were that the speech quotient obtained on the Griffiths Infant scale by 18-month-old children was predictive of general IQ scores when those children were 8 years of age. However, this relationship held only for females. "In summary, three studies indicate that vocalization in infancy may have special salience for females that it does not have for males with respect to predicting later mental performance" (McCall et al., 1972, p. 735). Three studies do not make a test, but clearly the results are suggestive of a new direction in infant intelligence testing.

Mention was also made of the fact that the total scores on infant intelligence scales are not necessarily devoid of all meaning. While total scores are not helpful in predicting subsequent test scores for most children, there is a category of children where such tests might be usefully applied. Children who score abnormally low on the infant tests are likely to obtain low scores of subsequent intelligence tests. In effect then, ". . . it has been possible to make fairly good prediction of future low intellectual status, especially when organic damage was apparent in infancy, but it has not been possible to make good predictions within the normal or superior ranges" (Reese and Lipsett, 1970, p. 536). This finding is perhaps not surprising since one purpose of developing these scales was to detect which children might have severe dysfunctions. Apparently such tests can be useful in the early detection of children who are likely to experience rather severe problems in their intellectual development. The predictive validities of infant tests in estimating subsequent IQ scores may be increased by limiting testing to children who are physically or developmentally abnormal, especially when such test scores are combined with the observations of pediatricians (Werner, Honzik, and Smith, 1968).

Sechrest (1967) has suggested that tests need to be evaluated on the basis of their power to increase knowledge over that obtained by more economical procedures. Tests should be judged as to their *incremental validity*. After reviewing many studies in which infant tests were compared to other sources of information, McCall et al. concluded that "these results imply that parental education may be a better predictor of childhood IQ than an assessment on the child during the first two years of life" (1972, p. 733). For the child of average or rapid development, the parent's socioeconomic status is a better predictor of subsequent intellectual development than are the results obtained from infant intelligence tests. When there is suspicion of defective development, such as mental retardation or brain damage, the infant scale may usefully be employed. In most cases, these tests will lack incremental as well as predictive validity.

The bulk of the data leads to the inference that infant scales are not measures of intelligence, if one means scores obtained on subsequent childhood intelligence tests. There is little to indicate that the use of these tests with very young children is justifiable, with the important exception of infants who may be severely disabled. In this case, the assessment should lead to differential diagnosis and intervention, such as would occur if it were established that the child was hearing impaired rather than severely retarded. At the same time, concern must be voiced for the children who are misdiagnosed as either pathological or normal. There is no compelling evidence to suggest that *false positive* and *false negative* instances of misdiagnosis are so few that we can feel comfortable in applying infant tests for individual diagnosis. We do not know that such tests increase our information above that which is obtained by ratings or observations made by parents, pediatricians, or sensitive and experienced child watchers. If the result is merely a slight increment in knowledge, the question must be asked as to whether such knowledge is worth depriving other children of the scarce and costly time of a professional psychologist or psychometrician.

The discouraging results obtained regarding infant tests have led researchers along two somewhat different empirical paths. Some are attempting to refine the psychometric approach, eliminating items which are not predictive and adding items which may be more useful and predictive of later scores. An example of such efforts is the work of Cameron, Livson, and Bayley (1967) on the relationships of infant vocalizations to subsequent intelligence scores.

A second approach is to emphasize the study of cognitive processes rather than the development of better test items (Kagan, 1971; Zigler, 1968). Determinants of attention, such as heart rate deceleration and inhibition of motor activity, become the types of behaviors studied in this approach. When the emphasis is upon cognitive processes, researchers focus on determinants of what might constitute encoding and decoding of stimulus inputs. The focus is upon how infants receive, organize, and respond to new information.

With the notable exception of the severely handicapped child, it is no longer possible to assume that infant intelligence tests, loaded at younger ages with measures of sensorimotor skills, yield useful information about subsequent IQ scores or academic success, which emphasize verbal skills.

CHILDHOOD INTELLIGENCE TESTS

We guess that by now almost everyone in this society has had some type of test of intelligence. It is a booming business, albeit a controversial one. In the remainder of this chapter we hope to familiarize you somewhat with the nature of the two most popular tests of children's intelligence, the Stanford-Binet (SB) and the Wechsler Intelligence Scale for Children (WISC). Following the description of these two important tests, we will look at some of the findings concerning influences upon test scores and what these scores have been interpreted to mean. We hope that you will get a sense of the complexity and ambiguity surrounding the usual measurement of intelligence.

Stanford-Binet

This test, originally published in France in 1905, has undergone five revisions. Its latest form was published in 1960 by Terman and Merrill (1960), while the test norms were updated as recently as 1972 (Terman and Merrill, 1973). The test is designed to assess individuals ranging in age from 2 to 18 years, but its use is probably mostly limited to children. In the latest revision, little new material was added and there were no changes in the format of the test, but there is a greater emphasis on word knowledge than in the 1937 version. In addition, items whose content was irrelevant to scholastic aptitude were eliminated in the 1960 scales (Cronbach, 1960).

There are 142 test items which are presented to the subject in order of difficulty, defined by the percentage of subjects who passed the item. Difficulty level is well established, as more than 4,000 individuals were recently tested to assure that items had not changed in this regard. As you can well imagine, any test which assesses individuals ranging in age from 2 to 18 years of age would have items which vary in content. To describe the nature of the items, we have adopted the analysis of the SB made by Anastasi (1961) and Freeman (1962).

> *Years 2–5:* At these age levels, the subtests involve manipulations of objects (placement of pieces in a simple form board, block building), recognition of body parts, the recognition of objects referred to by name and by function. Rote memory, the use of words in combination, verbal comprehension, and word knowledge are also assessed.
> *Years 6–12:* The child is tested for form perception, visual motor skills, rote memory, word knowledge, number concepts, and arithmetical reasoning.
> *Years 13–Superior Adult III:* At this level, visual analysis and imagery, visual motor skills, rote memory for digits, words and sentences, work knowledge, and problem-solving are assessed.

Memory, spatial orientation, numerical concepts, and language skills are tapped at scattered age levels throughout the test, using increasingly difficult items. For example, tests of memory may require the child to recall objects or the content of passages. Numerical tests start with simple counting and proceed to complex reasoning problems. The reliability of items within each age level seems adequate with the lowest reliability occurring at age level 3 and the highest at the Superior Adult II (Terman and Merrill, 1973). The final IQ score is a deviation IQ. The IQ score indicates the amount by which a person deviates from the average performance of individuals of his own age group. An IQ score of 100 reflects the average score for subjects within that particular age range. The standard deviation of the IQ score is approximately 16 points. In layman's language this means that given a random sample of children, approximately 68 percent will achieve scores on the SB between 84 and 116, while an additional 14 percent will obtain a score between 116 and 132. By the same token, another 14 percent will obtain scores between 84 and 68. Thus 96 percent of the children tested would be expected to obtain an IQ score between 132 and 68.

The test is administered individually to the child. The procedure of administration is to start the test at the level in which the child is likely to pass all of the items and proceed to the age level where the child fails all of the items. The subject has to have adequate vision, hearing, and oral speech for proper administration of the test. Sensory or language defects can seriously affect the score.

The 1937 and 1960 forms of the SB are heavily weighted with items which assess verbal abilities. Anastasi (1961) reports correlations between scores on the vocabulary test and the mental age of the child range from .71 to .83 for children 8 to 14 years old. Stormer's study of the 1960 revision of the SB indicated that the upper year levels contained items which primarily tap verbal abilities (Sattler, 1974). Ramsey and Vane (1970) also found similar results in their analysis of items used to test young children. There is little debate that the SB consists of many items which measure the verbal abilities of children. It also appears that other abilities are assessed at different age levels and that items at various age levels do not necessarily measure the same abilities as items in other parts of the test (Sattler, 1974).

The 1960 version of the SB has been accused of a variety of ills as well as virtues. Cronbach has written that this scale and its predecessor ". . . is an instrument efficiently designed for one particular function, namely, providing a single score describing the child's present level of general intellectual ability. It is interesting to the child, precise, and well standardized. The large amount of research on the scale gives a basis for interpreting results which no newer test can offer" (1960, p. 188). On the other hand, criticisms of the test have included the lack of assessment of the child's creativity, the emphasis upon verbal abilities, its lack of adequacy in assessing very superior students, and the various placement of items at particular age levels (Sattler, 1974). In addition it should be noted that adequate test performance requires, at the minimum, some experiences common in an urban culture. As Cronbach (1960) has written, "[it] is of dubious value for comparing culture groups" (p. 184).

Finally, mention should be made of the clinical uses of the SB test. For many decades, the hypothesis that one can make inferences concerning emotional or pathological conditions of the test taker on the basis of his SB scores has been entertained. Hypotheses concerning the revealing of pathological states through test performance have served to stimulate research and to provide substance to clinicians' diagnostic reports. The reasoning is that if an individual shows a wide range of *unexpected* successes and failures on the SB, the *scatter* or *variability* reflects the presence of some abnormality. If the child shows that he is capable of successfully performing one intellectual operation, subsequent failures on the items which require this operation reflect a kind of "mental block." Clinicians, psychologists, or special educators often attend to and attribute importance to variability or scatter in a test taker's performance on the SB. There are a number of ways in which scatter can be indexed. For example, scatter may be reflected by a subject ". . . failing a test at a given year level and passing a test at higher year levels" (Sattler, 1974). Indeed, Harris and Shakow (1937) were able to evaluate research which involved nine different methods for determining scatter. By and large, research attempts to validate clinical hypotheses concerning scatter have not been successful, and probably for good reason. A scattered performance by an individual may well reflect factors other than emotional disturbances. Scatter can be the result of factors intrinsic to the test, such as the unreliability of the items comprising the measure of scatter. Scatter can be related to characteristics of the person which are not reflections of pathological states. Examples are momentary lapses in the subject's cooperation with the examiner, or the not-so-momentary condition wherein the subject has acquired particular skills. Indeed, Liverant (1960) has pointed out that scatter in intellectual performances may be the rule rather than the exception for most of us. While clinicians may well be obligated to report that which they observe, and speculate as to the meaning of variations in test performance, it is clear that they must do so at considerable risk of error and should do so with considerable humility. The use of scatter on the SB might provide some interesting ideas about the child which require further exploration, but scatter in itself does not provide adequate demonstration of any attribution of the individual being tested.

The Wechsler Intelligence Scale for Children

The WISC is the Stanford-Binet's chief competitor. "The chief differences are in organization, in greater precision of the Binet at low mental ages, and in the greater variety of tasks in the Wechsler scale" (Cronbach, 1960, p. 189). The WISC is widely used for the assessment of intelligence in children ages 5 to 15. There is a form available for testing adults, the Wechsler Adult Intelligence Scale (WAIS), and one for children ages 4 to 6, the Wechsler Preschool and Primary Scale of Intelligence (WPPSI). The scale consists of twelve subjects, two of which are optional. Of the ten required subtests, five form the basis for the Verbal Intelligence score, while the remaining five comprise the tests making up the Performance Intelligence score. The two IQ scores can be combined to yield a Full Scale IQ score.

The Verbal Scale subtests, and items similar to those used, include:

1. General information: From what animal do we get milk?
2. Comprehension: What are some reasons we need fireman?
3. Arithmetic: If I cut a peach into thirds, how many pieces will I have?
4. Similarities: In what ways are a tree and a bush alike?
5. Vocabulary: Tell me what rainbow means.
6. Digit span (optional): Repeat the following numbers: 3-4-5-6-7-8.

The Performance Scale subtests of the WISC include:

1. Picture completion: The child is shown a drawing and is asked to indicate which part of the drawing is missing (for example, a missing nose from a drawing of a face).
2. Picture arrangement: The child is presented with several pictures which, when arranged properly, will depict a meaningful story.
3. Block design: The child is presented with a set of red and white blocks which are to be arranged to match a pattern demonstrated in a picture.
4. Object assembly: The child is presented with a jigsaw puzzle which must be arranged to yield a meaningful product, such as a face.
5. Coding: There are two coding tests, one appropriate for use with children 5 to 7 years, the second for children 8 to 15 years. The version suitable for the younger children presents them with pictures of various shapes, such as a star and a circle. Inside the shape is another symbol, a vertical line, a horizontal line, or a circle and so on. Below this presentation are five rows of symbols which have not been filled in. The child is shown how to match shapes to symbols, and during the test proper, is given two minutes to complete the task. The version of coding for the older child is essentially the same, but the visual stimulus is a set of boxes divided in half, the top half being a number between one and nine, the bottom half being geometric symbols. The child is given two minutes to complete the task.
6. Mazes (optional): The child completes a series of mazes which increases in difficulty.

Like the SB, the WISC was recently revised. The first form of the WISC was published in 1949, and this was somewhat altered in 1974 (Wechsler, 1974). The newer version is referred to as the Wechsler Intelligence Test for Children–Revised (WISC-R). Test revisions were based upon the responses of more than 2,200 children who were fairly representative of all children in terms of place of residence, socioeconomic status of the family, and race of the children tested. One alteration in the recent revision of the test was to raise the age range of the test. While the WISC was suitable for testing children 5 to 15 years of age, the WISC-R is appropriate for use with children 6 to 16 years. In addition, the new group of subjects tested to develop norms of performance included a proportional representation of nonwhites, thus correcting a serious shortcoming of the WISC. Finally, the content of items was changed so as to, among other things, give them a more contemporary ring than that of the 1949 test items. By and large, however, the format and the subtests are quite similar to those of the original WISC.

The reliability of the test is quite good, whether it is determined by the split-half method or the test-retest procedure. The reliabilities of the verbal and performance IQ scores as well as for the Full Scale IQ score is quite high, and all are higher than the reliabilities associated with the subtests of the WISC-R.

Like the SB, the WISC-R IQ score is a *deviation* score, with the average score being 100 and the standard deviation 15. Hence about 84 percent of children tested will obtain an IQ score no greater than 115. The highest 1 percent of individuals at any age level will have IQ scores over 135 and the lowest 1 percent will have IQs of 65 or below.

Insofar as the WISC-R is a relatively new test, research pertaining to it is sparse. However, given its similarities to the WISC, it is likely that the findings relative to that test might well characterize the WISC-R as well. We briefly present some of these findings.

A number of hypotheses have been generated about the significance of particular subtests for revealing components of intellectual and emotional functioning. These hypotheses are quite popular in spite of the failure to obtain empirical verification of them. The following discussion is based upon Sattler's (1974) review of these ideas.

The general information subtest is often considered a reflection of the child's cultural background and ability to remember that to which he has been exposed. The comprehension subtest is considered a measure of the child's social judgments and ability to use facts in a social and emotionally relevant manner. The arithmetic subtest is considered to be a good index of reasoning ability plus "numerical accuracy in mental arithmetic" (Sattler, 1974, p. 189). The similarities subtest is often thought to reflect verbal concept formation and logical thinking, while the vocabularly subtest is believed related to a variety of mental operations which involve language ability and general information. The digit span subtest is linked to attention and short-term memory, while the picture completion subtest is thought to assess ability to separate the trivial from important details in the environment. The picture arrangement subtest is considered a measure of nonverbal reasoning ability and the ability to plan ahead. There is some question of whether any reasoning tasks are entirely free from verbal processes (Bryan and Bryan, 1975). The block design subtest is linked to visual-motor coordination and ability to perceptually organize or make sense of the environment. The object assembly test is also considered a good estimate of perceptual organization. The coding subtest is thought to be a measure of the child's visual-motor coordination, speed of mental operation, and short-term memory, while the mazes subtest is considered a reflection of planning ability and perceptual organization.

While these clinical interpretations of subtests are popular, there is not much empirical support for their validity. Factor analytic studies of the WISC find that the test taps some five different abilities (Sattler, 1974). Sattler suggests that the WISC measures two types of verbal abilities. One type is verbal knowledge which is the result of formal education. The second is the ability to apply judgments following implicit verbal manipulations. The third and fourth factors are related to attentional abilities and to interpreting and organizing visually perceived information within a limited period of time. The fifth factor appears to have no psychological interpretation.

There have been attempts to employ the WISC as a diagnostic test of other than intellectual functions. Wechsler (1958) and Rappaport (1946) suggested that the diagnosis of emotional and mental states of a person might be made on the basis of the pattern, or scatter of subtest scores. Differences between Verbal and Performance IQ scores or differences between sets of subtest scores form the basis of scatter analysis. Since there are twelve subtests and three additional scores, there are many forms of scatter analyses. By and large, the use of scatter analyses has not increased our ability to make predictions about the emotional or social state of the individual. It has been found that individual subtest scores are not sufficiently reliable to yield information based on scatter analyses (McNemar, 1957). It is also apparent that even if groups can be discriminated using scatter analyses, the number of false positives and negatives is sufficient to preclude the use of a scatter analysis for individual diagnosis. In a strong statement against the use of scatter analysis, Cronbach wrote: "No objective treatment of the Wechsler scores has proved able to classify individual patients with a useful degree of accuracy. Indices representing 'scatter' of subtest scores—e.g., the range from highest to lowest subtest score—are worthless as diagnostic signs" (1960, p. 201).

So far we have presented the internal properties of the SB and the WISC. The format of the test, the types of test items, the relationship among test items, and the use of subgrouping test items to form judgments about the test taker have been described. Now we turn to critical questions which have been asked about the use of these tests. For instance, questions have been raised about what these tests predict, the stability of test scores, factors which make test scores unreliable, and the applicability of these tests to groups of children, particularly children from minority group backgrounds.

USES OF CHILDHOOD INTELLIGENCE TESTS

One of the questions asked is what behaviors do intelligence tests predict. It is clear that scores on one intelligence test do predict scores on other intelligence tests (Littell, 1960; Sattler, 1974). If you want to predict how well a person will score on the SB you might as well test the person with the WISC. Most of the time we are not interested in how one performs on different intelligence tests. The goals are usually more lofty than predictions of how persons respond to various intelligence tests.

Correlates of IQ Scores

"The man in the street, and often the unwary psychologist too, thinks of intelligence as something really existing 'out there'; something which the psychologist may or may not recognize successfully, and measure with more or less success. In these terms it would make sense to argue about whether a particular test 'really' measures intelligence. Such reification is utterly mistaken; there is nothing 'out there' which could be called intelligence . . . concepts only exist in the minds of scientists" (Eysenck, 1973, p. 1). The conceptualization of the nature of intelligence and what intelligence tests actually measure are two very different things. Many people believe that there is a "true intelligence" or a "potentional intelligence," a relatively constant ability perhaps genetically influenced which is instrumental in determining the child's behavior in a wide variety of situations. The search for culture-fair, culture-free tests of intelligence reflects the belief that there is a "potential intelligence" located under the skin which can and should be separated from cultural influences and experiential history (Liverant, 1960). When we examine the definition of learning disabilities, we see that potential intelligence is a mainstay in the definition against which academic failure is assessed. However, intelligence "is not an entity, nor even a dimension in a person . . . [Intelligence is] an evaluation of a behavior sequence from the point of view of its adaptive adequacy" (Tuddenham, 1962, p. 517).

Intelligence may also be defined on the basis of what intelligence tests predict. It is important to note that the meaning of a concept can be defined on the basis of the tests used to measure it. The meaning of the concept is defined on the basis of the behaviors which the test results predict. Cleary et al. suggest: "intelligence and other ability tests are useful to the extent to which they are correlated with socially relevant and important criteria, not whether they measure someone's conception of innate capacity" (1975, 23). Children's intelligence test scores predict which behaviors? Scores on these measures tell us something about the child, such as his social class and the attitudes of his parents (Bayley, 1970; Reese and Lipsitt, 1970; McClelland, 1973); but is that what we mean by the concept of intelligence? Surely we do not administer intelligence tests to ascertain parental education level, parental achievement demands, or other cultural influences upon test scores. We can obtain this kind of information by asking and observing parents. But these variables are important correlates of intelligence test scores.

Children's intelligence test scores do provide us with information about who is likely to do well in school and on tests of school achievement (McNemar, 1964; McClelland, 1973). Anastasi writes: ". . . the Stanford-Binet is primarily a measure of scholastic aptitude . . ." (1961, p. 208). The same can be said of the WISC. There is some evidence that intelligence tests are helpful in predicting future occupational success, although the degree of the test's power to do so is open to debate (McClelland, 1973; Sattler, 1974). There is some evidence that intelligence tests are useful in predicting performance on some laboratory tests of learning which involve verbal content, although it has by no means been shown that these tests measure learning ability in all tasks (Stevenson, 1970).

In sum, intelligence test scores are good predictors of performance in school work, learning tasks with high verbal content, other intelligence tests, parental social class, and perhaps future occupational success. It should not be surprising that intelligence test scores predict these particular variables. Middle-class parents emphasize the importance of school work and verbal skills. Verbal skills are in high demand in the performance of school work. Intelligence tests involve the measurement of verbal skills, and occupational success may depend upon school experiences, which are in turn dependent upon verbal skills.

There is general agreement as to what intelligence tests do not measure. They do not measure "inborn capacity" (Cronbach, 1960; McNemar, 1964) or learning ability (Stevenson, 1970). They are not culture free, they do not assess potential (Cleary et al., 1975). The scores are not constant, nor are they free from influences in the immediate situation.

The nature of what intelligence tests measure is pretty well summed up by an 11-year-old girl who was asked what it means to be smart. She responded: "When you are older you get a good job and more money. When you're young, you get good grades."

Constancy of Intelligence Test Scores

Intelligence test scores are often used in planning for a child's educational placement in the immediate and distant future. People who employ these tests hope that the test scores will help them read the murky crystal ball of future events. We thus ask about the stability of intelligence test scores across a long period of time. Does an individual's intelligence test score of his standing relative to peers change much over the course of three, five, or twenty-five years?

Constancy of intelligence test scores is assessed in two ways. The most frequently employed method is to correlate the scores obtained by the child at two or more distinct points in life. A correlation indicates the degree to which the child maintains his rank relative to others. If the ranking of the highest to lowest scoring children is the same on two testings, the correlation between the two tests will be perfect (see Table 5-1). The second method of assessment of intelligence test score constancy is to

TABLE 5-1: Correlation of relative rankings of intelligence test scores

Child	IQ at age 6	IQ at age 10
Gail	175	160
Lisa	160	110
Ara	150	109
Cara	110	108
Lynne	100	95
Donna	90	92
Justin	80	85
Danny	70	73
Peter	69	72
Sheri	65	68

Notice that the ten hypothetical children maintain the same relative rankings when tested at age 6 and at age 10. The correlation between the two tests would equal 1.00; that is, demonstrates a perfect correlation.

examine the child's change score across two testings. The interest in this method is in absolute scores rather than relative rankings.

Studies of the constancy of intelligence test scores during childhood indicate that the correlations of test scores obtained by children yield high correlations, particularly when children are more than five years of age. For instance, Bayley (1949) found that tests given to children older than six years were highly related to scores at age 18 years. The closer in time the administration of the two tests, the higher the correlation, and these correlations are likely to be .80 or higher. Correlations between tests administered at ages 15 and 18 were .96 (Bayley, 1949). Bradway, Thompson, and Cravens (1958) found correlations about .55 between two administrations of the SB after a lapse of twenty-five years. Even the scores obtained at ages 4 and 29 were rather highly correlated. "In terms of group trends, the long-range predictive validity of a Stanford-Binet IQ, especially when obtained with school-age children, is remarkably high" (Anastasi, 1961, p. 206). McMillan writes: ". . . it is safe to draw these conclusions from the longitudinal data: intelligence is a relatively stable human characteristic; as age increases, this characteristic becomes increasingly more stable; the correlations of IQ at two points in time increase as the age of initial testing increases and as the interval between testings decreases" (1977, p. 177).

Note that Anastasi refers specifically to *group trends*. People who are involved in studies of intelligence testing are making predictions on the basis of groups of people, but those who are concerned with school placement decisions are making predictions about individuals. While there are high correlations across time in IQ scores for groups, the perspective is considerably different when we examine the constancy of IQ scores across time for individuals. The evidence is abundant that there are frequent and marked changes in intelligence test scores for individuals. Honzik, Mac-Farlane, and Allen (1948) reported that more than half of their sample of children obtained changes in intelligence test scores greater that 15 points and that 9 percent changed more that 30 points. McCall (1970) found that average shift to be 24 points. McCall, Appelbaum, and Hogarty (1973) investigated the stability of intelligence quotients and test profiles of forty-eight males and sixty-six females who had had at least twelve assessments of intelligence between the ages of 3 and 13 years. The results were that the "average individual's *range* of IQ between 2½ and 17 years was 28.5 IQ points, one of every three children displayed a progressive change of more than 30 points, and one in seven shifted more than 40 points. Rare individuals may alter their performance as much as 74 points" (1973, p. 70). Baker, Sontag, and Nelson (1958) found that 62 percent of a sample of fifty children changed more than 15 points in their Stanford-Binet IQ scores between the ages of 3 and 10 years. It is quite clear that individual IQ scores are subject to marked shifts and that absolute scores are not constant.

The variation found in the absolute scores of individuals has important implications. An examination of Table 5-1 finds a single testing of Lisa and Ara might be very misleading if one makes educational and social decisions for these children at age 6 which determine their placement at age 10. If one is to use intelligence tests for the purpose of individual diagnosis, it is critical that the test be repeatedly administered to the child. This necessity has been given recognition, insofar as PL 94–142 mandates repeated testing on an annual basis.

A multitude of factors may contribute to the waxing and waning of an individual's IQ scores. Some moderate shifting is likely due to errors of measurement. A high or low score can be obtained by the child because he was good or bad at guessing that day or had good or poor rapport with the test giver. On retesting, a child's score is likely to be lower if it was high on the first evaluation and higher if it was low on the first evaluation. Additionally, IQ score shifts have been linked to a number of personal and social characteristics of the test taker. McCall, Appelbaum, and Hogarty reported that boys are more likely to show increases in IQ scores with age than girls, and girls who are "relatively more favorably disposed to traditional masculine roles tend to increase in IQ more than girls who are less so" (1973, p. 70). Low-income groups are less likely to show shifts than middle- or upper-income groups, or are likely to show decreasing scores with age. Personality characteristics of both children and parents have been associated with shifts in IQ scores. Children who are independent and competitive appear to be more likely to show shifts upward than children who are less independent and competitive. Parents who encourage children in their intellectual tasks and use moderate and rational discipline techniques are likely to have children who show upward increases in IQ scores (McCall et al., 1973). Thus, a host of factors has been found to be correlated with shifts in an individual's IQ scores across time.

Uses and Abuses

Whether the current debate and controversy concerning the use of intelligence tests within public schools reflects a more fundamental change in values which the public holds dear (Cronbach, 1975), or whether the controversy is more limited to simply the technology of testing, there is no question that public concern over testing is now very great. Professional journals are devoted to the issue, and apparently resolution of many of the problems is being achieved only within a courtroom setting. While controversy about intelligence testing is not new (Cronbach, 1976; Mac-Millan, 1977), the fervor against it is recent.

Intelligence tests and their cousins, aptitude tests, are used for at least two broad purposes: to determine the best educational and remedial program for individual children; and to limit an individual's subsequent opportunities for participation in particular kinds of educational programs. The original goals of the French commission that mandated Binet to devise a test was based on the former goal. Binet was aware of the need for special education, as well as the potential stigma attached to the receipt of such aid. He was concerned that decisions about school placements be as objective and free of capricious factors and personal biases as could be humanly possible. But it has been true that with limited resources to support higher education in this country, aptitude and intelligence tests have served to prohibit members of our society from the opportunity to obtain whatever bounty may be the result of obtaining an advanced education. The latter use of intelligence tests has fed the belief that intelligence tests represent another method to propagate prejudice and prohibit equal opportunities, thus eliciting ire and indignation from those affected. Organizations of persons who share these beliefs have moved legislators to take action against the use of intelligence tests. For example, the state legislature in California has voted twice against the use of group intelligence tests within the schools, only to have the governor veto the bill each time. It is nonetheless currently against state law in California to use an intelligence test for the purpose of identifying mentally retarded children. In addition there have been several court decisions that it is illegitimate to use intelligence tests for minority group children which have been standardized on children from the majority culture. Finally, PL 94–142 demands that tests used to evaluate individuals for diagnostic assessments must be administered in the child's native language.

Criticisms of testing have taken a number of forms. First, it has been argued that the tests were constructed without inclusion of adequate representation of minority group children. Until the 1974 revision of the WISC it was true that minority children were not appropriately represented in the sample used to develop the test. It is believed that the tests are inappropriate for use with children not represented in the construction of the test. Second, it has been stated that the content of the test items are culture bound, that children from minority groups have not had as much exposure to the experiences reflected in the items as children from the white middle class. Third, it has been suggested that language differences between children and between the minority group child and test examiner yield underestimates of the minority group child's intelligence. There has been concern that the examiner may be affected by his or her stereotypes of the minority group so as to seriously underevaluate the child's test scores. Finally, there is concern that the minority group child interacting with a white middle-class examiner might experience fear, anger, or anxiety, which in turn might adversely affect the child's test performance.

Happily, there have been a variety of responses to these concerns, some taking the form of research, some others the attempt to develop alternative methods of assessment. As mentioned, the revised WISC test in its restandardization did include an appropriate proportion of minority children. The attempts to produce a culture-free test have not been successful, nor are they likely to be and still be useful in yielding predictions concerning future academic performance.

Additionally, some limited research has suggested that some of these concerns may not have a basis in reality. Thus research comparing the scores of black children given an intelligence test in black dialect with those given the test in the standard manner has failed to demonstrate differences. Moreover, and more frightening, there is at least one study showing that intelligence tests given in Spanish to Mexican-American children yielded lower scores than the same test given in English (MacMillan, 1977). The problems associated with translating tests, a demand now made by law, are quite serious (Sattler, 1974). While there has been speculation that black children tested by white examiners may experience considerably more stress within the examination, the evidence on this point is somewhat mixed. There seems little doubt that negative interactions between the examiner and the child will tend to reduce the child's IQ score. However, the research which has found such effects have employed procedures which violate the procedures of administering the test and have employed procedures which are highly and probably unusually aversive (Sattler, 1974). The concern about the examiner's stereotypes and expectancies concerning the performances of a minority child has received mixed support from studies directly related to the intelligence testing situation (MacMillan, 1977). But studies testing such effects in interviewing situations and minority children's test performance have received mixed support from research directly related to the intelligence testing situation (MacMillan, 1977). Studies of these effects in interviewing and laboratory settings do suggest that examiner stereotypes and expectancies would have an impact on intelligence testing results (Hyman, 1954; Rosenthal, 1966).

There is little doubt that intelligence tests are discriminatory if you define intelligence as anything other than an estimate of performance on academic and verbal tasks. If intelligence means a child's ability to survive on the streets, to be creative, to be socially or interpersonally sensitive, to act appropriately and be adaptive in a wide variety of situations, to be clever, or to earn money, then one should not use intelligence tests. If one uses intelligence tests to predict these skills, then the general finding that minority children obtain lower scores than white middle-class children leads to a series of false, misleading predictions.

However, if intelligence tests are perceived as estimates of the likelihood of success in a school program which emphasizes verbal skills and abstract ideas, there is little question that the IQ is useful in making accurate predictions. In spite of the admitted difficulties associated with contemporary use of intelligence tests, they are among the best predictors of school performance. It is perfectly reasonable to challenge educational policies on the basis of contemporary educational practices. One might question, however, whether attacks upon an instrument which predicts the child's success, given these educational practices, will ultimately serve the child.

We appear to have come full circle in our uses, or abuses, of intelligence tests. These tests were originally developed to provide a basic evaluation of a child's mental abilities which would minimize the biases of teachers and the excessive influence of parental status and power. By denouncing and legally prohibiting the use of these tests we now appear to be opening the door to such biases and influences. It appears that once again, it will be personal opinions, be it of the teacher, the psychologist, the school administrator, the lawyer, or parents, arrived at through unknown paths and screened by personal beliefs that will determine the mental level of children who are in most need of careful evaluation for determining educational services. "The fact that any scientific instrument is popularly misused, however, does not in itself render it useless for the purposes for which it was intended. It simply underscores the fact that many test users have not been adequately trained" (Reese and Lipsett, 1970, p. 555). It is clear that the test is not useless for those purposes for which it was designed. The profession, but mostly the children, apparently will pay the consequences for our inadequately trained test users. The price that they will pay may be great indeed.

INTELLIGENCE AND LEARNING DISABILITIES

The chapter has thus far been focused upon the role of intelligence tests in capturing the essence of whatever we mean by intelligence. The IQ score is critical to the field of learning disabilities, since, by definition, we use this score to limit the group to which we channel our resources and energies. The IQ score is used to indicate "potential." A gap between the potential and performance on achievement tests is one method to define children as learning disabled. But is it true that IQ tests assess "potential," "underlying," or "true" scholastic capacity? Insofar as we have yet to define such terms as potential as other than the score on an IQ test, we are engaging in circular reasoning. Until such terms are better defined, answers cannot be forthcoming. It is not true that all "bright" children should learn in school, irrespective of the teacher, tasks, incentives employed, or the motives in operation. Nor is it true that all dull children are doomed forever to low scholastic productivity irrespective of the influence of motivational and contextual factors which influence them.

Learning Disabled vs. Mental Retardation

IQ scores are critical to the learning disability specialist, as these scores are used to limit the population to whom these services are available. While IQ scores form the legal basis on which to determine provision of services, types of children, and application of treatment, the question needs to be raised as to the actual adherence to this specification regarding normal intelligence as a requirement for classification as learning disabled. Ames (1968) reported that 24 percent of the children referred to the Gesell Institute for school learning problems had IQ scores below 90. Ames argues that complicated diagnostic interpretations of learning disabilities might be eliminated by recognition of the fact that such children do poorly in school because of low intelligence. Bryan (1972) examined the case histories of sixty-five children diagnosed as having learning disabilities at a prestigious hospital clinic. Virtually the same percentage of children had IQ scores below 90.

Birch and Belmont (1964) studied WISC patterns for retarded and normal readers. The retarded readers had scores below the 10th percentile on three of four reading tests. Belmont and Birch reported that the entire group of retarded readers had significantly lower IQs than normal readers. When the data were analyzed with the omission of the borderline 80–89 IQ subjects, the retarded readers were still significantly lower in IQ than normal readers. In a number of experimental studies, IQ differences between learning-disabled and control groups have been found to be significant. In each case learning-disabled children had lower IQs and in each case their performance on the experimental task was significantly poorer than that of the comparison group. In two of these studies the data were analyzed so as to control the intelligence differences among groups. In one (Dykman et al., 1971) the experimental differences between groups remained even after the intelligence differences had been eliminated; in the second (Browning, 1967) the differences between groups disappeared when intelligence was held constant between groups. Other researchers (Schwartz and Bryan, 1971) have restricted the range of intelligence from 85 to 115. Nonetheless, significant group differences resulted as learning-disabled children had lower intelligence levels than the comparison group.

It may be that a sizable percentage of children who are labeled as learning disabled could or should be diagnosed mentally retarded. A sizable minority of these children could be expected to do poorly in school on the basis of the results indicated by standardized tests of intelligence. This is not to say they do poorly in school because they have low intelligence. Insofar as we stress concern for what such a term as intelligence means, we do not intend to imply that low intelligence always causes poor academic performance. But whatever it is that contributes to academic success that is captured by intelligence tests suggests that these mysterious abilities, motives, or factors are frequently less represented in learning-disabled children than in random samples of children.

The inclusion or exclusion of below-average-IQ children from the learning disabilities category may depend upon a number of political, budgetary, and humanistic considerations. It may be that labeling children who are experiencing a host of developmental problems (e.g., mental retardation, emotional disturbance) as learning disabled will result in their experiencing less stigma and better educational opportunities. It may also be that inclusion of these children may retard the development of therapeutic interventions, as these, in turn, have been predicated upon the assumption of normalcy. Irrespective of these considerations in making placement and treatment decisions, the reality of the current situation is that many children labeled as learning disabled do obtain lower IQ scores than their peers. Perhaps the definition of learning disabilities or diagnostic policies should be changed. The question still remains as to whether "dullness" makes a difference. We have to consider the benefits of obtaining IQ scores and ask whether these scores really make a difference after all. It is of import, and empirically feasible, to determine whether obtaining a low IQ score leads to school programs which are better suited to the skills of the students or simply discourages teachers and pupils.

Factors Other Than Intelligence

It should be recognized that intelligence tests are often employed for the purpose of diagnosis of various conditions which are remotely, if at all, related to problem solving. Wechsler (1958) and Rappaport (1946) both have suggested that diagnoses of emotional and mental states of persons might be made on the basis of the pattern of intelligence scale subtests. For instance, if the scale score on the Verbal section of the Wechsler Intelligence Scale for Children (WISC) is higher or lower than the scale score on the Performance section, or if the result on the Digit Span test is markedly different from the Vocabulary test score, inferences could be made regarding the person's mental processes and emotional status. Differences in subtest or subscale scores are thus considered indicative of psychological processes and pathology.

Psychologists have conducted many research investigations to associate intelligence test profiles with psychological processes, personality traits, and pathology states (Frank, 1970). The results of these research efforts have indicated that groups of subjects cannot be differentiated on the basis of profile analysis of intelligence test scores. Even if these results were positive, the problem of the use of test profiles for diagnoses of individuals would still exist.

Researchers in the area of learning disabilities have followed the path of the psychologists, attempting to employ test profile analyses to determine the clinical status of children. Two general orientations have characterized research in this area. In the first case there has been an attempt to determine whether learning-disabled children can be discriminated from nondisabled children on the basis of discrepancies between verbal and performance scores on the WISC. In the second instance, the research inquires into whether a pattern of subtest scores might be uniquely associated with learning difficulties. Using either of the two above-mentioned approaches, the investigator serves as a Sherlock Holmes, trying to ferret out differences in subtest scores which might differentiate groups of children, and he does so on a post hoc basis with little theoretical direction.

Huelsman (1970) reviewed twenty-three studies of performance on WISC subtests by children with reading difficulties. In general, it has been found that children with reading difficulties obtain lower scores on Information, Arithmetic, Digit Span, and Coding relative to other subtest scores. Huelsman, however, investigated the WISC patterns of 101 underachievers and 56 achievers (defined on the basis of not having reading problems). These groups of children could not be differentiated on the basis of the total number of subtests in which they showed marked deviation from their own general performance. Overall scatter of scores did not differentiate the achievers and nonachievers. In addition, these groups were assessed in terms of their performance on Information, Arithmetic, and Coding subtests, as low scores on these three subtests have been associated by others with reading problems. In general, there were a greater number of underachievers than achievers who scored low on one or another of these subtests. But Huelsman underlines the finding that *individual* underachievers in reading do not necessarily demonstrate this pattern of low scores on these three subtests. Indeed, only 13 percent of the groups had poor performance on all three subtests, and only 11 percent showed low performance in two of the three subtests. It was also found that large deviations in particular subtest scores from the average score obtained by a particular child did not differentiate among children. In effect, achievers appear to have about the same incidence of high and low subtest scores as underachievers. Kender (1972) reached similar conclusions after a review of the literature of WISC patterns of poor readers.

The second issue was related to the discrepancies between Verbal and Performance scale scores. Huelsman reported that 61 percent of the underachievers had higher Performance than Verbal scores; only 38 percent of the achievers demonstrated a similar discrepancy. This does provide some support for the discrepancy notion, but note that if the discrepancy scores were used as a basis of diagnosis, 39 percent of the underachievers and 38 percent of the achievers would have been misdiagnosed. Huelsman writes,

> It appears advantageous at this point for research to turn away from searching for a WISC subtest pattern and to turn toward analysis of the possible significance of low subtest scores in the instructional program of individual children (1970, p. 545).

Recently, Keogh and associates have called for a closer examination of the differences in cognitive styles which may be associated with different types of learning disabilities. Keogh and Hall (1973) suggest,

It is time to begin differentiating the teaching methods in order to see the emergence of real clinical teaching, where the goal is a precise match between the cognitive style of the learner and the cognitive demands of the task. Specification of particular areas of strength and weakness through the proposed process analysis may provide some direction for individualized program planning, thus increasing the usefulness of the WISC in psychoeducational evaluation (1973, pp. 4–5).

In her attempt to study the cognitive styles associated with learning disabilities, Keogh has employed the WISC. Following the suggestions of Witkin, Dyk, Faterson, Goodenough, and Karp (1962), Keogh treats WISC subtest scores as reflecting three major factors.

The first factor, Verbal-comprehension, is comprised of scores on the subtests Vocabulary Information and Comprehension. The second, Analytic-field approach, is comprised of subtests Object Assembly, Block Design, and Picture Completion. The third factor, Attention-concentration, consists of Arithmetic, Coding, and Digit Span subtests (Keogh, 1973). Scores on these three factors constitute the assessment of cognitive styles which Keogh suggests will differentiate the learning-disabled from non-disabled children. In an attempt to test her hypothesis, Keogh, Wetter, McGinty, and Donlon (1973) compared the performances of clinically diagnosed educable mentally retarded, learning-disabled, and hyperactive learning-disabled boys on these three categories. The hyperactive learning-disabled boys were defined as children who had been referred for evaluation on the basis of learning problems and hyperactivity. As could be predicted, the retarded children scored significantly lower on all factors than did the two learning-disabled groups. The patterns of scores are, however, of interest. The retarded children scored significantly higher on the analytic-field approach than on the other two categories. The learning-disabled children, particularly hyperactive ones, scored lower on the attention factor relative to the other categories. In a follow-up study, Keogh and Hall (1973) enlarged the size of the sample and studied learning-disabled and retarded children. The same results were obtained, at least when investigating the performance of the boys. These findings appear to be stable. Groups of retarded and learning-disabled children demonstrate varying degrees of competence within certain psychological processes. At the same time, the overlap of performance of these children with members of other diagnostic groups is likely to be great, possibly sufficiently great to preclude the use of this classification scheme for the purpose of individual diagnoses. Keogh and colleagues have, nevertheless, demonstrated that learning-disabled children, *as a group,* appear to be deficient in attentional skills relative to verbal comprehension and field approach strategies. It is this deficiency that may differentiate these children from educable mentally retarded children. What is important about the emphasis upon cognitive styles of perceptual organization and problem solving is that a new and more refined direction in the understanding of the learning-disabled cognitive abilities and processes is provided. It is hard to dispute Keogh (1973) when she writes, "Many standardized psychological tests have limited usefulness in evaluation of exceptional children. Test results have tended to provide confirmation, not understanding, of exceptional conditions, in that traditional approaches to evaluation lead to summarizing, global scores which reflect intellectual achievement (IQ) or are heavily weighted in psychodynamic interpretations. Neither approach allows easy translation into educational or remedial programs for children with special educational needs" (pp. 98-9). Perhaps more refined analysis of cognitive styles will provide for such translations.

While agreeing that such theoretically directed research employing WISC scores will likely lead to important new insights about the cognitive processes of the learning disabled child, we also eschew the continuation of the Sherlock Holmes method of WISC analysis. The post hoc analysis of WISC subtest scores in which the investigator, without theoretical direction, simply searches to determine whether this or that pattern of subtest scores will differentiate the learning disabled from nondisabled is likely to be unproductive. The rationale for this negative prophecy stems from the low reliabilities of difference scores between subtests. Chance fluctuations which do affect scores are likely to have marked influence upon any particular pattern of scores "discovered" (McNemar, 1957). Until subtests have adequate reliability, there can be little hope for attempts to develop a diagnostic procedure based upon pattern analyses of subtests scores. In our opinion, the test is not sufficiently reliable to "reveal" stable subtest pattern differences among handicapped and nonhandicapped children.

Finally, a word about individual diagnosis employing such WISC analysis, a practice which we fear is all too frequent. It is clear that the degree to which these WISC patterns differentiate groups is insufficient to permit basing individual diagnoses upon such test scores, at least without the greatest humility. Errors in classification of individual children are likely to be so frequent that diagnostic use of subtest patterns is useless, at best, and damaging, at worst. Clinicians may wish to continue such diagnostic procedures in light of what they believe to be no alternative, but they should do it with awareness that many errors will be made.

INTELLIGENCE TESTS AND THE SCHOOLS

The use of intelligence tests within schools has been vigorously challenged. A primary reason for the attack has been the belief that intelligence tests are biased against ethnic and racial minority groups and that use of these measures deprives members of minority groups of valued opportunities in education. Insofar as ethnicity and race may be confounded or associated with socioeconomic status and lower social class members typically do more poorly on such tests relative to nonminority group persons, these charges have some credibility. Currently there are sophisticated debates concerning what criteria should be used to identify and evaluate the biases of tests (Schmidt and Hunter, 1974). There is no question that such debates will increase our knowledge and sophistication in the development of valid psychological tests. The problem is that in spite of admitted difficulties associated with intelligence tests, they are among the best predictors of school performance. If this is true, we must ask if academic achievement is primarily a function of adopting those values and skills associated with middle and upper socioeconomic classes. Intelligence tests appear to be biased instruments, in the sense that they measure factors associated with success in American schools. The test may be less at fault in the propagation of biases than the criteria by which it is being evaluated. Damage generated from the use of the intelligence test does not stem from the test itself, but from educators' assumptions about the nature of intelligence.

Whether the focus of concern is the learning-disabled child and/or ethnic and racial minority group members, it is folly to imbue intelligence tests with characteristics of constancy and unmodifiability and to assume that precise categorization of children or placement in classes can be made on the basis of such tests. Intelligence test scores can be used to suggest appropriate class placement for children at the very low end of the intelligence continuum. But there are children who score in the lower end of the normal range who subsequently blossom, and high-scoring children who wither (Robinson and Robinson, 1965). Are conceptions of intelligence, diagnostic procedures, classroom schedules, and teacher and parent expectancies sufficiently flexible to note and adjust to changes in the child?

We have relied too long on the intelligence test for information concerning the acquisition of information. Attention should be directed toward the classroom itself; to the demands made by the teacher, the skills necessary to meet the demands and the motives which sustain a child's endurance in what to most children is an aversive situation. By way of example, Carver (1974) has predicted the demise of standardized achievement tests and a revolution in educational measurement. Carver suggests that *psychometrics,* which emphasizes the normal curve and percentile rankings of students, will be replaced with *edumetrics,* a means of assessing the individual's gains within a specified curriculum. Evaluation in edumetrics will focus upon such questions as whether or not the student can read the curriculum materials and has learned the information the teacher has been presenting. While this approach does not eliminate some kind of assessment of the child's ability, intuitive or standardized, it does place the emphasis upon the material to be learned and the student's demonstration that he has or has not achieved this goal. This approach is promising for learning disabilities insofar as it removes the onus of proving the child has intelligence in this or that range and allows effort and resources to be placed in what we conceive as one proper area, the means by which children can successfully complete academic assignments, and, in the event of failure, the means to provide alternate routes to learning.

REFERENCES

Ames, L. B. "A low intelligence quotient often not recognized as the chief cause of many learning difficulties." *Journal of Learning Disabilities,* 1968, 1, 45–48.

Anastasi, A. *Psychological Testing.* New York: The Macmillan Co., 1961.

Baker, C. T., Sontag, L. W., and Nelson, V. L. "Individual and group differences in the longitudinal measurement of change in mental ability." In L. W. Sontag, C. T. Baker, and V. L. Nelson (eds.), "Mental growth personality development: A longitudinal study." *Monographs of the Society for Research in Child Development,* 1958, 23, No. 2, 11–83.

Bateman, B. "Learning disabilities—Yesterday, today, and tomorrow." *Exceptional Children,* 1964, 31, 167–177.

Bayley, N. "Consistency and variability in the growth of intelligence from birth to eighteen years." *Journal of Genetic Monographs,* 1949, 75, 165–196.

Bayley, N. "Development of mental abilities." In P. H. Mussen (ed.), *Carmichael's Manual of Child Psychology, Vol. 1.* New York: John Wiley & Sons, 1970.

Bersoff, D. N. "Silk purses into sow's ears: The decline of psychological testing and a suggestion for its redemption." *American Psychologist,* 1973, 28, 892–899.

Birch, H. and Belmont, L. "Auditory-visual integration in normal and retarded readers." *American Journal of Orthopsychiatry,* 1964, 34, 852–861.

Bradway, K. P., Thompson, C. W., and Cravens, R. B. "Preschool IQ's after twenty-five years." *Journal of Educational Psychology,* 1958, 49, 278–281.

Browning, R. M. "Effect of irrelevant peripheral visual stimuli on discrimination learning in minimally brain-damaged children." *Journal of Consulting Psychology,* 1967, 31, 371–376.

Cameron, J., Livson, N., and Bayley, N. "Infant vocalizations and their relationship to mature intelligence." *Science,* 1967, 57, 331–333.

Carver, R. P. "Two dimensions of tests: Psychometric and edumetric." *American Psychologist,* 1974, 29, 512–518.

Cronbach, L. J. *Essentials of Psychological Testing.* New York: Harper and Row, 1960.

Frank, G. H. "The measurement of personality from the Wechsler tests." In B. A. Maher (ed.), *Progress in Experimental Personality Research, Vol. 5.* New York: Academic Press, 1970.

Freeman, F. S. *Theory and Practice of Psychological Testing.* New York: Holt, Rinehart and Winston, 1962, 227–228.

Hindley, C. B. "The Griffiths scale of infant development: Scores and predictions from 3–18 months." *Child Psychology and Psychiatry,* 1960, 1, 99–112.

Honzik, M. P., Macfarlane, J. W., and Allen, L. "The stability of mental test performance between two and eighteen years." *Journal of Experimental Education,* 1948, 17, 309–324.

Huelsman, C. B., Jr. "The WISC subtest syndrome for disabled readers." *Perceptual and Motor Skills,* 1970, 30, 535–550.

Kagen, J. *Change and Continuity in Infancy.* New York: John Wiley & Sons, Inc., 1971.

Kender, J. P. "Is there really a WISC profile for poor readers?" *Journal of Learning Disabilities,* 1972, 5, 397–400.

Keogh, B. K. "Perceptual and cognitive styles: Implications for Special Education." In L. Mann & D. A. Sabatino (eds.), *The First Review of Special Education,* Philadelphia, Pennsylvania: JSE Press, 1973.

Keogh, B. K. and Hall, R. J. "Functional analysis of WISC performance of children classified as EH and EMR." Technical Report SERP 1973-A9 Graduate School of Education, University of California, Los Angeles, 1973.

Keogh, B. K., Wetter, J., McGinty, A., and Donlon, G. "Functional analysis of WISC performance of learning disordered, hyperactive, and mentally retarded boys." *Psychology in the Schools,* 1973, 10, 178–181.

Lewis, M. "Infant intelligence tests: Their use and misuse." *Human Development,* 1973, 16, 108–118.

Littell, W. M. "The Wechsler Intelligence Scale for Children: A review of a decade of research." *Psychological Bulletin*, 1960, 57, 132–156.

Liverant, S. "Intelligence: A concept in need of re-examination." *Journal of Consulting Psychology*, 1960, 24, 101–110.

McCall, R. B. "IQ pattern over age: Comparisons among siblings and parent-child pairs." *Science*, 1970, 170, 644–648.

McCall, R. B., Appelbaum, M. I., and Hogarty, P. S. "Developmental changes in mental performance." *Monographs of the Society for Research in Child Development*, 1973, 38, No. 3, 1–84.

McCall, R. B., Hogarty, P. S., and Hurlburt, N. "Transitions in infant sensorimotor development and the prediction of childhood I.Q." *American Psychologist*, 1972, 27, 728–748.

McClelland, D. C. "Testing for competence rather than for 'intelligence.' " *American Psychologist*, 1973, 28, 1–15.

McNemar, Q. "On WAIS difference scores." *Journal of Consulting Psychology*, 1957, 21, 239–240.

McNemar, Q. "Lost: Our intelligence? Why?" *American Psychologist*, 1964, 19, 871–882.

Pease, D., Rosauer, J., and Wolins, L. "Reliability of infant developmental scales during the first year of life." *Journal of Genetic Psychology*, 1961, 98, 295–298.

Rappaport, D. *Diagnostic Psychological Testing.* Chicago: The Yearbook Publishers, Inc., 1946.

Reese, H. W. and Lipsett, L. P. *Experimental Child Psychology.* New York: Academic Press, 1970.

Robinson, H. B. and Robinson, N. M. *The Mentally Retarded Child: A Psychological Approach.* New York: McGraw-Hill Book Co., 1965.

Schmidt, F. L. and Hunter, T. E. "Racial and ethnic bias in psychological tests: Divergent implications of two definitions of test bias." *American Psychologist*, 1974, 29, 1–8.

Schwartz, T. and Bryan, J. H. "Imitation and judgments of children with learning disabilities." *Exceptional Children*, 1971, 38, 157–158.

Sechrest, L. "Incremental validity." In D. N. Jackson and S. Messick (eds.), *Problems in Human Assessment.* New York: McGraw-Hill Book Co., 1967.

Wechsler, D. *The Measurement and Appraisal of Adult Intelligence* (4th ed.). Baltimore, Md.: Williams & Wilkins, 1958.

Witkin, H. A., Dyk, R., Faterson, H., Goodenough, D., and Karp, S. *Psychological Differentiation.* New York: John Wiley & Sons, 1962.

Zigler, E. "The nature-nurture issue reconsidered: A discussion of UZGIRIS' paper." *Proceedings of Peabody–NIMH Conference on Social-Cultural Aspects of Mental Retardation*, June, 1968.

6 | Behavior of the Learning Disabled

The most frequently mentioned characteristics of the learning-disabled child are hyperactivity and short attention span. In addition, other characteristics have been added. Common among these characteristics are behavior difficulties. The argument is not made that the learning-disabled child suffers an obvious physiological, nutritional, intellectual, or emotional difficulty, but rather that he behaves inappropriately. To a considerable degree, the difficulties of the learning-disabled child are social in nature. He is judged by others to act in ways which may be dissimilar to his peers, self-defeating in their consequences, or disruptive to the social organization of the family and classroom. The learning difficulties which children experience may be an outcropping of the behavior problems. Not sitting still, not paying attention, not initiating self-instructions affect the acquisition of information. Case studies of learning-disabled youngsters are replete with descriptions of untoward behavior, particularly within the testing situation, if not the classroom. Yet texts which outline intervention techniques have focused on learning tasks and procedures, not on remedies for behavior problems. Perhaps we feel more comfortable establishing programs to teach a child the difference between long and short vowels than we do in establishing a program for a child whom the teacher describes as unable or unwilling to work alone, to attend under the usual classroom conditions, to sit or stand still or to remain quiet. At the same time we recognize that if we could successfully program that child to work by himself, to be a self-starter, his learning the difference between short and long vowels would be greatly facilitated.

hyperactivity
short attention span
behavior problems

BEHAVIORAL CHARACTERISTICS

In this chapter we shall review the data available on the behavioral characteristics of the learning-disabled child. This information is organized into two sections. The first presents descriptions of these behaviors by parents, teachers, peers, educators, and clinicians. The second concerns the data relevant to the issue of hyperactivity. Hyperactivity is a central concept employed in discussions of learning disabilities and specialists should be aware of the limited amount of systematically gathered data available. There is not much research to discuss because not much research has been done.

Before reviewing some of the findings concerning the behavioral differences between the learning-disabled and the nondisabled child, some points concerning the diagnostic process itself should be made. It has long been recognized that labeling others deviant, inadequate, or emotionally ill is determined not only by the characteristics of the labeled person as evaluated and measured on certain tests, but also may be affected by the subjective characteristics or functions of the person doing the labeling (Becker, 1963). It has been noted that normal children are viewed by their mothers as experiencing many problems in growing up (Lapouse and Monk, 1964), and teachers view many children as evidencing hyperactivity without labeling them learning-disabled or pathological. What factors result in the labeling of the child as learning disabled? One might assume that the critical feature is an adequate IQ score and low academic achievement, but labeling does not appear to be that simple. How can the kindergarten and first-grade child, and indeed, the preschool child, be judged academically incompetent? The criteria for attaching a label to a child are being increasingly removed from the original definition of such problems, while other features of the child or his judge constitute, in part, the basis for labeling. There is no way to know how much "luck" plays a role in defining a child as inadequate, but it is certain that the role of the adult in responding to the child is critical. Moreover, once a child is labeled, it is likely that observers who "know" of the child's difficulties are likely to interpret a variety of behaviors as reflections of the pathological condition (Rosenhan, 1973). Thus, the diagnostic labeling of the child, whether correct or incorrect, is likely to have a profound influence upon others' judgments of the child. What might be tolerated antisocial behavior by the normal child becomes for the learning disabled a serious reflection of the "basic difficulties" which he is experiencing. As yet we know very little about the characteristics of the adult and child which might interact to affect the labeling process. Perhaps we should be studying adult tolerance for children's movements, fidgetiness, talking, and defiance within the classroom. What is clearly needed are studies concerning the individual differences among adults, teachers, and parents in their readiness to initiate the referral process, and those characteristics of the teachers or classroom situations which might be associated with quick, slow, or incorrect labeling and referral practices.

Parents' Observations

There are some limited data concerning how peers and adults view the learning-disabled child. Wender (1971) has categorized clinical data on children diagnosed as having minimal cerebral dysfunction within a developmental framework. Infants and preschoolers are reported by their parents to have been very active and restless. The child is likely to be described as one who walked early, and who, by virtue of getting around easily, was unintentionally destructive to household objects. Wender summarizes the parents' view of the child as reflecting an infant "King Kong," a perennial 2-year-old. Parents report further crises when the child enters school. To the considerable annoyance of others both at home and in school such a child is likely to be fidgety, appearing to be incessantly in motion. Parents describe these children as obstinate, sassy, bossy, stubborn, negativistic, disobedient, difficult to discipline, resistant to adult domination, and yet attempting to dominate peers. These terms reduce to the parents' perception that the child will not conform to their wishes. When the child reaches adolescence, he is described as manifesting poor impulse control, an inability to delay gratification and to persevere in tasks, and poor judgment and planning.

It should be noted that the adequacy of these data remains in doubt. Little information is given as to the sampling of parents. It is not known, for example, whether or not these parents are in the process of seeking help for their youngsters. If such were the case, it is likely that they would paint a gloomy picture of the youngster's behavior, emphasizing the child's inadequacies rather than his strengths. It is not known whether the parents are referring to their youngster's present behavior or behaviors which may have occurred in the distant past. Descriptions of the behavior of the preschool infant may have required a considerable amount of retrospection concerning events several years past. This point is important, because it is generally recognized that parents' recall of long past behavior of their children is likely to contain a considerable amount of error (Yarrow, Campbell, and Burton, 1970). The lack of details concerning the sampling and interviewing procedures makes a critical evaluation of the descriptive scheme forwarded by Wender impossible. Whether these descriptions reflect facts of stereotypes concerning these children remains to be seen.

Support for parts of Wender's descriptions is obtained from an excellent study by Owen, Adams, Forrest, Stolz, and Fisher (1971). These investigators interviewed the parents of educationally handicapped (California's term for learning disabilities) and noneducationally handicapped children. Parents selected from these two groups were matched on social class and race, age of youngster and the youngster's siblings. Mothers describe the learning-disabled child as having less verbal ability (in effect this meant that the child did not like to listen, was difficult to talk to, and had trouble expressing himself), had less ability to control his impulses and to structure the environment, and more anxiety than his siblings or nonhandicapped children. Unfortunately, the authors fail to provide sufficient information as to just what constitutes ability to structure an environment or to control impulses.

Strag (1972) asked parents of learning-disabled, mentally retarded, and normal children to complete a questionnaire in which they rated their children on items associated with behavioral and emotional disturbances and items indicative of neurological dysfunction. The comparison of the parents' ratings of learning-disabled and normal children revealed that these groups were differentially rated on several variables. The learning-disabled child was characterized as showing less consideration for others, less ability to receive affection, and more clingingness than normal children. Learning-disabled children were distinguished from the mentally retarded by being rated as less stubborn, more clinging, demonstrating greater jealousy, and being less able to receive affection than the mentally retarded youngster.

Putting these studies together, it would appear that parents perceive the learning-disabled child as clinging, yet unable to receive affection, and showing little impulse control, being rather uncontrolled in his emotional and motoric expressions. Birch and Belmont (1964) paraphrase parents' views of these difficult problems:

> Such technical descriptions as catastrophic behavior, perceptual impairment, perseveration, disinhibition, mimism, short attention span, exogenous behavior contagion, learning disability, Strauss syndrome, neurological impairment, and hyperactivity are translated by the outside world as spoiled, bratty, bad-mannered, ill-behaved, badly brought up, undisciplined, obnoxious, and by the other children as "queer" (p. 11).

While not all learning-disabled children can be so characterized, the fact that many can should be clearly recognized. While virtually unexplored, there seems little reason to question the assumption that the presence of a learning-disabled child may produce considerable stress and strain on the family unit. The difficulty is not simply that such children are not reading, but that they are not pleasant.

Noteworthy are several follow-up investigations involving hyperactive children, many of whom were experiencing school failures at the time of the initial referral (Mendelson, Johnson, and Stewart, 1971; Minde, Weiss, and Mendelson, 1972; Weiss, Minde, Werry, Douglas, and Nemeth, 1971). These three reports all indicated that parents, when interviewed several years subsequent to the initial referral, reported that a major problem confronting them with their child was that child's rebelliousness to both parents and society in general. If parents are experiencing interpersonal strain with their learning-disabled child, it is apparent that many will still be experiencing such strain even in the distant future. It seems many learning-disabled children remain unpleasant.

Teachers' Observations

Surprisingly few studies have been conducted concerning teachers' perceptions of the behavior of learning-disabled children. Recently, however, a number of investigations addressed to this issue have been conducted. Myklebust, Boshes, Olson, and Cole (1969) found that of forty-nine different tests, teacher rating of child behavior was the second best predictor as to whether the child would subsequently be diagnosed as learning disabled. Learning-disabled children were judged as being less competent in auditory comprehension (following directions, comprehending class discussions), spoken language (vocabulary, sentence length), orientation (time concepts), behavior, and motor ability (general coordination) than nondisabled children. Of particular interest was the teachers' judgment concerning the behavior of the learning-disabled child. Teachers rated these children as less cooperative, less attentive, less able to organize themselves, less able to cope with new situations, less socially acceptable to others, less accepting of responsibility, less able to complete assignments, and less tactful than nondisabled youngsters. In a subsequent investigation (Bryan and McGrady, 1972), teacher ratings were obtained on 183 learning-disabled and 176 control children on those items used by Myklebust and Boshes. The Bryan and McGrady results replicated the Myklebust and Boshes investigation, as all items pertaining to the behavior of the child were found to discriminate the learning-disabled from the nondisabled child. Behaviorally, then, the learning-disabled child is seen by the teacher as less desirable within the classroom than is the nondisabled child.

Keogh, Tchir, and Windeguth-Behn (1974) extended out knowledge concerning such teacher attitudes by obtaining teachers' views of learning-disabled and mentally retarded children. This study indicated that teachers were quite consistent in detecting behaviors which they associated with learning disabilities and that they made distinctions between learning-disabled and mentally retarded children. A high percentage of teachers associated the following characteristics with educationally handicapped children: aggressiveness (violent, cruel, destructive—66 percent of the teachers); hyperactive (63 percent); short attention span (44 percent); withdrawn (44 percent); no sense of responsibility or self-discipline (44 percent); poor interpersonal relationships (41 percent); parental problems (34 percent); disruptive (talking, noisemaking, 31 percent); disinterested, poor attitude toward school (28 percent); angry, hostile (28 percent); poor coordination (25 percent); low academically (25 percent); anxious and nervous (22 percent); demands a great deal of teacher time (22 percent); attention seeking (29 percent); loner (19 percent) (1974).

Unfortunately, results of follow-up studies would suggest that such characterizations of the learning-disabled child are likely to persist. Thus, Weiss et al. (1971) found that teachers of children who had been diagnosed as hyperactive four to six years previously reported them to be more restless, aggressive, and antisocial than comparison children.

The discriminable differences between learning-disabled and mentally retarded children from the teacher's perspective are that the teacher views the retarded child as having primary difficulty with school work, whereas the educationally handicapped child has behavior and personality difficulties. The learning-disabled child is hyperactive, has problems with his parents, has no sense of responsibility, is angry and hostile; the mentally retarded child is smiling, friendly, and lovable but unable to work with academic materials and abstractions.

Peers' Observations

So far we have seen that, by and large, learning-disabled children are viewed quite negatively by both parents and teachers. The question may also be raised as to how such children are evaluated by their peers. Bryan (1974a) has conducted two large-scale investigations designed to assess peer reactions to learning-disabled children. Children in sixty-two third-, fourth-, and fifth-grade classrooms were administered a sociometric scale. In each classroom there was at least one learning-disabled child, so that peer reactions to eighty-four learning-disabled children were obtained. Since peer popularity and peer rejection are not always highly correlated—that is, a child who is not popular is not necessarily rejected (Hartup, Glazer, and Charlesworth, 1967)—the sociometric test consisted of items designed to assess both a child's popularity and his rejection by others. Items to assess peer popularity included asking children to nominate three classmates whom they desire as friends, to sit next to, and to invite to their birthday party. Items to assess peer rejection directed the child to name three children they would not wish as friends, birthday party guests, or to sit next to in the classroom. When the learning-disabled child was compared to a randomly selected classmate of the same sex and race, it was found that this child was significantly less popular and significantly more rejected by his peers than the nondisabled child. This was particularly true if the learning-disabled child was both white and a girl. School problems of white girls are associated with considerably more rejection by peers than either black or white boys or black girls. Also noteworthy is the fact that while the peers of learning-disabled children do not view them as hyperactive, they do judge them as being worried and frightened, as children who never appear to have a good time, as being sad, not being neat and clean, not very good looking, and as children to whom nobody pays much attention. Peer assessments of these same children were made one year later in order to assess the degree to which the learning-disabled child's status with his peers remained stable over time (Bryan, 1976). This follow-up investigation assessed the peer popularity of white learning-disabled children, mostly males. The results replicated those obtained the previous year. Once again, these learning-disabled children were more rejected and less accepted by their peers than the randomly selected comparison child.

Parent, Teacher, and Peer Rejection

The data are convicing that the learning-disabled child is likely to be rejected or in conflict with parent, teacher, and peers. As yet, we know very little concerning the basis of such rejection, but studies toward this end are now being undertaken. In one investigation, Bryan (1974c) compared the interactions of learning-disabled, potential learning-disabled, and nondisabled children with children one year younger. Each child was brought to a laboratory and allowed to play a miniature bowling game. After playing the game, the child was informed that he was to teach a younger child how to play the game in such a way as to obtain high scores. In reality, the game scores were preset, but this was unknown to the participants. A younger child was then brought into the room, the experimenter left, and teaching lesson was initiated. The lesson was videotaped by a concealed camera for subsequent analysis.

There is some evidence that peer popularity and rejection are associated with children's use of social reinforcements, essentially praise and punishment (Hartup et al., 1967). The particular emphasis in the analysis of these tutorial sessions was the degree to which learning-disabled and nondisabled children employed such reinforcements. No differences were found. The adults who tested these children felt strongly that learning-disabled children did, in fact, act very differently from the nondisabled children while interacting with their peers, and insofar as these interactions were videotaped, all was not lost.

To check these intuitions, randomly selected videotapes were shown to a group of education students who had no knowledge concerning which of the children were learning disabled and which were not. Unlike the investigators, then, they were "blind." Each rater viewed videotapes which were no longer than four minutes in duration and was asked to rate each child as to his physical appearance, speech and language competence, academic achievement and attractiveness to other children. It was found that education majors rated the learning-disabled child as significantly less competent in speech and language use, as having lower academic achievement and attractiveness to peers than the nondisabled child. Physical attractiveness was the only item which did not differentiate the learning-disabled from the nondisabled child! Thus, strangers to learning and reading problems, inexperienced at evaluation and in dealing with young children, could view this short tape of a dyadic interaction and differentiate the learning-disabled from the nondisabled child.

While there are, no doubt, many factors which might contribute to this differing behavior by these children, one starting point is to focus upon the child's ability to accurately discriminate the various affective states in others. For this purpose Bryan (1974b) employed a test devised by Robert Rosenthal, which is known as the Pons. The test consists of a film and an audio tape. The film has forty segments which display an adult female expressing either positive or negative affects combined with dominant or submissive expressions. Examples of the situations used are: (a) positive/ dominant—an expression of motherly love; (b) positive/submissive— expressions of gratitude; (c) negative/dominant—nagging a child; (d) negative/submissive—asking forgiveness. Besides varying the affects and styles of expressions, the amount of information available to the child is also varied. On some occasions, the child views only the face of the actress, while on other occasions, the torso and face are viewed. The forty audio segments present the same affects, but the messages have been made uninterpretable by removal of high frequency sounds or by scrambling and resplicing the tape. The viewer-listener sees or hears emotional expressions without being able to understand any of the words spoken. The viewing child is instructed to indicate on a questionnaire which one of two statements best describes the scenario.

Taking care to ensure that the children had understood the questionnaire, Bryan found that learning-disabled children were less able to accurately describe the scenario than were nondisabled children. The learning-disabled child apparently has more difficulty in understanding subtle communications concerning affects than do nondisabled children. Difficulties in interpreting nonverbal social communications appear to persist into adolescence. Wiig and Harris (1974) administered a videotape of a young female's nonverbal expressions of anger, embarrassment, fear, frustration, joy, and love to learning-disabled and nondisabled adolescents. They report that learning-disabled adolescents made more substitutions than the control group in the labeling of the female's emotions. Furthermore, when the nondisabled adolescents made errors, they seem to be age specific errors, such as substituting embarrassment for display of love. But the errors made by the learning-disabled adolescents were more gross; for example, they were more likely to label positive emotions as judged by others as negative in nature. The special education teachers also rated the children who scored in the lower half of the distribution on the nonverbal test as poor in adaptive social behaviors in the classroom. To what degree this ability might be tied to their interpersonal difficulties with parents, teachers, and peers remains to be determined. Clearly, however, these findings provide a lead as to future possibilities concerning remediation efforts involving such children. The evidence indicates that many of the problems experienced by the learning-disabled child involve interpersonal interactions. Considerably more attention should be addressed to both the understanding and the remediation of these problems. Learning-disabled children do not suffer only from academic failure; many carry an additional burden of social failure.

CLASSROOM CONDUCT

In addition to studies concerned with the social interactions of children, research has been conducted within school settings to determine just how the learning-disabled child conducts himself. The focus of such research has been on two major issues: the degree to which the learning-disabled child focuses upon academic tasks; and the social relationships that such children experience with teachers and peers. Are such children disruptive, hyperactive, quiet, talkative, nontask-oriented, ignored, rejected, in attendance or absent during the school day? There is very little information available and the existing information is of very recent origin.

Forness and Estveldt (1971) studied children in the process of being referred for evaluation for academic difficulties. Observations were made within their classrooms to determine if, in fact, their behavior distinguished them from their classmates. These investigators studied twenty-four boys, 6 to 11 years of age, all having intelligence scores within the normal range, over a fifteen-month period within a regular elementary school classroom. Observers visited the classrooms over a period of two weeks and recorded the children's behaviors while they were engaged in small group reading and math instruction. A data coding cycle was set up so that the subject's behavior was coded for the first six-second interval; then the observer coded the behavior of each of the other children in that group and started the cycle again. The behaviors recorded were interactions, attending behaviors, and the responses of the teacher and peers. The results indicated that most of the time was spent in attending to the academic task at hand. More than 80 percent of the behaviors which occurred appeared to receive no overt response from anyone. The target subjects in the reading group attended from 22 to 78 percent, while the peers attended from 36 to 92 percent. The target children received more attention from teachers than peers and this attention was in the context of task-related help. The main difference between the target children and comparison peers was that related to attending behavior and their frequency of interaction with the teacher. It was noted that many of the nonreferred children attended to the school task less than half of the time; in fact, children who were referred were no less attentive than children who were not deemed as needing remedial help.

The finding that task-oriented behavior is less likely to be exhibited by learning-disabled than nondisabled children has received further support in several additional studies (Bryan and Wheeler, 1972; Bryan, 1974d). The method used in both studies was an Interaction Process Analysis. A behavioral code is developed which includes the behaviors defined as relevant to provide an accurate picture of the occurrence of behaviors in an elementary school class. The categories of behaviors which were recorded were: task-oriented behavior, nontask-oriented behavior, social interactions, and waiting. Task-oriented behavior was defined as "becoming engaged in a purposeful activity that has been prescribed for us by someone else" (Jackson, 1971, p. 84). This includes reading, library, art, and miscellaneous tasks (passing out paper to the class, watering the plants). Nontask-oriented behavior was defined as nonproductive behavior and/or activities the child was not supposed to be engaged in. This included such behaviors as staring out the window, roaming around the room, pretending to be attending (flipping the pages of the book with no observable signs of reading or writing), and singing during quiet time. Social interactions were defined as verbal and/or nonverbal behaviors emitted between two or more persons. The child's approaches to the teacher and peers, their responses to him, and their initiations to the child were included. Waiting was used to describe transitional periods, such as when the teacher organized the class activities for the day, when the class was changing activity, or when the individual child finished his work and was waiting for further instructions.

In the first study (Bryan and Wheeler, 1972), the results were that the learning-disabled child spent less time in task-oriented and more time in nontask-oriented behaviors than did comparison children. The learning-disabled children spent an average of 57 percent of their time in task-oriented behaviors compared to the comparison children's average of 70 percent. The learning-disabled children did not interact with the teacher more than did the comparison children; indeed, neither group interacted with her significantly (only 2 percent of the time was spent in such interactions).

In the second study (Bryan, 1974d), the goal was to determine whether learning-disabled children's task-oriented behavior would vary according to the task at hand (reading vs. music), whether the frequency and type of teacher/peer interactions would vary from the regular classroom to the special education setting, and to determine whether or not there are qualitative differences in the social interactions of these children.

As in the first study, the learning-disabled children spent less time in task-oriented behaviors and more time in nontask-oriented behaviors than comparison peers. While learning-disabled children spent an average of 68 percent of their time in task-oriented behavior, the comparison children devoted an average of 88 percent. Learning-disabled children spent an average of over 30 percent of their time on nontask-oriented behavior, while comparison children devoted but 11 percent of their time to such activities. The learning-disabled child was particularly "turned off" (spent less time than did comparison children) to lessons in arithmetic, language, and the arts (music, art, games). Finally, the learning-disabled children simply paid less attention to the teacher, irrespective of topic discussed, than did the comparison children.

Again the results of follow-up investigations of hyperactive children suggest that such lack of task orientation persists four to six years following the identification of the problem. Weiss et al. (1971) compared the classroom behaviors of twenty-four previously labeled hyperactive children with those not so labeled. Attempts were made to match these groups of children on the basis of age, sex, intelligence test scores, and classroom. Observers were used who were unaware of the diagnostic status of the children. They report findings which indicated that hyperactive children engaged in significantly more behaviors unrelated to classroom activity than did the comparison child. It was not that they found general excessive motor actions for hyperactive children, but rather that such children engaged in organized behavior (e.g., playing with a pencil) which was irrelevant to the school task at hand.

While we have focused upon the task orientation of the learning-disabled child, also of interest are the classroom interactions between learning-disabled children and their peers and teachers. In the previously described study by Bryan (1974d), such behaviors were noted.

The social interactions revealed that the learning-disabled and comparison children did not differ on the proportions of time they spent interacting with the classroom teacher (5.1 percent and 3.7 percent, respectively), or with peers (9.8 percent and 10.4 percent, respectively). There were very significant differences, however, in the patterns of interactions which the learning-disabled child had with teachers and peers. The number of times the adult responded to an initiation of contact by the child was very different for these groups. The teacher responded to 76.7 percent of the contacts initiated by comparison children, but only to 43.6 percent of the contacts initiated by the learning-disabled children. Whatever the reason for the lack of responsiveness by the teacher, the result is likely to be an increasing alienation between child and instructor. When the teacher did interact with the children, the nature of the teacher's interactions with the learning-disabled and comparison children differed. About 50 percent of the time that the teacher interacted with the learning-disabled child was devoted to helping him with his academic work. Only about 25 percent of the time the teacher interacted with the comparison child was devoted to academic matters. The teacher was more likely to interact with the comparison child for purposes of sending him on errands, eliciting his aid in organizing games, obtaining his help in helping other students, and other nonacademic matters.

The comparison of attending behavior and social interactions of learning-disabled children in the special education classroom and in the regular classroom revealed that the children engaged in more task-oriented behavior in the special classroom.

Also of interest was the nature of the reinforcements given these children by their teachers. While the learning-disabled children received as many positive reinforcements (statements of praise and approval) as did the non-disabled children, they also received more reproofs. The teachers appeared to be generally reluctant to respond to the learning-disabled child's attempts to initiate an interaction, did not employ more encouragement or praise for such children who might be in particular need of such encouragement, and tended to give such children more negative feedback. While in the resource room, the learning-disabled child interacted more with the teacher and received proportionally more positive and fewer negative feedbacks.

Peer interactions were also studied. As the reader will recall, the learning-disabled child is generally rejected by his peers. Classmates describe the learning-disabled child as untidy, not one whom one would wish for a friend, and one who tends to be ignored by other children within the classroom. The results of this observational study confirm at least one feature of the results of the sociometric studies. While learning-disabled and comparison children did not differ in the amount of peer interaction in which they engaged, the learning-disabled children were more likely to be ignored by peers than were comparison children when they initiated peer contact.

Subsequent investigations to determine those learning-disabled children's behaviors which may be "turning off" their peers has not thrown much light on the matter. Bryan, Wheeler, Felcan, and Henek (1976) found that learning-disabled children emitted a significantly greater number of statements indicating competition with their peers than nondisabled children, while Bryan and Bryan (unpublished manuscript, 1977) found that such children made more "nasty" statements to their peers than did comparison children. Both studies did demonstrate that peers were "turned off" by the disabled child, finding that the learning-disabled child received fewer statements of consideration and more statements reflecting peer rejection than did nonlearning-disabled children.

There seems to be little question that the learning-disabled child is likely to be rejected by parents, peers, and teachers. If you ask either adults or peers, by and large, they will tell you so. Moreover, analysis of the classroom situation suggests that the learning-disabled child's social life is rather different from that of other children. Apparently, he is more often ignored when attempting to initiate a social interaction, is less likely to be interacted with by the teacher for matters not essentially academic, gets more negative and less positive reinforcement from teachers than his nondisabled counterpart. In short, people do act as if they dislike the learning-disabled child. Whatever distinguishes the behavior of the learning disabled from the nondisabled in peer interactions is manifested very quickly. Strangers to children can reliably detect differences between learning-disabled and nondisabled children, and after viewing such interactions only a few minutes (Bryan, 1974e). As indicated, there is evidence that the learning-disabled child is somewhat disabled in detecting or correctly perceiving subtly expressed affective cues by others. One major source of the disabled child's difficulty with peers and parents may be linked to this type of insensitivity. Perhaps it is their faulty language, their intrusiveness, or all manner of possible combinations of such behaviors. We do not know. What we do know is that such children are not liked by others.

Finally, it should be noted that most remedial efforts are devoted to the correction of the learning-disabled child's reading, writing, or arithmetic failures. To our knowledge, virtually no remediation efforts are studied or recommended for the academic failure's social failures. This is perhaps justified, according to one's values and resources. However, ignorance concerning the disabled child's social difficulties is not justifiable. There is no question that they exist and that both parents and teachers should be alerted to that fact.

ORGANIC CAUSES OF FAILURE

The social and academic failure of the learning-disabled child has not been unrecognized by workers in this area and various explanations as to the etiological or causative factors have been advanced. While the exact site, processing, and nature of the defect are controversial, there are many who view the problem as organically based. Cruickshank, Bentzen, Ratzeburg, and Tannhauser (1961) suggested that

> hyperactivity is . . . defined to include much much more subtle deviations in behavior, and is more specifically considered to be related to matters of short attention span, visual and auditory distractibility, and disturbances in perception leading to disassociative tendencies. . . . All of these characteristics have been observed in individuals with definitely diagnosed brain pathology (p. 10).

While recognizing that many cases of hyperactivity may be more associated with emotional problems and may not demonstrate any organically significant deficits, the weight of their view is upon the degree to which these children have established cortical control of attention and perception. Johnson and Myklebust (1967) described cases of children with psychoneurological learning disorders as having "social imperception." These authors suggest that the parietal lobe of the right hemisphere of the brain is responsible for a child's inability to comprehend his social world. This brain damage is believed to affect the child's nonverbal skills, resulting in unintentionally reckless and tactless behavior.

Dykman and colleagues (1971) have developed an extensive research program to test the notion that learning disabilities are primarily a reflection of an attentional deficit and that this is the result of a breakdown in the reticular activating system of the brain. Brown (1973) also suggested that behavioral characteristics typical of learning-disabled children reflect individual differences in the maturation of brain centers responsible for the control of emotion. As such, it would appear that we are simply viewing individual differences in control for which we should have more tolerance. Brown argues that we expect differences in the rates at which children acquire motor-cognitive skills and we should extend this to expectancies concerning the child's development of self-control.

Finally, an interesting case has been made for the role of allergies in affecting children's behaviors. Franklin (1973) believes that the number of learning-disabled children who are sensitive to chemicals and additives used in drugs and foods is seriously underestimated and that many of the problems people experience are a result of this sensitivity. Somewhat supporting this position is a *Newsweek* article (1973) which reports the work of Feingold and his colleagues. Working with a group of twenty-five hyperkinetic children, they found that many had a history of allergies and had consumed large quantities of processed foods. A diet free of artificial flavors and coloring was reported to reduce these children's hyperactivity. These findings lack corroborative data from other systematic research, but are nonetheless intriguing.

PSYCHOLOGICAL AND SOCIAL CAUSES OF FAILURE

While the above-mentioned theorists have focused upon the role of organic dysfunctions in affecting the learning-disabled child's behavioral problems, others have looked toward psychological and/or social processes as possible causative factors. Friedland and Shilkret (1973) suggest that hyperactive behavior results from traumatic interactions with adults. It is argued that the child becomes hyperactive in order to avoid interpersonal relationships with adults within his environment. This explanation is not persuasive. By and large, hyperactivity itself is not the cause of social problems; rather it is how the activity is directed or its nature which turns others off (Pope, 1970). Additionally, there is little systematically gathered data suggesting that learning-disabled children avoid adults. In neither of the observational studies conducted by Bryan (Bryan and Wheeler, 1972; Bryan, 1974d) was it found that learning-disabled children attempted fewer interactions with the teacher than did nondisabled children. Avoidance conditioning does not appear to characterize the history or reflect accurately the behavior of such children. The "unsuccessful extrovert" (Wender, 1971) seems to better describe the children.

In her research involving hyperactive children, Barbara Keogh (1971, 1973) has advanced two hypotheses concerning psychological factors which may be important in understanding such children. She suggests that one view of the effect of hyperactivity is that of producing a deficit in information collection and/or processing. Hyperactivity reduces the amount of information the child can obtain under conditions where motor activity must be inhibited. You cannot run and read at the same time. The longer the period of hyperactivity, the greater the accumulation of the deficit of information. Keogh also suggested that hyperactive children may have different conceptual styles than nonhyperactive ones. Conceptual styles reflect individual differences in decision-making styles, particularly the time in which decisions are likely to be made (Kagan, 1965). Some persons take a long time to make a decision and make few errors. These individuals are said to have a reflective tempo. Other children tend to make rapid decisions and make many errors as well. These children are presumed to have an impulsive conceptual style.

Individuals who are reflective in their cognitive style have been found, when presented a task for which the *correct response is uncertain,* to more systematically scan the stimulus material, to be more anxious about making errors, to ask more relevant questions related to the problem-solving activity, to more efficiently use feedback information in their problem solving, and to exhibit greater self-generated verbal control over their behavior than individuals assessed as employing impulsive cognitive styles (Messer, 1976). While the research evidence is somewhat mixed in its results, there is some to indicate that learning-disabled children, as defined by reading or other academic failures, may show greater impulsivity in their cognitive styles than nondisabled children (Messer, 1976; Whalen and Henker, 1976). This important hypothesis certainly appears reasonable, since hyperactive children, many of whom may be learning disabled, are often described as responding too quickly for their own good, as lacking the ability to think things through, and as being unable to delay their responses. A more detailed examination of these hypotheses will be presented in the next chapter.

Other investigators have suggested that situational influences play an important role in eliciting maladaptive behaviors. It is not that the brain-damaged child is maladjusted because of the damage, but rather that such children are likely to find themselves in situations in which they are continually frustrated in achieving their hopes and aspirations (McReynolds, 1966). Owen and collaborators report that children with learning disabilities experience a family life which is quite different from that experienced by their siblings and other academically successful children. Families of learning-disabled and comparison children were rated by observers on the degree of organization of family living. The scale ranged from "family activities and schedules planned to give structure to family living rather strictly adhered to" to "practically no structure; disorganized pattern of living; lack of schedules or assigned responsibilities" (1971, p. 45). The authors concluded that the "educationally handicapped children lived in a family atmosphere that tended to be less well organized and less emotionally stable than the atmosphere of the control families" (p. 46).

Peck and Stackhouse (1973) hypothesized that learning-disabled children, in this case defined as reading problems, were experiencing difficulties as a result of intrafamilial conflict. To assess this hypothesis, fifteen normal and fifteen reading-problem families were asked to complete a thirty-eight-item questionnaire. Twenty items on which the mother, father, and son disagreed were then selected for the experimental task. The triad, operating as a unit, were asked to solve these twenty problems. Their interactions were recorded and later analyzed for the amount of time spent in solution of the problems, the percentage of time spent in silence, and for categories of types of verbal interactions. A comparison of the interactions for the reading-problem son, mother, and father with those of the comparison son, mother, and father teams revealed that the reading-problem families spent more time completing the decision-making tasks, more time in silence, and exchanged less explicit and more irrelevant information. Contrary to expectation, conflict was not more evident with the reading-problem groups; it was in fact less evident. The authors concluded that the ways in which reading-problem families interacted produced "mystification." In effect, they communicated in such a fashion as to avoid open disagreement, however legitimate, by misdefining the issues under discussion. The families appeared to argue about arguing and failed to reach a decision. The results of such interactions, if frequent within the home, may well be to teach the child how not to confront an issue and also how to remain stupid about things, issues, and people.

There is another interpretation to these results. Perhaps a general language problem exists within the families of learning-disabled children. It is known that there is a correlation between parental academic accomplishment and children's accomplishment, for reasons of either genes and/or example and/or tutorial efforts. Thus, Owen et al. (1971) reported that the parents of the educationally handicapped children had lower high school English grades than comparison parents. In addition, the fathers of these children had lower Wide Range Achievement Test scores than comparison fathers.

There is mounting evidence that the learning-disabled child experiences a very different social world than does the comparison child. He appears likely to be ignored, at best, or utterly rejected, at worst. In addition an impressive amount of follow-up data is accumulating which leads to the inference that such social rejection is likely to continue for many years. It is not likely to be a transient problem. The controversy as to the causative factors to this social rejection is, so far, marked more by speculation than by data. Considerably more effort should be addressed to the understanding and remediation of the social failures exhibited by these children.

HYPERACTIVITY

We have reviewed the few studies concerning other people's views of the learning-disabled child. But research into the behavior of disabled children has not been simply limited to the social status of such children. Perhaps the central characteristic associated with the learning-disabled child is that of hyperactivity. Virtually any discussions or readings about learning-disabled children indicate that a "hard sign" of such disabilities is hyperactivity.

It should be noted at the onset that our knowledge about learning-disabled children and hyperactivity is quite limited. We have found very few investigations addressed to the question of whether children diagnosed as learning disabled are also, independent of that diagnosis, considered hyperactive. This does not mean to say that some learning-disabled children are not hyperactive, and there is sufficient evidence to suggest that children whom some individuals call hyperactive will eventually demonstrate severe academic difficulties (Mendelson, Johnson, and Stewart, 1971; Weiss, Minde, Werry, Douglas, and Nemeth, 1971). There is little doubt that there is some overlap among these groups of children, but direct information about hyperactivity and learning disabilities is sparse. It may even be that neither brain damage nor hyperactivity is germane to the learning-disabled child; or it may be that both are. In the remainder of this chapter we will present some research studies concerning the motor activity of brain-damaged children (presumably the categorical cousins of the learning disabled), followed by a discussion of current concepts and characteristics of hyperactivity.

Motor Activity and the Brain Damaged

An ingenious study of motor activity in brain-injured children was conducted by Pope (1970). The study was undertaken with the realization that we have little quantification of levels of activity of children during their early school years. How can we say a child is too much or too little of something if we have no normative data?

Pope studied the activity level of two groups of children, each consisting of nineteen boys. One group consisted of children diagnosed as suffering from some form of brain injury; the other group was comprised of children with no damage. The children were between the ages of 7 and 11. So that differences between groups would not be obscured, drug treatment was suspended several days prior to the administration of the tests. Children were observed in four different situations: (a) when they were assigned to do a simple task and (b) a difficult task, (c) when they were in an undirected play situation and (d) when they were instructed to refrain from moving. The child's activity was measured by an accelerometer, a device developed by Schulman, Kaspar, and Throne (1965). The accelerometer is an automatically winding calendar wrist watch modified in such a way that there is a direct drive from the pendulum to the hands of the watch. Two of these devices were used for each child, one attached to a hand, the other to a foot. In addition, activity was assessed by a behavior recorder, a keyboard device for recording direct visual observations. The experimental area was a hospital ward in which the floor area was divided into four equal zones by means of tape. Each of these four areas contained identical equipment and toys. In the undirected play situation, the child was allowed to play in the playroom. The simple task situation to which the child was exposed was the administration of the Sequin Form Board test, a test in which the child is asked to place objects into an appropriate hole in a wooden board. For the difficult task, the child was asked to complete the Sequin Form Board test while the board was at an angle. Finally, the child was asked to sit quietly without leaving his seat for a period of five minutes. All other situations lasted for a fifteen-minute period. Children were observed through a one-way vision mirror. The activity recorded included the movement of the child across the zones, and within zones, and such behaviors as standing, sitting, and contact with available toys.

The results were somewhat dependent upon the situation in which the child was assessed, but generally indicated the following. When children were in a free play situation, brain-damaged children showed more gross motor activity and less attention to particular toys than did the control children. When a task demand, whether simple or difficult, essentially constrains movement in space, brain-damaged children are likely to show more energy expenditures within the space limits allowed. They will not leave the task to run in an open space, but will tend to show more movements and greater energy expenditures in the vicinity of the task than will control children. Finally, when instructed to inhibit motor behaviors, to sit still in a chair, the brain-damaged are less likely to demonstrate such inhibitions than are nonbrain-damaged children. It should be noted, however, that the children did persist in completing the task even though motor movements during the task situation were evident. It should also be noted that many of the brain-damaged children were less active than were the nondamaged ones.

While there is some reason, then, to believe that brain-damaged children may show evidence of hyperactivity, such behavior may not be so strongly associated with brain damage or so infrequently associated with nondamaged children as to warrant it useful in individual diagnosis. Moreover, it should be remembered that this evidence does not directly support the hypothesis that learning-disabled children will be hyperactive.

Distractibility

Other behaviors, in addition to hyperactivity, which might be associated with brain damage have also received some attention. For example, is brain damage associated with stupidity, distractibility, or short attention spans? A now classic study of the behavioral correlates of brain damage was conducted by Schulman, Kaspar, and Throne (1965). These investigators conducted an extensive study of the behavior of brain-damaged children in laboratory and commonplace settings. The children were between 11 and 14 years of age, obtained IQ scores ranging from 46 to 87, and lived in a residential school or attended a day school. These investigators administered a battery of standard clinical measures, such as the Wechsler Intelligence Scale for Children and the Bender-Gestalt tests. The children's activity was measured for three days by attaching two actometers or accelerometers to each child. Distractibility of the brain-damaged child, presumably a characteristic of the learning disabled as well, was assessed by the child's performance on four laboratory tests. One, the clock test, required the child to press a lever at the appropriate instant to prevent a mechanical mouse, which was moving around the clock, from being "trapped." The second assessment device, the box test, demanded that the child indicate the shape, color, or position of one of three boxes out of which a puppet popped at varying intervals. Third, a card test required the child to indicate whenever the picture of a baby appeared in a deck of 200 picture cards rapidly presented. Finally, a tone test was administered wherein the child was presented with a tape recording of various tones. The child's task was to indicate when a particular tone was presented.

This investigation was unique in several respects. First, the authors employed a multitude of measures to assess the same concept. Given imperfection of any one measure, the use of many measures lends greater confidence to any results obtained (Webb, Campbell, Schwartz, and Sechrest, 1966).

The assessment of activity across situations provides information concerning the generality of the findings. Questions were asked as to whether distractibility and hyperactivity were correlated with each other, or whether one or the other was correlated with neurological signs and psychometric test scores.

Some very surprising results were obtained. First, hyperactivity and distractibility are not general traits of the child; children show marked variations in both, given changes in the situation and task. Second, these two measures do not correlate with one another. The presence of hyperactivity does not guarantee the presence of distractibility. Third, the presence of neurological signs is likely to be correlated with *hypo,* not hyper, activity. In their summary of the results, the authors indicated that

> . . . individual diagnostic measures employed are not sufficiently reliable to be acceptable. . . . Measures used to measure "brain damage" do not co-vary significantly and tend instead to be separable into at least two loose types of measures. . . . Only one set of behaviors correlates significantly with both the diagnostic clusters and that correlation is in the wrong direction (1965, p. 74).

One response to the negative findings of this study is to conclude that brain damage, hyperactivity, and distractibility as syndromes or even as problems are figments of someone's imagination. Many professionals did turn their backs on the business of syndromes and brain damage as such. But let us reexamine the data. Each of these behaviors: hyperactivity and distractibility, were measured using different techniques. Each should be further evaluated as separate constructs, both complex and multidimensional. In the case of the distractibility measures, the child had to respond quickly and had to respond verbally or motorically. Not only was the child's ability to attend to a puppet or mouse being evaluated, but also his ability to organize himself motorically in order to respond by pressing a lever, pointing to a card or naming colors and shapes. Distractibility as assessed in this study would appear to be more related to the ability to call up words quickly, the ability to respond to a visual or auditory stimulus with a motor response, and the ability to sequentially order these responses. In retrospect, it appears unreasonable to assume that such diverse behaviors and abilities would be correlated.

Therefore, it is unforgivable that professionals, in this day and age, continue to talk about brain-damaged and/or learning-disabled children possessing personality characteristics as global distractibility or hyperactivity.

Current Views on Hyperactivity

Up to this point we have used the word *hyperactivity* to represent some unitary dimension residing in the person rather than its being affected by both the person and the situation. The use and overuse of the term have made it imperative to take a much closer look at the meaning of this term.

Approximately 3 to 20 percent of our school-age population is defined as hyperactive (Whalen and Henker, 1976). It is estimated that approximately 50 percent of all childhood behavior disorder referrals are for hyperactivity (Langhorne and Loney, 1976). Thus far in the book and perhaps in the field at large, the term *hyperactive* has been used to represent some unitary dimension residing in the person; that is, the characteristic of excessive activity which is usually maladaptive. Judgments about excessive activity, either formalized in rating scales or expressed within free interviews by either teachers, parents, or physicians usually serve as the criteria by which inferences as to hyperactivity are made. By whatever means and from whomever the judgments are obtained, it is clear that hyperactivity is generally thought of as an excessive expression of motor activity by a child. Insofar as so many children are labeled hyperactive, cause such concern, and receive drug treatments which have become quite controversial, it is not surprising that considerable evidence has recently been gathered concerning characteristics of children labeled hyperactive. The next section will describe some of these findings.

First and foremost, it is apparent that children who are labeled hyperactive are not by and large overactive. That is to say, hyperactive children do not appear to demonstrate greater activity levels than nonhyperactive children, at least in "unstructured situations." By unstructured situations, it is meant those situations which generally do not require the child to be task oriented, particularly when the task is that selected by someone other than the child. Whalen and Henker (1976), who have provided an excellent review of findings pertaining to hyperactivity, write, "It should be noted that the failure to find consistent differences in general activity level holds whether global ratings, behavioral observations, or electromechanical recordings are used to assess motoric response" (p. 1115). The hyperactive child is not a motoric machine run amok. Since hyperactive children are generally not more active than their nonlabeled counterparts, is there any evidence that they differ from other children on any type of motoric expression? Apparently there is. Whalen and Henker have reviewed evidence and suggest that "the issue is one of quality rather than quantity of movement, and the data indicate that hyperactive children may show atypically high levels of motor restlessness when an external agent (e.g., teacher or examiner) requires performance on a structured task. In other words, the difficulty may not be one of inordinately high activity levels, but rather an inability to modulate motor behavior in accordance with situation (and particularly social) demands" (p. 1115). Moreover, Whalen and Henker argue that it is not that the hyperactive child wiggles or jiggles excessively, even within a structured task situation, but rather that he seems to be more impulsive, less able to maintain vigilance or attention upon the task.

While general activity level has been thought to be the primary manifestation of hyperactivity, associated characteristics of this "condition" have also been postulated. There is apparent agreement among observers as to the nature of the characteristics. Hence hyperactive children are not only hyperactive, but show distractibility, short attention span, clumsiness, emotional lability, poor academic performance, antisocial behavior, poor peer relationships, low self-esteem, and irritability (Langhorne and Loney, 1976; Whalen and Henker, 1976). It is believed that such characteristics should be associated with hyperactivity and with each other. Most of the investigations concerned with the correlation of these behaviors have employed rating scales as their means of measurement. The results of these investigations have generally failed to find that the above-mentioned characteristics are associated with the diagnosis of hyperactivity or that they co-vary among themselves. The results of studies reviewed and completed by Langhorne and Loney (1976) suggest that correlations, if any, found between these characteristics are associated with the source of the judgment rather than the behavior of the judged. That is to say, the correlations among ratings which should not necessarily correlate, made by the same judge, are likely to be higher than the correlations found in ratings of the same behavior completed by two different judges! Given that judges, such as physicians, teachers, and parents, view the children in very different situations, and given that the differences between hyperactive and nonhyperactive children are manifested only in "structured" situations, then it is perhaps not surprising that these judges would not agree when evaluating the same child on the same behavior. They see different actions because of the situational differences in which they confront the child. In addition, there are difficulties associated with currently employed rating scales. While rating scales do generally differentiate children previously diagnosed as hyperactive from other children, they have been found to yield ratings rather unstable across time, and these ratings are frequently found to be uncorrelated with actually observed behavior (Whalen and Henker, 1976). It is probably not surprising, then, that given the unreliability of rating scales, the importance of the rater, and the lack of relationship between judgments and observations, that empirical demonstrations of a hyperactive syndrome have not been forthcoming.

In an attempt to make finer differentiations, a number of specialists have suggested that children might be usefully categorized into various types of hyperactive behavior. For example, Denckla (1973) has suggested three types of hyperactive behavior and has hypothesized, apparently on the basis of clinical observations, that various types of hyperactivity might respond differentially to various drugs. Denckla suggests that there are three different types of hyperactivity, only one of which will respond favorably to drug intervention. One type is characterized by the child demonstrating anxious, aggressive, destructive, unpredictable, and impulsive behavior, a kind of demonic emotionality. A second type of hyperactivity is that in which the child is placid, sweet, socially gauche, flits about aimlessly while accomplishing little, and is motorically clumsy. Neither of these types of children, according to Denckla, will respond well to drugs employed to alter their hyperactive behaviors. The third type of child is described as "on the go," very verbal and talkative, a happy child who fails to act his age, and a fidgety one who "thinks out loud" (p. 446). This type of child is described as responding well to the drug Ritalin.

Solomons (1971) has suggested that it would be heuristic to devise a classification scheme where finer differentiation is made with regard to hyperactivity. He suggests four categories. A child might show *hypokinesis,* a chronic low level of energy expenditure. Or he might demonstrate *fidgetiness,* constantly moving parts of the body while not locomoting in space. The third category is termed *overactivity.* The child does not stay in place the usual length of time. Finally, the category *hyperkinetic impulsive* is suggested to describe the impulsive, distractible, irritable, and hyperexcitable child. Solomons' categories reglect a one-dimensional scale ranging from low to high activity as he defines them. The scale may or may not be useful for the researcher or practitioner. Solomons, like Denckla, relates categories to the efficacy of types of drug intervention. He suggests that the hyperkinetic impulsive type of child may show behavioral improvement when treated by an amphetamine, while the fidgety type is more responsive to a tranquilizer.

A word of caution is in order. Clinical observations, apparently the data base for both Denckla and Solomons, are often fruitful generators of useful hypotheses to be tested, but they are notoriously poor sources of data. The observations of Denckla and Solomons need and certainly deserve further investigations. For example, neither investigator has presented evidence pertaining to the reliability of judgments when their particular classification systems are employed. Even with training, will people agree as to whether a particular child is overactive or fidgety, or flits about aimlessly but is not destructive? Indeed, the question remains as to whether any type of hyperactivity is independent of any other type of hyperactivity. Are destructive hyperactive children verbal children as well? Maybe yes, maybe no. This is an empirical matter and before any typology of hyperactivity can be accepted, independence of the types from one another needs to be demonstrated. Warnings aside, both Denckla and Solomons have made an important point, buttressed by research.

It is time to refine the global concept of hyperactivity and to focus upon the specific behaviors which lead observers to infer the presence of hyperactivity. Once this is done, then the relationships between such acts can be determined, and the concepts of hyperactivity will begin to take on additional meaning and utility.

While the foregoing discussion makes it clear we know very little about hyperactivity and whatever differentiates these children from others (excepting the taking of medication) it is likely to be situationally specific and it is more likely to involve attentional rather than gross motor problems. It is also clear that children labeled hyperactive have a rather bleak future, with or without medication. Already mentioned are the data pertaining to their problems involving parents and teachers.

Mention should now be made of other problems that the future holds in store for them. Weiss et al. (1971) in their five-year follow-up of children previously diagnosed as hyperactive found such children had shown no improvement in academic marks, had few friends, and that 15 percent of such children had been referred to the courts for significant antisocial activities. Mendelson et al. (1971) found that parents reported that over 50 percent of their hyperactive offspring demonstrated stealing, fighting, frequent lying, and over one-third had threatened to kill one or both of their parents. Indeed, 59 percent of the children in this sample had some contact with the police. These authors further report that over 50 percent of the sample indicated feelings of low self-confidence and social rejection by others. Fifteen percent of the sample had either talked about or had attempted suicide. Finally, as Whalen and Henker point out, the employment of drugs doesn't seem to make a difference, at least in terms of most of these behaviors.

In summary, it appears clear that the learning-disabled child is confronted with a social world in which he is disliked, at worst, or ignored, at best, by his peers, classroom teachers, and even, perhaps, his parents. Moreover, there is evidence to suggest that he has difficulty in understanding subtle messages concerning adults' affective states, a deficiency which might well be expected to lead to social rejection. It is increasingly obvious that it is a grave error to assume that the social world of the learning-disabled child is either benign or comparable to that of the nondisabled one. The data pertaining to the social rejection of the learning-disabled child appear to have important implications for the contemporary style of providing remediation while allowing the child to remain in regular classrooms (i.e., mainstreaming). While the mainstreaming approach might ultimately be more desirable than segregated classrooms, the possibility that the learning-disabled child will be rejected by peers and teachers alike should not be overlooked.

In spite of the emphasis of the concept of hyperactivity as a "hard sign" of learning disabilities, it is becoming increasingly clear that hyperactivity may or may not be associated with brain damage, brain damage may or may not be associated with learning disabilities, and hyperactivity may or may not be associated with learning problems. Children who are hyperactive are not hyperactive all the time, or in all situations or under all motivational conditions. What does seem to be the case in this uncertain domain of hyperactivity is that such children are not generally more motorically active than nonhyperactive children; that such children may show deficits in sustaining attention on tasks which others impose and which require of them some regulation of their behavior; that such children will, on follow-up studies, show high incidence of school failures, parental and teacher rejection, high aggressiveness and rebelliousness, frequent interactions with police and courts, and probably feelings of low self-esteem and despair. This is true whether they have or have not taken medication.

Finally, evidence concerning such situational variables as teacher tolerance, task difficulty, and social reinforcement is sparse. Yet, to understand the behavior of the learning-disabled child, these situational variables must be explored and their impact upon behavior detailed.

Whether called hyperactive or learning disabled, it is clear that the social difficulties experienced by these children are grave. In the future we hope that the learning disability specialist and the classroom teacher will be more sensitive and more helpful in aiding the deficit child in the acquisition of social skills. Public support for such actions, at least in the abstract, has recently been documented by Bader (1975). Bader surveyed a number of active parents and professionals involved with learning-disabled children. The majority of professionals and parents indicated that training of social perception should have at least as much or more emphasis than academic matters in educational planning; that achievement in the social sphere was at least as important, and perhaps more important, than achievement in academic matters; that regular classroom teachers should have the primary responsibility for such training; and that the earlier such training of the children is initiated the better. No doubt the specifics of the training procedure and the particulars of the content of the training will become a matter of dispute. Surely appropriate compromises can be worked out, so that efforts can be initiated to aid the learning-disabled child to understand others, as well as in learning numbers and words.

REFERENCES

Bader, B. W. *Social Perception and Learning Disabilities*. Des Moines, Iowa: Moon Lithographing and Engraving, 1975.

Becker H. *Outsiders*. New York: Free Press, 1963.

Birch, H. and Belmont, L. "Auditory-visual integration in normal and retarded readers." *American Journal of Orthopsychiatry*, 1964, 34, 852–861.

Bryan, T. "Peer popularity of learning-disabled children." *Journal of Learning Disabilities*, 1974a, Vol. 7. 261–268 (a).

Bryan T. "Social factors in reading disabilities." Paper presented at the meetings of the American Educational Research Association, Chicago, Ill., 1974b.

Bryan, T. "Peer interactions and sociometric choices." Unpub. manuscript, 1974c.

Bryan, T. "An observational analysis of classroom behaviors of children with learning disabilities." *Journal of Learning Disabilities*, 1974d, 7, 26–34.

Bryan, T. "Peer popularity of learning-disabled children: A replication." *Journal of Learning Disabilities*, 1976, 9, 307–311.

Bryan, T. "Stranger's Judgments of Children's Social and Academic Adequacy: Instant Diagnosis." Unpublished manuscript, 1974 E.

Bryan, T. and McGrady, H. J. "Use of a teacher rating scale." *Journal of Learning Disabilities*, 1972, 5, 199–206.

Bryan, T. and Wheeler, R. "Perception of learning-disabled children: The eye of the observer." *Journal of Learning Disabilities*, 1972, 5, 484–488.

Bryan, T. and Bryan, J. H. "Social interactions of learning-disabled children." University of Illinois at Chicago, unpublished manuscript, 1977.

Bryan, T., Wheeler, R., Felcan, J., and Henek, T. " 'Come on, Dummy': An observational study of children's communications." *Journal of Learning Disabilities*, 1976, 9, 661–669.

Cruickshank, W. M., Bentzen, F. A., Ratzeburg, F. H., and Tannhauser, M. T. *A Teaching Method for Brain-injured and Hyperactive Children*. Syracuse: Syracuse University Press, 1961.

Denckla, M. B. "Research needs in learning disabilities: A neurologist's point of view." *Journal of Learning Disabilities*, 1973, 6, 441–450.

Dykman, R. A., Ackerman, P. T., Clements, S. D., and Peters, J. E. "Specific learning disabilities: An attentional deficit syndrome." In H. R. Myklebust (ed.), *Progress in Learning Disabilities, Vol. II*. New York: Grune & Stratton, 1971, 56–93.

Forness, S. R. and Estveldt, K. C. "Classroom observation of learning and behavior problem children." Graduate School of Education, University of California, L.A., 1971.

Friedland, S. J. and Shilkret, R. B. "Alternative explanations of learning disabilities: Defensive hyperactivity." *Exceptional Children,* 1973, 40, 213–214.

Hartup, W. W., Glazer, J. A., and Charlesworth, R. "Peer reinforcement and sociometric status." *Child Development,* 1967, 38, 1017–1024.

Jackson, P. "Life in classrooms." In E. Hollander and R. Hunt (eds.), *Current Perspectives in Social Psychology.* New York: Oxford University Press, 1971.

Johnson, D. and Myklebust, H. *Learning Disabilities: Educational Principles and Practices.* New York: Grune & Stratton, 1967.

Kagan, J. "Reflection-impulsivity and reading ability in primary grade children." *Child Development,* 1965, 36, 609–628.

Keogh, B. K. "A compensatory model for psychoeducational evaluation of children with learning disorders." *Journal of Learning Disabilities,* 1971, 4, 544–548.

Keogh, B. K., Tchir, C., and Windeguth-Behn, A. "Teachers' perceptions of educationally high risk children." *Journal of Learning Disabilities,* 1974, 7, 367–374.

Langhorne, J. E. and Loney, J. "Childhood hyperkinesis: A return to the source." *Journal of Abnormal Psychology,* 1976, 85, 201–209.

McReynolds, L. V. "Operant conditioning for investigating speech sound discrimination in aphasic children." *Journal of Speech and Hearing Research,* 1966, 9, 519–528.

Mendelson, W., Johnson, N., and Stewart, M. A. "Hyperactive children as teenagers: A follow-up study." *The Journal of Nervous and Mental Disease,* 1971, 153, 273–279.

Messer, S. B. "Reflection-impulsivity: A review." *Psychological Bulletin,* 1976, 83, 1026–1052.

Minde, K., Weiss, G., and Mendelson, N. "A five year follow-up study of 91 hyperactive school children." *Journal of the American Academy of Child Psychiatry,* 1972, 11, 595–610.

Myklebust, H. R., Boshes, B., Olson, D., and Cole, C. "Minimal brain damage in children." Final Report. U.S.P.H.S. Contract 108–65–142. Evanston, Ill.: Northwestern University publications, June, 1969.

Owen, R. W., Adams, P. A., Forrest, T., Stolz, L. M., and Fisher, S. "Learning disorders in children: Sibling studies." *Monographs of the Society for Research in Child Development,* 1971, 36, No. 144.

Peck, B. B. and Stackhouse, T. "Reading problems and family dynamics." *Journal of Learning Disabilities,* 1973, 6, 506–511.

Pope, Lillie. "Motor activity in brain-injured children." *American Journal of Orthopsychiatry,* 1970, 40, 783–794.

Rosenhan, D. "On being sane in insane places." *Science,* 1973, 179, 250–258.

Schulman, J. L., Kaspar, J. C., and Throne, F. M., *Brain Damage and Behavior.* Springfield, Ill.: Charles C. Thomas, 1965.

Solomons, G. "Guidelines on the use and medical effects of psychostimulant drugs in therapy." *Journal of Learning Disabilities,* 1971, 4, 420–475.

Strag, G. A. "Comparative behavioral rating of parents with severe mentally retarded, special learning disability, and normal children." *Journal of Learning Disabilities,* 1972, 5, 631–635.

Webb, E. J., Campbell, D. T., Schwartz, R. D., and Sechrest, L. *Unobtrusive Measures: Nonreactive Research in the Social Sciences.* Chicago: Rand McNally, 1966.

Weiss, G., Minde, K., Werry, J. S., Douglas, V., and Nemeth, E. "Studies of the hyperactive child: A five-year follow-up." *Archives of General Psychiatry,* 1971, 24, 409–414.

Wender, H. *Minimal Brain Dysfunction in Children.* New York: Wiley-Interscience, 1971.

Whalen, C. K. and Henker, B. "Psychostimulants and children: A review and analysis." *Psychological Bulletin,* 1976, 83, 1113–1130.

Wiig, E. H. and Harris, S. P. "Perception and interpretation of nonverbally expressed emotions by adolescents with learning disabilities." *Perceptual and Motor Skills,* 1974, 38, 239–245.

Yarrow, M. R., Cambell, J. D., and Barton, R. V., "Recollections of childhood—A study of the retrospective method." *Monographs of the Society of Research in Child Development,* 1970, 35, No. 5.

7 | Information Processing

The most important new theoretical concept is that of a human being as a sampler of the information around him. . . . We are born into a world of constantly fluctuating stimulation. We sample from this flux, we do not experience it totally. We formulate ideas about our sampled "bits." We construct expectations and concepts. We test these concepts in various ways, and often revise them on the basis of our tests. . . . (Farnham-Diggory, 1972, p. xxxi).

Emphasis upon how children process information in their attempt to know the world about them has been the heart and soul of the field of learning disabilities. Theories, assessment techniques, and remediation programs have often been addressed to the role of children's perceptions and memory in academic performance. Assessments are made concerning the differential effectiveness the child might exhibit in processing or understanding visual or auditory signals, and remediation attempts are directed toward improving the child's ability to process information in the deficit sensory channel. Lying behind these efforts is the implicit belief that the learning-disabled child is particularly deficient in the reception, coding, or retrieval of information presented to him in a particular sensory channel.

The behavior of concern in information processing consists of all sorts of things. Attention, perception, labeling of perceptions, storage of perceptions, and the connection and integration of information perceived in different modalities all fall under the general topic of information processing. Virtually all activities from sensation to language are included.

FOCUSED ATTENTION

The phenomena of focused attention has long been a central issue in the field of learning disabilities. Attention deficits were included in one of the earliest constellations of traits, the Strauss syndrome, subsequently considered a type of learning disability (Torgesen, 1975). The importance of attention has not waned over the years. Teachers and other professionals concerned with learning-disabled children frequently indicate that attentional problems are among the important difficulties faced by learning-disabled children (Keogh, 1973). One group of researchers and theorists defined attentional problems as the most central and important characteristic of learning-disabled children (Dykman et al., 1971).

What is attention? Do children show attentional deficits, and if they do, does this mean they have learning disabilities? And if they are learning disabled, under what conditions and in what manner are such deficits demonstrated? From an educational perspective, attention refers to the child's ability to focus attention selectively upon the task at hand, a task usually determined by the classroom teacher. While there are a variety of other definitions of attention, the Kagan and Kogan (1970) one is offered here: "One can define selectivity of attention (or focused attention) as the degree to which thresholds are selectively lowered for one class of stimuli relative to others" (Kagan and Kogan, 1970, p. 1297). This definition carries important implications. First, attention reflects the "drawing power" of both the task and potential distractors from the task. Attention is thus intimately associated with distraction. Second, potentially competing stimuli are not limited to external stimuli, but may reflect conditions internal (e.g., thoughts) and external (e.g., noise) to the person. Third, attention may be affected by changes in the stimuli, as well as the child. Making the stimuli more complex, less redundant, more sharply contrasted than its competitors may increase attending behavior (Pick and Pick, 1970).

Theorists and researchers involved with the study of attention differ as to the meaning of various research findings. But there does seem to be general agreement on several important points. A number of investigators have indicated that attention is a very complex event; that attention should not be construed as some unitary characteristic or trait of an individual. Rather, several processes, each affected by different events, comprise this thing we call attention (Kagan and Kogan, 1970; Kawabe, 1976; Keogh, 1973; Pick and Pick, 1970). This means that there are a variety of behaviors which comprise attention and that while these behaviors are correlated with one another, they are not very highly correlated (Keogh and Margolis, 1976).

Furthermore, there is evidence that we undergo physiological changes at various stages of involvement in tasks. As children start to attend to a task, the pattern of physiological responses is quite different from a little later, when they are concentrating on that task. For example, in the initial stage, as children start to attend to a task, cardiac rates decrease and skin resistance increases. When concentrating on a problem, cardiac rate increases and shows increased variability, and there is a decrease in skin conductance. When a child is concentrating, the pupil of the eye dilates, in contrast to the initial stages of attention. In effect, attending behaviors are only partially correlated. Thus, investigators now hypothesize that attention consists of a variety of critical behaviors, each affected somewhat differently by varying conditions. We should no longer speak of attention without specifying just which process of attending is critical to the problem.

Although theorists use somewhat different terminologies to describe components of attention, there seems to be agreement that at least three components should be treated as conceptually unique. The orienting response (Kawabe, 1976; Pick and Pick, 1970; Rohwer, 1970), or in Keogh's term (1973) "coming to attention" is one important component. The second is the child's ability or strategy in scanning and focusing upon the appropriate stimulus material (Dykman et al., 1971; Kawabe, 1976). In effect, a child first becomes aroused, comes to attention, but then has to focus on the critical features of the task. The third component of attention is the ability or motivation to sustain attention, to focus on the critical features of the task across a period of time. This component is usually referred to as vigilance or maintenance (Pick and Pick, 1970).

Coming to Attention

The first component of attention, the orienting response, appears to be pretty primitive; it is a response or reflex which can be evoked in most animals at a very early stage of their development (Kessen, Haith, and Salaptek, 1970). The response consists of rapid arousal of the organism which includes a physical orientation to the task plus visual movements which better prepare the animal to receive information from the external environment. This response can be elicited by any discriminable change in the environment. For example, when a teacher yells "pay attention" or "be quiet" there should be orienting response by children. As most teachers can no doubt attest, the arousal state does not last long; it habituates very quickly.

"Coming to attention" behavior has been related to learning disabilities, at least theoretically. Strauss and Lehtinen (1947) suggested that learning-disabled children overreact to external stimuli, responding too vigorously to changes in stimulus conditions. Keogh and Margolis (1976) hypothesize that hyperactive children fail to engage the task at hand because they have difficulty in focusing upon the appropriate task features. It is not clear whether this reflects weak orienting behavior or excessively strong orienting behaviors. That is, the child may not attend either because of weak arousal or because of arousal to too many competing stimuli. While orienting responses have been given considerable theoretical weight in discussions of the attentional deficits of learning-disabled children, there has been little attention to this problem by researchers in learning disabilities.

In our discussion the orienting response has thus far been rather narrowly defined. Keogh and Margolis (1976) suggest that part of "coming to attention" is the organization of the perceptual field; selection of the correct stimuli to focus upon from the vast array within the environment. Other investigators prefer to conceptualize organization of the perceptual field as distinct from the orientation response.

We will next consider the available data concerned with learning-disabled children's difficulties in perceptual organization.

Focusing and Scanning

Once a child is aroused, assuming he cares to attend, attentional problems still may be evidenced. Two difficulties may crop up. First, the child may not be able to adequately organize what he sees. He may be distracted by irrelevant features of the stimulus array. The child is thus unable to determine the critical features of the task and respond appropriately. He literally can't get his act together. The second problem occurs when the child believes he has it together, but hasn't. The first problem is referred to as reflecting field dependence (Keogh, 1973); the second problem reflects impulsivity (Kagan and Kogan, 1970). To make matters more complex, field dependence is associated with impulsivity (Messer, 1976). Thus children who are field dependent, that is, who are strongly affected by irrelevant features of the perceptual field, are also likely to be somewhat impulsive, that is, to make quick and erroneous judgments.

Primarily through the efforts of Barbara Keogh, there has been some research on the relationship of field independence/dependence to learning disabilities. Keogh has hypothesized that learning-disabled children are likely to have difficulty organizing perceptual inputs and are likely to focus on the irrelevant features of such inputs. She argues that learning-disabled children have relative difficulty in separating the field (i.e., what is important) from the ground (i.e., what is not important). Keogh (1973) reports the results of several unpublished studies which support the hypothesis that perceptual organization difficulties might characterize children who do, or will, experience academic difficulties.

In a study conducted by Watson, it was found that reading ability was correlated with ability to ignore irrelevant features of a stimulus display. Becker found that high risk kindergarten children were less able to ignore irrelevant features than low risk children. Finally, Keogh and Donlon (1972) compared the performances of severely and mildly learning-disabled boys on a variety of tasks, one of which was to assess field dependence. There were no differences in the performances of these groups, but the authors compared the performances of the mildly and severely disabled groups with the performance of nondisabled children studied by other investigators. This comparison suggested that mildly and severely learning-disabled children perform more poorly than nondisabled children. The evidence that learning-disabled children may be relatively more field dependent than nondisabled children is sparse, but seductive. There should, and hopefully, will be more research directed toward this intriguing issue.

It has also been hypothesized that learning-disabled children are impulsive; that is, they fail to reflect upon the possibilities of several explanations or responses in situations where the correct response is uncertain. Before examining how impulsive behavior may be related to attentional behaviors, let us consider how impulsivity is most frequently measured. The most popular test of reflectivity-impulsivity is the Matching Familiar Figures Test (MFFT: Kagan, Rosman, Day, Albert, and Phillips, 1964). The test requires the child to study a picture of a familiar object (the standard) and then indicate which of six other pictures are identical with the standard. One of the six choices is identical, the remaining five are similar to the standard. There are two practice and twelve test items. Impulsive children are defined as children who make many errors and/or make their choices very quickly. Reflective children take their time and/or make fewer errors. Studies of impulsivity are related to questions of attention, since many investigators have focused upon the scanning or visual strategies used by children as they match the figures to the standard. In summarizing these studies, Messer (1976) indicates that impulsive children are less systematic and more global in viewing the test items. "In particular they do not scan the distinctive features as systematically as reflectives" (p. 1037). The relationship of scanning strategies to academic and cognitive failure has not been directly studied, but comparisons of reflective and impulsive children find impulsive children have less adequate short term auditory memory, less adequate short term visual memory, less competency solving mazes, and even less skillfulness playing the card game Hearts (Messer, 1976).

Given the apparent importance of impulsivity in affecting learning, it is reasonable to ask whether learning-disabled children might be characterized as impulsive. There is evidence to support this characterization. Keogh and Margolis (1976) reported that learning-disabled boys make a greater number of erroneous judgments on the MFFT than achieving boys. Kagan (1965) found that scores on the MFFT were predictive of oral reading errors one year later. Keogh and Donlon (1972) found severely learning-disabled children were more impulsive than mildly disabled children, although the mildly disabled group had scores comparable to those obtained by other investigators for normal achieving children. In addition, Kagan (1965) reported that impulsive first grade children were less able than reflective children to match the experimenter's spoken word with one of five words presented visually. Thus there is evidence which suggests that impulsivity may well play an important role in the life of the learning-disabled child. The impulse to impulsivity also appears to be amenable to correction, and correction is likely to be beneficial to the academic life of the child. Studies which report corrective measures are extremely important and are discussed in Chapter 12.

Vigilance

The third important component of attention is the child's ability to sustain his efforts upon a task. Until a task is completed or a problem solved, the child's resistance to external distractions (e.g., noise) or internal distractions (e.g., boredom) plays a significant role in affecting what the child learns. Vigilance is typically assessed by measuring the quality of the child's performance on an easy task which requires sustained attention under monotonous conditions. Usually, but not always, the child is asked to respond to easily discriminated signals which are presented at irregular intervals without forewarning. Measures of vigilance include the failure of the child to notice the signal, responding to the incorrect signal, or the time he takes to respond to the signal.

There is increasing evidence that children who are experiencing academic difficulties and children considered as high risk for academic failure demonstrate difficulties in sustaining their attention to easy but long and boring tasks. Messer (1976) reviews studies the results of which suggest that impulsive children show slower reaction times in their responses to signals than comparison children. Whalen and Henker (1976) report that hyperactive children identify fewer correct and more incorrect signals than nonhyperactive children. But the evidence is not limited to impulsive and hyperactive children who may or may not have learning disabilities; it is more direct. Children with reading difficulties have slower reaction times to correct signals than nonreading disabled children (Noland and Schuldt, 1971). Keogh (1973) reports that Margolis, in an unpublished study, found vigilance scores related to both reading achievement and teacher ratings of student's academic achievement. It is interesting to note that intelligence quotients were correlated with reading achievement, but not with vigilance. It seems that intelligence quotients and vigilance may independently contribute to a child's reading achievement.

Additional support and refinement of the hypothesis that learning-disabled children have difficulties maintaining attention is found in the results of a study by Anderson, Halcomb, and Doyle (1973). They reported that learning-disabled children made fewer correct detections and more incorrect responses to the stimulus signal than nondisabled children. When the authors subclassified the learning-disabled group as hyper-, normo-, or hypoactive, differences between learning-disabled and normal children could be attributed to the hyperactive children. These findings were essentially replicated and extended in a subsequent study by Doyle, Anderson, and Holcomb (1976). In this investigation, learning-disabled children again emitted more incorrect responses than comparison children, and once again most of these differences were attributable to the hyperactive learning-disabled group. The frequency and duration of children's viewing of a distractor was also assessed in this study. The results were that learning-disabled children looked more often and for longer periods than nondisabled subjects. Moreover, the hyperactive were more likely to be distracted than the hypo- and normoactive children. The results of these two studies suggest that vigilance problems associated with learning-disabled children may be particularly acute, and perhaps limited to, the hyperactive learning disabled.

In summary, there is increasing evidence that children with learning disabilities suffer from attentional problems, at least in focusing, scanning, and maintaining attention. So far, much of the theorizing concerning attentional deficits has been focused upon physiological explanations. Thus Dykman et al. (1971) suggested that such deficits are a reflection of something amiss in the reticular activating system. Kagan and Kogan (1970) have hypothesized that between the ages of 5 to 7 years, important changes in brain chemistry occur which are critical to the development of sustained attention. Perhaps these speculations will be relevant to the attentional problems suffered by the learning-disabled child. However, it is clear that learning-disabled children do learn, and that they are not always inattentive (Bryan, 1974). It is clear that motivational and environmental features will affect the attention of all youngsters, including the learning disabled.

Whatever factors contributing to the attentional problems of the learning-disabled child, it is imperative that such problems not be overlooked in either diagnostic or remediation efforts. They are there, and they can be both measured and remediated. We will have more to say about this in the later chapters.

THE MODALITIES AND INFORMATION PROCESSING

There are certain assumptions frequently made concerning information processing. One is that there is a developmental sequence in the acquisition of skills used for processing information presented through various channels. For instance, it has been assumed that children learn in one modality (auditory or visual) *before* they learn to integrate information presented in both modalities. A second assumption is that the crux of the learning-disabled child's difficulty is a breakdown in information processing and that the more specific the identification of that breakdown, the more useful the analysis. Care is taken to diagnose the degree to which memory problems reflect a deficiency in remembering information presented auditorily (auditory memory) or visually (visual memory). A third assumption is that effective treatment can be initiated when an information processing deficiency has been specified. These assumptions have underestimated the complexity of information processing.

The remainder of this chapter will be devoted to a discussion of auditory, visual, and cross-modal integration. Information will be presented concerning the developmental sequence, assessment techniques, and general research data in each of these areas.

AUDITORY PROCESSING

The detection of the signal is the first step in making sense out of what is heard. Although signal detection occurs prior to information processing, it is important for the learning disability specialist to be sensitive to problems of acuity. The lack of awareness by diagnosticians concerning the distinction between acuity and comprehension has produced misdiagnoses which have caused no small amount of pain to all concerned. Acuity problems are easily misinterpreted as problems associated with the processing of auditory information. As a result deaf children have been misdiagnosed and treated as mentally retarded, emotionally disturbed, or aphasic (DiCarlo, 1960; Reichstein and Rosenstein, 1964).

Hearing acuity is assessed by an audiometer, an instrument which permits assessment of the capacity to hear different sound frequencies (pitch) at different decibel (loudness) levels under different sound conditions (pure tones, words). A screening assessment of children's hearing is typically performed within the schools at periodic intervals. Most people are acquainted with "flat" hearing losses in which the child can hear various pitches if they are presented loudly enough. Thus, they can hear both high frequency sounds, such as *s, f,* and *t,* and low frequency sounds, such as *m, n,* and *b,* when these sounds are presented loudly. But there are other kinds of hearing losses in which the child or adult can hear some sounds but not others. In "nonflat" hearing deficits, the child may respond appropriately when some sounds are quite soft and not respond to sounds that are quite loud. For example, a child may not hear the *s, f,* and *t* presented reasonably loudly, but will hear the low frequency sounds.

When teachers and parents are unaware of a problem of hearing acuity, the child is likely to be misunderstood, because his responses in school and home settings appear erratic and unpredictable. Consider, for example, the child trying to do phonics and spelling when he cannot hear the difference between *f* and *s.* The child who hears part of the message may signal his confusion by constantly asking for a repeat of the message, withdrawing , responding incorrectly, or waiting until he can observe his classmates and imitate them as best he can.

It is not difficult to detect a severely hearing-impaired child or to recognize that if a hearing problem is suspected, the child should be referred for a hearing test. But it is considerably more difficult to distinguish between a hard-of-hearing and a learning-disabled youngster. A hearing test may well resolve the issue of whether the child is hearing impaired or not, provided that he does not have a fluctuating hearing loss because of recurring infections or seasonally based allergies. But a hearing test may not resolve the issue when the child cannot or will not respond to the test itself. What is one to make of a child who fails to respond when he hears (or does not hear) a bleep from the audiometer? Suppose the child has a severe language problem and is not easily understood. Thus, a difficult differential diagnosis is that of discriminating an aphasic from a hard-of-hearing child. Goldstein, Landau, and Kleffner (1960) examined 183 children who were diagnosed as aphasic or deaf. They reported that there were few etiological categories which helped distinguish these two groups of children. Of the children labeled aphasic, 32 percent did not exhibit neurological abnormalities, and about 40 percent of both the aphasic and deaf children had abnormal electroencephalograms. Moreover, it should be noted that the presence of a hearing loss does not preclude an aphasia in a child. Merklein and Briskey (1962) assessed the hearing of children with aphasia and found that many such children did suffer from a high-frequency (high pitch) hearing loss. The conscientious teacher should be sensitive to the fact that hearing problems often cause school related problems.

Auditory Perception

Auditory perception has been defined as:

> A system specialized for dealing with temporally (serially organized) stimulus patterns. To the extent that verbal symbolic system is linked to the auditory sensory modality, it must be characterized as a sequential processing system. . . . [The] verbal system is also sequentially organized as a symbolic system by virtue of its syntactical nature; the grammar of a language involves a temporal ordering of its elements. All language has a form which requires us to string out ideas even though their objects rest one within the other. . . . There is flexibility in the sequential ordering but . . . the information conveyed depends on what came before and what is yet to come in the sequence . . . (Paivio, 1971, p. 33).

Learning in the classroom, or in any situation which involves responding to sounds, requires the child to be able to sort the auditory signal into meaningful units, order these units temporally, remember them, and respond appropriately. Classroom activities, particularly responding to teacher instructions, require the child to listen to what the teacher says, produce the appropriate response, and to do so easily, quickly, and automatically (Rosner, 1973). The child must perceive the message, select the salient details, and produce a response. The complexity of the process depends upon the meaningfulness of the verbal units being used, as well as the length of the message and the task demanded of the child. It is one thing for a child to be directed to get his coat and quite another for him to process a long series of instructions, presented in complex sentences, which demand a serial performance. The child who does not process this type of information quickly and as well as his peers finds himself expending an inordinate amount of time and energy trying to make sense out of what is heard and the implications of this message for what he is to do. At the perceptual level auditory information processing demands that the child attend, receive, discriminate, and remember the signals as long as the task requires. The ability to do this is measured by the appropriateness of the child's verbal or motoric responses. One approach to understanding children's auditory information processing is to consider the tests developed for assessment of problem children and the resulting intervention programs. Perceiving sounds is measured by the child's ability to assign appropriate meanings to the sounds presented, memory span for sounds, ability to discriminate differences and similarities across sounds, skill in sequencing a string of sounds and comprehension of others' speech. All of these behaviors have been the targets of diagnosticians.

Assumptions Concerning Auditory Processing

There are at least three important assumptions concerning these behaviors which should be noted. The first is that each of these behaviors is thought to represent or to be part of the auditory processing system. This suggests that if one of these behaviors is measured, generalizations concerning other behaviors within the auditory processing system can be made. For example, if the child shows a deficiency in memory span, the assumption can be made that he will be likely to show less adequate responses in discriminating sounds, sequencing sounds, comprehending others or assigning appropriate meanings to the auditory inputs. The second assumption is that these defects are associated with and indeed contribute substantially to inadequate school performance. The third assumption is that remediation is facilitated by training the child on tasks which include only stimuli and responses within the auditory modality. It is thought that to train a child to learn a list of words, he should hear the words and be required to speak the words. Both the input and output are within one modality. This is believed preferable to having the child see the words and then speak them where the input modality differs form the output modality (Johnson and Myklebust, 1967).

Children with learning disabilities have been noted to have difficulties on some of these auditory tasks, but the reliability of the first assumption has not been fully established. For instance, auditory discrimination of sounds is commonly assessed by having the child indicate whether two words sound the same or different (Wepman, 1958). Some children will perform poorly on this task, and presumably such children are thought to have deficiencies in their auditory processing (not just their ability to discriminate sounds). Wood (1971) found, however, that while discrimination of sounds was correlated with the child's age and his verbal intelligence, it was not correlated with the child's committing speech distortions, substitutions or omissions. Wood then raises some question as to whether these various measures actually do assess a single process or whether these behaviors are diverse and relatively uncorrelated with one another. A question is raised then about the first assumption. But if these measures do not correlate with one another, how good is one measure in predicting school achievement? While it is clearly an empirically answerable question, as it stands now, assumption two rests more on faith than fact.

The third assumption, that remediation efforts involving deficits in auditory processing are best treated by focusing upon inputs and outputs which involve auditory activity, has also been challenged. Brooks (1958) found that the use of a verbal response system to facilitate short-term memory of sounds interfered with the child's acquisition of the material. It was found that a child's learning of sounds was assisted by having him commit a response based upon visual inputs (i.e., having him point). The implication is that learning is facilitated if the child can use different information channels to receive and respond. This really should not be very surprising, since memory is intimately tied to the child's ability to make meaningful associations to the stimulus. However these associations are made, whether through visual or auditory cues or responses, meaningful associations should improve memory (Underwood, 1964). Although much progress has been made toward understanding auditory processing, both the manner in which responses are associated, if indeed they are, and how the learning-disabled child might be helped to better master his social and academic skills through modality training have yet to be completely determined.

Development

Irrespective of the adequacy of current conceptions about the auditory processing system, it is important for parents and teachers alike to have some understanding about the appropriate development of the processing of auditorily presented stimuli. The developmental sequence involved has been outlined by Zigmond and Cicci (1968). The authors indicated that the area of the brain considered critical in at least one aspect of auditory processing of information, Broca's area, matures later than brain areas which control various kinds of motor movements. Not until the infant is 17 months old does Broca's area reach the anatomical differentiation observed to exist in other motor centers by 11 months of age. According to Zigmond and Cicci, the infant can discriminate the sounds around him by five to six months of age. At this time the infant can distinguish familiar and unfamiliar sounds and can localize sounds outside his visual field. By 8 months of age the infant responds to "no-no," can imitate speech sounds and the intonations of another's voice. By 12 months the child can stop an activity upon hearing "no" (should he so decide) and can follow simple commands. By 15 to 17 months the child can respond to "give me that" when the request is accompanied by a gesture and can point to body parts such as the nose, eyes, and hair.

A rapid increase in the ability of the child to comprehend language follows. These understandings are integrated with expressive language development as the child learns to appropriately say and combine strings of words. By 2 years of age a child can select objects which others name. By age 2½, the child can identify objects by their use, and by age 3, the child recognizes the names of colors, adjectives like *big* and *little,* and can follow simple commands which use prepositions. A child, by age 2, can reproduce two digits by 3 years, three digits; by 4, four digits. Memory for short sentences appears about age 4. These are simple yardsticks to assess whether or not auditory information processing and receptive language development are progressing at expected developmental rates.

Testing Auditory Perception

There are a variety of means by which to assess auditory perception. At the preschool age, informal observations can be made of the child's responses to sound-making toys, his responses to auditory signals from different areas of the room, and by noting whether the child associates a sound with an event (e.g., the ringing of a telephone with the object telephone). Can the child discriminate familiar voices; does he respond to simple commands, such as "give me," or "show me"? Learning disability specialists and the classroom teacher can also make informal assessments. For example, to assess the child's auditory discrimination (skill in distinguishing sounds), the teacher may ask the child to repeat words and take note of his inaccuracies in pronunciation (Stephens, 1970). If the child incorrectly pronounces the word, then it is possible that the sounds are not being correctly discriminated. Of course, the error may also be due to a hearing acuity problem, an attention problem, or a problem in the child's simply getting his tongue to mind his brain. At least the teacher should be alerted to the presence of a problem which should be more systematically assessed. Teachers can also informally assess auditory memory, both of immediate and delayed recall. Immediate recall can be assessed by having the child repeat a series of numbers or words immediately after hearing them. Delayed recall, clearly important to academic achievement, might be assessed by having the child hear a short story on which his recall is later tested (Stephens, 1970). Obviously, all of these informal methods, and indeed most of the standardized ones which will be discussed, are quite imperfect. Children's reproductions can be affected by many things, notably familiarity with or interest in the material being presented. But like the story of the gambler who played on the rigged roulette wheel because it was the only wheel in town, the learning disability specialist, like other professionals, must often use far from perfect methods in an attempt to understand the child.

Standardized tests of intelligence, achievement, and specific diagnostic techniques tap the various components of auditory information processing. Items on the Cattell Infant Intelligence Scale (Cattell, 1947), the Wechsler Intelligence Scale for Children (Wechsler, 1949), and the Stanford-Binet Intelligence Test (Terman and Merrill, 1960) assess the child's ability to comprehend and express auditorily received material. Many assessments are indirect insofar as they measure language rather than simple responses to auditory signals. But any test which requires a child to respond verbally is, after all, tapping auditory processes. By way of example, items on the Binet from the 2- to 5-year-old levels ask the child to identify objects by name, by use, and identify pictures of objects by use. Evaluation is based on the ability to closely follow directions, to use words in combination, and the rote memory for increasingly lengthy spans of numbers.

In addition to informal techniques and intelligence tests, there are a variety of standardized tests designed specifically for the assessment of a child's auditory information processing. There are essentially three areas of auditory processing which have been of interest to learning disability specialists: auditory reception, auditory discrimination, and auditory memory.

Auditory reception tasks assess the degree to which children understand what is told them. Do they comprehend verbal messages? Initial assessment should have established that the child is neither retarded nor hearing impaired; yet many children do not comprehend relatively simple verbal inputs. Thus, in administering the Illinois Test of Psycholinguistic Ability (ITPA), the examiner reads a short statement to the child and the child is required to respond "yes" or "no" to the sense of the statement (Kirk, McCarthy, and Kirk, 1968). On another subtest the child is required to fill in the final word to complete a short verbal statement given him.

Auditory discrimination refers to the child's ability to recognize whether symbols heard are alike or different. The most well-known test for such an ability is the Wepman Test of Auditory Discrimination (1958). In this test, the child indicates whether two words sound the same or different. In a laboratory setting, a child may be asked to indicate the similarity of tones (Dykman et al., 1971).

Auditory memory is measured by the child's ability to repeat verbally a series of words or numbers immediately after their presentation. The Digit span subtest on the Wechsler Intelligence Scale for Children (WISC) requires the child to repeat a series of numbers orally presented to him. This is presumed to assess his auditory memory. The ITPA and the Stanford-Binet Intelligence test also included such tasks. The Detroit Test of Learning Aptitude (Baker and Leland, 1935) has subtests in which the child is asked to repeat words and sentences, and to follow verbally presented orders by the tester. These tests are measures of immediate, short-term memory in which the child is asked to repeat words or digits immediately after hearing them. His adequacy in doing this is related to the number of units, the rate with which the verbal units are presented, the meaningfulness of these units, and the child's attentiveness during the task.

We have, for purposes of illustration, mentioned some standardized tests which have been designed to assess these particular forms of auditory information processing. It would be remiss, however, not to point out that simply designing a task to measure an event is not the same as measuring it. The tests referred to may or may not have validity in detecting auditory processing and may or may not be applicable to particular groups of children.

The ITPA, for example, appears to have reasonably good reliabilities among the subtests. However, the validity of this test has been seriously challenged by Hammill and Newcomer (1975) in their review of research relevant to the test. These authors conclude that the test cannot be employed with confidence to identify school children who may develop difficulties or for purposes of diagnosing an already present difficulty in either reading, spelling, or arithmetic. Moreover, they argue that the test should not be used to develop educational programs or for purposes of determining children's individual styles of learning. Insofar as the original form of the test has been shown to be influenced by examiner characteristics, and is highly correlated with intelligence test scores, it may not be surprising that the original hopes associated with the development of the test have not been fulfilled (Carroll, 1972; Chase, 1972; Hammill and Newcomer, 1975).

The Digit span subtest of the Wechsler Intelligence Scale for Children is also reported to have rather low reliabilities, and for the 10½- and 13½-year-old child it has the lowest reliabilities of all subtests (Wechsler, 1949). Thus, individual diagnosis of auditory memory by this subtest alone is not warranted.

As is evident, neither informal nor formal methods of assessing a child's auditory information processing tell us much about process. These methods are not "pure tests" but may be contaminated by the child's school learning, his skill in reproducing sounds which may reflect not auditory processing but his ability to talk, or by other activities he may be involved in between the time the inputs are made and the reproductions required. The tests may tell us about stable differences between children which may affect their classroom performance, whatever the source of the differences. To better understand the processing of auditory information, laboratory experiments are an important source of information. The results of some of these experiments will now be reviewed.

There are many ways to study auditory processing within the laboratory. Studies have typically employed one of three techniques in attempts to understand this process. One technique used to study the developmental sequence of processing complex auditory stimuli is to present some auditory stimulus (words, tones, or numbers) masked by background noise (Impellizzeri, 1967). This procedure is particularly relevant to learning disabilities, because many believe that learning-disabled children may be unusually distracted by environmental noise. This method is concerned with the child's ability to focus upon the relevant auditory signals and to exclude attention to masking sounds.

A second method involves lengthening the time intervals between parts of words and thereby disrupting the hearing of a chain of sounds as a word. Instead of words, the child hears isolated sounds. His task is to put the sounds together. This method is an analogue to phonics learning. The learning-disabled child, with an auditory processing problem, may have more difficulty in integrating these sounds into a meaningful unit than will the nonlearning-disabled child.

The third method employed is to present two words which are very similar in sound and require the child to make a discrimination between them. This method involves an auditory discrimination task.

Several studies have outlined the development of auditory processing. Impellizzeri (1967) studied 5- to 8-year-old boys and girls who were free of any apparent abnormalities. Words which were partially erased were presented to these children. Sometimes these partially erased words were presented closely in time, sometimes not. Subjects were asked to indicate the words presented, initially by repeating the word heard, later to both repeat the word and point to a picture which identified the word. Impellizzeri found that older children were more likely to give the correct response than younger ones.

In another study, Maccoby and Konrad (1966) employed a dichotic listening procedure in which normal kindergarten, second-, and fourth-grade children heard on some occasions two voices presented to both ears or, on other occasions, each voice presented to a different ear. Subjects were to repeat the word spoken by one voice. These investigators found that correct responses were more frequent for the older than younger child and that for both the younger and the older children, the dichotic listening condition was easier than when both voices were presented to both ears. Children did show the effects of practice, improving in their performance as their opportunity to perform increased. In addition, children show fewer errors when presented multisyllable words than single-syllable ones. Children become more familiar with words as they age and are consequently better able to process auditory inputs as a function of this familiarity.

Age effects may be different for children of one social class than for children of another. Peisach (1965) asked first- and fifth-graders from both lower- and middle-class families to produce words which had been deleted from speech samples of teachers and children also of varying social class backgrounds. Her results indicate the complexities involved in auditory information processing. Differences in the performances of children from varying social classes became evident to the fifth-graders, but not to the first-graders. Hence, with increasing age, social class differences become more significant. Fifth-grade girls performed better on this task than did fifth-grade boys if both boys and girls were from the lower class. Indeed as Rohwer (1970) has indicated, one popular hypothesis is that such social class differences are associated with differential development of auditory processing abilities. The hypothesis is based upon the assumption that the noise level in the homes of the lower social class families is high and thus interferes with perceptual learning. Unfortunately, the research evidence that is available does not lend much support to the hypothesis: as yet, the issue has not been settled.

Of particular interest to the learning disability specialist is the ability of the learning-disabled child to process auditory information. There have been several studies addressed to this concern.

Auditory Signals and the Disabled Child

Rourke and Czudner (1972) compared normal and brain-damaged children in their attention to auditory signals. The child's task was to press a key with the onset of a high-pitched sound and to release the key when a low-pitched sound was presented. These investigators found that young normal (6 to 9 years) and older children (10 to 13 years), brain-damaged and normal, did not differ in their attentiveness to the auditory signals. Young brain-damaged children did evidence difficulty in performing these tasks. Rourke and Czudner hypothesize that the older brain-damaged child has managed to recuperate from his earlier attentional deficits.

Grassi (1970) did not find such recuperation when he assessed the performance of brain-damaged adolescents and compared them to their peers who were deemed either as normal or as evidencing behavior problems. In this study, subjects were asked to record each time an auditory signal was presented. Grassi found that normal children performed best on this task, followed by behavior-disordered children, with the brain-damaged children doing least adequately. From this study, then, evidence is forthcoming that brain-damaged children, even in adolescence, have relatively more difficulty in attending to auditory tasks than do nonbrain-damaged children. Factors other than brain damage influence attention as indicated by the finding that behavior disordered children did did appreciably worse than normal children.

Other sources of evidence also point to the difficulty of learning-disabled children in dealing with auditorily presented information. Dykman et al. (1971), in a series of studies, compared the performances of learning-disabled and normal children in their ability to discriminate sounds for purposes of obtaining a reward. The task required children to attend to the tones, to remember which of the tones led to a reward and which did not, and to remember what to do when they heard the tones. The results reveal that brain-damaged children had greater difficulty than normal children in discriminating the tones, were less able to follow instructions, and were less able to profit from practice in learning how they could receive the reward. McReynolds (1966) found that aphasic children 4 to 8 years of age were less able to discriminate sounds and showed slower improvement with practice than normal children when discrimination had to be made with sounds embedded in the context of nonsense syllables. A simple auditory perceptual problem in the aphasic was not evidenced; rather the performance deterioration was a function of the complexity of the auditory signal presented. Doehring and Rabinovitch (1969), using very different methods and samples, also arrived at a similar conclusion based upon their results.

Short Term Memory and the Disabled Child

Connors, Kramer, and Guerra (1969) investigated the role of short term memory in word synthesis in a comparison of learning-disabled and normal children. Short term memory was measured by children's ability to remember numbers presented to them on a dichotic listening task. Auditory synthesis was assessed by the children's ability to indicate the correct word which had been presented to them in elements. While learning-disabled children performed significantly less adequately on the word synthesis task, little difference was found between the groups on the dichotic listening task. These investigators concluded that short term memory problems are not critical to deficits in auditory processing as assessed by the word synthesis method.

A comparison was made of the ability to learn a list of words presented auditorily by tape recorder and visually by pictures on slides. Bryan (1972) found that both learning-disabled and comparison children learned the list of words with fewer trials when the stimulus was visual. But the learning-disabled children were significantly less adequate than the comparison group learning under both the auditory and the visual treatments.

Certain results are pervasive in these research studies even though the researchers use very different tasks, different kinds of samples, and are testing very different hypotheses. First, the learning-disabled child, however defined, does appear to have difficulty in dealing with information presented auditorily. But, by and large, it does not appear that such children find simple discriminations of sounds difficult. Rather, decreases in performance are most evidenced when the auditory information is complex, either because it is associated with masking noise, involves words rather than tones, or is embedded in irrelevant stimuli. Second, a pervasive, recurring result reported across studies is the lack of improvement with practice. Learning curves which present the adequacy of performance as a function of the number of learning trials to which the child has been exposed show that the learning-disabled child learns at a slower rate than do comparison children. One implication of this finding is that the learning-disabled subject may not have a qualitatively different means of processing auditory information, but rather may simply be slower in learning from such information. The differences may not be a function of perception or discrimination of sounds, but rather the means by which he can use the information in such a way as to be able to remember it and use it appropriately. It is certainly not clear at this point how the auditory signal is related to those factors which have been found to differentiate the learning-disabled from the normal child.

Remediation Techniques

Various suggestions have been offered as to the appropriate remediation techniques for children evidencing auditory difficulties. The suggestions range from offering fairly simple classroom exercises to fairly explicit and elaborate programs. All of the suggestions have one thing in common. No one knows with any degree of certainty that any of them will work, much less just what part of the program might be responsible for whatever improvements might be shown by the child. Like imperfect tests, however, imperfect treatments will have to be tried. After all, children do have difficulties that cannot wait for treatment until science becomes sophisticated regarding them. Until that time does come, the learning disability specialist and the classroom teacher will have to continue to try to help those children in need. It is hoped that the activities prescribed for improving auditory discrimination, memory, attending, and sequencing will correct the child's deficit in dealing with the particular training materials and that this correction will be evidenced in other classroom activities which require the same general skills.

A variety of suggestions to help the young child attend to auditory stimuli have been offered (Johnson and Myklebust, 1967; Lerner, 1971; Zigmond and Cicci, 1968). Teachers are encouraged to allow the child to practice listening. They may have the child clap his hands upon hearing one of a number of stimulus sounds, or the child may be requested to tell how many times he heard a sound. Variations in such practice might be created by changing the complexity of the task and by requiring of the child a variety of responses to indicate his detection of the sound. Training children to discriminate one sound from another, to string sounds together, should start at the level of the child. You do not start by demanding discriminations of sounds with which he is unfamiliar. For young children exercises are suggested which try to assist the child in becoming aware of sounds within his natural environment. Progressions are then made to excercises involving discriminations among consonants and vowels. Activities in rhyming and word games for sounds follow. Initially, the sounds to be discriminated are distinctly different; as the child progresses, finer discriminations are required from him.

Auditory memory exercises include placing objects in front of the child and instructing him to complete a string of commands. The child can be required to follow a series of commands which revolve around a written exercise. The commands can be taped and the child completes the exercise by following the taped instructions. Some suggest working directly on auditory memory by having the child attempt to increase the number of digits, or words, he can recall at one time. Nursery rhymes, finger play, and poems are considered useful in auditory memory training (Lerner, 1971). Relating stories, facts of stories, and making up stories are all believed to stimulate better auditory memory.

There is really little evidence to support the efficacy of such exercises in increasing children's academic performance. We don't know whether the exercises work, and if they work, just what their effects will be in increasing the academic performance of the learning-disabled child. It is our bias that remediation should focus on teaching the child that academic related behavior in which he is deficient. For instance, if the child appears to have difficulty comprehending teacher instructions when these are presented before the entire class, activities should be devised to assist this child in comprehension of speech and language under similar circumstances. Tape recording of the teacher's voice and peer voices with background noise could be used for treatment. The focus of the exercise then is not upon improving auditory memory or sequencing or some particular skill, but rather in improving the behavior which is causing the child difficulty by using tasks and situations most similar to those surrounding the deficit.

A model of this approach has been developed by Lindamood and Lindamood (1969) for remediation of reading difficulties. The program is designed to help the child understand the sounds of our language and to learn to associate sounds in sequences with patterns of syllables and words. The child is additionally taught the correspondence of oral patterns and the graphic symbol patterns (written words) which are used to represent them.

Consonants and vowels are grouped according to similarities in mouth formation and the child is taught labels to facilitate the association between the formation and the letter. Examples are "lip poppers" for *p* and *b;* "scrapers" for *k* and *g*. In a step-by-step progression the child, using colored wooden blocks, is led to make discriminations among sounds. Visual and tactile manipulation of blocks provides practice in tracking the order of sounds presented sequentially. Initially, isolated sounds in short sequences are presented; later longer strings of more complex sound combinations are tried.

To aid the child in associating letters and sounds, games like Bingo are recommended. Such games allow practice of recall of sounds and letters, left-to-right orientation, position in space, start and stop points, order and sequences, plus responses to auditory and visual cues. The child learns to read by working with exercises and games which use auditory, visual, and tactile representations of sound and symbol relationships, progressing from single sounds and symbols to complex combinations. There is no focus upon training within a single modality in this program. The emphasis is upon using all the modalities in order to aid the child. A detailed outline of the program has been put into a manual which is available.

While the efficacy of this program and others has not been convincingly demonstrated, it is possible to train young mentally retarded children's listening skills. Ross and Ross (1972) trained one group of educable mentally retarded (EMR) to listen in a training program ten weeks in duration. The program consisted of the children playing games which required "extensive repetition of listening skills," with the experimenters using material and social rewards and peer exemplars as aids. In addition, the experimenters paid careful attention to both the timing of the verbal instructions given and the task demands made on the child. They reported that the EMR children who went through the training performed more adequately than EMR children not so trained on such tests as story comprehension, following directions, digit span, and repeating sentences. A total listening test score, a combination of ten such tests, was much greater for those EMRs who received the training than those who did not. While it is still not clear what components of the Ross and Ross training program made the difference, it is clear that differences in listening skills were found and that listening to auditory signals is a teachable skill. Noteworthy is the fact they used all modalities, along with a variety of reinforcements, in order to accomplish this.

There is really no reason to believe that deficits in attentional skills and auditory processing of information cannot be remediated. Children do learn these skills. What seems unwise, however, are those remediational efforts which limit themselves to working through and upon but one modality. Remediation efforts should employ, in our opinion, any of the child's skills in affecting the remediation of any particular problem.

VISUAL INFORMATION PROCESSING

> Our eyes are general purpose instruments for feeding the brain with comparatively undoctored information, while the eyes of animals possessing simple brains are more elaborate, for they filter out information which is not essential to their survival, or usable by the simple brain. It is this freedom to make new inferences from sensory data which allows us to discover and see so much more than other animals. . . . We do not perceive the world merely from the sensory information available at any given time, but rather we use this information to test hypotheses of what lies before us (R. L. Gregory cited by Farnham-Diggory, 1972, p. 411).

Visual perception, understanding a visual stimulus and perceptual-motor functions, wherein a complex and coordinated act is performed in response to a visual stimulus, have been theoretically linked to learning disabilities since the conception of the field. Integrating the early work of Werner (1948), Strauss and Lehtinen (1947), and Piaget (1954), various professionals have advocated that learning disabilities are the result of an insufficient development of visual perception and visual perceptual-motor skill, the result of which adversely affects the child's ability to achieve those cognitive skills necessary for adequate academic performance. The perceptual deficit hypothesis has been nurtured, promulgated, and sold by both special educators and professionals within the field of vision. There has been widespread consensus regarding the importance of the linkage of visual inputs to motor skills and to cognitive development in affecting the child's academic skills (Barsch, 1967; Cruickshank, 1972; Frostig, 1972; Getman, 1965; Kephart, 1973; 1971). It is not surprising that assessment and intervention programs have been developed which are based on this belief.

Before discussing the available data on visual information processing as it applies to the field of learning disabilities, several points need to be made. When people refer to perception and perceptual handicaps, they usually mean visual perception and perceptual-motor inadequacies. Visual perception concerns professionals in a number of fields, such as optometrists, psychologists, and educators. Perhaps because of the many professional hats thrown into the perceptual handicap ring, there is a healthy body of data as well as confusion regarding visual information processing. Finally, the same three basic assumptions made about the relevance of auditory information processing are implicitly made about visual information processing. That is, it is often assumed that a deficiency in one component of the visual processing system implies a deficit in another component, that such deficits are associated with poor academic performance and that remediation is facilitated by training the child on tasks which include only stimuli and responses within the visual modality.

Development of Vision

Before considering the role of vision in affecting learning-disabled children, a brief overview of the general development of vision will be discussed. Starting at the beginning, even the newborn sees, but not very well. The newborn demonstrates a number of eye movements, which suggests that visual inputs are being received. For example, children under five days of age will show a preference for one visual array over another, will track a horizontally moving object, though not very well, and will show changes in pupil dilation which indicate adaptations to light intensity. While the vision of the newborn is far from perfect, he is receiving visual inputs. The visual acuity of the newborn has been estimated between 20/150 and 20/400.

Changes of the visual system occur as the child matures. By one month, the infant apparently can perceive complex stimuli, that is, will show a preference for a visual display of stripes, checks, or patterns over displays which are homogeneous or which show little change in colors and shading. Until about four months of age, the infant has difficulty in adjusting his eyes so as to perceive distant objects: the child seems to have a fixed focus point of about eight inches from his body. By four months, however, the child is able to adjust his eyes to receive information about more distant objects. By this time the child should be able to recognize familiar objects and people.

Initially the infant and young child will tend to be farsighted, but as the eyes mature the young child tends to become nearsighted. Ordinarily, these states are self-correcting, but occasionally they are not. There is some debate as to the age where the self-corrections are completed, some placing the attainment of 20/20 visual acuity at age 6, others at age 10 (Lawson, 1968; Kessen et al., 1970; Pick and Pick, 1970). It is interesting to note a few findings relevant to visual information strategies. Compared with adults, children tend to be less efficient visual processors. For example, when searching for a letter among rows of letters, young children take longer to detect the target than do older children, who in turn take longer than young adults. Additionally, if the target letter is among letters which are frequently confused with the target, then younger children are particularly likely to be negatively affected. Younger children show considerable confusion with such a background relative to young adults. Children are also less likely to attend to the most informative features of a picture, and tend not to consider the whole visual display when compared to adults (Pick and Pick, 1970). Studies suggest then that the young child will be less efficient at visual processing of information, scanning less effectively and more narrowly, as well as being more negatively affected by certain backgrounds than will older children or young adults.

The Eye and Learning Disabilities

There are three major parts in the visual processing system: the eye muscles (ocular-musculator); the eye, which among other things acts as a transducer; and the occipital lobe of the cortex, which acts as a visual processor (Chalfant and Scheffelin, 1969). Distinctions must be made between eye defects which have nothing to do with reading, eye defects which may be related to reading efficiency, and reading deficits which reflect faulty cognitive management of visually presented information. The role of the vision field grew from concern for visual acuity to much more sophisticated concern for coordination of visual skills and training of such skills to improve cognitive processes.

Examination by an eye practitioner includes a check for acuity, how well a child can see from how far. For normal vision it is necessary to have 20/20 vision or better either uncorrected or corrected by refraction (with glasses) and good stereopsis (both eyes working together to produce a single image to the brain). There are two common types of visual errors, those involving refractive errors and those concerning binocular vision. A refractive error is the result of a defect in the eye lens (Lerner, 1971) and there are three such types of errors. One is called *myopia* (nearsightedness). While this problem can develop anytime, it is likely to show an increase in incidence around age 11 and 12 for girls and 13 to 14 for boys (Tanner, 1970). Myopia is characterized by visual images coming to a focus in front of, rather than on, the retina. This results in the child having difficulty seeing distant objects. A second refractive error is called *hyperopia* (farsightedness). Here the visual images are brought to a focus behind the retina, with the result that the child has difficulty in seeing objects which are near him. The third type of problem is called *astigmatism.* Here the lens fails to correctly transmit the light or image to the retina, with the consequence that the child sees blurred images.

Binocular vision concerns how well the two eyes coordinate in bringing together two visual inputs to produce one visual image. There are three principal processes involved, the coordination of extraocular and intraocular muscles, the fusion of the monocular images into a single perception, and the individual's personal response to the visual stimulus (Park, 1969). The binocular defects which occur in children are *strabismus, inadequate fusion,* and *aniseikonia.* Strabismus occurs when one of the eyes strays from the proper direction, so that both eyes do not look at the same thing at the same time. This, believe it or not, is called a squint. Inadequate fusion is a defect in which the eyes do not accommodate to get a monocular effect. Simply put, one eye is adjusted to see at a different distance than the other. Aniseikonia is a condition in which the images of an object fixated are unequal in size or shape in the two eyes (Lerner, 1971).

There appears to be agreement that refractive defects do not contribute to reading difficulties or learning disabilities. Refractive problems are just as likely to occur in academically high achievers as in poor readers. Indeed, good readers appear to have a higher incidence of myopia than poor readers, although there does seem to be a higher incidence of hyperopia among poor than good readers (Lerner, 1971).

Severe binocular problems also seem unrelated to learning disabilities. According to Krieg and Windsor (1974), many severe binocular problems can be solved by the organism. A person with a severe binocular problem will suppress one of the retinal images and become visually monocular. When the reading deficiency is caused exclusively by a binocular deficiency, an internal adjustment to monocular vision alleviates the reading deficiency. However, it should be noted that milder binocular difficulties might be associated with reading defects. As early as 1930, Eames (Lawson, 1968) compared good and poor readers to find that children with reading problems showed less ability to maintain coordination between the two eyes over long periods. It is now believed that if a child is struggling to maintain fusion or has any kind of mild binocular difficulty, his struggle will have an adverse effect upon his reading skills.

Visual Defects and Reading Failure

Lawson (1968) summarized the studies which relate ophthalmological factors to reading and learning disabilities. Early work, namely Orton's, focused on the eye as it reflected the development of cerebral dominance. Many characteristics seen in dyslexic children, such as reversals of letters and mirror writing, were interpreted as symptomatic of slow cerebral development. Others focused on the abilities of good and poor readers to coordinate the movements of the eyes, irregularities in depth perception, and astigmatism. By and large, early studies, such as those conducted by Witty and Kopel (Lawson, 1968), reported that fusion, muscle balance, visual acuity, and refractive errors were not related to the ability to read. Ocular dominance and hand preference, and the match of these, were also investigated and also found to be unrelated to reading achievement. As late as 1964, Belmont and Birch assessed the hand-eye preference and left-right awareness of retarded readers. Left-right awareness did have some relationship to reading skills, but hand-eye preferences did not.

Other areas of concern were the speed with which the reader could recognize words and the amount of information which could be processed at one moment by the reader. The factors which influence the span of perception is the efficiency of the visual mechanism, the kind of reading material, the size of type, the language background of the reader, and the ability to organize what is seen at each fixation. Lawson points out that the average reader cannot be trained to read at high speeds. In addition, he specifies studies to indicate that mirror reading and the tendency to make reversals are psychological, and that good readers may make reversals and poor readers may not. All in all, these studies do not support early interpretations of the symptomatic behaviors of children who failed to learn to read as related to eye acuity, hand-eye preferences, or cerebral dominance.

Vision Training

While Lawson has challenged the notion that poor readers invariably have some visual defect, Greenspan (1972) provides an extensive summary of studies, several of which support the efficacy of optometric training programs. Perceptual and perceptual-motor training, according to Lawson, can improve visual functioning, which in turn will result in improved reading ability. It is not that all children with reading problems have visual defects, but that children with visual defects can benefit from certain visual exercises which then will improve their reading. There are a number of questions concerning the source of this improvement, however, as there are a variety of explanations that can be offered to account for it. In the studies reviewed by Greenspan, training techniques included more than one exercise. For example, they might use a combination of the following: exercises in gross motor skills, body balance, fine motor skills and hand-eye coordination, oculomotor skills and tracking, form perception, tachistoscopic perception, auditory perceptual training, to name a few. When such exercises work, it is difficult to explain just what the child is learning which improves his visual information processing and his reading.

Other kinds of eye training, such as attempts to increase the child's reading speed or the number of words a child sees at one glance or eye movements across the page, have not met with success. In effect, when there is a shift from training the eye to receive the visual stimulus to training the child to understand what he sees, optometric training should be put aside.

There are really two difficulties associated with the evaluation of the efficacy of optometric training programs. The first is the nature of the sample. Often children are studied whose only apparent deficiency is lack of reading skills. It would be naïve to assume that all poor readers have poor vision. There are many possible causal factors associated with poor reading, poor vision being only one. In using such subjects, instead of children who have known eye defects, the possibility of determining the efficacy of such programs is reduced. Second, the training programs involve a lot more than simply ocular exercises. For example, Painter's (1966) training program included gross motor and body balance activities, body image training and motor responses to visual and auditory stimuli. This program involved more than ocular training by requiring cognitive learning as well.

Because of the popularity of and confusion regarding optometric training for the learning-disabled child, a prestigious committee of ophthalmologists, optometrists, otolaryngologists, and learning disability specialists studied the programs in use (Helveston, 1969). The following conclusions were drawn.

1. Children with learning disabilities, be it dyslexia or reading under-achievement, have the same incidence of ocular abnormalities (refractive and binocular) as children who are normal achievers reading at grade level.

2. These abnormalities should be corrected.

3. Since clues in word recognition are transmitted through the eyes to the brain, it has become common practice to attribute reading difficulties to subtle ocular abnormalities presumed to cause faulty visual perception. . . . There is no peripheral eye defect which produces dyslexia and associated learning disabilities. Eye defects do not cause reversals of letters, words, or numbers.

4. Treatments which depend upon visual training (muscle exercises, ocular pursuit, glasses) or neurologic organizational training (laterality training, balance board, perceptual training) have no scientific support to claims of improvement of academic abilities.

5. Beware of such limited training. It is expensive, and may delay more beneficial intervention.

6. Glasses are important for the correction of ocular defects. Other than this they play no role in specific treatments of any academic problems.

7. Learning disabilities, dyslexia, reading retardation, school under-achievement . . . are educational problems. Ophthalmologists should offer the knowledge and expertise of their science, in the identification of specific ocular defects, early recognition of problems, and appropriate medical intervention.

A variety of tests have been offered to the learning disability specialist which are purported to assess the visual perceptual abilities of children. Tests either entirely or partially devoted to assessing visual perception have entered the market with alarming rapidity. Tests devised to assess visual perception, including the Illinois Test of Psycholinguistic Abilities (ITPA), the Developmental Test of Visual Perception (DTVP), Detroit Test of Learning Aptitude, the Perceptual Motor Survey, and the Winterhaven Perceptual Forms test, to name a few, have been offered to the testing specialist.

As would be expected, the hypothesis and claims of these test constructors have been questioned and put to a variety of empirical tests. Essentially, two questions have been asked. One has been whether the tests are internally valid; that is, whether the items of the test correlate with one another in such a fashion that the test is measuring what it is supposed to. If, for example, it is found that items that are presumed to be measuring auditory information processing are highly correlated with those assessing visual information processing, one would be unlikely to conclude that the test is measuring two different types of information processing.

The second question is whether the tests have any practical utility. Can deficient children be discriminated from nondeficient ones on the basis of their scores on the tests? Can predictions of children's school performance be made on the basis of their performance on the tests?

Testing Visual Processing

The following discussion concerns the research pertaining to two very popular tests of visual processing, the ITPA and the DTVP. These tests are focused upon because of the relatively large number of research projects concerned with them and also because of their apparent popularity with the learning disability specialists. It should be said, however, that many research questions have not been answered and that definite statements concerning these tests are relatively few.

Studies concerned with the internal consistency of a test, that is, the degree to which the items correlate with one another in the appropriate manner, have employed a statistical technique called factor analysis. This technique attempts to determine the fewest number of concepts or "factors" which can account for the correlation among all items of the test. By and large, reviewers of the factor analytic studies of the ITPA suggest that this test does not measure nine different processes, as originally believed, but a lesser number. Meyers (1969) suggested that the test measures six and possibly seven separate abilities, at least when using an early edition of the test. With regard to the test's assessing some ability which uniquely reflects visual processing, the evidence is discouraging. Uhl and Nurss (1970) found that the intercorrelations of the items could be reduced to but three or four dimensions and that there was no evidence that the visual processing tests were simply or solely measuring visual processing. Burns and Watson (1973) found that the visual processing items did tend to correlate, but that these were also correlated with subtests presumably assessing language ability. Thus, tests which are designed to assess visual processing also tap, to some degree, language skills.

In support of this finding were the results obtained by Huizinga (1973). He found that the Visual-Motor tests of the ITPA correlated .69 with scores on the Stanford-Binet Intelligence scale, and .56 and .54 with the verbal and performance scores, respectively, of the Wechsler Intelligence Scale for Children. Scores on these intelligence tests are markedly affected by children's verbal skills and thus the results suggest, but do not prove, that the visual processing subtests of the ITPA tap language as well as visual skills. As Carroll (1972) has written, "A casual inspection of the subtests will reinforce the conclusion that many of them, even the 'non-language' ones, measure a 'vocabulary' factor, or rather, a factor having to do with the range of cultural experiences to which the child has been exposed" (p. 442). He points out that in the Visual Association subtest "the child may be shown an item requiring him to make a distinction between a microscope and a telescope" (p. 442). Such associations involve more than simple visual processing; they also involve language skills and/or a variety of everyday experiences. Similar conclusions, with their unfortunate implications, have been reached by Hammill and Newcomer (1975).

Another popular device for assessing visual processing is Frostig's Developmental Test of Visual Perception (DTVP). This test consists of five subtests which are presumed to tap five different aspects of visual perception. However, it has generally been concluded that the test measures but one perceptual ability rather than the five originally postulated (Chissom, 1972; Mann, 1972). As Mann has pointed out, "Profile analysis and specification of areas of perceptual strength and weakness are patently not feasible on the basis either of reliability or of factor analysis data" (p. 872).

In general, the internal consistency of these two popular tests of visual processing, the ITPA and the DTVP, indicate that they do not measure those separate abilities which were originally hypothesized as being assessed by the tests. This does not necessarily mean that neither test has any practical usefulness. Questions can be posed as to whether these tests do make predictions about the children's school performance, and whether test performance is changeable as a result of particular kinds of training programs.

As yet there is very little evidence suggesting that these tests assess what their developers had originally hoped to measure. With regard to the ITPA, Carroll (1972) points out that there is no reason to assume that the test would have any validity when applied to other than white middle-class children and warns against employing it when assessing disadvantaged children. But even for white middle-class children, the utility of the ITPA is quite questionable. Carroll suggests that the test has no validity in predicting future reading scores, a conclusion also reached by Hammill and Newcomer (1975). Indeed these latter investigators, after reviewing the research pertinent to the ITPA, have concluded that the test is of little value either for assessing present deficits, predicting future deficits, or for the development of remediation programs. Studies of the predictive power of the DTVP yield mixed results. Chissom (1972) and Mann (1972) suggest that the weight of the evidence is that the test can yield useful predictions of children's reading in the first and second grades, but Chissom points out that the test may be of little value in aiding one to predict specific reading difficulties. On the other hand, Hammill (1972) has argued that there is no good evidence suggesting that the test has predictive value in assessing reading skills.

In summary, it does appear that the test constructor's hypothesis concerning which abilities are being measured by the test have not been substantiated empirically. Factor analytic studies of both tests suggest that the individual subtests within them are not measuring independent abilities, but rather abilities that are reflected in more than one subtest. Second, the practical usefulness of these tests in aiding testers to make difficult diagnoses has been far from established. There is a dearth of evidence to substantiate that these tests are powerful predictors of school achievement, more specifically reading levels, or that subtle differences among children are easily detected through the tests.

Visual Processing and the Learning Disabled

The surface of the visual information processing system has yet to be scratched, but there is an increasing number of experiments designed to assess differences between the learning-disabled and the nondisabled child on such functions as visual memory, attention to visual stimuli, and general rapidity in visual processing.

Lyle and Goyen (1968, 1974) and Goyen and Lyle (1971a, 1973) have conducted a series of research studies addressed to the general issue of whether retarded readers perceive visual inputs as well as adequate readers. Using tachistoscopic presentations of various visual stimuli, such as geometric lines or letters of the alphabet under different rates of presentation and incentive conditions, they have compared young and old, adequate and retarded readers. They have consistently found that younger retarded readers, below 8.5 years, perform less well than older retarded and all young and old normal readers. The difference in performance in younger retarded readers was related to their relative inefficiency in noting critical details of the visual stimuli and this was related to their slowness in processing visual information relative to other children.

It is unlikely that in the academic world many children get less than a one-second exposure to the visual materials they are expected to master. In this sense, the results of the Lyle and Goyen experiments have limited applicability. Nonetheless, it is important to note that these investigators have raised an interesting challenge to the belief that poor readers have a perceptual problem. What might be important is the time that children spend in focusing upon the visual stimulus and the amount of effort involved in discriminating the relevant features which aid in coding the material for purposes of remembering it. The results of the Lyle and Goyen experiments should also be noted for their age-related findings. Differences occur primarily for retarded readers under 8½ years of age. This suggests that younger retarded readers may be characterized by perceptual and perceptual-motor difficulties, while older children may differ with regard to their verbal or intellectual skills.

Visual Memory

There have been a number of studies addressed to possible differences in visual memory of the learning-disabled and nondisabled child. Doehring (1960) compared short-term visual memory of aphasics, deaf and normal children and reported that aphasic children performed less adequately than did the remaining two groups of children. Unfortunately, the aphasic children also had lower intelligence test scores than the remaining two groups and thus interpretation of the results is somewhat ambiguous. The role of visual memory for sequences in normal and disabled readers around 8½ years of age was studied by Guthrie and Goldberg (1972). They presumed that visual sequential memory is necessary for the comprehension of written sentences and word recognition. They tested children on the Benton Visual Retention test, which requires the child to identify a "correct" form from several incorrect alternatives. Additionally, children were tested on a subtest of the Illinois Test of Psycholinguistic Abilities in which the child is requested to reconstruct from memory a series of geometric shapes in the proper sequence. It was found that the tests of visual sequential memory did, by and large, correlate with several measures of reading. The exception to this was that no significant correlation was found between the ITPA subtest and reading ability in children previously defined as reading disabled. The Benton Visual Retention test showed the most significant correlations with reading skills for both normal and disabled readers. The authors suggest that the reason for the Benton test's success revolves around the additional demands placed upon the child. The Benton test requires the subject to remember both the form and the direction of the form, a requirement absent in the ITPA. In effect, then, it is still not clear as to how great a role visual sequencing memory plays in determining the reading skills of the child.

Visual Sequencing

Poppen, Stark, Eisenson, Forrest, and Wertheim (1969) conducted a study on the visual sequencing of aphasic children. There were nine aphasic children in the study, ages 6 to 12½, and nine normal children, ages 7 to 11½. Children were exposed to visual inputs by means of flashing lights onto keys in various sequences. The children's task was to press the keys in the right sequence at the end of the visual sequence presented to them. The delay following the presentation of the sequence and the child's key pressing was varied from two seconds to twenty-seven seconds. It was found that normal children made fewer errors than aphasic children, that errors increased with an increase in the delay between the stimulus presentation and the child's responses, and that the delay had a greater effect upon the aphasics than the normal children. Additionally, each child was tested on the auditory and visual memory subtests of the ITPA, the Knox Cube Tapping test and the Auditory Vocal Sequencing with Language test. Aphasics demonstrated inferior performance on all tests when compared to the normal children. They concluded that aphasic children have a general deficit in the ability to sequence information which underlies and causes general problems in language and learning. On the other hand, it is quite conceivable that language problems lead to sequencing problems, insofar as language deficits may well interfere or decrease the child's capacity to code and retrieve information.

Dykman, Ackerman, Clements, and Peters (1971) investigated children's impulsivity in response to visual cues (certain flashing lights on a panel). In one study, twenty-six children with minimal cerebral dysfunction and twenty-six nondisabled children were investigated. The task confronting the child was to press a lever in response to particular flashing lights and to refrain from pressing the lever to other flashing lights. Children were scored as to whether they committed impulsive errors (pressing the button to the wrong visual stimulus) and as to their rapidity in making the correct response. The minimal brain-damaged children committed more impulsive errors and responded less quickly when correct than did the comparison children, particularly after practice.

Dykman et al. extended and replicated these results using learning-disabled children. In this study, learning-disabled children were divided on the basis of school and parent reports into hyperactive, normoactive, or hypoactive children. The performances of these groups were compared with those of nondisabled children on a task similar to that previously used. The results were that learning-disabled children made more errors in following instructions and showed greater impulsivity in their responses than nondisabled children. Response latency to visual signals, measured under several different conditions, was consistently longer for the learning-disabled children than the nondisabled ones. Unfortunately, the age of the nondisabled children was greater than that of the disabled ones and, therefore, these differences can be attributable to general maturational factors. Of interest is the fact that hypoactive children were slower to respond in a variety of situations than either the hyperactive or normoactive learning-disabled child.

Dykman et al. suggest that learning-disabled children cannot attend to visual signals with the same competence as normal children and that some types of learning-disabled children, such as the hypoactive child, are much slower in processing visual signals than other types, such as hyperactive ones.

Pursuing similar lines, Czudner and Rourke (1970) studied reaction time in brain-damaged children. The purpose of the study was to assess the ability of brain-damaged children to maintain a state of readiness to respond to a visual light stimulus and to compare the reaction time of brain-damaged and normal children. The brain-damaged subjects were fifteen children diagnosed as having cerebral dysfunction with a mean age of 10.7 years; comparison subjects were fifteen children with a mean age of 10.5 years. All subjects were exposed to two experimental procedures. The experimental apparatus had a telegraph key and two lights, a white warning light and a red reaction time light. All subjects were exposed to two procedures: in one series of trials, the preparatory interval which occurred between the onset of the warning signal and the onset of the reaction time stimulus was the same; in the second, the preparatory intervals were varied for 2, 4, 6, or 8 seconds. The results of the study indicated that the brain-damaged children tended to perform slightly better on the regular than irregular preparatory interval trials; but the same results occurred for the normal group. As with Dykman et al., it was found that the overall performance of the brain-damaged group was inferior to that of the control group.

Little in the way of general conclusions can yet be offered regarding the visual processing of learning-disabled children. It does appear that learning-disabled children are no more likely to suffer from visual acuity problems than are nondisabled children. It appears as well that learning-disabled children have problems in maintaining attention, and in determining what to pay attention to. This problem is not simply in the processing of visual stimuli, but is present in the case of processing auditory stimuli as well. Aside from these few generalizations, little more can be offered regarding the differences between learning-disabled and nondisabled children in processing visual stimuli.

The lack of information concerning differences can be attributed to many factors. First, studies in visual information processing which are relevant to this field have focused upon a variety of aspects of such processing. The work has been broad in the topics addressed, but not very deep on any particular topic.

Second, the performances by the child which have been used to index such processing have been many, but rarely repeated in more than one study. Thus, reaction time, errors in response, and errors in following instructions have been used by particular investigators. The results from different laboratories are often not comparable.

Third, many of the tests employed in studies as measures of the child's competence in visual processing have a certain intuitive validity, but not necessarily an empirical one. It remains to be determined whether such measures as the Frostig (1964) are, in fact, assessing visual processing of the child. If these measures are not valid, then the findings of any particular study employing them are open to serious question.

Fourth, many of the studies of visual processing which have reported group differences between learning-disabled and nondisabled children also report differences between these children in terms of age and scores on intelligence tests (Doehring, 1960; Dykman et al., 1971; Browning, 1967). Interpretations of such results, therefore, are not obvious.

Finally, tests which are made to assess the same visual processing activity have been found not to correlate with each other (Guthrie and Goldberg, 1972). This suggests that if the tests are measuring something, they are not measuring the same thing. All of these considerations suggest that the hypothesis that learning-disabled children have particular difficulties in processing visual stimuli has not yet been supported.

CROSS-MODAL INFORMATION PROCESSING

So far, we have discussed information processing through single modalities, the auditory and visual systems. But it is clear that information is obtained through the integration of material introduced through separate modality channels. It is reasonable to be concerned with the procedures or mechanisms through which cross-modal integration occurs. Within the field of learning disabilities, three sources gave impetus to concern with cross-modal integration. One source was the incidence of reading problems. While it was initially believed that reading was primarily associated with visual processing, a view under challenge (Hammill, 1972), more recently it has been recognized that learning and comprehending written material are also highly related to auditory stimuli. Children do not learn to read by seeing the written word, but rather by both seeing it and hearing it. The realization of the importance of auditory as well as visual processing in affecting reading achievement stimulated a hypothesis that children who have difficulty learning to read suffer a deficit in the ability to process information from two or more modalities.

A second stimulant to the study of cross-modal integration has come from studies of lower animals which suggest that animals cannot perform tasks which require cross-modal integration. These findings led to the hypothesis that the capacity for language may be a critical variable in affecting cross-modal processing (Ettlinger, 1967).

A third source has been studies involving brain-damaged humans. Studies have been conducted with individuals who have suffered trauma to the corpus callosum, a major fiber tract which connects the right and left sides of the brain. If the left-side language section of the brain is disassociated from the right side of the brain, the difficulty for the individual to verbally respond to a stimulus presented to the right hemisphere is greatly increased (Gazzaniga, Rogen, and Sperry, 1965; Sperry, 1964). These results dovetail with those reported in studies involving lower animals.

Studies concerning deficit populations, such as brain-damaged or reading-disabled children, have increasingly focused upon their abilities to integrate information across or between modalities. Insofar as there is a ". . . discrepancy between the sensory input and the finished product" (Gibson and Gibson, 1962, p. 5), the process of cross-modal integration has received attention within the field of learning disabilities.

Integrating Information

Laboratory and developmental studies of integrative information processing have employed a variety of procedures and measures. One approach is to assess the individual's ability to make judgments as to whether complex stimuli presented to two different modalities are the same or different. For example, in a procedure devised by Birch and Belmont (1964, 1965), a subject might be presented with a complicated series of long and short sounds and be asked to match the sounds with one of several patterns of dots and dashes presented to him visually. A second method is to present to the individual information in two modalities, visual and auditory or visual and tactile, and ask the subject whether or not the stimuli are equivalent. Another method has involved various adaptations of the Broadbent (1958) dichotic listening task. In this case, subjects might be presented with information through two modalities at a very rapid speed. The subject is asked to recall the information presented. Of interest is whether the testee remembers the information in order presented (e.g., auditory, visual, auditory, visual, etc.) or whether the individual differentially recalls visual rather than auditory materials or auditory rather than visual stimuli.

Presumably, such tests give the learning disability specialist information concerning the testee's ability to process and organize information from two modalities. The learning-disabled child is hypothesized to differ from the nondisabled in his organization, as inferred from his recall, of the material. Individual differences in the organization of such material are assumed to reflect neurophysiological differences.

Several studies have been concerned with the development of cross-modal processing. Birch and Lefford (1963) studied the development of the ability to process visual, haptic, and kinesthetic information in 145 children, 5 to 11 years of age. These researchers presented a stimulus object to the child so that he could look at it, feel it with his hands without looking at it (haptic presentation), and/or trace it with a stylus (kinesthetic presentation). The child was presented with a stimulus by one means and then asked to judge whether a second stimulus was the same or different from the standard stimulus. As would be expected, the number of correct judgments increased with age of the child. Materials presented visually and then judged by feeling were easiest. Materials presented visually and tested kinesthetically, and information presented kinesthetically and tested haptically were more difficult. Schevill (1973) also found that first-graders were better able to integrate cross-modal information than children in kindergarten. While it is clear that the research into the development aspects of cross-modal integration is hardly complete, the evidence does suggest that this ability is associated with the age of the child.

Considerable work has been conducted concerning cross-modal integration by deficit populations. Studies have been completed which have tested these processes in psychiatrically disturbed adolescents, schizophrenic children, retarded readers, brain-damaged individuals, and even malnourished children (Freides, 1974). Of particular interest to learning disability specialists is the work concerning the retarded reader, both because of its direct relevance to his work and because there is a fair amount of evidence concerning these children's cross-modal integration.

An early study by Birch and Belmont (1964) seems to have had considerable influence on many of the subsequent investigations concerning cross-modal integration in retarded readers. These investigators hypothesized that integration of auditory and visual stimuli is basically what is required in the act of reading and that children unable to read might very well demonstrate a deficit in this type of task. Retarded readers in the Birch-Belmont study were 150 boys, ages 9.4 to 10.4, who had scored at the lowest 10 percent level on at least three of four reading tests. Normal comparison subjects were 150 boys randomly selected from boys who were not in the lowest 10 percent of readers. The experimental task was a multiple choice problem in which children had to indicate which tap pattern heard was identical to one of three dot patterns seen. Results were that retarded readers performed significantly more poorly than comparison subjects. The authors concluded that the inability to make such auditory-visual equivalence judgments is an underlying and major source of reading retardation.

The finding that retarded readers perform significantly more poorly than nonretarded ones on cross-modal integration tasks has been reported by a variety of other investigators (Birch and Belmont, 1965; Blank and Bridger, 1966; Muehl and Kremenak, 1966; Schevill, 1973; Senf, 1969; Senf and Freundl, 1971). Whether readers are compared with nonreaders in terms of their responses to two inputs (Birch and Belmont, 1964), their quickness in giving their responses (Freides, 1974), or their recall of information (Senf, 1969; Senf and Freundl, 1971), it does appear that good readers perform more competently than do less adequate readers.

Evaluation of Tests and Studies

Things are not that perfectly clear, however. First, it should be noted that many investigators who have studied cross-modal integration in deficit groups have generally failed to determine whether such failures of integration are problems of integration or problems within a modality, a point correctly made by Schevill (1973) and Freides (1974). For example, can one argue that a child has an integration problem of auditory and visual stimuli if, in fact, the child may have a deficiency in one modality? Before the conclusion is reached that cross-modal deficits distinguish good from poor readers, more carefully controlled research wherein intramodality competence is demonstrated must be conducted.

A second question is the degree to which cross-modal integration is uniquely associated with the learning-disabled child. Is the learning-disabled child particularly likely to have problems in cross-modal integration? Apparently, children with many various types of problems have been studied and they also suffer from cross-modal integration difficulties. It has been suggested and presumably demonstrated that the schizophrenic, the emotionally disturbed and malnourished suffer from such difficulties.

A question might also be asked whether cross-modal integration difficulties are evidenced by the child in his daily social intercourse with peers and adults. Is the learning-disabled child more likely to remember verbal or visual inputs, and will he be particularly insensitive to contradictions between these two sources of information? There have been only two studies conducted on the question and apparently no such gross or massive deficit in functioning occurs (Schwartz and Bryan, 1971).

Freides (1974) has recently published a valuable review of the research in this area. While we will go into some detail concerning his conclusion, it is clear that the phenomenon of cross-modal integration is more complex than has been assumed heretofore. Freides has recently challenged some commonly held beliefs concerning this process and has advanced some provocative hypotheses. First, the assumption that cross-modal integration of information is more difficult than intramodal processing has not been empirically supported. Second, the assumption that specific difficulty in cross-modal processing would distinguish brain-damaged and learning-disabled children from nondisabled children cannot be claimed because deficit groups have been found to have as much difficulty in processing intramodal tasks as cross-modal ones. Freides further suggests two hypotheses which appear buttressed by the data. One is that the information received by the child is translated into the form required by the task at hand. The second hypothesis is that each modality has particular aptness for handling certain kinds of information. Spatial information appears to be translated into a visual code, temporal information into an auditory code.

Freides has also summarized some basic differences between audition and vision which should be noted. Complex auditory and visual information appear to be stored in a different manner. Apparently, memory for things heard and seen show different patterns of decay. Additionally,

> visual memory for words favored the early inputs of the sequence (primacy), whereas auditory memory favored the later inputs (recency); . . . retrieval of information increased with faster auditory inputs and slower visual inputs . . . (p. 307).

No doubt knowledge will increase concerning the processing of information and cross-modality integration. As yet, however, considerable caution should be maintained when arguing that learning disability, and particularly reading deficiencies, are attributable to the child's deficit in integrating information from two or more modalities.

REFERENCES

Anderson, R. P., Halcomb, C. G., and Doyle, R. B. "The measurement of attentional deficits." *Exceptional Children,* 1973, 39, 534–539.

Barsch, R. H. *Achieving Perceptual Motor Efficiency.* Seattle, Wash.: Special Child Publication, 1967.

Birch, H. and Belmont, L. "Auditory-visual integration in normal and retarded readers." *American Journal of Orthopsychiatry,* 1964, 34, 852–861.

Birch, H. and Lefford, A. "Intersensory development in children." *Monograph of the Society for Research in Child Development,* 1963, 28, serial #89.

Birch, H. and Belmont, L. "Auditory-visual integration, intelligence, and reading ability in school children." *Perceptual and Motor Skills,* 1965, 20, 295–305.

Blank, M. and Bridger, W. "Deficiencies in verbal labeling in retarded readers." *American Journal of Orthopsychiatry,* 1966, 36, 840–847.

Broadbent, D. E. *Perception and Communication.* New York: Pergamon, 1958.

Brooks, L. R. "Spatial and verbal components of the act of recall." *Canadian Journal of Psychology,* 1958, 22, 349–358.

Browning, R. M. "Effect of irrelevant peripheral visual stimuli on discrimination learning in minimally brain-damaged children." *Journal of Consulting Psychology,* 1967, 31, 371-376.

Bryan, T. "The effect of forced mediation upon short-term memory of children with learning disabilities." *Journal of Learning Disabilities,* 1972, 5, 605-609.

Bryan, T. "An observational analysis of classroom behaviors of children with learning disabilities." *Journal of Learning Disabilities,* 1974d, 7, 26-34.

Burns, G. W. and Watson, B. L. "Factor analysis of the revised ITPA with underachieving children." *Journal of Learning Disabilities,* 1973, 6, 371-376.

Carroll, J. B. "Review of the Illinois Test of Psycholinguistics." In O. K. Buros (ed.), *The Seventh Mental Measurements Yearbook, Vol. II.* New Jersey: The Gryphon Press, 1972, 7, 819-823.

Cattell, P. *The Measurement of Intelligence of Infants and Young Children.* New York: Psychol. Corp., 1947.

Chalfant, J. and Scheffelin, M. "Central processing dysfunctions in children: A review of research." NINDS Monograph No. 9. Bethesda, Md.: U.S. Department of Health, Education, and Welfare, 1969 (Task Force III).

Chase, C. I. "Review of the Illinois Test of Psycholinguistics." In O. K. Buros (ed.), *The Seventh Mental Measurement Yearbook, Vol. II.* New Jersey: The Gryphon Press, 1972.

Chissom, B. S. "Review of Frostig DTVP." In O. K. Buros (ed.), *The Seventh Mental Measurements Yearbook, Vol. II.* New Jersey: The Gryphon Press, 1972.

Connors, C. K., Kramer, K., and Guerra, F. "Auditory synthesis and dichotic listening in children with learning disabilities." *Journal of Special Education,* 1969, 3, 163-170.

Cruickshank, W. M. "Some issues facing the field of learning disability." *Journal of Learning Disabilities,* 1972, 5, 380-388.

Czudner, G. and Rourke, B. P. "Simple reaction time in brain-damaged and normal children under regular and irregular preparatory interval conditions." *Perceptual and Motor Skills,* 1970, 31, 767-773.

DiCarlo, L. M. "Differential diagnosis of congenital aphasia." *Volta Review,* 1960, 62, 361-364.

Doehring, D. "Visual spatial memory in aphasic children." *Journal of Speech and Hearing Research,* 1960, 3, 138-149.

Doehring, D. and Rabinovitch, M. S. "Auditory abilities of children with learning problems." *Journal of Learning Disabilities,* 1969, 2, 467-475.

Doyle, R. B., Anderson, R. P., and Halcomb, C. G. "Attention deficits and the effects of visual distraction." *Journal of Learning Disabilities,* 1976, 9, 48-54.

Ettlinger, G. "Analysis of cross-modal effects and their relationship to language." *Brain Mechanisms Underlying Speech and Language.* New York: Grune & Stratton, 1967.

Freides, D. "Human information processing and sensory modality: Cross-modal functions, information complexity, memory and deficit." *Psychological Bulletin,* 1974, 81, 284-310.

Frostig, M. *Frostig Developmental Tests of Visual Perception.* Palo Alto, Calif.: Consulting Psychologists Press, 1964.

Frostig, M. "Visual perception, integrative functions and academic learning." *Journal of Learning Disabilities,* 1972, 5, 1-15.

Gazzaniga, M. S., Bogen, J. E., and Sperry, R. W. "Observations on visual perception after disconnection of the cerebral hemisphere in man." *Brain,* 1965, 88, 221-236.

Getman, G. "The visual-motor complex in the acquisition of learning skills." In J. Hellmath (ed.), *Learning Disorders, Vol. 1.* Seattle: Special Child Publications, 1965.

Gibson, J. J. and Gibson, E. J. "Perceptual Learning: Differentiation or Enrichment?" *Psychological Review,* 1965, 62, 32-44.

Goldstein, R., Landau, W. M., and Kleffner, F. R. "Neurologic observation in a population of deaf and asphasic children." *Annals of Otolaryngology, Rhinolaryngology and Laryngology,* 1960, 69, 756-767.

Goyen, J. D. and Lyle, J. G. "Effect of incentives upon retarded and normal readers on a visual associate learning task." *Journal of Experimental Child Psychology,* 1971a, 11, 274–280.

Goyen, J. D. "Short term memory and visual discrimination in retarded readers." *Perceptual & Motor Skills,* 1973, 36, 403–408.

Grassi, J. "Auditory vigilance performance in brain damaged, behavior disordered, and normal children." *Journal of Learning Disabilities,* 1970, 3, 302–304.

Greenspan, S. B. "Research studies of visual and perceptual-motor training." Optometric Extension Program, Duncan, Oklahoma, 1972.

Guthrie, J. T. and Goldberg, H. K. "Visual sequential memory in reading disability." *Journal of Learning Disabilities,* 1972, 5, 41–46.

Hammill, D. "Training visual perceptual processes." *Journal of Learning Disabilities,* 1972, 5, 552–559.

Helveston, E. M. *The Role of the Ophthalmologist in Dyslexia.* Dayton, Ohio: Institute for Development of Educational Activities, Inc., 1969.

Huizinga, R. J. "The relationship of the ITPA to the Stanford-Binet Form L-M and the WISC." *Journal of Learning Disabilities,* 1973, 6, 451–456.

Impellizzeri, I. H. "Auditory perceptual ability of normal children aged five through eight." *Journal of Genetic Psychology,* 1967, 111, 289–294.

Johnson, D. and Myklebust, H. *Learning Disabilities: Educational Principles and Practices.* New York: Grune & Stratton, 1967.

Kagan, J. "Reflection-impulsivity and reading ability in primary grade children." *Child Development,* 1965, 36, 609–628.

Kagan, J. and Kogan, N. "Individual variation in cognitive processes." In P. H. Mussen (ed.), *Carmichael's Manual of Child Psychology.* New York: John Wiley & Sons, Inc., 1970. Vol. 1.

Kagan, J., Rosman, B. L., Day, D., Albert, J., and Phillips, W. "Information processing in the child: Significance of analytic and reflective attitudes." *Psychological Monographs,* 1964, 78 (1, Whole No. 578).

Kawabe, K. K. "Attentional deficits in learning disabled children." *Division for Children with Learning Disabilities Newsletter,* 1976, 2, 35–41.

Keogh, B. K. "Perceptual and cognitive styles: Implications for special education." *Review of Special Education,* 1973.

Keogh, B. K. and Margolis, J. "Learn to labor and to wait: Attentional problems of children with learning disorders." *Journal of Learning Disabilities,* 1976, 9, 276–286.

Keogh, B. K. and Donlon, G. "Field dependence, impulsivity, and learning disabilities." *Journal of Learning Disabilities,* 1972, 5, 331–336.

Kephart, N. C. *The Brain-Injured Child in the Classroom.* Chicago: National Society for Crippled Children and Adults, 1963.

Kephart, N. C. *The Slow Learner in the Classroom.* Columbus, Ohio: Merrill, 1971.

Kessen, W., Haith, M. M., and Salapatek, P. H. "Infancy." In P. H. Mussen (ed.), *Carmichael's Manual of Child Psychology.* New York: John Wiley & Sons, Inc., 1970. Vol. 1.

Kirk, S., McCarthy, J. J., and Kirk, W. D., *Illinois Test of Psycholinguistics Abilities: rev. ed.* Urbana, Ill.: University of Illinois Press, 1968.

Krieg, F. J. and Windsor, M. M. "Visual factors in reading disability." Paper presented at the Conference of the American Education Research Association, Chicago, Ill. April, 1974.

Lawson, L. J. "Ophthalmological factors in learning disabilities." In H. R. Myklebust (ed.), *Progress in Learning Disabilities, Vol. I.* New York: Grune & Stratton, 1968, 147–181.

Lerner, J. W. *Children with Learning Disabilities.* Boston: Houghton Mifflin, 1971.

Lindamood, C. H. and Lindamood, P. C. *Auditory Discrimination in Depth.* Boston, Mass.: Teacher Resources Corp., 1969.

Lyle, J. G. and Goyen, J. D. "Visual recognition, development lag, and strephosymbolia in reading retardation." *Journal of Abnormal Psychology,* 1968, 73, 25–29.

Lyle, J. G. "Effect of speed of exposure and difficulty of discrimination upon visual recognition of retarded readers." Unpublished manuscript, 1974.

McReynolds, L. V. "Operant conditioning for investigating speech sound discrimination in aphasic children." *Journal of Speech and Hearing Research,* 1966, 9, 519–528.

Maccoby, E. E. and Konrad, K. W. "Age trends in selective listening." *Journal of Experimental Child Psychology,* 1966, 3, 113–122.

Mann, L. "Review of Frostig DVTP." In O. K. Buros (ed.), *The Seventh Mental Measurements Yearbook, Vol. II.* New Jersey: The Gryphon Press, 1972.

Merklein, R. A. and Briskey, R. J. "Audiometric findings in children referred to a program for language disorders." *Volta Review,* 1962, 64, 294–298.

Messer, S. B. "Reflection-impulsivity: A review." *Psychological Bulletin,* 1976, 83, 1026–1052.

Meyers, C. E. "What the I.T.P.A. measures: A synthesis of factor studies of the 1961 edition." *Educational and Psychological Measurement,* 1969, 29, 867–876.

Muehl, S. and Kremenak, S. "Ability to match information within and between auditory and visual sense modalities and subsequent reading achievement." *Journal of Educational Psychology,* 1966, 57, 230–239.

Newcomer, P. L. and Hammill, D. D. "ITPA and academic achievement: A survey." *The Reading Teacher,* 1975, 28, 731–741.

Noland, E. C. and Schuldt, W. J. "Sustained attention and reading retardation." *Journal of Experimental Education,* 1971, 40, 73–76.

Painter, G. "The effect of a rhythmic and sensory motor activity program on perceptual motor spatial abilities of kindergarten children." *Exceptional Children,* 1966, 33, 113–116.

Park, G. E. "Ophthalmological aspects of learning disabilities." *Journal of Learning Disabilities,* 1969, 2, 189–198.

Pavio, A. *Imaginary and Verbal Processes,* New York: Holt, Rinehart and Winston, 1971.

Peisach, E. C. "Children's comprehension of teacher and peer speech." *Child Development,* 1965, 36, 467–480.

Piaget, J. *The Child's Conception of Numbers.* New York: Humanities Press, 1952.

Pick, H. L. and Pick, A. D. "Sensory and Perceptual Development." In P. H. Mussen (ed.), *Carmichael's Manual of Child Psychology.* New York: John Wiley & Sons, Inc., 1970. Vol. 1.

Poppen, R., Stark, V., Eisenson, J., Forrest, T., and Wertheim, G. "Visual sequencing performances of aphasic children." *Journal of Speech and Hearing Research,* 1969, 12, 288–300.

Reichstein, J. and Rosenstein, J. "Differential diagnosis of auditory defects: A review of the literature." *Exceptional Children,* 1964, 31, 73.

Rohwer, W. D. Jr. "Cognitive Development and Education." In P. H. Mussen (ed.), *Carmichael's Manual of Child Psychology.* New York: John Wiley & Sons, Inc., 1970, Vol. 1.

Rosner, J. "Language arts and arithmetic achievement, and specifically related perceptual skills." *American Educational Research Journal,* 1973, 10, 59–68.

Ross, D. M. and Ross, S. A. "The efficacy of listening training for educable mentally retarded children." *American Journal of Mental Deficiency,* 1972, 77, 137–142.

Rourke, B. P. and Czudner, G. "Age difference in auditory reaction time of 'brain damaged' and normal children under regular and irregular preparatory interval conditions." *Journal of Experimental Child Psychology,* 1972, 14, 527–539.

Schevill, H. S. "Longitudinal kindergarten-first grade perceptual study: Temporal ordering and first grade reading." Paper presented at the annual meeting of the American Educational Research Association. New Orleans: February, 1973.

Schwartz, T. and Bryan, J. H. "Imitation and judgments of children with learning disabilities." *Exceptional Children,* 1971, 38, 157–158.

Senf, G. M. "Development of immediate memory for bisensory stimuli in normal children and children with learning disorders." *Developmental Psychology,* 1969, 1, 1–28.

Senf, G. M. and Freundl, P. C. "Memory and attention factors in specific learning disabilities." *Journal of Learning Disabilities,* 1971, 4, 94–106.

Sperry, R. "Neurology and the mind-brain." In R. Isaacson (ed.), *Basic Readings in Neuropsychology.* New York: Harper and Row, 1964.

Stephens, T. M. *Directive Teaching of Children with Learning and Behavioral Handicaps.* Columbus, Ohio: Charles E. Merrill, 1970.

Strauss, A. and Lehtinen, L. *Psychopathology and Education of the Brain-injured Child.* New York: Grune & Stratton, 1947.

Tanner, J. M. "Physical growth." In P. H. Mussen (ed.), *Carmichael's Manual of Child Psychology (Vol. 2).* New York: John Wiley & Sons, 1970.

Terman, L. M. and Merrill, M. A. *Stanford Binet Intelligence Scale.* Boston, Mass.: Houghton Mifflin Co., 1960.

Torgesen, J. "Problems and prospects in the study of learning disabilities." In M. Heatherington (ed.), *Review of Child Development Research.* Chicago: University of Chicago Press, 1975. Vol. 5.

Uhl, N. P. and Nurss, J. R., "Socio-economic Level Styles in Solving Reading Related Tasks." *Reading Research Quarterly,* 1970, 5, 452–485.

Underwood, B. J. "Degree of Learning and the Measurement of Forgetting." *Journal of Verbal Learning and Verbal Behavior,* 1964, 3, 112–119.

Wechsler, D. *Wechsler Intelligence Scale for Children: Manual.* New York: The Psychological Corporation, 1949.

Wepman, J. *Auditory Discrimination Test.* Chicago: Language Research Associates, 1958.

Werner, H. *Comparative Psychology of Mental Development.* New York: International Universities Press, 1948.

Whalen, C. K. and Henker, B. "Psychostimulants and children: A review and analysis." *Psychological Bulletin,* 1976, 83, 1113–1130.

Wood, N. E. "Auditory perception in children." Social and Rehabilitation Service Research Grant (RD-2574-5), University of Southern California, Los Angeles, Calif., March, 1971.

Zigmond, N. K. and Cicci, R. *Auditory Learnings.* San Rafael, Calif.: Dimensions Publishing Co., 1968.

8 | Language Disorders and Learning Disabilities

The most prevalent conditions to be found among specific learning disabilities are those in which language abilities have been impaired (McGrady, 1968, p. 215).

Early theorizing concerning delayed language development of learning-disabled children was based on analogy to the brain-injured adult aphasic. The assumption was made that similar physiological processes characterized children who never developed speech and language and adults who had had speech but lost it. The category of childhood aphasia served to separate children with deficits in language development from children with language deficits which were attributable to mental retardation, hearing impairments, or emotional problems. Since the field of learning disabilities historically has been concerned with the diagnosis and treatment of brain-injured children, aphasic children have been of interest to specialists within this field.

Characteristics of language disturbances were cited in Clements' (1966) report on children with minimal brain dysfunction. These language dysfunctions included: aphasia, impaired discrimination of auditory stimuli, slow language development, and frequent mild speech disorders. As language and thought are integrally connected, thinking deficits are also related to language problems. Thinking deficiencies were named as poor ability for abstract thinking and concept formation, thinking which is concrete, poor short-term memory, disorganized thinking, thinking which appears to be autistic, and thought perseveration. Kirk and Kirk (1972) describe the study of learning disabilities as

> a relatively new educational approach which involves handicapped children with specific disorders in perceiving, thinking, talking, reading, writing, spelling, arithmetic, and related disabilities primarily in the communication process (p. 12).

Although language disorders are firmly established in the history and definitions of learning disabilities, they have been very much underestimated and understudied. It is our bias that language disorders may be a central problem for learning-disabled children and also might be reflected in a wide variety of problems, including reading and attentional deficits.

It is also our belief that a number of different types of research on language development can and should be related to the field of learning disabilities. Studies of the development of syntactic and semantic competence, the relationship of language to conceptual development, the acquisition of reading skills, and the social communications of children appear to be germane to the work of learning disability specialists. Whether or not our biases are correct, the area of language development has been relatively understressed within this field. In the remainder of this chapter we shall discuss the assessment techniques relevant to the measurement of language and the empirical data available concerning the language skills of learning-disabled youngsters.

LANGUAGE DEVELOPMENT

There is evidence that language is learned rather than instinctive, that development proceeds in predictable stages, and that this development requires an intact nervous system (Dale, 1972). It also appears that early vocalizations are not simply incorrect imitations of adult speech, but reflect the child's conceptual development (Piaget, 1954). Language production is affected by the child's ability to understand that others may have a point of view different from his own, that objects can exist without being in view, and that one can employ words to refer to abstract events or phenomena. The stages at which language skills appear can be marked within a fairly restricted timetable, but the order of appearance of these skills is more predictable than the specific age. While it is also apparent that an enormous amount of language development occurs by the time a child reaches four years of age, language development continues for years thereafter (Lee, 1974; Menyuk, 1963; Palermo and Molfese, 1972).

Because of the rapid, massive development of language, most studies of language acquisition have been conducted with children 1½ to 3 years of age. McNeill (1970) specifies three basic foci of researchers in psycholinguistics. Researchers have been concerned with phonetic development, the production of speech sounds, such as the ages at which children use *r* or *sh* in their spoken language. Another area is the emergence of the grammatical system. In this case the researcher examines the child's ability to use forms of grammar, such as negatives or interrogatives. Finally, the experiential conditions which affect the development of language meaning have been studied.

Prelinguistic Period

McNeill (1970) provides an excellent review of the field of psycholinguistics. Summarizing language development benchmarks, McNeill indicates that normal children start to babble about 6 months of age, say their first word at 10 to 12 months, combine words at 18 to 24 months, and have a syntactic system virtually complete by 4 to 5 years of age. Initial sound production finds infants use more vowels than consonants, with the consonants emerging later. Sounds produced during the first year of life are made in the back of the mouth with a gradual shift to sounds produced in the front of the mouth. Parents' claim to the contrary, vocalizations are made by the infant before he emits true words.

The initial period of prelinguistic life seems to be fairly immune from all but severe traumas. Brain damage, physical trauma, or serious health problems might affect early vocalizations. But even hearing-impaired infants exhibit the early stages of vocalization. Parents may describe them as quiet or more quiet than their siblings, but they do vocalize. Hearing-impaired infants' vocalizations tend to decrease as they age and there may be a failure to demonstrate later stages of prelinguistic development. They fail to imitate sounds (echolalia), or demonstrate jargon (speech made up of nonsense sounds with correct sounding rhythm and voice inflection).

Some theorists, Lenneberg (1967) and Chomsky (1967), for instance, argue that language is a biologically guaranteed skill of man. There have been, however, a number of demonstrations that prelinguistic development can be affected by environmental events. Spitz (1946) reported that the vocalizations of infants were depressed when they were placed in institutions which provided them with little human or environmental stimulation. Brackbill (1958) demonstrated that an adult's smiling and hugging in response to an infant's vocalization resulted in an increase in the infant's vocalization. Brackbill also found that cessation of the adult's contingent hugging and smiling resulted in a decrease in infant vocalizing. While prelinguistic development will occur in many types of environments, and in the face of various abnormalities, it is clear that prelinguistic development can be altered through deprivation or reinforcements.

Comprehension and Meaning

While the tape recorder is the primary instrument used to study language acquisition, its usefulness is limited when examining comprehension. There are standardized tests to assess children's comprehension of language. Interest in the child's ability to understand language spoken by others was stimulated by concern for aphasics, and it is intimately linked to clinical practice. In this context standardized tests which include assessments of language comprehension have been used. The REEL Scale (The Bzoch-League Receptive-Expressive Emergent Language scale, Bzoch and League, 1972) and the NSST (Northwestern Syntax Screening test, Lee, 1970) are two well-known comprehension tests. In the REEL scale, assessment of comprehension is achieved through parental interview; on the NSST the child is asked to indicate which of two pictures describes a statement made by the examiner. Experimentally, various forms of the missing word approach have been devised in which the child is asked to add the appropriate endings to words embedded in sentences (Berko, 1958; Lerea, 1958).

The development of comprehension is intimately tied to the development of the meaning of language, which is in turn tied to the acquisition of concepts. Initially, word meanings are vague to the child (e.g., "dog"). With experience the child comes to learn the names of things, the salient attributes of various concepts, and those attributes which do not belong to the concept. Long after a child uses a word he is still acquiring attributes and experiencing the meaning of that word in different settings (Pflaum, 1974). Meanwhile the child is also coming into contact with related words or concepts (e.g., "animals") and forming words groups, or semantic clusters. The acquisition of meanings and concepts is a process which continues well beyond the primary years and is a process not easily subjected to simply learning of categories and the organization of a rule system. While the acquisition of the phonological and syntactic systems seems to be quite automatic and natural, the acquisition of meaning requires many experiences, trials, corrections of errors, and more direct teaching by adults.

While knowledge concerning language comprehension is sparse relative to language production (McNeill, 1970), information is available as to its course of development. Benchmarks of the development of comprehension during the first 24 months are based on the Bzoch-League REEL scale; and from Binet and Gesell from 24 to 60 months. Sample items from each age level follow.

0 to 12 months: (Bzoch and League, 1972, p. 22)
Respond with gross reflexes to sudden loud noises.
Localize the source of sounds or voices.
Recognize and distinguish familiar sounds and voices.
Understand the general meaning of speech utterances with different rates and inflectional patterns (e.g., warning, loving).
Recognize and respond to some familiar words uttered in connected speech (e.g., names of family members).
Respond appropriately to some simple commands, questions, and statements in a manner that indicates some discriminate language decoding skills.

12 to 24 months: (Bzoch and League, 1972, p. 23)

Increased interest in the names of things.

Increased ability to understand some new words each week.

Interest in listening to rhymes, songs, or jingles.

Ability to identify one familiar object from among a group of several familiar objects when the object is named.

Increased ability to follow simple directions and commands.

Ability to learn new words by associating the names of smaller parts of whole known objects.

Remember and identify two or more familiar objects from among a group of four familiar objects when asked to do so in a single request.

Ability to learn new words by association in categories (such as foods).

Understand and carry out three requests combined in a single utterance: learn new words almost daily;

recognize the names of almost all common objects or pictures of such objects;

understand the meaning of some complex sentences.

Increased interest in learning and listening to the meaning and reason of words and sentences.

24 to 36 months: (Binet and Gessell)

Understands direct vocative better (i.e., "Peter kick the ball," instead of, "You kick the ball").

Likes to listen for reasons of language as well as of sound.

By listening acquires sense of descriptive power of words.

Listens to simple stories, especially liking those he's heard before.

Understands two prepositions.

Identifies at least six of the following pictures from names: dog, cup, shoe, house, flag, star, leaf, basket, book.

Understands three prepositions.

Identifies pictures from name (at least seven of the following: dog, cup, house, flag, clock, star, leaf, basket, book).

36 to 48 months:

Learns to listen and listens to learn. (Single word spoken by mother may instantaneously reorganize whole stream of activity.)

Suggestions take effect.

Memory span lengthening – recalls events of yesterday.

Beginning to distinguish between black and white.

Generalization common in comprehension – in, on, under.

Distinguishes one and many.

Listens and can be reasoned with verbally.

Listens to longer and more varied stories.

Tends to reenact in body postures and gestures what is told in a story.

Comprehends: what do you do when hungry, thirsty, or tired.

48 to 60 months:

Can single out one word and ask its meaning whereas formerly reacted to sentence as a whole.

Genuine interchange of ideas remains limited.
Tries to use new words, can define some simple ones.
Considerable time looking at books—likes to be read to.
Understands some abstract words (connectives, colors).

Phonemic Development

Phonology refers to the study of the emergence and production of single
sounds and the rules whereby sounds are combined in sequences appropriate
to the language. There is a good deal of data concerning the emergence
of individual sounds. This may be due to the longer history of attention
given articulation problems in the field of speech pathology. Knowledge
as to the rules governing the sequencing of sounds is more limited (McNeill,
1970).

Developmentally, children across cultures emit sounds of their language
and other languages during the babbling stage. Sounds of other languages
drop out of the babbling repertoire (Berry, 1969). By age 2 much of the
child's sound production may be difficult or impossible to understand,
but by age 3 about 90 percent of the normal child's utterances can be
interpreted by the adult listener (Templin, 1957). Templin has provided
useful guidelines to the developmental sequence of sound production. The
expected age of acquisition is that age at which 75 percent of the children
can be expected to produce that sound in either the initial, medial, or
final parts of words (Table 8-1).

Vocabulary Development

The number of words used by children and the number of words used
in sentences have been traditional guides to assessing language development.
Between the ages of 1½ and 4, the child acquires an impressive number
of words. It has been estimated that the child's vocabulary increases from
460 to 910 words between the middle of his second year to 3 years. By
4 years, the child has a vocabulary of about 1,500 words (Berry, 1969).
Table 8-2 presents some developmental norms associated with vocabulary
growth.

Syntactic and Expressive Language Development

Counting the number of words children use does not account for the
major contemporary thrust of students of language development. As a result
of the efforts of Noam Chomsky and colleagues, the emphasis within the
field of psycholinguistics shifted from studies of word counting to defining
"deep structure," the underlying meaning of sentences. Children do not
merely spout isolated words when they begin to acquire a vocabulary; their
utterances of words reflect unspoken and perhaps unknown sentences.
Before the child is able to use sentences, he can use a word to reflect

TABLE 8-1: Development of sound production

Age	Phonemes and Phoneme-blends
3 years	Vowels: ē, i, e, a, o, u, oo, ōō, ō, ô, a, ûr Diphthongs: û, ā, i, ou, oi Consonants: m-, -m-, -m, n-, -n-, -n, -ng-, -ng, p-, -p-, -p, t-, -t-, -t, k-, -k-, b-, -b-, d-, -d-, g-, -g-, f-, -f-, -f, h-, -h-, w-, -w- Double-consonant blends: -ngk
3.5 years	Consonants: -s-, -z-, -r, y-, -y- Double-consonant blends: -rk, -ks, -mp, -pt, -rm, -mr, -nr, -pr, -kr, -br, -dr, -gr, -sm
4 years	Consonants: -k, -b, -d, -g, s-, sh-, -sh, -v-, j-, r-, -r-, l-, -l- Double-consonant blends: pl-, pr-, tr-, tw-, kl-, kr-, kw-, bl-, br-, dr-, gl , sk , sm-, sn-, sp-, st-, -lp, -rt, -ft, -lt, -ft Triple-consonant blends: -mpt, -mps
4.5 years	Consonants: -s, -sh-, ch-, -ch-, -ch Double-consonant blends: gr-, fr-, -lf
5 years	Consonants: -j- Double-consonant blends: fl-, -rp, -lb, -rd, -rf, -rn, -shr Triple-consonant blends: str-, -mbr
6 years	Consonants: -t-, th-, -th-, -th, v-, -v, -th-, -l Double-consonant blends: -lk, -rb, -rg, -rth, -nt, -nd, -thr, -pl, -kl, -bl, -gl, -fl, -sl Triple-consonant blends: skw-, -str, -rst, -ngkl, -nggl, -rj, -ntth, -rch
7 years	Consonants: -th-, -th, z-, -z, -zh-, -zh, -j Double-consonant blends: thr-, shr-, sl-, sw-, -lz, -zm, -lth, -sk, -st Triple-consonant blends: skr-, spl-, spr-, -skr, -kst, -jd
8 years	Double-consonant blends: -kt, -tr, -sp

SOURCE: *Certain language skills in children* by Mildred C. Templin, Child Welfare Monograph No. 26. University of Minnesota Press, Minneapolis, © Copyright 1957 by the University of Minnesota. P. 51.

TABLE 8-2: Vocabulary growth as a function of age

Age (years, months)	Number of words	Increment
0; 8	0	
0; 10	1	1
1; 0	3	2
1; 3	19	16
1; 6	22	3
1; 9	118	96
2; 0	272	154
2; 6	446	174
3; 0	896	450
3; 6	1222	326
4; 0	1540	318
4; 6	1870	330
5; 0	2072	202
5; 6	2289	217
6; 0	2562	273

SOURCE: Adapted from Smith, M. E. An investigation of the development of the sentence and the extent of vocabulary in young children. *University of Iowa Studies in Child Welfare,* 1926, 3, No. 5.

a complex event. For example, the child who says "milk" may be crying over spilled milk or may be indicating a desire for more milk. The context in which the word is uttered is likely to influence the listener's interpretation.

The initial words used by children about 18 months old are called *holophrastic* and *telegraphic*. Holophrastic speech "refers to the possibility that the first single word utterances of young children express complex ideas" (McNeill, 1970, p. 1074). To develop holophrastic speech requires the child to be able to name things, and there is speculation that holophrastic speech is linked to action (for example, the child may get up from a chair and say "walk") and to emotional states. Telegraphic speech refers to the first multiple word combinations of the child. Like a telegram certain words are omitted; for example, "me milk."

Children's speech at this age is described as having two classes of words, *pivot* and *open* (Braine, 1963). Pivot class words are always accompanied by open class words. For instance, a pivot class word may be "my" accompanied by an open class word "mommy." Children's utterances will vary as the pivot word may precede or follow the open word, or the child may use the open word without a pivot word. The initial linguistic skills of the child are described by noting the use of telegraphic and holophrastic speech.

There does appear to be consensus that the young child's two- and three-word sentences indicate that he is applying his own rule system to his language production. In effect, children apply several rules in the generation of these short sentences. According to Pflaum (1974) children show an early use of subject and object in their sentences (e.g., "it doggie"), will combine verbs and objects (e.g., "see train"), and unite subjects and verbs (e.g., "I see"). Children also combine words to reflect modification ("more hot"), conjunction (e.g., "and hot"), genitive (e.g., ownership meanings such as "daddy mitten"), and locational structures (e.g., "banana table"). Children make the same combination of words as adults, but in the early stages of language development they fail to verbalize the whole message. Children's language, while imperfect in terms of adult grammar, does appear to focus on the critical element of the message they wish to communicate.

According to Lee (1974) the child quickly acquires the ability to use pronouns and negatives, to ask questions, to join sentences, and to use infinitives, participles, and gerunds. There is thus much syntactic growth during the second and third years of a child's life. We see that the average length of a child's sentence increases to 4.7 words by age 4 years, and that the importance of this expansion is in the way children's additional words function in their sentences.

Pflaum (1974) describes the rapid expansion of children's syntactic development, using the acquisition of verb forms as an example. According to Pflaum, there are two early major events in the development of verb forms. One is the use of "-ing" (e.g., "I making coffee"). This is an example of the use of auxiliary verb forms. Adults use auxiliary words to accompany verbs to express tense, indicate questions, make negative statements, and to show passive voice. Young children use auxiliary verb forms in past tense forms (e.g., "He feeled it"). The second major factor in developing verb forms at this time is the acquisition of the verb "to be" (the copula). Once children start to use these verb forms they have the mechanics for full sentences.

Yet another important change in the use of verbs occurs when children start to form negative sentences. The progression of learning negatives has been exemplified in Klima's study (1964). Children proceed from attaching a negative ("no") to a holophrase and then positioning negative words within the sentence. This is followed by using auxiliary verbs with transformational rules. The initial sentences of the child are thus quite simple and consist of a noun and a verb; by 36 months of age children employ very complex sentences.

The child's acquisition of questions also occurs during this time period. Children initially ask questions by raising the pitch of their voice. The intonation is the tag that signals the asking of a question (e.g., "ball go?"). Children then ask questions by beginning their sentences with wh-words (who, where, why). The most advanced stage occurs when children ask questions by inverting the order of words in the sentences. This inversion appears to be one of the first transformations, or transformational rules, acquired by children. Transformations are rules which permit us to change words around and put sentences together. In a few months children change from using "who that" to "see my doggie" to "does lions walk?". While not having learned all the rules of adult language, by 3½ years of age children are nearly as competent as adults in their ability to ask questions.

Another major change which occurs during this same time frame is the acquisition of inflections, word parts which make nouns plural and which then result in noun-verb agreement. The order of acquisition appears to go from noun plurals, to possessive, and finally verb inflections. By 3½ years children's sentence structure is amazingly adult-like, for children's uses of verb forms are quite sophisticated. The acquisition of transformational rules is well under way.

During the 3½- to 6-year period children's language continues to grow in complexity. Menyuk (1963) studied the language production of nursery school and first-grade children. There were syntactic similarities among these two groups in the frequency of production of various linguistic structures. Both groups emitted contractions ("didn't"), possessives ("Mary's hat"), pronouns ("he can"), adjectives ("brown hat"), infinitive complements ("I wanted to do it"), main clause conjunctions ("He sang and Mary danced."), and conjunctions with deletions ("Mary sang and danced"). With other kinds of transformations there is a shift in the frequency of occurrence, with first-graders more frequently using these transformations than nursery school aged children. Thus first-graders more frequently than nursery school aged children use: relative clauses ("The man who sang is old"); "because" sentence embedding (". . . because he said so"); particle separation ("put down the box"); reflexives ("I did it myself"); imperatives ("Shut the door"); passives ("The boy was hit by the girl"); participial complement ("I saw her washing"); "if" sentences embedding (". . . if you want to"); "so" sentencing embedding (". . . so he will be happy"); compound of nominals ("You have to clean clothes"); iteration ("to make them clean").

According to Pflaum (1974) children first learn subject and predicate, then sentence parts which make their simple sentences more like those of adults; followed by rules which allow them to form compound and complex sentences. This progression of development is believed to mirror the hierarchical character of language by generative grammarians.

At the same time it appears that as children develop "socially," they also learn to make assessments of the situation and the persons who are their listeners. Shatz and Gelman (1973) completed three studies of 4-year-old children's ability to modify their communications to accommodate the age of their audience. Under varying conditions the 4-year-olds were asked to relay information to an adult and to a 2-year-old listener. Four-year-olds used speech to communicate to 2-year-olds which differed from their speech to adults. Communications to the 2-year-old contained more short, simple utterances and more attentional utterances. The younger the listener, the greater the simplification in the 4-year-old's communications.

Bzoch and League (1972) have outlined the development of spoken language during the first two years. The Bzoch and League manual for the REEL scales of receptive and expressive language development specify the following events as occurring during the first two years of life (1972, pp. 23–24.)

0 to 12 months:
. . . cry frequently with some variety in force and patterns, and to produce random reflexive vocalizations from time to time.
Signal developing hunger, by use of a specific differentiated cry or vocal pattern.
Communicate several states of pleasure or discomfort or pain through specific vocal signals that provide early vocalized social interaction with the mother.
Babble in chains of two or more syllables with increasing use of back vowels.
Respond to vocal stimulation by babbling and sometimes by attempting to imitate the specific sound heard:
. . . "talk" to objects and people in jargon patterns;
. . . use some true words in interpersonal communication to satisfy wants or needs (p. 23).
12 to 24 months:
. . . express wants and needs by using some true words in combination with other vocalizations and gestures.
. . . name more objects (and pictures of objects).
Development of speaking vocabulary from ten to twenty words.

Combine words into short, simple sentences.

More rapid development of expressive vocabulary.

Increased use of simple sentences consisting of four or more syllables.

Expansion of the speaking vocabulary to 100–150 words.

Increased use of two- and three-word sentences, coupled with decreased use of jargon utterances;

. . . speak regularly in sentences of two or more words, with expansion of the speaking vocabulary to more than 250 true words.

Borrowing again from Binet and Gesell, expressive language development from ages 24 months to 60 months includes the following skills:

24 to 36 months:

Often talks while he acts and acts while he talks.

300 words in vocabulary; reaches about 450 words.

Names of things, persons, actions, and situations greatly predominate.

Adverbs, adjectives, prepositions in minority.

Pronouns "mine," "me," "you," and "I" coming into use in approximately that order.

In same sentence expresses intention and action. (Peter slide down.)

Jargon may have disappeared, but not singsong which often made jargon musical. Singsong sentences.

Does not relate experiences in well-defined past tense.

Pleasure in matching words with objects.

Language is *beginning* to be used more extensively as communication for wants, needs, ideas. Simple experiences are verbal.

Tries to use words in telling his physical needs or answering simple questions, but does not carry on conversation.

Carries on "conversation" with self and dolls.

Asks names of things, "what's this?", "what's that?"

Sentence length of two words on the average.

Names three to five objects.

Refers to self by name.

Identifies many pictures by name.

Sentence length of three words on the average.

Repeats four syllables (two words).

36 to 48 months:

Vocabulary of nearly 1,000 words. Averages 900; reaches about 1,500 words.

Words become instruments for designating percepts, concepts, ideas, relationships.

Indulges in soliloquy and dramatic play in order to match his words and phrases and syntax. Combines acting and talking. Fits action to word and word to action in his monologue.

Asks questions to which he already knows the answers.

Uses language easily to tell a story or relay an idea to someone else.

Plurals, past tense, personal pronouns, prepositions such as "on."

Refers to self as "I."

Knows last name, sex, name of street on which he lives, and a few rhymes.

Speech may be infantile, but usually understood even by those outside the family.

Sentence length average of three to four words; reaches average of four to five words

Long sentences—compound and complex.

Nonpresent situations dealt with verbally.

Generalizations common in talking.

Complete sentences are used.

Number concept barely goes beyond "one," "two," and "many."

Can count to four or more by rote.

Powers of generalization and of abstraction are present.

Speaks of imaginary conditions: "suppose that" and "I hope."

Speech is forthright, not likely to carry on long conversations.

Plays with words.

Verbal rather than verbose (associative thinking).

May have imaginary playmate, but communicating is sketchy rather than organized and dramatic play does not long sustain a role.

Can tell lengthy story mixing fact and fiction.

Can carry on lengthy conversation with adults and children, though may make grammatical errors and misuse words.

Aggressiveness may appear in words as well as actions; calls names and brags.

Talks about everything, to gain social rapport and to attract attention.

Questions at a peak, not always interested in explanations but more interested in how answers fit own thought.

Speech quite understandable, although some traces of infantile speech may remain.

48 to 60 months:

Vocabulary of 1,900 words; reaches about 2,200 words.

Sentence length averages four to five words.

Can count ten objects. Can tell his age.

Can carry a plot in a story and repeat a long sequence accurately.

Talks without infantile articulation.

Answers to questions more succinct and to the point.

Questions for information, not merely social intercourse or practice in speaking.

Defines in terms of use. ("A horse is to ride.")

Language essentially complete in structure and form.

Uses all types of sentences, including complex sentences with hypothetical and conditional clauses.

Uses conjunctions more freely, but generally frequency of parts of speech same as at four years.

Less literal and concrete than formerly.

Dramatic play full of practical dialogue and commentary which has to do with everyday functions (kitchen, grocery store, etc.). Good deal of talk with these. Function is to clear ideas and relationships through words rather than indulge in make-believe.

Distinguishes left and right hand in self, but not others.

Lacks power of explicit reasoning.

Names primary colors.

Physical Interference with Development

Lenneberg (1967) has described the effects of brain damage, whether or not genetically caused, upon language and speech development. His hypoth esis is that during language development, the effects of brain damage will be more debilitating as the child ages. The impact of physical assaults upon the brain is thought to have different effects upon language development depending upon the age of the child and the severity of the damage sustained. According to Lenneberg, the child who suffers a lesion will experience delayed but normal development of language if the child is younger than about twenty months of age at the time of the trauma. This recuperation is attributed to the equipotentiality of the cerebral hemispheres at this age, which allows the nondamaged areas of the brain to assume the functions of the damaged sections. At this time, symptoms and prognosis are the same irrespective of the side of the brain which suffers damage. The delay in language development is thought to reflect the delay of the nondamaged areas in assuming the functions of those parts suffering the lesion.

During the 21- to 36-month period of the child's development, brain damage to the language areas of the brain (left hemisphere areas) will produce greater debilitation. This period of development is the major one in which the child develops language, and a lesion at this time necessitates repetition of previous language learning. According to Lenneberg, however, spontaneous recuperation of the language deficits produced will be evidenced.

Children who suffer damage between the ages of 3 to 10 will demonstrate aphasic symptoms similar to those exhibited by brain-damaged adults, but spontaneous recuperation is still possible. Interestingly and importantly for the learning disability specialist, Lenneberg has hypothesized that children suffering such damage during this period of their lives may demonstrate reading and writing handicaps.

If the lesion occurs during the 11- to 14-year period, the child will exhibit aphasic symptoms, and some of these symptoms may persist as residual deficits. By this time, lateralization of brain functioning has occurred and the nondominant hemisphere can no longer take over as it did during younger age periods. The child now retains problems which resemble those of the adult who suffers brain damage, such as expressive and receptive language deficits.

A final point needs to be made concerning language deficits, physical assaults, and childhood aphasia. It is entirely reasonable to assume that some children who suffer brain damage also suffer aphasia. But we agree with Birch (1964) when he argues that there is a difference between the fact of brain damage and the concept of brain damage. Apparently, Birch's well-taken point is that diagnosticians will illogically argue that because a child has a language deficit, he must be brain damaged. Such is not logically or empirically the case. Because brain-damaged children may have trouble talking, or more correctly, in employing language, does not mean that all children who have language problems suffer from brain damage.

Nonphysiological Interference with Development

Children, even without physical evidence of brain damage, may well show delayed language development. What is the nature of the delay? Do such children simply resemble younger children, or is their speech production different in quality as well as quantity from their peers? What are the implications of delayed language development?

Menyuk (1969) studied the linguistic competence of language-delayed children between 3 and 6 years of age and compared their performances with children not suffering such delay. In the study, children's speech was obtained in response to a projective test, conversation with an adult and a peer, and by having the child repeat a list of grammatical and nongrammatical sentences. Menyuk reports that at no age level did the syntactic structures of the language-delayed children match those employed by the normal children. The second finding was that the language-delayed children resembled each other in the linguistic structures employed, irrespective of their age. The 3-, 4-, and 5-year-old language-delayed children used similar syntactic structures in their verbal productions.

There were two major findings: language-delayed children were similar to each other across the age range of 3 to 6, and were different in their expressive language from nondelayed children irrespective of their age. The normal child was found to be more sophisticated and competent in using grammatical structures. The characteristics of the language-delayed child included: using sentences which seem to be "reflections of a basic 'unmarked' grammar" (p. 130); articles were omitted; the verb phrase was almost never expanded; incorrect usage of words was frequent and grammatical rules were ignored (e.g., "My like guns," p. 134); the simple transformational structures produced were generated by the operation of conjoining elements (e.g., "I want milk" and "I want cookies" rather than "I want some milk and cookies"); and failure to produce correct negatives and questions.

In addition, some of these children failed to speak at all and others spoke with correct syntax but with such poor articulation that they were unintelligible. In the linguistically deviant children, there seemed to be,

TABLE 8-3: Sentences by normal and language-delayed children

Normal-speaking 3; 0	Deviant-speaking 3; 0
Do you see it over there?	Which mine?
I want the fire engine to talk.	I go wash hands.
He's going up the ladder.	He's go there.
There's a fire and here's the ladder.	My like gun.
The monster's not coming.	Not take mine.
He isn't coming.	This is not buttoned.

SOURCE: Menyuk, P. Sentences Children Use. Research Monograph No. 52. Cambridge, Mass: The M.I.T. Press, 1969.

in general, a static state of nondevelopment between the ages of 3 and 6 years in the production of sentences. When asked to repeat sentences, the language-deviant children repeated sentences omitting phrases or using the final part of the sentence. The difference between normal and deviant children was that the errors made by normal children reflected their efforts to correct ungrammatical sentences, but the linguistically deviant children's productions reflected nongrammatical modifications of transformations. While sentence length and the ability to repeat sentences was not related for the normal children, it was highly related for the deviant children. The 3-year-old literally repeats the last word or part of the sentence. The language-delayed 5-year-old could repeat a sentence better than a 3-year-old, but was still limited in his ability to understand and repeat the sentence. Menyuk hypothesizes that the performance of the language-delayed child reflects poor auditory memory and suggests that such a deficit will have profound effects upon the child's subsequent ability to expand the rules in his grammar, and observe more contextual constraints (i.e., be sensitive to the grouping of words to convey particular meaning). When a young child cannot remember more that two or three morphemes (the smallest meaningful unit within a sentence), he is at a considerable disadvantage in developing his language through his everyday experiences. The degree to which such a child can form hypotheses about sentence production, or understand and generate sentences, will be sorely limited. Table 8-3 presents some examples of the sentences produced by normal and language-delayed children.

Lee (1974) also has described many of the language acquisition difficulties of children with language delays. The following is a summary of the Lee studies.

Whereas normal speaking children learn to use complicated linguistic structures by age 4 years, language-delayed children have great difficulty in the acquisition of a variety of such structures. For instance, children learn to use pronouns very early, but language-delayed children have an inordinately difficult time learning pronouns. The use of negatives is apparently easily achieved by normal speaking children. They learn to use no, and, then add not; but language-delayed children cling to the use of "no" or just add "no" to the end of sentences. Children learn to ask two kinds of questions, yes-no and "why" questions.

Yes-no asks for confirmation of something as right or wrong and "why" questions ask for information. But children with delayed language seldom ask "why" questions and they have difficulty learning to make the interrogative reversal (e.g., "What that is"). The absence of the use of questions reflects both linguistic and conceptual shortcomings. To use questions the child has to understand yes and no, and have the concepts of time and causality. Normal children learn to join sentences using conjunctions, an early appearing conjunction is "and." But language-delayed children may just put words in a series and omit the conjunction or they may use an inappropriate one. The language-delayed child is similarly delayed and inconsistent in his acquisition of infinitives, gerunds and participles.

LANGUAGE AND LEARNING DISABILITIES

Children who have been labeled as learning disabled have been described as demonstrating inadequate language development. Indeed Kirk and Elkins (1975) found in their survey of the characteristics of children enrolled in Child Service Demonstration Centers that remediation emphasis was frequently upon language skills. They report that 43 percent of the children being serviced were involved in some form of language remediation efforts.

Research and Observations

Owen, Adams, Forrest, Stolz, and Fisher (1971) interviewed parents of learning-disabled children, their siblings, and nonrelated peers. The parents reported that such children, in comparison with siblings and other children, had less adequate verbal skills as well as other difficulties. The fathers perceived the *main* difference between the learning-disabled and comparison children to be verbal ability. In this monograph, the investigators divided the learning-disabled children into categories which were associated with various problems. Children were divided into five groups, those who had a history or organic or physical abnormality, those who had high WISC performance scores relative to their verbal scores, those who had relatively low IQ scores, those who had relatively high IQ scores, and those who demonstrated some emotional difficulties. Children designated within the first three categories appeared to demonstrate language deficits. Children who had some history of medical difficulties appeared to have receptive and expressive language problems and difficulty in reproducing auditory stimuli. Children with high performance scores relative to their verbal scores (fifteen IQ points or higher was the criterion for inclusion) appeared to have problems of articulation in which they made distortions ("mushy" sounds such as *shss* for *s* sounds), substitutions, and omissions of sounds. The errors seemed to be related to difficulty in sequentializing auditory stimuli (e.g., *aminal* for *animal*). Also of interest was that the mothers and siblings also evidenced language problems.

The children categorized as belonging to the relatively low IQ score group (IQ scores between 90 and 99 on the Wechsler Intelligence Scale for Children) showed both problems of articulation and in expressive and receptive language. Mothers described these children as having difficulty listening in school, being difficult to talk to, and as having a history of limited sound production. Siblings and parents of these children did not exhibit language problems.

Children of the remaining two groups, that is, those with relatively high IQ scores (scores ranging between 117 and 154), and those with some emotional problems, did not appear to have language problems.

There are two important hypotheses which can be derived from the results of the Owen et al. study. First, language problems might well be extensive in that population of children called learning disabled. Second, many learning-disabled children may have or are suffering from delayed language development. But caution in interpretation of these findings is warranted. The analysis of learning-disabled children's language was based on post hoc partitioning of the subjects and may reflect the influence of "chance" factors. Additionally, the data were based upon the recollections of the children's parents, and such recollections are often both unreliable and invalid.

While the Owen et al. investigation has suggested the importance of language deficits in learning disabilities, other researchers have provided more direct evidence about such deficits. By and large, the results support the idea that learning-disabled children do exhibit language problems. Moreover, these language problems are not only pervasive but are also enduring. Let us review some of the research in this area because the results pinpoint potentially important areas for intervention as well as future study.

First, there is the "bad" news. There is one study which apparently fails to support the language deficit hypothesis. Bartel, Grill, and Bartel (1973) studied normal and learning disabled children's language, using the technique of free association. Changes in linguistic development are noted through the analysis of children's associations to stimulus words. Thus, children move from using syntactic associations, where the response to a stimulus word is based upon a description or function of that word (e.g., apple—eat; apple—red) to paradigmatic associations, where a response to the stimulus word is to indicate the class in which the stimulus word belongs (e.g., apple—fruit). While the investigators found that younger children were less likely to give advanced associations than older children, no differences were found between the learning-disabled and the nondisabled children. The authors suggest that the learning-disabled children performed as well as the nondisabled ones because of the nature of the task. The response required of the child was immediate; it required no memory, no extended attention, and no sequencing of information. These disappointing results seem similar to many others in which differences between groups are not found when the task employed is simple and does not make demands on attention, memory, or sequencing skills.

Now for the "good" news. Several studies have reported differences in the linguistic abilities of learning-disabled and nondisabled children. Irrespective of whether the children were defined as learning disabled, dyslexic, or poor readers the findings are consistently in favor of the nondisabled comparison groups.

Semel and Wiig (1975), for example, assessed learning-disabled and nondisabled second- through seventh-graders on language production and comprehension. These assessments were based upon the Northwestern Syntax Screening test, a test described in Chapter 10. Their results indicated that learning-disabled children were significantly inferior to nondisabled ones in both language production and language comprehension of syntactic structures. More shocking was the degree to which learning-disabled children showed language problems. Over half of these children scored below the tenth percentile in expressive language, while over three-quarters of them scored below the tenth percentile in language comprehension. According to Lee (1974), who developed the test, such performances by children even younger than those employed by Semel and Wiig would signal the need for extensive evaluation and intervention efforts.

Fry, Johnson, and Muehl (1970) compared oral language of second-graders, some of whom were good oral readers, others of whom were considered poor oral readers. Their analysis was based upon the children's story tellings in response to twenty pictured stimuli. Analysis was made of the children's communication units, grammatically independent clauses with any of their modifiers. A variety of variables were analyzed, including the types of linguistic patterns used, the number and length of communication units, as well as incomplete communication units.

Three major differences discriminated the good from the poor readers. One was the size of the speaking vocabulary and fluency. The good readers appear to have larger speaking vocabularies and were also more fluent. A second difference was the type of linguistic patterns used by the above- and below-average readers. It was found that below-average readers were more likely to use subordination in the subject position, whereas above-average readers used more subordination in the predicate position. The below-average group made greater use of a category of "movable expression (phrase or subordinate clause) of purpose, cause, or condition. . . . 'The mother didn't have anything because she wasn't hungry' . . ." (p. 127), whereas more of the above-average readers were likely to use the subject-predicate (clause) satellite of the verb. . . . 'Before they wrote a story they had to stand up and pledge' . . ." (p. 129). The authors then hypothesize that subordination itself may not distinguish groups of good and poor readers, but the position of the subordination may reflect linguistic development. The third difference between groups was the finding that the below-average readers used the "existence" type of sentence more than the above-average readers. An existence type of sentence starts with "there" followed by a form of the verb to be (e.g., "There's a dog"). The authors hypothesize that the below-average readers employ more existence type sentences than the above-average readers because they are less skilled in organizing, integrating, and telling a coherent story. These children appear to be likely to enumerate picture content, whereas the better readers were more likely to create a meaningful story.

Using considerably different measures, Vogel (1974; 1977) also studied the oral syntax of dyslexic and nondyslexic boys. She found that dyslexic boys were not as competent as "normal" boys in detecting whether a sentence they heard was a statement of information or a question. The same relative competencies were found in tasks involving repeating sentences and in filling in a word deleted from a spoken paragraph. Vogel also examined groups' differences in performing on two tests of morphology, one of which used meaningful words, the other nonsense words. Dyslexic boys, on both tasks, demonstrated less knowledge of morphological rules than did nondyslexic boys.

Wiig, Semel, and Crouse (1973) obtained similar results on a test of morphology employing nonsense words. Four groups of children were tested. Ten 3- and 4-year-olds were designated as high-risk children on the basis of neurological involvements. A second group of ten children of approximately the same age served as the control group. These children showed no signs of neurological impairment. A third group of ten children were of school age (8 to 10 years) and were drawn from a population of learning-disabled children who presumably had no speech or language disorders. Finally, a fourth group of ten subjects of approximately the same age as the learning-disabled group, and who were academically competent, served as the control for the third group.

When comparing the young children, the high-risk and their control group, it was found that the normal children were much better than the high-riskegroup, particularly on sentences involving the progressive tense, the third person singular, and the past tense of verbs. Likewise, when comparing the learning-disabled with their control children, the learning-disabled children performed much less competently. Unlike their peers, the learning-disabled children could not form plural forms of possessives, or form the progressive tense, a transformation that the 3- and 4-year-old normals could accomplish.

The fascinating aspect of the study was that close inspection revealed that high-risk and learning-disabled children who apparently had adequate language development in fact did not. These results again suggest that linguistic development, and the conceptual development that corresponds with it, may well be delayed or different for the learning-disabled child.

So far we have discussed studies related to comprehension and morphology. Now we will look more closely at language production, by describing one investigation in which a battery of tests was employed and another which was an experiment within a laboratory setting.

Wiig and Semel (1975) compared the performances of learning-disabled and nondisabled adolescents on a battery of tests which presumably assess semantic production abilities. They found that the learning-disabled adolescents were less competent than their peers on naming verbal opposites, formulating sentences, defining words, and retrieving words descriptive of pictures. Learning-disabled adolescents were also slower and less accurate in responding to test items, and unlike control subjects, were less likely to detect their incorrect responses. Observers also rated the subjects' conversational speech. Learning-disabled adolescents were found to differ from their peers on both phrase length and grammatical form.

Using quite a different format to assess language production, Bryan and Pflaum (in preparation) conducted an experiment to obtain a linguistic analysis of children's social communications to both a same age child and a younger, same sex child. One-half of the child communicators were learning disabled; the remaining communicators were not. All were fourth- and fifth-grade males and females. The results of the experiment indicate that children's communications depend upon whether the child is disabled, whether the child is a learning-disabled boy or girl, and whether the target of the communication is a peer or a younger child. Communications are a complex matter. As a group, the learning-disabled children differed from comparison children in their length of utterances, the complexity of their utterances, the number of clauses used, and the variation of the length of their sentences. In all instances, learning-disabled children performed less competently than did the nondisabled ones. However, these differences were, in fact, attributable to the performances of learning-disabled males. Learning-disabled females were as linguistically competent as the nondisabled girls. Noteworthy also was the fact that while the learning-disabled girls and the nondisabled girls and boys were all sensitive to whether they were communicating to a same age or younger child, learning-disabled boys did not make adjustments in their speech according to the age of the target of communication.

In summary, there is considerable evidence that learning-disabled children show pervasive and enduring language problems across a wide variety of language tasks. It should be stressed, however, that the great bulk or research on this matter has employed boys, not girls, as subjects. The results of the Bryan and Pflaum study strongly suggest that such language problems may be more typical of learning-disabled boys than learning-disabled girls.

At least with regard to learning-disabled boys, there is a good deal of information specifying the particulars of these language problems. These problems fall primarily into the two major linguistic categories of syntax and semantics. For example, in the area of syntax, learning-disabled males have been found less competent than comparison children in dealing with inflections, and the comprehension and creation of complex sentences. In terms of semantics, they are less able to define words, create sentences, classify objects into categories, show less adequate sentence production, and are less skilled at recognizing their errors.

But there is more to language development than simply the acquisition of generative grammar. Children must not only develop the use of phonemes, morphemes, and syntax, but must also know when to use them in everyday discourse. As the child develops, there is an increasing number of situations which demand of him not simply primitive motor responses, but linguistic ones as well (Flavell, Beach, and Chinsky, 1966).

Mediation

Mediation, what goes on within the organism after seeing a stimulus and before making a response, has been long thought to be critical in facilitating the child's learning, be it a motor, a conceptual, or an interpersonal skill (Flavell, Beach, and Chinsky, 1966). While the various forms that such mediation might take are often disputed, many theorists agree that one important form of mediation is language (Bandura, 1969; Kohlberg, 1969; Luria, 1966; Osgood, Suci, and Tannenbaum, 1957; Vygotsky, 1962). If, and how, the child uses language in his problem-solving activity is deemed particularly critical to his development.

There is evidence that as the child ages, he will rely increasingly upon his self-generative language in order to encode and deal with problems. For example, Flavell, Beach, and Chinsky (1966) noted that the spontaneous verbalizations by the child increased with age. Miller, Shelton, and Flavell (1969) found that children began to employ self-instructions by age 3½ and by age 5 children's self-instructions were as facilitating as those generated by the researchers.

It is also clear that all children do not generate an adequate set of instructions or rehearse the instructions given them by the experimenter. Many children do not appear to mediate the problem at hand. This lack of mediation might be due either to a vocabulary lack, a production deficiency, or the child may have the words but fail to use them in the problem-solving capacity, a mediation deficiency. An important question, then, is the degree to which children might be trained toward greater mediational efforts.

There is now evidence to suggest that children can be trained to use covert self-instructions in approaching learning tasks and that such training will facilitate their performance of these tasks. Of particular relevance to the learning disability specialist are two studies of verbal mediation which employed hyperactive children (Palkes, Stewart, and Kahana, 1968; Palkes, Stewart, and Freedman, 1971). Children, ages 7 to 13, were defined as hyperactive on the basis of receiving psychiatric treatment for that symptom. Those children who had received directions to orally instruct themselves to think before they act, to listen, to stop before they responded, performed significantly better on the Porteus Maze tasks than children who had not received directions or written instructions.

Bandura, Grusec, and Menlove (1966) tested 6- to 8-year-old children in their imitation of a model they had observed. One group of children was instructed to verbalize all the actions of the model as they observed the scene. A second group was given no instructions relevant to verbalizations, while the third group was instructed to verbalize material which would interfere with their verbal codings of the model's behavior. As expected, children who verbalized the actions of the model showed more imitation than those who passively observed, and those who passively observed showed greater imitation of the model than those who were told to verbalize competing material.

The utility of directions to produce self-instructions has also been demonstrated with training adults. For example, Meichenbaum (1971) was able to reduce adult females' fears of snakes by having them observe a model who verbalized intentions and techniques while herself approaching and handling a snake. Those who observed a vocal model subsequently showed less fear of the snake than those women who viewed a nonvocal model.

It is clear that much remains to be determined about the effectiveness of instructions to self-instruct. Sometimes such instructions are simply ineffective (Bryan, 1972). Sometimes they may simply interfere with learning the adequate performance of a skill (Bandura, Grusec, and Menlove, 1966; Miller, Shelton, and Flavell, 1969). While we do not know all of the parameters affecting the power of self-instructions, certainly there are enough data to suggest that they may play an important role in problem-solving activities of children and may also play an important future role in the remediation of some forms of learning disabilities.

Social Relations

Compared to data on other effects, there is relatively little information available concerning the language production of learning-disabled children and the social repercussions of their defects. It is our belief, however, that language problems are crucial for the disabled child and that such problems might be the cause of a variety of his interpersonal difficulties (Bryan, 1974a; Keogh et al., 1974; Owen et al., 1971).

Entwisle (1975) has argued forcibly for the importance of rather subtle language factors in affecting the social and academic life of the child. As she correctly notes, children not only acquire basic grammar and language skills, but they also learn how to use various styles of language, what to say when and to whom. She refers to this knowledge as "sociolinguistic competence." This competence requires learning a large number of variations in style and timing. The child is expected to learn to use different phonology, grammar, vocabulary, pitch, and loudness when speaking in various situations and to various parties, and when expressing various attitudes or feelings. This competence is attributed to familial interactions, primarily in the form of modeling the family's own style of language deployment. For example, if the family relies on physical forms of punishment rather than verbal control of behavior, the child may well enter the classroom quite ill-equipped to respond to the typical verbal control techniques of the teacher. Similarly, it has been well demonstrated that children do imitate the language habits of the adults around them (Adams and Hamm, 1971; Bandura and Kupers, 1964). If the models are poor, the child's performance is destined to be similarly inadequate.

Whatever the cause of such incompetence, evidence indicates that the learning-disabled child does not exhibit the same degree of linguistic competence as do his nondisabled peers. But even if the incompetencies are of such a nature as to produce sociolinguistic incompetence (a fact yet to be demonstrated), will he be at a disadvantage within the classroom, and if so, what is the nature of the disadvantage?

There is evidence that teachers' expectancies of children's performances are relevant to the eventual performance of the child (Seaver, 1973). Is there evidence that language factors will affect either these expectancies or, more importantly, the behavior of the teacher toward the child? Rist (1970) has provided some provocative, if not altogether persuasive, observations on this point. This investigator conducted a longitudinal study of black children who entered kindergarten and whose teacher was black. He observed the class at the beginning of the term and found that within a few days the children had been more or less divided into three groups. The groups were differentiated on the basis of how far they sat from the teacher. Interestingly, the teacher's behavior toward the children was rather predictable on the basis of these stable seating arrangements. Thus, the children who sat closest to the teacher were more likely to be allowed to help her. They were asked to perform such activities as leading the pledge and running errands. Moreover, the closest students engaged in more verbal interactions with the teacher than did children of the remaining groups. What distinguished the groups of children besides their seating arrangements was whether they spoke to the teacher using standard English or black dialect. The children closest to the teacher spoke most frequently in standard English; the children furthest removed from her spoke black dialect. Interestingly, when they entered the first and then the second grades, the children's spatial arrangements continued to reflect the pattern of the kindergarten years.

This study is not conclusive, since the results might simply reflect the biases or idiosyncrasies of a single teacher. Yet this may not be the case, and if this teacher is typical of many others, future teachers should be very sensitive to their own treatment of children with language styles differing from their own. Moreover, the learning disability specialist will be confronted with children who have not only subtle language deficits, but obviously different language styles as well. The speech and language of learning-disabled children are readily discernible from nondisabled children of the same age, sex, and socioeconomic status. In the chapter on behavior the authors cite a study which is worth repeating for this discussion (Bryan, 1974e). College students who had no previous interactions with or knowledge about the children they viewed on videotape were asked to rate them on a variety of characteristics. Some of the children were learning disabled, some were not. All were videotaped during an interaction they had with a younger peer involving their giving instructions to the younger child on bowling. These students rated the adequacy of the language of the learning-disabled child significantly less that that of the nondisabled ones. This discrimination was possible after viewing the interaction of the children no longer than four minutes!

Many of the academic and behavioral characteristics associated with learning disabilities in many children may reflect language disorders. Admittedly, language may be one factor among many, or language problems may reflect other problems. But there is good reason to believe that language disorders have been much underestimated in explanations of learning problems. First, learning disability is often a synonym for reading failure, and both reading failure and learning disabilities have been linked to low scores on measures of verbal intelligence (Birch and Belmont, 1965). Second, many of the studies of other factors, such as auditory or visual information processing, find that the discriminating variable between the learning-disabled and comparison child is verbal rather than nonverbal or perceptual stimuli (McGrady and Olson, 1970).

One hypothesis is that many of the behavioral characteristics associated with the learning-disabled child reflect language disorders, albeit perhaps subtle ones. Short attention span, for example, may well reflect a language disability, and thus may be a symptom rather than a cause of deficit learning by the child. Children who have difficulty in attaining early levels of comprehension or learning the syntax and semantic rules of language may miss a great deal of information which they are expected to learn. Commands may not be heeded, readings understood, or sociolinguistic competence obtained. An evil cycle may thus be set into motion, in which the child's conceptual development lags, and the expectancies and affective responses of adults toward the child further deprive him of the needed remediational training, which in turn increases his conceptual incompetence. When this occurs, a cumulative deficit may result. Language is intimately linked to conceptual development. Any decrease in language skills would reciprocally affect conceptual development adversely.

When a child fails to respond as expected to parents, it seems reasonable that parents will become irritated, upset, and/or confused and will have difficulty socializing, understanding, and controlling this child. In addition, a child whose behavior is seen as erratic, unpredictable, and uncontrollable, and who has difficulty in understanding or in expressing himself, will not elicit positive feelings or high expectations from others. Not only will parents feel less affection, but lower expectations are also associated with differential treatments—all to the disadvantage of the child.

REFERENCES

Adams, G. R. and Hamm, N. H. "A test of the 'contiguity' and generalized imitation theories of imitation learning." Paper presented at the meetings of the Society of Research & Child Development, 1971.

Bandura, A. *Principles of Behavior Modification.* New York: Holt, Rinehart & Winston, 1969.

Bandura, A., Grusec, J., and Menlove, F. "Observational learning as a function of symbolization and incentive set." *Child Development,* 1966, 37, 499–506.

Bandura, A. and Kupers, C. A. "Transmission of patterns of self-reinforcement through modeling." *Journal of Abnormal and Social Psychology,* 1964, 69, 1–9.

Bartel, N. R., Grill, J. J., and Bartel, H. W. "The syntactic-paradigmatic shift in learning-disabled and normal children." *Journal of Learning Disabilities,* 1973, 6, 518–523.

Berko, J. "The child's learning of English morphology." *Word,* 1958, 14, 150–177.

Berry, M. F. *Language Disorders of Children: The Basis and Diagnoses.* New York: Appleton-Century-Crofts, 1969.

Birch, H. G. and Belmont, L. "Auditory-visual integration, intelligence, and reading ability in school children." *Perceptual and Motor Skills,* 1965, 20, 295–305.

Birch, H. G. *Brain Damage in Children: The Biological and Social Aspects,* Baltimore, Maryland: Williams and Wilkins, 1964.

Brackbill, Y. "Extinction of the smiling response in infants as a function of reinforcement schedule." *Child Development,* 1958, 29, 115–124.

Braine, M. D. S. "On learning the grammatical order of words." *Psychological Review,* 1963, 70, 323–340.

Bryan, T. "The effect of forced mediation upon short-term memory of children with learning disabilities." *Journal of Learning Disabilities,* 1972, 5, 605–609.

Bryan, T. "Peer popularity of learning-disabled children." *Journal of Learning Disabilities,* 1974, 7, 261–268 (a).

Bryan, T. "Stranger's Judgements of Children's Social and Academic Adequacy: Instant Diagnosis." Unpublished manuscript, 1974 (e).

Bzoch, K. R. and League, R. *Assessing Language Skills in Infancy.* Gainesville, Fla: The Tree of Life Press, Inc., 1972.

Chomsky, N. "Review of Skinner's verbal behavior." In L. A. Jakobovits and M. S. Miron (eds.), *Readings in the Psychology of Language.* Englewood Cliffs, N.J.: Prentice-Hall, 1967.

Clements, S. D. "Minimal brain dysfunction in children." NINDS Monograph No. 3, Public Health Service Bulletin #1415. Washington, D.C.: U.S. Department of Health, Education, and Welfare, 1966.

Dale, P. S. *Language Development.* Hinsdale, Ill.: Dryden Press, 1972.

Entwisle, D. R. "Socialization of language behavior and educability." In M. Machr and W. Stallings (eds.), *Culture, Child and School.* Monterey, Calif.: Brooks/Cole Publishing Co., 1975.

Flavell, J. H., Beach, D. R., and Chinsky, J. M. "Spontaneous verbal rehearsal in a memory task as a function of age." *Child Development,* 1966, 37, 283–299.

Fry, M. A., Johnson, C. S., and Muehl, S. "Oral language production in relation to reading achievement among select second graders." In D. J. Bakker and P. Satz (eds.), *Specific Reading Disability.* Netherlands: Rotterdam University Press, 1970, 123–159.

Keogh, B. K., Tchir, C., and Windeguth-Behn, A. "Teachers' perceptions of educationally high risk children." *Journal of Learning Disabilities,* 1974, 7, 367–374.

Kirk, S. A. and Elkins, J. "Characteristics of children enrolled in the Child Service Demonstration Centers." *Journal of Learning Disabilities,* 1975, 8, 630–637.

Kirk, S. A. and Kirk, W. P. *Psycholinguistic Learning Disabilities: Diagnosis and Remediation.* Urbana: University of Illinois Press, 1972.

Klima, E. S. "Negation in English." In J. J. Fodor and J. A. Katz (eds.), *The Structure of Language.* Englewood Cliffs, N.J.: Prentice-Hall, 1964.

Kohlberg, L. "Stage and Sequence: The Cognitive Developmental Approach to Socialization." In D. S. Goslin, ed., *Handbook of Socialization Theory and Research.* Chicago, Ill.: Rand-McNally, 1969, 347–480.

Lee, L. L. "A screening test for syntax development." *Journal of Speech and Hearing Disorders,* 1970, 35, 103–112.

Lee, L. L. *Developmental Sentence Analysis.* Evanston, Ill.: Northwestern University Press, 1974.

Lenneberg, E. *Biological Foundations of Language.* New York: John Wiley & Sons, 1967.

Lerea, L. *The Michigan Picture Language Inventory.* Ann Arbor: University of Michigan, 1958.

Luria, A. *Higher Cortical Functions in Man.* New York: Basic Books, Inc., 1966.

McGrady, H. J. "Language pathology and learning disabilities." In H. R. Myklebust (ed.), *Progress in Learning Disabilities,* New York: Grune & Stratton, 1968, 199–233.

McGracy, H. J. and Olson, D. A. "Visual and auditory learning processes in normal children and children with specific learning disabilities." *Exceptional Children,* 1970, 36, 581–589.

McNeill, D. "The development of language." In P. H. Mussen (ed.), *Carmichael's Manual of Child Psychology, Vol. 1* (3rd ed.). New York: John Wiley & Sons, 1970, 1061–1161.

Menyuk, P. "Syntactic structures in the language of children." *Journal of Child Development,* 1963, 34, 407–422.

Menyuk, P. *Sentences Children Use.* Cambridge, Mass.: MIT Press, 1969.

Miller, S. A., Shelton, J., and Flavell, J. H. "A test of Luria's hypotheses concerning the development of verbal self-regulation." Paper presented at the meeting of the Society for Research in Child Development, 1969.

NaLDAP Centerfold, November, 1976.

Osgood, C. E., Suci, G., and Tannenbaum, P. *The Measurement of Meaning.* Urbana, Ill.: University of Illinois Press, 1957.

Owen, R. W., Adams, P. A., Forrest, T., Stolz, L. M., and Fisher, S. "Learning disorders in children: Sibling studies." *Monographs of the Society for Research in Child Development,* 1971, 36, No. 144.

Palermo, D. S. and Molfese, D. L. "Language acquisition from age five onward." *Psychological Bulletin,* 1972, 78, 409–428.

Palkes, H., Stewart, M., and Freedman, J. "Improvement in maze performance of hyperactive boys as a function of verbal-training procedures." *Journal of Special Education,* 1971, 5, 337–342.

Palkes, H. and Kahana, B. "Porteus maze performance of hyperactive boys after training in self-directed verbal commands." *Child Development,* 1968, 39, 817–826.

Piaget, J. *The Construction of Reality in the Child.* Translated by M. Cook. New York: Basic Books, Inc., 1954.

Pflaum, S. W. *The Development of Language and Reading in the Young Child.* Columbus, Ohio: Chas. E. Merrill, 1974.

Rist, R. C. "Student social class and teacher expectations: The self-fulfilling prophecy in ghetto education." *Harvard Educational Review,* 1970, 40, 411–451.

Rosenthal, R. and Jacobsen, L. *Pygmalion in the Classroom.* New York: Holt, Rinehart & Winston, 1968.

Seaver, W. B. "Effects of naturally induced teacher expectancies." *Journal of Personality and Social Psychology,* 1973, 28, 333–342.

Semel, E. M. and Wiig, E. H. "Comprehension of syntactic structures and critical verbal elements by children with learning disabilities." *Journal of Learning Disabilities,* 1975, 8, 46–52.

Shatz, M. and Gelman, R. "The development of communication skills: Modifications in the speech of young children as a function of listener." *Monographs of the Society for Research in Child Development,* 1973, 35, No. 5.

Spitz, R. "Hospitalism: A follow-up report on investigation described in Volume I, 1945." *The Psychoanalytic Study of the Child, Vol. II.* New York: International Universities Press, 1946.

Templin, M. C., "Certain Language Skills in Children." *Child Welfare Monograph,* No. 26, Minneapolis: University of Minnesota Press, 1957.

Vogel, S. A. "Syntactic abilities in normal and dyslexic children." *Journal of Learning Disabilities,* 1974, 7, 103–109.

Vogel, S. A. "Morphological ability in normal and dyslexic children." *Journal of Learning Disabilities,* 1977, 10, 35–43.

Vygotsky, L. S. *Thought and Language.* Cambridge, Mass.: MIT Press, 1962.

Wiig, E. M. and Semel, E. M. "Productive language abilities in learning-disabled adolescents." *Journal of Learning Disabilities,* 1975, 8, 578–588.

Wiig, E. M., Semel, E. M., and Crouse, M. A. B. "The use of English morphology by high-risk and learning-disabled children." *Journal of Learning Disabilities,* 1973, 6, 457–465.

9 | Reading and Mathematics

Reading is a perceptual process, a response, a developmental task, an interest, a means of learning and of communication (Dechant, 1964). In the United States, reading instruction dates back more than 200 years, with the method and materials used reflecting each period's religious and educational beliefs and cultural needs. The technological nature of today's society and the public's concern for equal opportunities for its citizens has led to an increasing interest in the reading achievement of citizens. The public's concern has generated a wealth of data about reading and the techniques appropriate for its development. Because the failure to learn to read is frequently defined as a learning disability, information about reading becomes important to specialists in the field.

DYSLEXIA

Historically, reading failure was linked to adult aphasia and was called dyslexia, a medical term which connotes defective reading associated with a neurophysiological disorder. Dyslexia is a syndrome in which a child has unusual and persistent difficulty in learning the components of words and sentences, in integrating segments into words and sentences, and in learning other kinds of representational systems, such as telling time, directions, and seasons. Often the child has a history of delayed language development, and sometimes a history of soft neurological signs. Invariably, the child has concomitant problems in writing and spelling. The characteristics of dyslexics seemed to form a syndrome which Gerstmann (1940) described as consisting of problems in reading, space-form disability, left-to-right disorientation, dyscalculia (difficulty in math), dysgraphia (difficulty in writing), and finger agnosia (inability to meaningfully interpret stimuli gathered by the fingers).

Clinicians have reported various characteristics of the dyslexic child and these descriptions have gained a certain degree of acceptance within the field. Many of these characteristics appear, on closer study, not to be evidenced by these children, but nonetheless are still considered applicable.

Be that as it may, the composite picture of the child experiencing reading problems, according to clinical lore, is that he has perceptual, linguistic, motor, and social skills less mature or in some respects deviant from his peers. Clinicians report that by age nine or ten the language and speech of dyslexic children seem adequate, and aberrant behavior (mainly hyperactivity) has diminished. Reading, writing, and spelling problems are marked by persistent errors, which while common for young children, is not for older ones. Such problems as making reversals, omissions, or substitutions while reading, spelling, and writing are evident. Specifically, the dyslexic child is believed particularly likely to commit errors of spatial direction and sequential ordering. Directional confusion in reading results in prolonged difficulty in differentiating similar-looking letters (b-d, p-q). Difficulty in sequencing appears when the child reverses the position of letters and numbers (was-saw, 14-41). Oral reading is marked by slow, word-by-word reading. Arithmetic and spelling performance will mirror the problems in deciphering the reading code (Edgington and Blackmon, 1962). These particular difficulties have frequently been attributed to presumed difficulty in the child's visual perception.

It has also been noted that the dyslexic child is often confused about words relating to time and direction. For example, confusions include *up* for *down, go* for *stop, now* for *later,* and *first* for *last.* It should also be noted that it is believed that dyslexic children reflect their reading problems in their speech, and apparently have or did have a history of problems of auditory discrimination (Owen et al., 1971). Thus, dyslexics, who may or may not have accompanying articulation errors, may show peculiar grammatical constructions, wherein prefixes and suffixes are confused and distorted.

Since there are so many children committing so many errors of reading with so many people studying them, it is hardly surprising that a variety of proposals as to how such children should be subcategorized has been made. Rabinovitch and Ingram (1962) have proposed dividing reading retardation into three major diagnostic categories: (a) primary reading retardation, (b) brain injury with resultant reading retardation, and (c) secondary reading retardation. The primary reading retardation group evidences a number of symptoms. These include difficulties in both visual and auditory information processing (cannot translate letters and letter combinations into meaningful concepts, cannot translate sounds into letter symbols); left-right directional confusion with or without mixed laterality; broader language deficits (difficulties in name finding, imprecise articulation, and primitive syntax); a specific concept symbolization deficiency in orientation and body image problems. The primary reading retardation case is presumed to be neurologically based, often familial in origin, and related to parietal lobe dysfunction. The group with brain injury with resultant reading retardation is similar to adult aphasics and has a history of some kind of brain injury, such as birth trauma, encephalitis, or head injury. The secondary reading retardation group has the normal potential to read but fails to do so as a result of environmentally induced problems (e.g., poor schooling) or emotional-motivational problems (e.g., negativism, depression, anxiety, psychosis).

Boder (1971) suggests three categories of dyslexics. Group 1 is the *dysphonetic dyslexic*. In this group the child has a limited sight vocabulary in which he can easily read only a small number of words. When this child encounters a word he does not know, he is at a loss as to how to decipher it. He may try to guess, using the first or last letters of words, but essentially he has no phonics or word analysis skills. For this child, reading from context is easier than reading single words because his speaking vocabulary is sufficiently large to allow him to employ clues embedded in the context to infer the puzzling word.

The second category proposed by Boder is *dyseidetic dyslexic*. This child has difficulty remembering the appearance of letters or words. Apparently, such a child has difficulty recognizing the whole word and infers the letter or word from analysis of the component parts. Unlike children categorized as dysphonic dyslexic, these children read analytically by sounding out familiar and unfamiliar combinations of letters. The child can read phonetically a list of unknown words. This child may spell poorly, as he is likely to spell phonetically.

The third group is *mixed dysphonetic-dyseidetic dyslexic*. Boder refers to these children as "hard core" dyslexics. Such a child has neither the visual nor the auditory means to decipher the written word and may remain a nonreader unless he receives intensive help. Even then, remediation is slow and painful. The urge on the part of the child to withdraw from trying to read is quite understandable.

Common to all three types of dyslexics is difficulty in spelling. Boder indicates that normal readers can spell correctly to dictation about 70 to 100 percent of the words in their sight vocabulary. Dyslexic children in the dysphonetic and mixed groups usually spell no more than 40 percent of the words in their sight vocabulary.

Several theorists have suggested that children with reading problems can be divided into two groups, visual and auditory or visual and verbal dyslexia (Bateman, 1969; Kinsbourne, 1973; Lyle, 1969).

Johnson and Myklebust (1967) divide reading retardation into two major categories, visual and auditory dyslexia. Visual dyslexics have visual discrimination difficulties and confuse letters or words which appear similar. These children make discriminations about visual configurations which are accurate, but these are made slowly. Many of the children appear to make spatial and orientation errors by reversing and inverting letters. Visual memory shortcomings are presumed to affect the child's ability to follow and remember sequences of symbols.

The auditory dyslexic has difficulty making the association between the visual presentation and sounds heard, as well as discriminating sounds, particularly short vowels. For such children, thinking of rhymes or listening for parts of words and making associations to other words are very difficult tasks. Separating words into components or reuniting segments into wholes are also very difficult for these children, as are problems in remembering auditory symbols and stringing them into sequences. As a result, words may be mispronounced or distorted.

We have reviewed some of the important taxonomies proposed for viewing the dyslexic child. But noteworthy is the fact that children can be categorized in an infinite number of ways. In evaluating taxonomies, remember that good ones differ from poor ones on one basis, that group members should bear important similarities with one another as well as important differences from others not within their group. Whether a proposed taxonomy does in fact accomplish this is an empirical matter, not solved by armchair speculations. The verbal-visual taxonomies do appear to have some empirical support; that is, children do appear to respond in one or another of these fashions (Lyle, 1969). Whether the remaining proposals for such categorizations will be useful will be determined by future researchers. As of now, these proposals reflect hypotheses, not empirically validated groupings.

As the field of learning disabilities has expanded, reading problems have become a major focus of its practitioners. The magnitude of the reading difficulty necessary for a child to be defined and labeled as learning disabled or dyslexic has been reduced. More and more children with fewer and fewer problems now come within the province of the learning disability specialist. The child need not exhibit all or even any of the associated characteristics of dyslexia to be considered a severe reading problem. If a child in the first or second grade is six months or more below expected reading skills, or if an older child is one year or more behind in reading achievement (as defined by standardized tests), an evaluation and intervention program is justified.

READING PROBLEMS

A considerable number of United States citizens are illiterate. Sartain (1976) has suggested that approximately 13 percent to 15 percent of the population can be so considered, and if you employ as a criterion of literacy an ability to read and understand federal income tax directions, the percentage increases to 20 percent! While it is clear that, by definition, dyslexic children have grave difficulties in reading, it would be a mistake to conclude that all children who experience reading problems should be considered dyslexic; that is, as one whose reading problems are somehow tied to his internal states, either physiological or intellectual (Boyd, 1975). Sartain estimates that approximately 10 percent of the children in this country have difficulty in reading, and of those, about 2 percent should be considered "real" dyslexics. Because the basis used for discriminating dyslexic children from those who are having reading problems is quite unclear, the validity of Sartain's estimate is also unclear. But it is clear that the perspectives concerning reading problems do vary considerably from the learning disability specialist to the reading specialist.

Within the field of learning disabilities, definitions of dyslexia are well embedded within the medical model framework and the attempts to discover those personality and physiological correlates associated with reading difficulties. The focus then is upon the child. The reading experts, on the other hand, emphasize to a greater extent the role of events external to the child which might be associated with reading problems.

Sartain (1976), for example, indicates that the most common cause of reading disability is simply poor teaching. Additionally he suggests that poor home and community environments are important determinants of reading failures. Likewise, Boyd (1975) also cites either poor teaching or radical changes in instructional methods as reasons for the creation of reading problems. The focus is then upon the environment. While it may sound trite to write that environmental forces can play an important role in affecting reading achievement, this perspective should be kept in mind so that it is not neglected during the search for the personal characteristics of children with reading problems. It is easy to become immersed in the study of personality and social forces presumably affecting the child with reading problems, and thus neglect such environmental effects as instructional methods.

ETIOLOGY OF READING PROBLEMS

Many theories have attempted to account for failure to learn to read in the absence of mental retardation and environmental deprivation. The majority of explanations have dealt with presumed physical inadequacies or medical problems. Reading problems have been associated with genetics by Hermann (1959) and Critchley (1964); and with events before, during, and after birth by Kawi and Pasamanick (1959) and Ernhart, Graham, and Eichman (1963). Dukman, Ackerman, Clements, and Peters (1971), Geschwind (1968), and Wender (1971) offer the explanation of minimal cerebral dysfunction, although they differ in opinion as to the specific dysfunction involved. These theoretical stances have generated three major hypotheses to explain reading retardation. Reading retardation has been viewed as a result of either perceptual deficits, inadequate sensory integration, or specific deficiencies in verbal intelligence.

Perceptual Deficit Hypothesis

The most popular explanation for reading failure has been that children have difficulty in the perception (discrimination, memory, translation) of visual symbols. This emanated from Orton's (1937) observations of reading retardates who reversed letters in reading and writing. Proponents of this hypothesis focus upon directional confusion (Hermann, 1959); difficulties in figure-ground perception (Bender, 1938; Strauss and Lehtinen, 1947); deficits in visual analysis and synthesis (Birch and Belmont, 1964); perceptual motor problems (Cruickshank, Bentzen, Ratzeburg, and Tannhauser, 1961; Frostig, 1964; Kephart, 1963); and disturbances in optical control (Getman, 1965). Using the same behaviors, others have interpreted reading disabilities as reflections of deficits in attention or organization of visual arrays, verbal labeling, and verbal rehearsal (Hutson, 1974: Lyle, 1969; Lyle and Goyen, 1968; Vellutino, 1974).

To determine which factors might be related to reading retardation, Lyle (1969) did a factor analytic study of fifty-four retarded and fifty-four adequate readers, 6 to 12 years old. A battery of tests was administered to each child. Included were tests of reversals in oral reading and spelling; writing reversals (from dictation); the WISC; Graham and Kendall memory for designs; spelling and arithmetic tests, along with data concerning perceptual skills, lateral dominance, and hand-eye dominance. Lyle found that there were two distinct factors, unrelated to each other, associated with reading retardation. One set of related items consisted of tasks in which there was a strong perceptual component. Letter and sequence reversals in reading and writing, and to a lesser degree memory designs, were intercorrelated and associated with reading retardation. The second factor consisted of items which required verbal skills. These included spelling, arithmetic, arithmetic information, and coding subtests of the WISC. The verbal factor was also related to reading achievement. Lyle did not find reading disability related to mixed laterality, crossed hand-eye dominance, or the Gerstmann syndrome. Reading-disabled children below 8 years were particularly likely to demonstrate difficulties on the perceptual tasks. Among the older adequate and inadequate readers, perceptual disturbances were less discriminating.

Lyle found that not only did the younger deficit readers demonstrate inadequate performance on perceptual skills, but that they also had a history of delayed language acquisition. Lyle concluded that there are two major kinds of reading retardation. One is nonverbal and related to perceptual skills; the second is verbal. The perceptual factor appears to be more characteristic of younger retarded readers, the verbal factor more characteristic of older retarded readers.

Programmatic research to investigate the perceptual skills involved in reading has been undertaken by Lyle and Goyen (1968), Goyen and Lyle (1971 a,b; 1973) and Vellutino and associates (Vellutino, Pruzek, Steger, and Meshoulan, 1973; Vellutino, Steger, and Kandel, 1972). Lyle and Goyen

(1968) investigated visual recognition of forty second- and third-graders, twenty of whom had reading deficits, defined by reading at least nine months below grade level. Through the use of a tachistoscope, children were presented with letters of the alphabet commonly confused by deficit readers, with fifteen lines simpler in form than letters and fifteen two-dimensional line drawings which represented the contours of four-letter words. The child viewed one figure and then had to indicate which one he had seen from a multiple choice response card. Children's responses were obtained under three conditions: immediately following the tachistoscopic presentation, after a short delay, and with three consecutively presented stimuli. In the latter condition, children were required to indicate the order of presentation. To prohibit verbal labeling or rehearsal and kinesthetic rehearsal, the children had to clasp their hands and recite multiplication tables aloud before the presentation and while waiting for the response card. Children were tested on several occasions.

The results were that the retarded readers performed significantly more poorly on all the tests than did the adequate readers, although the magnitude of differences was related to the age of the children. While retarded readers committed more of all kinds of errors, it was the young retarded readers who erred the most. Lyle and Goyen interpreted these results to indicate that young retarded readers do have a perceptual deficit.

Lyle and Goyen (1974) compared the performance of twenty-one retarded and twenty-one nonretarded readers, 6 and 7 years old, on speed of processing information, perceptual discrimination, and short-term memory. Reading retardation was defined as at least 9 months below age level for 6-year-olds and at least one year below age level for 7-year-olds. Children briefly viewed tachistoscopic presentations of thirty pairs of rectangular shapes; one-half were the same, the remaining different from each other. Some children viewed both items of the pair simultaneously, thus short-term memory was not involved. Other children viewed each item of the pair separated by a two-second delay. A third group viewed the items separated by a seven-second delay. The results replicated earlier studies (Lyle and Goyen, 1968; Goyen and Lyle, 1971 a,b), indicating that retarded readers experience difficulty in visual recognition tasks which require rapid information processing. When stimuli are presented rapidly, retarded readers have more difficulty than adequate readers in subsequently recognizing these stimuli. It should be noted, however, that retarded readers performed as well as adequate readers when judgments had to be made on identical pairs. Differences between adequate and inadequate readers resulted when the items of the pair were different; retarded readers were more likely to judge the items as equivalent. It appears that poor readers either have difficulty in making perceptual discriminations or they have a verbal bias which leads them to report stimuli as equivalent.

There was no evidence that retarded readers have deficits in short-term memory. Additionally, there were no effects found for the administration of rewards for competent performance (Goyen and Lyle, 1971 a, b).

Learning to read has been compared to mastery of a paired-associate learning task. In studies of paired-associate learning, subjects must learn to combine two stimuli so that upon presentation of one the person can recall the second. In reading, the child must learn to associate two stimuli, visual symbols with their respective sounds. To study the relationship of visual recognition memory to children's performance on a paired-associate task, Samuels and Anderson (1973) divided children into two groups, those with good and those with poor visual recognition memory. The children were then presented with two paired-associate learning tasks, one presumed to be easy and the second difficult. The child's intelligence test scores, visual recognition memory, and performance on the easy paired-associate task were unrelated. Performance of the hard paired-associate task was related to visual recognition memory and to vocabulary and total reading scores on the California Achievement test.

The evidence for perceptual problems underlying reading deficiencies is quite mixed. Vellutino and colleagues (Vellutino, Steger, DeSetto, and Phillips, 1975; Vellutino, Harding, Phillips, and Steger, 1975; Vellutino, Pruzek, Steger, Meshoulan, 1973; Vellutino, Steger, and Kandel, 1972) have failed to find, in spite of considerable effort, that the reading-impaired child suffers from perceptual deficits. Perhaps failure to find perceptual differences between adequate and inadequate readers reflects methodological flaws, inadequate sample definitions, or a variety of other factors. Nonetheless, the consistent findings of Vellutino and colleagues that reading-disabled children do not differ from adequate readers on perceptual discriminations raises serious questions as to the adequacy of the perceptual deficit hypothesis.

Vellutino and colleagues argue against the perceptual deficit hypothesis of reading dysfunction. In place of the perceptual deficit hypothesis, they suggest reading difficulties are the result of the child's failure to label perceptual experiences and that the child's cognitive operations are faulty.

At first blush, the results of the Vellutino and the Lyle and Goyen studies appear to be contradictory. Lyle and Goyen find evidence that perceptual deficits may be characteristic of young deficit readers but not older retarded readers. The Vellutino et al. studies often employed children somewhat older than the children in the Lyle and Goyen studies. Second, the differences in presentations in the studies may affect children's ability to employ mnemonic devices. Lyle and Goyen used rapid tachistoscopic presentations and in one case (1968) prohibited the children from employing their mnemonic devices by requiring them to clasp their hands and recite multiplication tables. In the Vellutino et al. studies the children might have been able to use their own cueing systems. These methodological differences might serve to mask perceptual differences in deficit and adequate readers.

The role played by visual perception has been an elusive and perhaps exaggerated one. The results of several studies indicate that auditory, rather than visual, perception may be particularly important in facilitating reading.

Kinsbourne (1973) administered a battery of tests of auditory and visual processing and associative learning. The visual tests measured the child's ability to discriminate forms; the auditory test required the child to repeat a pair of speech sounds, repeat three phoneme series, and indicate whether two words sounded the same or different. The associative part of the battery included having the child learn a nonsense word which was to be associated with a shape.

The test was administered to several hundred first-grade children, and then readministered to them in their classrooms at varying times during the next two years. These items were correlated with the children's scores on the Metropolitan Reading and Arithmetic tests. Kinsbourne found that the factor which discriminated good from poor readers was the increase in the performance on the *auditory* tests from the first to the second testing session. Neither performance nor improvement on the visual tests were predictive of reading achievement.

Rosner (1973) produced results very similar to those of Kinsbourne. First- and second-grade children were administered a visual analysis test, which required the child to copy designs, and an auditory analysis test, in which the child is asked to listen to a meaningful word and then repeat it with a sound omitted. Scores on these tests were related to scores on the Stanford Achievement Tests. It was found that the auditory analysis test was related to word reading, paragraph meaning, spelling, and word study skills. There was not a significant relationship between the visual analysis test and reading scores, although the visual analysis test did correlate with arithmetic scores. Similar difficulties with auditory rather than visual stimuli by dyslexic children have been reported by Estes and Huizinga (1974) and Zigmond (1966).

On the basis of the evidence, it would seem that the role of visual perceptual dysfunctions in producing reading retardation has probably been overestimated. There is evidence that such dysfunctions may characterize the young child, but even that evidence is mixed. Language, attention, auditory processes all come to bear upon the acquisition of reading, and any failures in such acquisition may reflect these processes. Indeed, there is evidence of the role of auditory processes in affecting reading performance and no doubt future work in the area of reading will further delineate their role.

Deficits in Cross-modal Information Processing

A second popular explanation for reading failure is the difficulty in integrating auditory and visual information. Several researchers have found that reading-disabled youngsters are less competent than adequate readers in making associations between auditory and visual stimuli. This area was first initiated by the studies of Birch and Belmont (1964), Blank and Bridger (1966), and Blank, Weider, and Bridger (1968). Senf and Freundl (1971) and Vande Voort and Senf (1973) have offered evidence that disabled readers were less able than adequate readers on a variety of tasks which required associating visual and verbal stimuli.

As has been pointed out in Chapter 7, Information Processing, many studies concerned with cross-modal integration have failed to control for intrasensory processing or for the verbal demands placed upon the child. The same general comment can be made regarding such studies which employ the dyslexic child as subject. Studies which determine that one group of children is worse than another on either visual or auditory processing cannot infer that one group has a problem in cross-modal integration, because the difficulty might be attributable to failure in intrasensory processing. Zigmond (1966) found that 9- to 12-year-old dyslexic boys performed significantly worse than nondyslexic ones on various auditory tests and in paired-associate tasks, which, presumably, required cross-modal integration of inputs, although groups were comparable in the visual tasks. The failure of the dyslexic child to perform adequately on the paired-associate task might be due either to (a) auditory processing difficulties or (b) cross-modal integration problems.

Cross-modal integration is likely to be facilitated by the linguistic development of the child. The child who can connect, through labels, the visual and auditory signals is probably more likely to make an adequate response than one who does not or cannot apply such labels. Insofar as the linguistic development of the learning-disabled child is likely to be different and less adequate than that of nondisabled children, differences in cross-modal integration among dyslexic children may reflect a linguistic deficit rather than a sensory processing difference. Indeed, in one study which attempted to remove the verbal components involved in most tests of intra- and intersensory processing, no differences between the dyslexic and nondyslexic children were found (Vellutino, Steger, and Pruzek, 1973).

Recently, there has been some tendency to move away from concepts involving intra- and intersensory auditory and visual processing toward conceptualizing stimuli as either involving spatial or temporal features (Blank and Bridger, 1966; Freides, 1974). Freides has argued that separating stimuli according to their spatial and temporal nature may be more efficacious than focusing upon whether the stimuli have a visual or auditory component. He suggests that the visual system is best suited for processing stimuli with spatial features, while the auditory system is best able to process stimuli with temporal features. He suggests that with age these features of the auditory and visual systems become even more specialized and thus there is a diminution rather than an integration of modalities. Future learning disability specialists should be sensitive to the spatial-temporal as well as the auditory-visual features of the tasks confronting children.

Verbal Deficits

A third explanation for reading retardation is that poor readers have a deficit in verbal skills. There is both direct and indirect evidence to support this view. Indirect evidence stems from the studies of information processing and of the developmental histories of retarded readers. In the information processing studies, there are invariably group differences in favor of normal readers when the experimental task requires the child to process auditorily presented linguistic information, and rarely are there group differences when the task is strictly one of visual recognition demanding no linguistic skills. Studies which investigate the developmental histories of retarded readers report a very high incidence of linguistic developmental difficulties and delays in the acquisition of language.

On the basis of the evidence, it appears reasonable to assume that reading reflects a two-step process. In the beginning, reading may be highly dependent upon certain perceptual skills, such as discriminations among phonemes and graphemes. After adequate discriminations are learned, competent reading may require more advanced conceptual skills. The question remains whether we are talking about two groups of children with reading deficits: one group who have perceptual problems but who may be academically successful when they learn the discriminations, and a second group who are successful initially but experience school difficulties because of verbal deficits. The data suggest that there is only one group of children, a group who demonstrates a history of difficulty with reading, or decoding processes, even at a young age (Owen et al., 1971).

Whether or not reading acquisition is a two-step process which the reading-disabled child cannot master, there is evidence to support the hypothesis that reading retardation is associated with language difficulties. Hutson (1974) has provided a summary of this evidence. She points out that language is a central factor in auditory and visual perception of complex stimuli, including words; that verbal mediation serves as an important facilitator in dealing with such stimuli; that disabled readers are generally found to have lower verbal intelligence scores than competent readers and that studies of language skill differences among good and poor readers find differences in the areas of phonemics, semantics, and syntax, always to the detriment of the poor readers. Hutson concludes:

> Although the ability to read, as a multifaceted phenomenon, is potentially subject to interference from several sources, a principal dimension along which good and poor readers differ is language skill. These differences are not always apparent at the lower levels of difficulty, but become evident in tasks of sufficient complexity to tap differences in the use of language, awareness of language, and in knowledge of more advanced language patterns (p. 4).

The verbal problems of children destined to have reading difficulties are evidenced at the onset of these difficulties. Indeed, the frequency of children with both early verbal and reading problems led Rabinovitch and Ingram (1962) to propose a subcategory to the classification of dyslexia, primary reading retardation. As previously mentioned, Owen et al. (1971) also found that reading difficulties were associated with early problems with language development. Likewise, DeHirsh, Jansky, and Langford (1966) developed a battery of tests, many of which contained items tapping language skills, in order to predict which child might have reading difficulties. The test, given to kindergarten children, did have some success in prediction, although it also yielded many false negatives and positives. DeHirsch and his colleagues felt that the reading, writing, and spelling difficulties of the school failures they tested reflect a comprehensive verbal-symbolic disturbance.

The evidence pertaining to the correlation of verbal or language problems with reading difficulties is not limited to studies of the young child. The relationship holds for older children as well. Blank, Weider, and Bridger (1968) found that reading retarded and nonretarded first-grade children differed in their performances on tasks which required verbal coding, with retarded readers performing less adequately than nonretarded ones. Vellutino (1974) summarizes research conducted on differences in phonemic analysis by good and poor readers. Generally, it is found that normal readers are linguistically more sophisticated, as they have greater verbal fluency and better syntax than poor readers. When defective and adequate readers read aloud, the defective readers commit more errors by repeating nonsense words as "real" words, and when they err in reading "real" words, they err by distorting the vowels, particularly those in the middle or final positions of the words. Vogel (1974) compared good and poor readers, ages 7 and 8, on their performances on a variety of tests which were administered orally and often required spoken responses from the child. Again, it was found that poor readers were less adequate than good readers in their language skills. To make matters worse, there is evidence to suggest that language handicaps of the poor reader will slow his learning of meaningful sentences. Weinstein and Rabinovitch (1971) divided fourth-graders into two groups, good and poor readers. The children were then given a paired-associate task and a task in which they had to repeat four sentences, two structured and two unstructured. The structured sentences were constructed by inserting a word in certain positions in a sentence. The unstructured sentences consisted of random insertions of this word into the sentence. The groups did not differ in their learning of the paired-associate test. They were able to learn the correct verbal response to the stimulus word. The groups differed, however, in their learning of the sentences. Good readers learned structured sentences faster than poor readers, and good readers learned the structured sentences faster than the unstructured sentences. Poor readers learned the structured and unstructured sentences at the same rate. The results suggested that for adequate readers, good syntax either facilitated the learning or bad syntax disrupted it. For the poor reader, syntax apparently failed to make any difference in their learning; they learned as if they were unaware of it. To compound the problem, Freidlander and Cohen de Lara (1973) found that children with relatively poor language skills were more likely to prefer distorted and relatively unintelligible speech than children with good linguistic skills, and children with poor language skills may be less likely to attend to meaningful language inputs.

The evidence concerning perceptual deficits and cross-modal integration as important processes in the production of reading difficulties has, at best, received rather equivocal empirical support. The data on verbal deficits and reading problems is much stronger. There is evidence that children who have difficulty learning to read have language deficits, and this relationship has been found in studies using a wide variety of language measures with relatively mildly handicapped youngsters. These findings may have important implications for efforts at early detection of learning problems. We know that language development undergoes tremendous growth during the preschool years, but it is also becoming apparent that language development continues well into the elementary school years (Palermo and Molfese, 1972). Such development has been linked to school achievement. In detecting or predicting learning disability during the preschool years, that is, in predicting reading achievement, it is very likely that attention should be withdrawn from the study of simple perceptual and motor skills and be directed instead toward a finer analysis of the child's language abilities.

Reading retardation has been studied from the perspectives of deficits in perception, sensory information integration, and verbal abilities. It is clear that problems in learning to read are multifaceted, as studies have demonstrated differences between retarded and adequate readers in various reading skills, using children of varying ages and severity of reading inadequacy and varying techniques of measurement.

The samples of children used to study reading retardation have ranged from 5 to 11 years of age, and, not surprisingly, the results found are somewhat dependent upon the age of the sample used. It appears that young children who have reading difficulties may have perceptual ones as well, particularly if the perceptual tasks involve auditory stimuli. Whether their faulty performance is due to a perceptual or linguistic problem remains to be seen. The younger child may do more poorly on tests which presume to tap more purely visual perceptual processes, but the evidence is mixed.

When differences are found between good and poor readers at an early age, they are differences of amount, not type. The patterns of errors made by retarded and adequate young readers have been found to be the same, except that poor readers make more errors than adequate ones (Lyle and Goyen, 1974; Kinsbourne, 1973). Apparently, it is not until the child is well into his primary school years that patterns of errors distinguish the good from the poor reader. The limited amount of information available suggests that good readers make more errors than poor ones when the stimuli used are somewhat familiar (Vellutino, 1977; Willows, 1974). It is likely that good readers allow intrusions of errors because of the overlearning of words which appear similar to the stimuli. Poor readers have weaker habits for omitting these erroneous but similar words, and thus intrusion errors are not likely to occur.

One of three major hypotheses advanced concerning reading deficiencies, which suggests the presence of verbal deficits, has received considerable empirical support. Whether the researcher looks to phonemic analysis, syntax, comprehension, or the use of verbal labels in learning a task, the retarded reader has a more difficult time than the adequate reader. There is little support for the perceptual deficit hypothesis, although this conclusion is somewhat dependent upon the definition of perception. There are certain perceptual tasks which discriminate good and poor young readers, but there are many which do not. It is difficult in light of these mixed results to believe that as a group poor readers have a gross visual or visual-motor defect when these inadequacies are only occasionally found and are dependent upon the methodology involved. While the hypothesis might be intuitively compelling, the evidence is not.

TEACHING READING

How shall we teach children to read? No single approach in twenty-seven years of research on teaching reading has overcome or eliminated reading disabilities in children at the first-grade level (Lohnes, 1973).

Studies of teaching methods reveal a quagmire of unrelated theories, methods, and poor research designs. Chall (1970) summarizes research from 1910 to 1965 and Diederich (1973) from 1960 to 1970. Chall points out that in many studies the authors fail to indicate how children were divided into experimental and control groups, how much time was given to reading treatments, how teachers were selected, whether the teachers, in fact, taught the method they were assigned to teach, and, finally, failed to specify the contents of the teaching program. Diederich points out that there is more research on reading than on any other subject taught in school, more than 1,000 studies each year. In spite of this, there are *no* important facts about methods of teaching reading which are incontestable.

Moreover, the research on teacher characteristics associated with good reading programs has likewise failed to yield many results. The results lead to the conclusions that teacher training may well be unrelated to teacher effectiveness and that bright, friendly people are better at teaching reading than dull, disagreeable ones (Diederich, 1973).

While the data pertaining to the best method of teaching reading have yielded little fruit, there is a good deal of evidence to suggest that most children do learn to read, and do so under a variety of teaching techniques. For instance, Graeme and Harris (1970) used dictionary skills to teach word recognition to retarded readers, Hollingsworth (1970) taught reading by having children read aloud and in unison with the teacher (impress method), and Humphrey used a game approach in increasing children's reading skills. There is no doubt that reading can be taught and that disabled readers can be helped (Balow, 1965).

The issue is not whether children can be taught reading—after all there are millions who can read—but just what is the best method to do so. For years there has been controversy, not only in the United States but elsewhere, as to how to best teach reading (Samuels and Schachter, in press). The controversy has focused on two very different approaches, the holistic and the subskill approaches, which reflect quite different notions of the nature of learning to read.

The holistic view, characterized by the works of Goodman and Goodman (1976), Goodman and Burke (1972), and Smith (1973), is based on the idea that reading and speaking are both processes of meaningful communication; that reading involves the obtaining of meaning from someone else's written word. The unit of instruction should be that which carries meaning, be it phrases, sentences, or paragraphs. It is also believed that the teacher should employ the child's own language and experiences to initiate reading instruction, thus facilitating the communication of the written material. The approach of Goodman and colleagues to teaching reading has been well spelled out (Goodman and Burke, 1972), but as yet, studies concerning the efficacy of this approach have not been published. There is no doubt, however, that some will be soon.

The subskill perspective, represented by the work of Samuels and his co-workers (Samuels, 1973; Samuels and Jeffrey, 1966; Samuels and Schachter, in press), approaches reading as a complex skill comprised of various subskills which must all be initially mastered before adequate reading is achieved. Advocates of this method believe that these subskills must be first taught, mastered, and integrated before one becomes concerned about meaningfulness of the material. While the holistic approach accepts the notion of subskill mastery, supporters of this method believe that these subskills are important only when the child evidences problems in understanding meaningful material.

Although the best method for teaching reading is still unknown, we can say with some assuredness that programs which include phonics instruction appear to yield better results than programs which employ whole-word methods (Diederich, 1973). A classic study of reading methods was conducted by Bliesmer and Yarborough (1965). Ten reading programs were compared at the first-grade level. Five of the programs used phonics, emphasizing letter-sound relationships and pronunciation rules to synthesize whole words. Five programs used the analytic approach, emphasizing teaching many whole words recognized on sight. Later the children learned to analyze the sounds in the words. The assignment of teaching method to classroom was attained by having principals draw lots. Teachers were then randomly assigned to method, but no inexperienced teachers were included. Intensive training and supervision throughout the year were given to help the teachers. The amount of reading time each day was specified to be no more than 45 minutes. First-graders were randomly assigned to rooms and given the Metropolitan Reading Readiness and California Test of Mental Maturity at the start and the Stanford Achievement tests at the end of the treatment. The Stanford tests included measures of word reading, paragraph meaning, vocabulary, spelling, and word study skills. The achievement of children in the five phonic groups was compared to that of the five groups of children who received a whole-word method technique. Of the 125 comparisons made, the skill level of the phonically trained children exceeded those who received the whole-word method in ninety-three instances. In no case did the whole-word method show itself to be superior to the phonics technique.

Similar conclusions were reached by Gurren and Hughes (1965) after a review of competent research studies comparing children who had intensive phonics instruction with those who did not. All the studies yielded results which favored the phonetic approach to the whole-word method. The phonics approach has also been urged by Bateman (1969).

Samuels and Schachter (in press) have suggested specific components of reading programs which have been thought of as outstanding. These authors identified these components as including: clearly stated objectives which were achievable; teachers trained in the instructional method; instruction administered on an individual or small group basis; highly organized and preplanned lessons relating to the objectives; both teachers and children devoting considerable time and effort to instruction; parental involvement; the use of additional personnel when needed; the continuous assessment of the children's progress. Additionally, Samuels and Schachter indicate that other critical variables may include actual time spent on reading instruction, high expectations for the children's performances, the utilization of positive reinforcements, and extensive pupil evaluations.

Teaching Dyslexics

Aside from the emphasis on phonics, other teaching techniques suitable for aiding the dyslexic child have been offered. Bryant (1965) has suggested some important principles that should be borne in mind when dealing with reading-disabled children. The first principle is based upon the observation that dyslexic children have difficulty in retaining the detailed image of a word. They may recognize a word on one line and fail to recognize it on the next. Details of word configurations need to be explicated frequently. Writing and tracing the word might be useful insofar as such activities require the child to attend to the details of the word. In light of this suggestion, it should be noted that Johnson and Myklebust (1967) indicate a variety of exercises that might facilitate the child's skill in discriminating differences between the shapes of letters and words.

The second principle offered by Bryant is based upon the rather well-documented evidence that dyslexic children have difficulty in learning the connection between graphemes and phonemes. Bryant suggests teaching these associations one or a few at a time until they are well learned. He further argues that the teacher should use words rather than isolated sounds or syllables.

A third suggestion by Bryant is that the child should not be allowed to practice incorrect responses. The incorrect response which is learned will interfere with subsequent performance. A fourth suggestion pertains to teaching discriminations. When the child cannot discriminate letters or sounds which are similar, Bryant recommends teaching one until it is well learned before introducing learning trials on the second element. The fifth suggestion is that there should be frequent reviews of the child's reading skills. Improvements may be short-lived and teachers should be alerted to the possibilities of worsening performances by the child and the need for follow-up remediation.

Information Coding

Studies of the verbal coding deficits of dyslexic children point to other helpful remediation techniques. The results of the studies lead to the inference that the efficacy of many teaching efforts involving dyslexic children might be enhanced if instructions on how to code and organize information are included. Strategies for dealing with and coding the information essential to reading may be critical in aiding the dyslexic child to read. Both the clinical observations of Frostig (1972) and the experimental results of Palkes, Stewart, and Kahana (1968) and Pakles, Stewart, and Freedman (1971) suggest that the performance of children can be effectively altered by the use of verbal instructions as to how to proceed in learning and by teaching the child to explicate his course of action for himself.

The data to date suggest that teaching the child verbal or other coding strategies for learning may well help him learn to read. But dyslexic children are a heterogeneous lot. The large individual differences among this group called dyslexic indicate that children will not respond equally to particular strategies and that the future will bring further refinements of classification and treatment of reading-disabled children. The now popular area of study called ATI (aptitude by treatment interaction) reflects efforts in this direction. Different coding strategies may be necessary for different children. For example, Levin (1973) and Levin, Devine-Hawkins, Kerst, and Guttman (1974) have provided some evidence regarding the interaction of individual differences and the efficacy of various encoding techniques. Levin found that visual imagery instructions (e.g., think of a picture which might flow from the text) did not aid children who were reading more than one year below grade level. Visual imagery instructions did help children who were not this deficient.

In a second study, Levin et al. (1974) found that children who could learn words best by viewing their pictorial representations would also demonstrate better learning on a reading comprehension task when given instructions to use visual imagery than when they were given instructions to read the words. The children who did poorly on learning words from pictures did not benefit from the imagery instructions. These authors concluded that there is a large group of children for whom the instructional strategy concerning encoding will make a large difference. These authors have made a significant contribution in initiating studies which will aid in identifying those individual characteristics and instructional variables which should be joined in aiding children's reading competence.

A particularly interesting set of studies was reported by Lovitt and Hansen (1976a, b) concerning a reading training program for dyslexic boys. What makes these studies interesting is that they employed as reinforcements for reading improvement the opportunity for the poor readers to omit further studying of reading lessons! In their studies the first step was to determine the correct reading levels for seven boys, ages 8 to 12. The diagnostic phase employed as reading material the Informal Reading Inventory and the Lippincott Basic Reading series. The instructional phase employed the Lippincott series. To determine the boys' reading level prior to the introduction of the instructional technique, the boys' reading behaviors were assessed across several days and across several levels of difficulty. The investigators hoped to place the boys at a reading level which would motivate them to further work without creating much frustration. Boys were placed at the reading level where they demonstrated an ability to meet three criteria: read forty-five to sixty-five words per minute; have an average incorrect rate of reading words between four and eight words per minute; and an average comprehension score of 50 percent to 75 percent correct on test-related questions.

The instructional technique was as follows. Children orally read 500 words each day and responded in writing to twenty to thirty comprehension questions. The reading material was divided into four sections. When students' performance on any one section was found to be 25 percent better over a seven-day period than their performance on the diagnostic tests, the student was allowed to skip the rest of the material on that section of reading and begin the next section. When students failed to increase their reading performance 25 percent, they were given contingent drills. Given the student's particular problems, he might practice reading more quickly, or more accurately, or with more comprehension. The authors thus refer to their program as the "skip and drill" method.

Lovitt and Hansen report that after exposure to the program, five of the seven students were reading at grade level within six months, and all were reading at that level by the end of the school year. Since the results could be attributed either to the skip method, to the drill method, or to the combination of the two, these investigators further studied the question of whether the skip and drill combination or simply the drill or the skip components of the training accounted for the results. They reported that the skip and drill and the skip methods produced the greatest improvements in reading rates and reading errors, although the children who received the drill-only treatment showed the greatest improvement in comprehension of the reading material.

It seems, from these results, that children with reading problems may well be "turned off" to redundancy in reading materials and that reading gains might be considerably facilitated by eliminating such redundancy in their reading lessons. It should be noted, however, that the design of their studies was such as to not include control groups which would indicate just what the students might have learned irrespective of the treatment.

DYSCALCULIA

Mathematics is a specialized and abbreviated language, a highly technical jargon. Mathematical constructions are only symbols which have meanings in terms of relationships. Numbers have no substance and mathematical data are arbitrary sounds or marks called symbols. "Behind these symbols lie the boldest, purest, coolest abstractions mankind has ever made" (Langer, 1957, p. 21). *Dyscalculia* is the term used to describe difficulty in mastering mathematical concepts and/or computations. Like dyslexia, the difficulty has been linked to a breakdown in the functioning or development of the central nervous system.

In general, it is thought that children who have difficulty learning to read do not have comparable difficulties learning mathematics and conversely, children having difficulty learning mathematics will not necessarily have problems with reading (Johnson and Myklebust, 1967; Kosc, 1974). There have been attempts made to develop a taxonomy of learning disability syndromes in which dyscalculia represented a syndrome distinct from dyslexia. There is evidence that performance on different kinds of readiness measures differentially predict children's subsequent performance on reading and mathematics tests (Rosner, 1973). At the same time, however, there may well be an overlap of skills necessary for obtaining competence in both reading and mathematics so that it is unlikely that these problems are entirely independent. Our understanding of dyscalculia is greatly complicated by the interrelationship of the comprehension of mathematics with other language or symbolic systems (Dienes, 1963; Piaget, 1952).

Chalfant and Scheffelin (1969) summarize the basic skills needed by the child to successfully undergo the various stages of mathematics learning. One essential characteristic is intelligence, or those skills tapped by intelligence tests. General intelligence accounts for the major variance in mathematics learning. A second major factor appears to be spatial ability, "ability to comprehend the nature of elements within a visual stimulus pattern" (p. 121). The child must know up and down, right and left, that four objects are four objects, whether in a row, column, or pile, or indicated by the symbol 4. A third factor associated with mathematics learning is the child's verbal ability, which may be another way of saying his intelligence. Mathematics is a form of language and any language development deficit may affect the learning of mathematical symbols and operations. The child needs to be able to label and use words related to magnitude, conservation, time, and numbers. A fourth skill is the child's approach to problem solving. The method by which the child compares and organizes the data prior to the solution of the problem, be it presented in verbal, arithmetical, or spatial forms, will critically affect the product given by the child. Finally, Chalfant and Scheffelin suggest neurophysiological processes may impede the acquisition of mathematical operations.

As we have so often seen in relation to other problems labeled learning disabilities, considerable attention has been paid to the role of neurophysiological deficits in producing dyscalculia. Here, as elsewhere, theory by analogy was attempted. If brain-damaged adults have problems with mathematics, then children with problems with mathematics might be brain damaged.

Clinical Observations of Adults

Most of the research on dyscalculia stems from clinical studies of adults who have suffered brain trauma. In 1919, Henschen observed that number blindness (i.e., a failure to recognize a number) could occur without word blindness and vice versa. Henschen defined calculation as a mental process which requires a series of thinking tasks, so that dyscalculia could result from lesions in the occipital, parietal, frontal, and temporal lobes of the cortex (Chalfant and Scheffelin, 1969). In his work with brain-damaged adults, Goldstein (1948) also noted the presence of dyscalculia, apparently with sufficient frequency to propose subcategories of this problem. For many years, it was erroneously believed that dyscalculia was one part of the Gerstmann syndrome, a syndrome associated with known brain damage (Benton, 1959). The historical linkage between dyscalculia and brain damage has been a relatively long one.

Given this history, it is not surprising that there have been attempts to link dyscalculia empirically to brain damage in adults, apparently with some success. One type of dyscalculia suggested is parietal dyscalculia. According to Luria (1966), adults suffering from parietal lobe trauma and dyscalculia would exhibit the following problems: incorrect alignment of one row of figures under another, inability to memorize numbers, particularly those with more than one digit, inability to arrange numbers in the order of their magnitude, inability to count backwards, inability to enumerate odd or even numbers in a series. The person may also have difficulty manipulating operational symbols (e.g., plus, minus), because they may be unable to comprehend the symbol and/or execute the reading and/or writing of figures.

A somewhat different parietal dyscalculia has been described by Luria (1966) and Goldstein (1948). Insofar as traumatic involvement with both the parietal and occipital lobes is presumed, Goldstein employed the term *visual agnosia*. Individuals so afflicted have been characterized as having a loss of spatial organization and visual discrimination and as being unable to copy or reproduce the direction of a symbol or the entirety of a geometric design. Paradoxically, these individuals are said to understand the concept of number, the nature of groups, or methods of calculation. It is believed that the closer the lesion to the occipital lobe, the more visual in nature the problems. Thus, the patient may have particular problems in understanding the directionality of symbols. For example, the patient might have great difficulty in understanding carats, the signs indicating more than or less than.

When lesions occur in the other sections of the brain, other forms of dyscalculia may occur. When the lesion occurs in the frontal or frontal temporal regions of the cortex, there is associated disintegration of skilled movements and complex intellectual operations. Calculations may be slow and the repertoire of strategies might be greatly diminished. Addition may be carried out, but slowly and by counting the series one element at a time. The most simple multiplication must be relearned, often without accompanying insight as to the correctness of the answer, much less alternative strategies for arriving at that answer. The operations of computation require laborious effort (Chalfant and Scheffelin, 1969).

More recently, there has been an emphasis upon the functions of the left and right sides of the brain as they may affect dyscalculia (Cohn, 1961; Curry, 1966; McFie, Piercy, and Zangwill, 1950). It has been increasingly realized that it is too simplistic to assume that one side or the other of the brain would have great influence over the occurrence of dyscalculia. Curry (1966), after summarizing the literature relevant to this issue, indicates that verbal functions are mediated in the left hemisphere, nonverbal functions in the right hemisphere. To the extent that nonverbal functions are facilitated by verbal skills, the left hemisphere has an important role in coping with nonverbal stimuli. The right hemisphere is dominant in the process, but probably only slightly so.

These works with adults served to provide both important information concerning dyscalculia and brain damage in adults and to form the underpinning of analogies to the child with deficits in mathematical competence.

Observations of Children

The same general concerns dictating the observations of adults with dyscalculia guided that of children with similar difficulties. Problems with mathematics were considered to reflect brain dysfunctions which differed in nature from those involved in disrupting verbal development. It was presumed that dyscalculia reflected disturbances in the nondominant hemisphere of the brain, while dyslexia was an outcropping of trauma to the left hemisphere of the brain (Johnson and Myklebust, 1967).

Children with dyscalculia have been variously described. Kalaski (1967) describes such children as having difficulties with spatial relationships. For example, they may have trouble learning the concepts of up and down, right and left. They are described as having difficulty understanding size relationships, and if this is so, they will have trouble mastering number concepts. Motor disinhibition is also said to characterize such children, and impulsivity, which interferes with their ability to manipulate objects in the environment and consequently to master basic concepts of mathematics. Left-right confusions are said to be evident in such children as well as habits of perseveration (an inability to shift psychological sets). Finally, Kalaski indicates that dyscalculic children will have language difficulties which prevent adequate mastery of mathematics. Johnson and Myklebust (1967) have described the dyscalculic child as having difficulty learning to count meaningfully, master cardinal and ordinal systems, perform arithmetic operations, and visualize clusters of objects as groups. They also suggest that such children find it difficult to associate auditory and visual symbols, to understand the conservation of quantity, to remember sequences of arithmetic steps, and to choose principles for problem-solving activities, to name but a few. At the same time, these children are described as having good auditory and verbal abilities.

Kosc (1974) has presented an extended taxonomy of dyscalculia in which he suggests the following terms be adopted:

1. *Verbal dyscalculia:* Wherein the child has difficulty understanding mathematics when presented orally or under conditions in which a verbal response is required.
2. *Practognostic dyscalculia:* Wherein the child is unable to adequately manipulate objects, symbolic or otherwise, for purposes of arithmetic.
3. *Lexical dyscalculia:* This condition refers to problems in reading mathematical symbols (e.g., numbers, operation signs).
4. *Graphical dyscalculia:* This refers to a difficulty in writing mathematical symbols.
5. *Ideognostical dyscalculia:* A problem in which the child has difficulties in understanding mathematical ideas and relationships, and in doing mental calculations.
6. *Operational dyscalculia:* In this condition, the child is said to have difficulty in carrying out operations. Thus the child may add rather than subtract, divide rather than multiply.

It is distressing to report that the amount of systematically gathered information on childhood dyscalculia is appallingly small. The characteristics enumerated in this section have been based upon clinical observation and rarely demonstrated by a more rigorous method. Indeed, even the data presented by Kosc were such as to suggest that distinct types of dyscalculia were not found. Moreover, the frequency of problems experienced by dyscalculic children, whether in spatial orientation, time sense, or what have you, have rarely been compared to those of the nondisabled child. Aside from clinical observations, we are quite in the dark about the nature of dyscalculia.

The lack of data concerning mathematics disorders may reflect cultural values, values which consider mathematics achievement of less concern than reading achievement. Cawley (in press) reports that children's failure in mathematics is extremely frequent but that such failures have not generated much interest among mathematics specialists. Cawley notes that these specialists have been more interested in preparing students for college than generating effective learning techniques for "slow learners."

Like those who specialize in reading, experts in mathematics attribute failure to achieve in this area to causes different from those usually considered by special educators. According to Cawley, math educators attribute failure in mathematics to the complexity of the material, the method of instruction, and the mastery of prerequisite skills. Mathematics educators are more likely to place blame for failure on methods and materials than on the child's deficits.

While the data are incredibly scanty concerning the arithmetic achievement or difficulties of learning-disabled children, Smith and Lovitt (1973; 1976) have been studying the effects of various teaching techniques on the arithmetic achievement of seven learning-disabled boys, ages 8 to 11 years. In one report of three studies (1973) they examined the effectiveness of a modeling procedure to help advance math skills. In this study, the child's math level is determined by using the Key Math test and a battery of tests involving computational arithmetic. The child's mathematics program designed and employed problems the child could not compute, but which involved prerequisite skills the child had demonstrated. In the first study, the child was given a demonstration of how to work the problems by the teacher, and the teacher left the demonstration problem (the model) with the child (model plus demonstration condition). The results were that three children went from a zero baseline (inability to compute any of the problems) to 100 percent correct in one day; while all but one child improved dramatically on a weekly posttest.

In a second study, the children were given feedback by the teacher in the form of corrections and markings of the child's errors. In this treatment none of the children raised their median percentage score above zero during the seven to eight days of this treatment. Smith and Lovitt then started the demonstration plus model condition with this group and the performance of the four children receiving this treatment rose to 100 percent.

In a third study, Smith and Lovitt investigated the questions as to whether it was the demonstration of the problem or the learning of the problem and its solution for the child which accounted for the children's dramatic improvements. It was found that three children improved on the condition in which they received only the teacher's demonstration, but only one child improved without it. Smith and Lovitt recommend that both demonstration and model techniques be used, and that the same technique might be appropriate for spelling and handwriting problems.

Smith and Lovitt (1976) also investigated the issue of whether reinforcements would be more or less effective at different points in mathematics performance, these being the stage of acquisition (before the child knows how to do a particular computation) and the stage of proficiency (when the child practices a newly acquired skill so that it becomes more automatic).

In the first experiment, the boys were given arithmetic problems which required knowledge of rules which the boys had not yet mastered and which thus required that they attain new skills. In the second experiment, boys were given arithmetic problems which they could solve, but on which they worked very slowly. In the first experiment, it was found that the boys' mathematics performance did not improve with contingent rewards, points which could subsequently earn them a toy. In the second experiment, however, there was great improvement in mathematics performance, whether the rewards were free time or points towards a toy. Smith and Lovitt thus conclude that reinforcements will not facilitate performance if the children have not yet attained initial skills necessary for arithmetic. Once children have mastered the initial prerequisite skills for solutions, reinforcement contingencies can be very effective in improving the children's performance.

Before concluding this chapter, several points need to be emphasized. First, we really do not know very much about the academic problems of learning-disabled children. This ignorance is traceable, in part, to the long-standing influence of the medical model and its traditions upon the conceptualizations and practices of the specialists in the field. For example, the reader may have drawn the conclusion from the material we have presented concerning dyscalculia that such problems are the result of neurological impairment. We believe that what is reflected is the influence and the approach of the medical model (as described in Chapter 2) in the understanding of learning disabilities. The medical model is not necessarily a bad one, but it has focused attention and energies upon processes other than the acquisition of reading and arithmetic.

It has only been within the recent past that problems of learning-disabled children have been given some priority in the concerns of specialists. It is likely that in future years considerably more data pertaining to these problems will be available. Of course we have no guarantee that such attention will yield a rich harvest of useful educational techniques and programs. For example, our track record vis-à-vis the understanding of the acquisition of reading skills has not been earth-shattering. But after all, reading and arithmetic reflect very complex intellectual processes and we may be many years away from understanding them.

REFERENCES

Balow, B. "The long-term effect of remedial reading instruction." *The Reading Teacher,* 1965, 18, 581–586.

Bateman, B. "Reading: A controversial view." In L. Tarnopol (ed.), *Learning Disabilities.* Springfield, Ill.: Charles C. Thomas, 1969.

Bender, L. "A visual motor Gestalt test and its clinical use." *American Orthopsychiatry Association Research Monograph,* 1938, No. 3.

Benton, A. *Right-Left Discrimination and Finger Localization.* New York: Hoeber-Harper, 1959.

Birch, H. G. and Belmont, L. "Auditory-visual integration, intelligence, and reading ability in school children." *Perceptual and Motor Skills,* 1965, 20, 295–305.

Blank, M. and Bridger, W. "Deficiencies in verbal labeling in retarded readers." *American Journal of Orthopsychiatry,* 1966, 36, 840–847.

Blank, M., Weider, S., and Bridger, W. J. "Verbal deficiencies in abstract thinking in early reading retardation." *American Journal of Orthopsychiatry,* 1968, 38, 823–834.

Bliesmer, E. P. and Yarborough, B. H. "A comparison of ten different beginning reading programs in first grade." *Phi Delta Kappan,* 1965, 500–504.

Boder, E. "Developmental dyslexia: Prevailing diagnostic concepts and a new diagnostic approach." In H. R. Myklebust, *Progress in Learning Disabilities, Vol. II.* New York: Grune and Stratton, 1971.

Boyd, J. E. "Teaching children with reading problems." In D. Hammill and N. Bartel (eds.), *Teaching Children with Learning Behavior Problems.* Boston, Mass.: Allyn and Bacon, 1975, pp. 15–60.

Bryant, N. D. "Some principles of remedial instruction for dyslexia." *The Reading Teacher,* 1965, 18, 567–572.

Cawley, J. F. "An instructional design for children with learning disabilities: Emphasis on secondary school mathematics." In L. Mann and L. Goodman (eds.), *Teaching the Learning-Disabled Adolescent.* Boston, Mass.: Houghton Mifflin, in press.

Chalfant, J. and Scheffelin, M. "Central processing dysfunctions in children: A review of research." NINDS Monograph No. 9. Bethesda, Md.: U.S. Department of Health, Education, and Welfare, 1969 (Task Force III).

Chall, J. *Learning to Read: The Great Debate.* New York: McGraw-Hill, 1970.

Cohn, R. "Dyscalculia." *Archives of Neurology,* 1961, 4, 301–307.

Critchley, M. *Developmental Dyslexia.* London: Heinemann, 1964.

Cruickshank, W. M., Bentzen, F. A. Ratzeburg, F. H., and Tannhauser, M. T. *A Teaching Method for Brain-injured and Hyperactive Children.* Syracuse: Syracuse University Press, 1961.

Curry, F. "A comparison of left-handed and right-handed subjects on verbal and nonverbal dichotic listening tasks." Unpublished doctoral dissertation, Northwestern University, 1966.

Dechant, E. V. *Improving the Teaching of Reading.* Englewood Cliffs, N.J.: Prentice-Hall, 1964.

DeHirsch, K., Jansky, J., and Langford, Q. *Predicting Reading Failure.* New York: Harper and Row, 1966.

Diederich, P. B. II. "Research 1960–1970 on methods and materials in reading." ERIC Clearinghouse on Tests, Measurement & Education. Princeton, N.J.: Educational Testing Service, 1973.

Dienes, Z. *An Experimental Study of Mathematics Learning.* London: Hutchinson, 1963.

Dykman, R. A., Ackerman, P. T., Clements, S. D., and Peters, J. E. "Specific learning disabilities: An attentional deficit syndrome." In H. R. Myklebust (ed.), *Progress in Learning Disabilities, Vol. II.* New York: Grune & Stratton, 1971, 56–93.

Edgington, R. and Blackmon, L. "Helping children with reading disability." Child Guidance Study Unit. University of Arkansas Medical Center, Little Rock, 1962.

Ernhart, C. B., Graham, F. K., Eichman, P. L., Marshall, J. M., and Thurston, D. "Brain injury in the preschool child: Some developmental considerations." *Psychological Monographs,* 1963, 77, 17–33.

Estes, R. E. and Huizinga, R. J. "A comparison of visual and auditory presentations of a paired-associate learning task with learning disabled children." *Journal of Learning Disabilities,* 1974, 7, 35–42.

Freides, D. "Human information processing and sensory modality: Cross-modal functions, information complexity, memory and deficit." *Psychological Bulletin,* 1974, 81, 284–310.

Friedlander, B. Z. and Cohen de Lara, H. C. "Receptive language anomaly and language/reading dysfunction in 'normal' primary-grade school children." *Psychology in the Schools,* 1973, 10, 12–18.

Frostig, M. *Frostig Developmental Tests of Visual Perception.* Palo Alto, Calif.: Consulting Psychologists Press, 1964.

Gerstmann, J. "Syndrome of Finger Agnosia: Disorientation for Right and Left, Agraphia and Acalculia." *Archives of Neurology and Psychology,* 1940, 44, 389.

Geschwind, N. "Neurological foundations of language." In H. R. Myklebust (ed.), *Progress in Learning Disabilities, Vol. I.* New York: Grune & Stratton, 1968.

Getman, G. "The visual-motor complex in the acquisition of learning skills." In J. Hellmath (ed.), *Learning Disorders, Vol. 1.* Seattle: Special Child Publications, 1965.

Goldstein, K. *Language and Language Disturbances.* New York: Grune & Stratton, 1948.

Goodman, Y. M. and Burke, C. L. *Reading Miscue Inventory Manual: Procedure for Diagnosis and Evaluation.* New York: Macmillan Publishing Co., Inc., 1972.

Goodman, K. and Goodman, Y. "Learning to read is natural." Paper presented at conference on theory and practice of beginning reading instruction. Pittsburgh, April, 1976.

Goyen, J. D. and Lyle, J. G. "Effect of incentives upon retarded and normal readers on a visual associate learning task." *Journal of Experimental Child Psychology,* 1971, 11, 274–280 (a).

Goyen, J. D. "Effect of incentives and age on the visual recognition of retarded readers." *Journal of Experimental Child Psychology,* 1971, 11, 266–273 (b).

Goyen, J. D. "Short term memory and visual discrimination in retarded readers." *Perceptual & Motor Skills,* 1973, 36, 403–408.

Gurren, L. and Hughes, A. "Intensive phonics vs. gradual phonics in beginning reading: A Review." *Journal of Educational Research,* 1965, 58, 339–346.

Hermann, K. *Reading Disability.* Copenhagen: Munksgaard, 1959.

Hutson, B. A. "Language factors in reading disability." Paper presented at the American Educational Research Association, Chicago, Ill., April, 1974.

Johnson, D. J. and Myklebust, H. *Learning Disabilities: Educational Principles and Practices.* New York: Grune & Stratton, 1967.

Kalaski, L. "Arithmetic and the brain-injured child." In E. C. Frierson and W. B. Barbe (eds.), *Educating Children with Learning Disabilities.* New York: Appleton-Century-Crofts, 1967.

Kawi, A. and Pasamanick, B. "Prenatal and paranatal factors in the development of child-hood disorders." *Monographs of the Society for Research in Child Development,* 1959, 24, #4.

Kephart, N. C. *The Brain-Injured Child in the Classroom.* Chicago: National Society for Crippled Children and Adults, 1963.

Kinsbourne, M. "Perceptual learning determines beginning reading." Paper presented at the meeting of the Eastern Psychological Association. Philadelphia, Pa., 1973.

Kosc, L. "Developmental dyslexia." *Journal of Learning Disabilities,* 1974, 7, 165–177.

Langer, S. K. *Philosophy in a New Key.* Cambridge: Harvard University Press, 1957.

Levin, J. R. "Inducing comprehension in poor readers." *Journal of Educational Psychology,* 1973, 65, 19–24.

Levin, J. R., Devine-Hawkins, P., Kerst, S. M., and Guttermann, J. "Individual Differences in Learning from Pictures and Words: The Development and Application of an Instrument." *Journal of Educational Psychology,* 1974, 66, 296–303.

Lohnes, P. R. "Evaluating the schooling of intelligence." *Educational Researcher,* 1973, 2, 6–11.

Lovitt, T. C. and Hansen, C. L. "The use of contingent skipping and drilling to improve oral reading and comprehension." *Journal of Learning Disabilities,* 1976, 9, 481–487 (a).

Lovitt, T. C. and Hansen, C. L. "Round one–Placing the child in the right reader." *Journal of Learning Disabilities,* 1976, 9, 347–353, b.

Luria, A. *Higher Cortical Functions in Man.* New York: Basic Books, Inc., 1966.

Lyle, J. G. "Reading retardation and reversal tendency: A factorial study." *Child Development,* 1969, 40, 833–843.

Lyle, J. G. "Effect of speed of exposure and difficulty of discrimination upon visual recognition of retarded readers." Unpublished manuscript, 1974.

Lyle, J. G. and Goyen, J. D. "Visual recognition, developmental lag, and strephosymbolia in reading retardation." *Journal of Abnormal Psychology*, 1968, 73, 25–29.

McFie, J., Piercy, M. F., and Zangwill, O. L. "Visual-spatial agnosia with lesions of the right cerebral hemisphere." *Brain*, 1950, 73, 167–190.

Orton, S. *Reading, Writing, and Speech Problems in Children*. New York: W. W. Norton, 1937.

Owen, R. W., Adams, P. A., Forrest, T., Stolz, L. M., and Fisher, S. "Learning disorders in children: Sibling studies." *Monographs of the Society for Research in Child Development*, 1971, 36, No, 144.

Palermo, D. S. and Molfese, D. L. "Language acquisition from age five onward." *Psychological Bulletin*, 1972, 78, 409–428.

Palkes, H., Stewart, M., and Freedman, J. "Improvement in maze performance of hyperactive boys as a function of verbal-training procedures." *Journal of Special Education*, 1971, 5, 337–342.

Palkes, H., Stewart, M., and Kahana, B. "Porteus maze performance of hyperactive boys after training in self-directed verbal commands." *Child Development*, 1968, 39, 817–826.

Piaget, J. *The Child's Conception of Numbers*. New York: Humanities Press, 1952.

Rabinovitch, R. D. and Ingram, W. "Neuropsychiatric considerations in reading retardation." *The Reading Teacher*, 1962, 15, 433–438.

Rosner, J. "Language arts and arithmetic achievement, and specifically related perceptual skills." *American Educational Research Journal*, 1973, 10, 59–68.

Samuels, S. J. "Effect of distinctive feature training on paired associate learning." *Journal of Educational Psychology*, 1973, 64, 164–170.

Samuels, S. J. and Anderson, R. H. "Visual recognition memory, paired-associate learning, and reading achievement." *Journal of Educational Psychology*, 1973, 65, 160–167.

Samuels, S. J. and Jeffrey, W. F. "Initial discriminability of words and its effect on transfer in learning to read." *Journal of Educational Psychology*, 1966, 57, 337–340.

Samuels, S. J. and Schachter, S. W. "Controversial issues in beginning reading instruction: Meaning versus subskill emphasis." In S. W. Pflaum-Connor (ed.), *Evolving Issues in Reading*. National Society for the Study of Education. San Francisco: McCutchan, in preparation.

Sartain, H. W. "Instruction of disabled learners: A reading perspective." *Journal of Learning Disabilities*, 1976, 9, 489–497.

Senf, G. M. and Freundl, P. C. "Memory and attention factors in specific learning disabilities." *Journal of Learning Disabilities*, 1971, 4, 94–106.

Smith, D. D. and Lovitt, T. C. "The use of modeling techniques to influence the acquisition of computational arithmetic skills in learning-disabled children." In E. Ramp and G. Semb (eds.), *Behavior Analysis: Areas of Research and Application*. Englewood Cliffs, N.J.: Prentice-Hall, 1975.

Smith, D. D. and Lovitt, T. C. "The differential effects of reinforcement contingencies on arithmetic performance." *Journal of Learning Disabilities*, 1976, 9, 21–29.

Smith, F. *Psycholinguistics and Reading*. New York: Holt, Rinehart and Winston, 1973.

Strauss, A. and Lehtinen, L. *Psychopathology and Education of the Brain-injured Child*. New York: Grune & Stratton, 1947.

Vande Voort, L. and Senf, G. M. "Audiovisual Integration in Retarded Readers." *Journal of Learning Disabilities*, 1973, 6, 170–179.

Vellutino, F. R. "Alternative conceptualizations of dyslexia: evidence in support of a verbal-deficit hypothesis." *Harvard Educational Review*, 1977, 47, 334–354.

Vellutino, F. R. "Psychological factors in reading disability." Paper presented at the meeting of the American Educational Research Association, Chicago, Ill., April, 1974.

Vellutino, F. R., Harding, C. J., Phillips, F., and Steger, J. A. "Differential transfer in poor and normal readers." *Journal of Genetic Psychology*, 1975, 126, 3–18.

Vellutino, F. R., Pruzek, R. M., Steger, J. A., and Meshanlon, U. "Immediate Visual Recall in Poor and Normal Readers as a Function of Orthographic-Linguistic Familiarity." *Cortex*, 1973, 9, 368–384.

Vellutino, F. R., Steger, J. A., DeSetto, L., and Phillips, F. "Immediate and delayed recognition of visual stimuli." *Journal of Experimental Child Psychology,* 1975, 19, 223–232.

Vellutino, F. R., Steger, J. A., and Kandel, G., "Reading Disabilities: An Investigation of the Perceptual Deficit Hypothesis." *Cortex,* 1972, 8, 106–118.

Vellutino, F. R., Steger, J. A., and Pruzek, R. M. "Inter- vs. intra-sensory deficit in paired associate learning in poor and normal readers." *Canadian Journal of Behavioral Science,* 1973, 5, 111–123.

Vogel, S. A. "Syntactic abilities in normal and dyslexic children." *Journal of Learning Disabilities,* 1974, 7, 103–109.

Weinstein, R. and Rabinovitch, R. D. "Sentence structure and retention in good and poor readers." *Journal of Educational Psychology,* 1971, 62, 25–30.

Wender, H. *Minimal Brain Dysfunction in Children.* New York: Wiley-Interscience, 1971.

Willows, D. M. "Reading between the lines: Selective attention in good and poor readers." *Child Development,* 1974, 45, 408–415.

Zigmond, N. K. and Cicci, R. *Auditory Learnings.* San Rafael, Calif.: Dimensions Publishing Co., 1968.

III | DIAGNOSIS, ASSESSMENT, AND REMEDIATION

In Part II, the preceding six chapters, we have presented current information on the characteristics and behaviors of learning-disabled children. Such knowledge is important in sharpening your evaluation of contemporary clinical practices, the major topic of concern in Part III. We believe that armed with this knowledge concerning the progress in the field, the elimination of myths, and the development of facts, you will be better able to judge which clinical practice is likely to yield fruit and which is not. You can discriminate between methods which incorporate assessments of the "known" characteristics and those scrutinizing traits which have been presumed to be, but in reality are not associated with, learning-disabled children.

The following chapters describe how learning disability practitioners go about their business. The first chapter focuses upon clinical procedures that are often employed but which do not include standardized tests. The second chapter is devoted to various standardized tests, while the third chapter discusses attempts to change the child's behavior.

It should be noted at the outset that because we present a procedure or a test, it does not mean that we endorse it. Indeed, some standardized tests which we describe in detail are probably not very good tests. We have presented such material not to train you to administer, score, or interpret it, but rather to give you some familiarity with clinical practitioners' activities. Thus, the standardized tests in Chapter 11 have been selected for discussion on the basis of their apparent popularity and widespread use and not their validity.

It is our belief that there is still much to be learned about the diagnosis and remediation of the learning-disabled child. The research which has been conducted so far has not indicated the preeminence of any particular approach. In Chapter 12, then, we have presented some remediation techniques not because of their known efficacy but because of their potential usefulness and their current controversial natures. These approaches may be hints of where future developments will go, but are not do-it-yourself kits for the remediation of learning disabilities. We hope that these chapters will give you an insight into current practices, and perhaps some useful guides as to how you might develop more helpful methods to serve your future clientele.

10 | Clinical Assessment Procedures

The terms *learning disabilities, minimal cerebral dysfunction,* and *educationally handicapped* are generic terms for a very wide variety of children's learning problems. The children who were the original inspirations for the development of the field of learning disabilities evidenced severe problems. These extreme cases of brain damage, language pathology, and hyperactivity provided the stimuli which elicited theories and therapies from diagnosticians in various disciplines. These diagnoses—medical, educational, and psychological—were subsequently extended to an ever widening group of children who all had in common some problem in development, learning, or behavior. Many types of diagnostic evaluations became a part of the multidisciplinary approach to learning disabilities, because it was found that these children's problems cut across several child care areas. The rationales, methods, and materials used by various professionals will be discussed in this chapter.

PURPOSE OF DIAGNOSIS

There are three primary rationales or functions of diagnosis: it may serve scientific, therapeutic, or moral functions. In a scientific enterprise, events, objects, or persons must be categorized within specified dimensions so as to stimulate further knowledge. Thus, children may be diagnosed as schizophrenic, autistic, or normal, for the purpose of studying one or more of each group. The goal is to increase our knowledge about persons who share the defining characteristics. In therapeutic enterprise, a diagnosis may categorize a person as a member of a specific group in order to better understand the individual and the situational constraints upon his activities.

The goal in this case is to provide appropriate therapeutic intervention. Finally, and unfortunately, diagnosis may be a case of name calling, in which the professional propagandizes the desirability or undesirability of particular behaviors. Often the propaganda follows establishment lines, but uses a language of technical jargon rather than religious rhetoric (London, 1964). A neutral example of the latter point, from the standpoint of this text, are the recent debates among psychiatrists and between psychiatrists and representatives of the Gay Liberation movement as to whether homosexuality reflects mental illness.

Each of these rationales for diagnosis is relevant and important. Science has progressed through the taxonomies which have been developed in various mental health fields; people have benefited from diagnostic links with therapies and education; and perhaps, with the decline of the theologian, a new spokesman for morality is needed within our culture. At issue is the particular hat, scientific, therapeutic, or moralistic, which the professional diagnostician chooses to wear. While the public may be confused about the differences among these enterprises, the evaluator cannot afford to be. It is of critical importance that the professional learning disability expert make discriminations among these functions in his own diagnostic evaluations.

The criteria used to judge the adequacy of a diagnosis will vary according to the function the diagnosis serves. A diagnosis whose purpose is the advancement of scientific knowledge must meet contemporary standards set for good science. Both the method used and the resulting evidence determine the evaluation of such diagnoses. The evaluation of therapeutic diagnostic procedures rests with the degree to which the diagnosis-specified treatment reduces the negative behaviors, increases the child's happiness, competence, or whatever is at issue. Like the scientific enterprise, however, empirical evidence is required before an evaluation of the diagnosis can be claimed. Perhaps the moral enterprise is reducible to political or persuasive criteria. If the diagnostic proclamations inhibit bad (pathological) behavior or facilitate good (normal, adjusted) behavior in large segments of the population, diagnosis may be adequately serving its moral purpose.

DIAGNOSTIC MODELS

Diagnostic models used in the field of learning disabilities differ from one another in rather radical ways. The old and new models are related to the different hypotheses regarding childhood pathology which were discussed in Chapter 2. A diagnostic evaluation in the context of the medical disease model focuses upon the assessment of abilities and/or attributes of the "patient" in a search for the etiology or causes of symptoms. Amelioration of symptoms is expected to occur through the elimination of their causes. The presumption is that unless one understands the source of difficulty (which resides within the patient rather than in the environment), one cannot make an accurate diagnosis or appropriate prescriptions for treatment. In the psychometric or statistical model, there is somewhat less concern for etiology, but the search is on through the use of standardized tests for those skills and inadequacies which are the cause of the child's problems. The procedure in which knowledge is demanded of the stimulus (etiology) which elicits the response (symptom) before the implementation of remedial efforts has been vigorously attacked by Skinner and his followers (Skinner, 1971). While this model is not logically correct, it is nevertheless a prominent model subscribed to by many clinicians throughout the country.

The social systems model is radically different from the medical disease model. Perhaps the increasing popularity of this approach is a backlash against the shortcomings of the medical disease and psychometric approaches to childhood pathology. In this context, the position taken seems to be that most problems children experience are attributable to the imperception, incompetence, or limitations of significant persons in their environment. Diagnosis and treatment are directed toward evaluation and changes in the environment, not in the assessment of the child. Proponents of this approach have attempted to attenuate the degree to which children are labeled as defective and/or isolated into separate school programs. This practice is supported by the observation that children who share the same label and even the same problem are, in fact, quite heterogeneous. The labels and associated segregated programs generate and sustain stereotypes which are not, in fact, descriptive and certainly not helpful for such children.

But if one does not look at the cognitive and personality characteristics of the child, what does one look for? The social systems model certainly does call our attention to the difficulties which may result from the biases of diagnosticians, the aspirations of parents, the incompetencies of some teachers, and the hazards to individual welfare faced when dealing with bureaucracies. But the focus of attention is on the manipulation of large units or samples, not on intervention and assistance for individual children.

A behavioristic approach is easily incorporated into this model, particularly that segment of behaviorism which uses operant conditioning as a diagnostic and intervention approach. Thus, a child's aberrant behaviors are controlled by the reinforcement or reward strategies of individuals in the child's environment. The diagnosis of learning disabilities would be the evaluation of teachers', parents', and peers' responses to the behaviors of the child. For instance, is the child rewarded for poor performance? Is there a lack of reward for competent or desirable behaviors? Or is the child ignored for both?

Whichever model proves to be the most helpful and enlightening, it is important to realize that definitions of what is normal (good) or abnormal (bad) behavior vary from place to place, from person to person, and from time to time. Definitions of children's behavior as deviant, maladaptive, inappropriate, and incompetent may be as much reflections of the world around the child as they are reflections of the child himself (Becker, 1963).

Another important point to remember when thinking about children who have been defined as abnormal is that everybody has problems, a point frequently forgotten by mental health workers. According to parents, many children who are never seen in any diagnostic setting have many difficulties. Behaviors, traits, habits, and circumstances currently thought to be uniquely associated with some form of pathology have been found in children never defined as abnormal in any way. A classic study conducted by Lapouse and Monk (1964) reported that more than 50 percent of mothers of normal (e.g., nonclinic) children rated their children as overactive or as having seven or more problems! Problems were more numerous in children 6 to 8 years of age, and declined during the ages 9 through 12. Not surprisingly, boys were the problem, not girls. Evidently, parental management of boys presents greater difficulties than girls; hence, the greater frequency of reported problems.

A third point to consider in diagnosis is that discrimination should be made between transient problems and problems which are likely to be chronic or produce other, more severe, difficulties for the child. It is obvious that a child with hearing and vision defects will not be suffering from a transient developmental difficulty. But the child who experiences a school phobia may well require minimal intervention on the part of professionals. The professional should not overdramatize or overgeneralize ordinary children's problems which may soon be eliminated through social, parental, or developmental forces. As long as professional skills are in greater demand than the supply, limited resources must be judiciously applied. When other social forces can act as therapists, by all means let them do the work.

Finally, it should be remembered that definitions of problems are intimately tied to developmental levels. Once a learning-disabled individual drops out of school, becomes a marginal graduate, or leads a routine existence of work and family rearing, he may no longer be defined as abnormal. He may remain illiterate, but he is no longer of concern to school officials. Chronic difficulties are those which require continuous institutional or professional resources. The learning-disabled child may escape the definition of deviance by virtue of aging.

To summarize, definitions of normalcy, pathology, and disabilities are culture bound. Significant persons must view the attributes of a child as negative and defective in order to bring the child to the attention of specialists in intervention. As a result of the desire for academic achievement within our culture, numerous diagnostic approaches have flourished, outstripping our skills in evaluation of their empirical worth. It must also be remembered that many of the behaviors defined as problems in children may be normal variants of development, magnified by parental and teacher intolerance of these behaviors or the adults' sophistication regarding current theories. Diagnosis should not be simply the evaluation of a child, but an evaluation of the labelers as well (Becker, 1963).

MULTIDISCIPLINARY TEAM APPROACH

The following discussion outlines those procedures typically employed in a multidisciplinary approach to children with academic difficulties. These procedures are used by professionals in varying disciplines in contributing to the best therapeutic program for the child. The very heterogeneity of children with learning problems, both across diagnostic categories and within any one category, has resulted in the inclusion of diagnosticians with varying perspectives. In some cases the multidisciplinary team approach is to administer a wide range of medical, psychological, and educational measures to the child. In other cases the team is comprised primarily of the classroom teacher, learning disability teacher, and school psychologist, whose approach is to use the evaluations made within the school. In the case of the wider use of professionals, the team approach using medical as well as psychological and educational evaluations, the goal is to determine the primary causes of the problem. The team is responsible for determining which of the diagnostic categories best describes the child's problem and which type of educational program is best suited for this child. Once a child has been assigned to the learning disability category, the diagnostic evaluation becomes focused upon the exact nature of the learning problem. Mental retardation, emotional problems, and hearing and vision impairments are presumed to be ruled out or of secondary importance. Instead of tests concerned with personality functioning or intellectual assessment, the child is given tests of specific skills believed to be related to academic achievement. Some of these tests have become an accepted part of the learning disabilities specialist's arsenal.

The professional members of the diagnostic team typically include the psychologist, pediatrician, neurologist, electroencephalographer, social worker, teacher, and, sometimes, speech therapist and audiologist.

It should be noted that the typical team is better staffed than that proposed in PL 94-192. The proposed rules require that the team consist of the child's regular teacher, a teacher with training in the area of specific learning disabilities, and "at least one additional individual certified, licensed, or approved by the state educational agency to conduct individual diagnostic examinations of children, such as a school psychologist, speech clinician, or remedial reading teacher" (p. 52406).

The age of the child is one major determinant with which these professionals become involved. If problems are noted in the infant or during the preschool years, the parents are likely to seek medical advice. But if the problem is not severe or does not evidence itself before the child enters school, he may be assessed through the procedures established by the school district, in a hospital clinic, or by a private practitioner. Analysis reveals that different professionals are qualified to do overlapping jobs. The social worker and the psychologist consider a case history an important source of information. The educational specialist and the psychologist are trained to administer educational and diagnostic tests. A pediatric neurologist, pediatrician, or family physician may administer a medical examination. Which professional becomes involved depends on who notices the problem, and the availability of resources within the school or community.

Referral: The First Step

Phase one of the diagnostic process is the referral. Who makes referrals? Why? When? Where do people go? What is the diagnostic significance of the referral system? We know very little about the referral process in learning disabilities. The information so far available stems primarily from studies of the labeling of minority group members as mentally retarded by the school system (Mercer, 1973). Studies of this issue have sensitized social service workers to the influence of the socioeconomics, religion, race, and educational statuses of the persons who do the referring. It is possible that the outcome of a child's case may be significantly affected by the "who" as well as the "why" of the referral.

Referrals can be initiated directly or indirectly by anyone who comes into contact with the child. Parents, teachers, school nurses, social workers, or the courts may initiate a referral. Referrals are made when the person who makes the referral becomes upset by the behavior of the child, or is pressured by someone else who has become concerned about that child. Families have traditionally sought the advice of the family doctor, while schools usually follow prescribed procedures for making referrals.

The age of the child may or may not be a critical factor in the referral process. When the child is very disturbed (e.g., a child who has developed no expressive language by four years), it is more likely that help will be sought in the preschool period. The timing of referral once the child is in school does not preclude the possibility that the child has evidenced developmental difficulties in the preschool period (Owen et al., 1971).

Socioeconomic Factors in Referral

The socioeconomic level of the family and the degree to which this is similar or dissimilar to that of others in the local school district affect the referral process. It has been documented in the mental retardation literature that affluent families are more likely to use the available institutional services to obtain desired help (Farber, 1968; Rowitz, 1973). Moreover, the socioeconomic status of the family is likely to influence the diagnostic label as well. Children from poor families are more likely to be labeled mentally retarded than children with the same intellectual levels from more affluent backgrounds (Mercer, 1973).

It seems likely that the facilities necessary to render services to learning-disabled children are more likely to be available and exploited by children of the more affluent than those of the lower socioeconomic levels. Judging from the availability and distribution of resources within the field of mental retardation (Mercer, 1968), it is likely that resources for diagnosis and program development in learning disabilities are likewise more available to affluent than nonaffluent school districts.

In addition, it may be more likely that when children of the poor are seen for diagnosis their problems will be construed as the result of cultural disadvantage and not specific learning disabilities, even though the definition of learning disabilities specifically excludes problems whose cause may reflect cultural definitions. In the absence of careful individual evaluations, it may be tempting to attribute the failures of the poor to cultural deprivation and the failure of the wealthy to specific learning deficits. The concentration of learning disabilities specialists' efforts upon the children of the affluent is in the process of changing. Professionals are becoming more aware of and sensitive to specific learning disabilities, outside of the influence of cultural differences; just as attention is being carefully given to distinctions between mental retardation and the consequences of poverty (McCandless, 1964). Such biases in the distribution of resources and within the referral system should be considered by the individual teacher, learning disabilities specialist, or diagnostician when dealing with the individual problem child.

THE PSYCHOLOGICAL EVALUATION

The purpose of conducting a psychological evaluation is to assess the child's emotional and intellectual status. Three primary processes contribute to the information needed by the diagnostician to make this assessment. These include: (a) observation of the individual in the clinic and other settings; (b) the administration of standardized tests, such as the Stanford-Binet test of intelligence and the Rorschach Ink-blot test; and, (c) the obtaining of case history material. On the basis of the information gleaned from these three procedures, the psychologist usually specifies the diagnostic category to which a child belongs, makes recommendations for treatment, and sometimes offers some predictions about expectations for future performance. It should be noted that different processes are used to obtain the same information. While we will describe as separate the procedures used in a diagnostic evaluation, the information obtained from these processes overlaps. The parents, for example, are asked questions about early development of the child's use of language. In a manner appropriate for the child's age, an assessment of the child's current language is also made by the diagnostician in the observation and in the standardized test phases of evaluation.

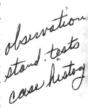

Clinical Observations

Psychological literature has a good deal of documentation on the difficulties of drawing inferences on the basis of observation of behavior. Recording statements of persons in a Gallup-type opinion poll, observing the intellectual level of a rat, or the behavior of psychiatric patients is fraught with procedural problems (Goffman, 1961; Hyman, 1954; Rosenhan, 1973; Rosenthal, 1966). The probability of biases in clinical observations is quite great. The attitudes and expectancies of the observer may well influence what he views and what he bothers to record, in memory or on paper. A number of personal characteristics of the child, irrelevant from the theoretical standpoint of learning disabilities, may well influence the observer's judgments. For example, when adults observe two children guilty of identical misbehavior, the prettier of the two children will be less condemned (Dion, 1972).

But there are several methods by which observer error can be reduced. First, it is helpful to observe and record the behaviors of the child, rather than the inferences on what has been observed. The psychologist who reports that a child is preschizophrenic without specifying both the behaviors of the child which prompted this diagnosis and the situation in which these behaviors occurred does no one a service and may do great disservice. The observer must know which behaviors to focus upon and this requires a good theory behind the recording process. A great deal of time must be devoted to the collection of observations in order to obtain a reasonably large sample of the child's daily activity. It is also time to recognize that the administration of a standardized test alone no longer comprises adequate diagnostic information; indeed results of a Rorschach are no longer considered even useful information. Diagnosis is a demanding task which requires a great expenditure of time and thought.

Observations of the child should be conducted in a variety of settings, for different situations may well provoke different kinds of behaviors. Children who are experiencing learning problems should be seen not only within the office of the psychologist, but in the classroom or home setting as well. Observational information may be collected in an informal or formal manner. For example, one might note how the child moves. Is his gait awkward? How does the child respond to sounds, to whom does the child speak, and does he initiate interpersonal contacts or does he merely respond when spoken to?

Observations in the clinical and school settings extend beyond the collection of information on the child's responses to others. As persons are confronted with tasks to perform, their behaviors change as the tasks vary in difficulty. The behavior and language of the child as he attempts to do frustrating work can be indicative of the type and extent of the problem he is experiencing. Beginners in diagnostics and student teachers often become concerned when they see a child who appears to be fatigued. But fatigue can be an important indicator of task difficulty level for that child. Most children can outlast a clinician, even the young college student, in endurance. Fatigue, yawning, restlessness, fidgetiness may be diagnostic cues of stress, frustration, and boredom. Change the activity to one that is fun and these cues may disappear. The information the diagnostician obtains from observations of the child's language, speech, and willingness to communicate, changes in affect, responses to failure and success are all integrated into his interpretation of diagnostic test performance.

Observations should be made of four areas of child functioning: physical appearance, movement, attention, and interpersonal relationships. Wender (1971) described a small fraction of children with minimal cerebral dysfunction as part of a pediatric subgroup, the funny-looking kid ("FLK") syndrome. These are children who have a higher incidence than would be predicted of physiognomic abnormalities of a type also associated with schizophrenia and mental retardation. These abnormalities are "anomalies of the epicanthus (a fold of skin in the eye) and ears; high arched palate; short incurving fifth finger; single palmar crease; abnormally long third toe; syndactylism of the toes; strabismus and, perhaps, abnormally shaped skulls" (p. 29). Physicians are trained to make such observations, but as teachers and diagnosticians we should also be alerted to characteristics which make us feel this child is "different."

Perhaps more critical, insofar as a larger group of learning-disabled children may be involved, is the question of physical appearance in terms of standards of beauty. There is a relationship between physical attractiveness and social popularity (Lindzey and Byrne, 1968), and children who are unattractive may be more likely to be viewed as learning-disabled than their more attractive counterparts. We must ask ourselves to what extent the child's appearance affects our responses and judgments.

Observations should be made of the way the child moves. Learning-disabled children have been described as clumsy and awkward. This has been related to perceptual-motor difficulties. The child who spills paint or trips over everyone's feet is likely to be having difficulties making appropriate judgments of spatial relationships. He is also likely to be very irritating to adults, who tire of mopping up after spills. The observer should note whether the awkward movements are related to gross motor movements. Is the child clumsy when he has to move his whole body or does the problem seem more specific to manipulation of small motor movements? Watch the child as he walks (runs) down the hall, climbs steps, and participates in gym activities. Observe the child as he tries to get his gym shoes tied or sharpen a pencil. Observations of the child's skills in manipulating common utensils and his ability to perform common motor movements have implications for remedial intervention.

Children with learning disabilities are notorious for not paying attention to school-related tasks (Bryan and Wheeler, 1972; Bryan, 1974d), and the Dykman et al. (1971) hypothesis regarding these children is based upon a theory of an organically based attentional deficit syndrome. It may be that inattention changes as children age. In kindergarten the child's inattention is associated with inappropriate, aggressive types of behaviors—at least according to teachers (Keogh and Tchir, 1974). If the child with learning disabilities is contained within the regular elementary classroom, rather than segregated into special self-contained classes, it may be because he learns to "pass" in the absence of learning to pay attention by flipping the pages of his book, fussing with materials on his desk, attending to one book and then to another and then back to the first book. He is not inattentive in the same way as a kindergartener who refuses to be quiet during nap time, but he is still inattentive. Teachers complain that learning-disabled children work only when they are on a one-to-one basis with the teacher. They are inattentive much of the remainder of the time. The observer should note the amount of time the child is and is not attentive; what he does when inattentive; if there is a difference in the activities to which he is more or less attentive; and under what conditions he is able to attend. As with the observation of motor skills, there are both diagnostic and remedial implications for this type of information.

Observations are made of the kinds and amounts of interactions the child has with teachers, peers, and, if possible, parents. It has been reported that children with learning disabilities are rated as less socially desirable than comparison peers (Bryan, 1974a). Studies to determine what types of interactions learning-disabled children have with teachers, peers, and parents suggest that these relationships are different from those held by comparison peers. Parents report feeling less affection for learning-disabled children than for siblings (Owen et al., 1971) and Bryan (1974d) reported that learning-disabled children are ignored significantly more often than academically successful children by both teachers and peers. What behaviors are to be observed which may account for these findings?

Wender has described these children as "unsuccessful extroverts." Children with learning disabilities, in general, do not appear to be withdrawn, neurotic children. They do try to interact with others, but their attempts seem to go astray. The goal of the observations of the child's interpersonal behaviors would be to determine the degree to which the child does interact with others, and the adequacy or inadequacy of these interactions. Is this the child who makes insulting remarks, who responds inappropriately to situations in the classroom, who fails to pay attention to instructions, and then vociferously interrupts to demand he be told what to do? Again, such information has implications for therapeutic intervention.

Structured Classroom Observations

The rules and regulations for learning disabilities which were written to implement the Education for All Handicapped Children Act of 1975 (Public Law 94–142) specifies that the diagnostic procedures for identification of children as learning-disabled must include an observation of that child. It is proposed that the observations of the child's academic performance are to be made in the child's regular educational setting or in one deemed appropriate by the state (Federal Register, 1976, p. 52407). In addition, the written report summarizing the diagnostic assessment of the child is to include a statement of the relevant behavior noted during the observation, although the proposed rules and regulations fail to define "relevant behavior." In any case, it is likely that many learning disability teachers and/or school psychologists do classroom observations either in the course of diagnosis or teaching. Given the mandate for classroom observations, it seems appropriate and timely to consider more structured and systematic ways of performing observations.

A number of structured observations scales have been developed and used for research and teacher evaluation. The primary focus of these techniques has been on classroom teachers, rather than upon individual children. Flanders (1970) and Good and Brophy (1973) have done extensive work in this area. The Flanders Interaction Analysis includes ten categories which are recorded in a way that provides an interaction matrix. The ten categories include: teacher responses (accepts feelings, praises or encourages, accepts or uses ideas of pupils); questions (teacher asks questions); initiation (teacher lectures, gives directions, criticizes, or justifies authority); responses (student responds to teacher); initiation (by student); and silence (or confusion). The purpose of the analysis is to understand teacher behaviors and student responses to teachers in order to give teachers feedback on their teaching styles and their impact upon students. Good and Brophy (1973) have suggested a variety of observation codes which focus more on individual children. But their research has really emphasized both how the teachers' expectations influence their behaviors toward children, and the impact of these behaviors upon the children. Flanders and Good and Brophy are important references in the area of observational techniques.

These authors' techniques might be considered to comply with the proposed observation requirement of PL 94–142. The advantages and disadvantages should therefore be pointed out. Their methods do include assessments of teachers' behaviors, teaching style, and responsiveness to children. Insofar as we are trying to effectively mainstream learning-disabled children into regular classrooms, inclusion of teacher responsiveness to learning-disabled children (or children they might have referred for special services) is critically important.

Unfortunately, it is not clear that the world is ready for an interactional model in which teacher behavior is the critical focus in diagnosis. So let us consider structured observations which focus on the individual child. First, let us assume that the diagnostic team may want to devise their own structured approach to observations, for various referral problems with which they will be confronted. In classroom observations, it is important not only to observe the child of interest but also another child, so that appropriate comparisons can be made. Excepting perhaps selecting a comparison child of the same sex and race, the designation of the comparison child should be randomly determined. That is to say, after locating all of the children of the same sex and race as the target child, one should be randomly selected to serve as the comparison child. The reason for this action is that it allows one a better evaluation of whether the target child's behaviors reflect some personal disposition on his part, or rather reflect some environmental forces which are determining most students' behavior.

A second critical matter is that of deciding just what is to be observed, and that, in turn, may well determine just how one goes about making the necessary observations. It is important to realize that most of the child's behaviors during the school day cannot be observed. It is simply too difficult. Whatever behaviors are deemed important, agreed-upon techniques for observations must be established a priori. There are a number of methods of recording observed behavior. These include *time sampling,* for example, recording the child's behavior the first ten seconds of every minute. Another method is *event recording,* which involves noting each time a particular behavior occurs. An additional technique is the *running record,* in which the observer tries to record everything that the child does during an extensive period of time. While novices appear to feel more comfortable with this technique, it is likely to be very time-consuming, difficult, and to yield unreliable results. Perhaps this technique is suited only for the very experienced.

Recent studies using observational techniques for studying the learning-disabled child's behavior within the classroom have suggested some categories of behavior which might be useful in diagnostic practices (Bryan, 1974d; Bryan, Wheeler, Felcan, and Henck, 1976). These categories include: on-task behavior (doing that which the teacher wants); off-task behavior (doing what one is not supposed to be doing); and social interactions (initiations and responses by the child to others and others to the child). Given the particular problem of the child, other categories may also be of importance. For example, it might be relevant to note whether the child is engaged in a group activity, or a one-to-one interaction with the teacher. One might wish to observe the children only during periods where specific academic topics, such as reading, are being presented. It is probably also important to note the quality or content of the child's social interactions. For example, does the teacher typically praise or punish the child, and if so, how frequently? In general, however, the common problems of the learning-disabled child, such as difficulty in attending structured tasks imposed by others, difficulty in persisting at a task, or problems in social relationships, should be reflected in classroom observations.

A desirable outcome of classroom observation should be a quantified picture of the children's behavior. To accomplish this, one need only count the number of times the particular categories of behavior occurred, and the total number of behaviors recorded. The observer then transforms these subtotals into percentages by dividing the subtotal for each category by the total number of behaviors recorded. These resulting percentages provide a picture of the individual child's life in the classroom in terms of individual subject areas, and interactions with other persons in the classroom. By performing the same calculations for the comparison child, one can form an idea of the lives of children in that class. This should help contribute specific information for the development of an individualized education plan. The information can also be used for feedback purposes with the classroom teacher.

Before leaving this topic, however, a few caveats should be issued. First, it is important that the observer be unbiased; otherwise, he will surely note what he expects to note. If it is at all possible, the observer should not be told prior to making an observation which of the children being observed is the "potential problem." Second, observations are crude measures. In effect, using observations for individual diagnosis, like using standardized tests, yields many false positives (where a "normal" is diagnosed as a learning-disabled child) and false negatives (where a learning-disabled child is deemed "normal"). Observational techniques thus join the multitude of other very imperfect techniques employed in individual diagnostic pursuits. It is necessary not only to live with this fact but to recognize it as well.

Empirical findings linking specific behaviors with specific diagnostic categories either reflect the obvious or are absent. But there are some observations which would appear helpful in better understanding the child of concern. Children who are mentally retarded do not respond in the same ways as emotionally disturbed or deaf children. The deaf child will probably not respond to spoken commands if he has his back to you and is playing with a toy. He is likely to respond eventually to your presence, as deaf children have been observed to have the habit of frequently checking their environment visually even when engrossed in some activity (Myklebust, 1954), and the hearing-impaired respond when another person enters their visual fields. The emotionally disturbed child may avert eye contact and not respond when you are in his field of vision, while the brain-damaged child, usually the hyperactive type, responds erratically. Children with learning disabilities have been observed to have poor, slow, immature language development, to be hyperactive, to display aggressive behavior in preschool and school years, and poor attention for academic activities in the following school years. Distinctions as to which category may be the most appropriate diagnostic category for a particular child can be obtained by observing the child in the clinic, classroom, and home. The majority of characteristics associated with the learning disabilities label and those best obtained from observation appear to be behavioral (Clements, 1966).

The Interview

The interview is a powerful technique for obtaining important information from a parent and teacher. It is most important for the interviewer to be aware of the potential biases which can influence the answers given by the respondent. Persons being interviewed are very sensitive to the responses, verbal and nonverbal, of the interviewer, particularly if there are social class differences between them (Hyman, 1954). If a simple smile, nod, grunt, or groan is given consistently to a particular word or theme, it is likely to increase the frequency of the respondent's answer. It is clear that the expectations of the interviewer as to how the respondent will answer a particular question are likely to influence in subtle ways the answer to the question, generally in the direction of confirming the expectation (Hyman, 1954; Rosenthal, 1966). The attitudes of the interviewer regarding the topic under discussion are also likely to influence the respondent, again subtly, to respond in a way which indicates agreement with the attitudes of the interviewer. The interviewer then may tend to elicit, by apparently subtle and undramatic actions, statements which tend to confirm either expectations of the respondent and/or the interviewer's attitudes toward the topic under consideration.

Aside from these unwanted sources of influence, the interviewer is likely to go astray in yet another way. Unless very careful recordings of the respondent's answers are made, the degree to which the interviewer's recall of the information will be flawed will be truly amazing! Lapses of only a few hours between the hearing and the recording of an interview will produce massive amounts of failures of both omission and commission in subsequent reports (Hyman, 1954).

Interviewer errors aside, what are the sources of bias likely to be introduced by the interviewee? In general, the longer the time span the interviewee is asked to recall, the less reliable the recall (Hyman, 1954). A parent may quite accurately recall how he disciplined his child the day before the interview, but his opinions of how he managed his child several years earlier are likely to be rather distorted. In a most important study, Yarrow, Campbell, and Burton (1970) found that parents' recall of past child-rearing events was such as to view the early period as a happier and easier time than it in fact was and to reshape their recall to conform to their perceptions of the present personality of the child. Distortions are more likely to be introduced in the discussion of personally important events than in statements concerning facts not so ego-related (Hyman, 1954). For example, people are more likely to make themselves appear more socially acceptable in reporting how they treat their children than in reporting their place of employment, their age, or their income. Generally, in the case history material the interviewer is dealing extensively with material that is particularly likely to be distorted by the respondent in the direction of making that respondent or spouse, or offspring more "acceptable" to the interviewer.

There is also some evidence to suggest that social class and race differences between the interviewer and respondent may affect the nature of the responses obtained. Apparently, lower-social-class respondents are more likely to acquiesce to the expectations of a middle-class interviewer than are middle-class respondents. Moreover, black persons may be more reluctant to admit to socially undesirable behaviors to white interviewers than are white respondents (Hyman, 1954). It behooves learning disability specialists to be sensitive in their dealings with members of other races or classes to the possible biases such differences may produce.

From the above discussion, it is clear that the interview is far from flawless as a technique for gathering information. Indeed, it was these flaws which gave rise to standardized testing methods (which have other flaws). All biases can never be eliminated; some imperfections of the interview will inevitably remain. It is possible, however, to employ techniques which might reduce some of the distortions arising from the interview material. Perhaps one of the simplest methods for gaining greater veracity from the interview is to make immediate recordings of what is being or has been said. Memories, of either the interviewer or interviewee, are not to be highly trusted. Second, when asking the respondent to report on behaviors which might reflect negatively upon him, cast the question in euphemisms. One does not need to ask a mother whether she neglects a child when she can be asked if she feels too busy to give the child the time that she would wish to devote to him. Introduce such questions with an "everybody does it" theme. Provide the respondent with a sense that his "sinning" is not unique, that it is a problem most people experience.

Case histories should be recorded, as much as possible, in a descriptive manner, specifying examples on which inferences are based. Diagnosticians should transcend the labels used by the parents. Obtain and record the behaviors committed by the child which lead the parent to the inference drawn. The description that the child is lazy or disorganized gives us little information. That the child cannot tie his shoes, fails to respond to requests or commands, and stays in his room daydreaming is of considerably greater interest. Alternative interpretations of information can be made when an interviewer has time to reflect upon what people have told him. Descriptive data, in addition to some educated guesses, provide the information needed to construct such alternative explanations.

Finally, the interviewer should not just record negative examples of behavior. As Goffman (1961) and Rosenhan (1973) have pointed out, the mental health workers are likely to either focus on only negative or socially undesirable behaviors of the patient or are likely to construe the most everyday type of behavior as reflecting pathology. We suspect the same bias may result when viewing any child defined by someone, particularly an expert, as a problem child. It is important to determine the strengths as well as the problems of any child, because the strengths of the child may well affect the interpretations given the particular problems.

In one of the author's experiences, a mother of a third-grade girl was so concerned about her child's shyness in the classroom that with the school's support she sought private psychological help. The mother had allowed the child to see a private practitioner for a brief period. The psychological diagnosis given this young girl was preschizophrenic and the withdrawal behavior in the classroom was interpreted as a sign of autistic tendencies. At the start of the school year, this author was asked to diagnose the girl and to treat her, if necessary. Upon discussions with the child's new classroom teachers and her social worker, it was discovered that the girl was a straight A student throughout her school career and that her

shyness was probably more related to some transitory interpersonal stresses within the classroom than to a preschizophrenic condition. The straight A record certainly did not speak of autistic daydreaming within the classroom. The author advised the parents not to seek further help and suggested to the teachers that this child would likely be much better socially adjusted during the upcoming school year. After several months, the social worker involved with this case called the author to congratulate him on his very effective therapy. Apparently, she had the mistaken impression that the author was the child's therapist and was seeing this girl on a regular basis. She informed the author that the girl had made considerable improvement.

Because of the fallibilities of the interview, the diagnostician must also rely upon other procedures in the diagnosis of children. The following sections will describe the procedures employed in evaluating a child with academic difficulties. First we will describe the process for obtaining a case history, a procedure which relies heavily upon interviewing as a source of data collection. Then we will discuss the neurological examination.

The Case History

A major step toward understanding the child's learning problem is an intensive interview with the parents. Vital information regarding the nature of the problem, its history, and the effects it is having upon the child and his family is obtained by discussing the problem with the family. A successful intervention program for a learning problem in many cases requires the understanding, support, and cooperation of the child's family.

The questions posed in taking a case history may vary among diagnostic models. The information determined to be important in a model concerned with the etiology of the problem as the basis for developing an intervention program is different from the information gathered by use of a model exclusively concerned with changing the child's behavior. The latter data focus more intently on current actions and skills of that child. In the medical disease model, clinicians are concerned about the etiology of the problem. Case history taking in the behavioristic approach either assumes the other questions about etiology were asked by someone else or that the problem's solution does not depend upon such information.

Specification of etiology is very much a shot in the dark. The assignment of children to discrete categories of problems on the basis of the case history and/or the entire evaluative process currently is impossible. Nonetheless, that does not mean we should stop trying to improve the state of knowledge concerning sources of problems, nor does it mean that we should turn our backs on the problems children and families experience outside the four walls of the classroom. In Chapter 12, Remediation, we place great emphasis upon specification of discrete academic problems and the solution thereof through behavior modification programs. But we do not find this obviates the need to know more about the problems this child may be experiencing elsewhere. The existence of a spelling problem may test out as related to a deficit in short-term memory or inability to make associations between sounds and symbols, and this can be academically programmed. But to stop at this point prevents learning that this type of deficit, as measured by test performance, may reflect the inability to attend to a wide variety of tasks, from teacher directions to television. It does not provide clues that the child is really more interested in playing cops and robbers; hates his mother or little brother and wants to get even with an intrusive family or a family which has branded him a dope; or that he has hypoglycemia, which affects his energy levels for any sustained activity.

Children have histories. And children's families have histories. Many of the academic failures or maladaptive behaviors manifested may be related to the family circle and family problems.

Initially, the case history requires obtaining basic information about the child and his family. Birth dates, ages, employment status, religious affiliation, church attendance, and the existence of such problems in other family members is specified. The family's religious background is noted because there are some rare diseases which appear more frequently in some religious groups than others. Autism and Tay-Sachs disease are more often reported in Jewish families than in families of other religious backgrounds (Rimland, 1964). Religious affiliation is also correlated with attitudes about mental and emotional problems and is specifically related to attitudes toward handicapped children (Farber, 1968; Gurin, Veroff, and Feld, 1960). Farber, for instance, has reported that devout Catholic families were more accepting of a mentally retarded child, as their faith provided them an explanation for the occurrence of this problem. This is not to suggest that Catholic parents are more loving or devoted to their children than other families, but that religious beliefs may provide a supportive cushion when things go wrong.

Information concerning the occupational status of the family may be useful in gauging the family's attitudes toward their problem child. Presumably, the upward bound or upper-class family will experience more distress in the presence of a handicapped child than families less affluent or less ambitious (Farber, 1968). Perhaps the less affluent or more poorly educated families contend with so many other difficulties that it is difficult for them to invest much energy in this particular problem. Perhaps they begin with different expectancies for the futures of their children and are not so engaged with their aspirations for themselves or their children. Perhaps we have not accurately tapped the consternation they experience. In any case, differences have been reported for the responses to handicapped children by families of differing socioeconomic levels.

The effects of a learning-disabled child upon the family unit have not, as yet, been systematically studied. Dunn (1973) summarized the findings of the effects which a retarded child has upon the family. Those effects which may apply to learning-disabled children's families indicate increased conflict within the family, affect the degree to which the family participates in community activities, and exert a restrictive effect upon an older sister or extra freedom for older brothers.

When getting the case history, information is sought regarding the educational histories of family members. A major theory of the cause of one learning disability, dyslexia, is that it is genetically linked. Bakwin (1973) recently reported a study of reading disabilities in twins which corroborated Hallgren's contention that reading disabilities are inherited and familially linked. A high degree of concordance of reading disabilities was found by Bakwin, who reported that 84 percent of monozygotic twins compared to 29 percent of dizygotic twins shared reading problems. He concludes that reading disabilities which cannot be attributed to cultural difference or disadvantages are principally genetic.

Whether or not reading problems are genetically linked, another study also reported a higher incidence of school problems in the parents of educationally handicapped children compared to academically successful children (Owen et al., 1971). This study also reported a higher incidence of related academic problems in siblings of educationally handicapped children. It may be that the parents are less competent at communicating preacademic skills to these children, with a subsequent disadvantage in their performance upon reaching school. While this hypothesis is speculative, the need for the information is an important factor in considering intervention. For instance, does the family need specific instruction on how to help this child organize his school work?

The parents' chief complaint or major concern regarding the child provides some insight as to when the problem was noticed and by whom. The severity of the problem may be indicated by the age at which parents became concerned about the child. The earlier the problem was noted, the more severe it was and, perhaps, the more it distressed the family members. The course of action followed by the family upon discovery of the problem should be noted, at the very least for the purpose of avoiding duplications among professional workers.

Case history information should include information about the pre-, peri-, and postnatal periods as experienced by the infant and by the mother. One factor related to developmental problems appears to be the age of the mother at the time of the child's birth and the existence of other siblings. There is some evidence to suggest that births which occur late in a woman's life, particularly late first births, are more likely to be associated with subsequent difficulties in the child. Of particular concern are conditions associated with birth trauma and brain damage. Rubella (German measles) in a pregnant woman is well known to be associated with blindness, cardiac disorders, mental deficiency, and deafness. Rh incompatibility is likewise associated with brain damage (Kawi and Pasamanick, 1959).

The condition of the child at birth and immediately thereafter has been demonstrated to be significant for later development. Knobloch and Pasamanick (1959) reported that such conditions as prematurity, low birth

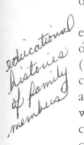

(margin handwritten notes) educational histories of family members

(margin handwritten notes) when problem noticed & by whom. What action taken.

(margin handwritten notes) pre, peri, & post natal information (diseases, traumas) problems during birth

weight, toxicity in the mother, or accidents during birth could all result in "sublethal clinical neuropsychiatric syndromes." Graham, Matarazzo, and Caldwell (1956) studied 346 infants and found that the 81 children who had suffered either anoxia, mechanical birth injury, or infection demonstrated a lower threshold for pain, poorer vision, greater irritability, and more muscle tension than children not so affected during birth. Of great importance are the results of a follow-up study of these children three years later. Children who had experienced anoxic states were not inferior on perceptual motor tasks, but showed neurological signs, behavioral problems of hyperactivity, and inferiority to comparison children on all the tests of conceptual functioning. The children who had been born prematurely did not show neurological signs, but were inferior on concept formation tasks. It was thus suggested that differential competencies in learning and performance could be directly related to events which occurred during birth (Graham, Ernhart, Thurston, and Craft, 1962).

To summarize, many conditions can cause developmental problems. These include abnormalities of gestation, metabolic disorders, virus infections of the mother and newborn, blood-type incompatibility, and poisoning of the fetus due to lead, carbon monoxide, drugs and other substances ingested by the mother (Dunn, 1973, p. 77). According to Dunn, there has been a shift in thinking recently regarding the importance of events at birth in causing brain damage. It is now believed that abnormal events at birth may be the result of a problem which may have arisen any time during the gestation period, which then led to a difficult, problem birth.

Information is sought regarding the medical history and medical status of the child. In the days before the development of penicillin and other drugs, many childhood diseases had debilitating effects. Mumps, measles, and several other such childhood diseases are no longer viewed with the same degree of seriousness. However, the diagnostician is still concerned with any medical problems the child may have had or is still having. Illness which prohibits the child from attending school for long periods or at critical periods (e.g., when prereading skills are taught) might well have deleterious effects upon the child's academic performance.

We would like to suggest that the diagnostician heed complaints from the child or parents regarding physical symptoms. For instance, when a child complains of feeling tired, is losing weight, or falls asleep earlier than would be expected, it is incumbent upon the parents to seek a medical evaluation. All too often parents are told by diagnosticians, both medical and psychological, that the child's problem is emotional.

The next area in the case history should cover the developmental history of the child. At what age was the child able to sit, walk, or speak his first words? When did the child become toilet-trained or wash his face? The child's physical maturation provides a general idea of the integrity of the nervous system. The age at which infants perform a number of rhythmic automatic activities has been studied, with the finding that children later diagnosed as handicapped achieved these milestones later than normal infants. A group of 200 normal infants from age 1 month to 12 months were compared with retarded and cerebral-palsied infants on hand sucking, foot kicking, lip biting, body rocking, toe sucking, and tooth grinding (Kravitz and Boehm, 1973). The age of onset for these activities ranged from 2.7 to 10.6 months for normal infants, while for cerebral-palsied and Down's-syndrome infants these appeared later than 12 months. It is noteworthy that many or all of these behaviors are often considered abnormal; yet great numbers of normal children can be expected to manifest them. It is not the occurrence of the behavior which is associated with severe difficulties, but the age at which such behaviors appear. Children who have severe problems are likely to manifest such behaviors later than the normal child. One could say that the normal child shows his abnormalities earlier than the abnormal child. Or, maybe abnormal means doing things later and longer.

Detailed and complete normative data can be collected in a way which yields a quantifiable assessment of the child. The ages at which children usually accomplish developmental milestones have been gathered and arranged statistically to permit comparison with peers much in the way any standardized test is arranged. One such scale is the Vineland Social Maturity scale developed by Edgar Doll (1947; 1953). This scale has items arranged in six-month intervals from birth to eighteen to twenty-one years. The items are developed to tap maturation in five areas considered critical and all-inclusive in child development. The items are scored so that a social quotient somewhat like an intelligence quotient can be obtained for comparisons of the child's social development to that of his peers. The scale can also be "double scored" so that a child suffering a particular handicap does not lose credit for the items which tap the skills precluded by that particular handicap. A child who cannot walk unaided is scored in two ways. One way subtracts for things he cannot do; the second credits the child for items specifically related to ambulation. As such the child can be compared with peers, can be evaluated intra-individually, comparing one area of development with another, and can be scored so as not to penalize him for his handicap. Differential diagnosis of young children may by aided by such a method. For instance, the mentally retarded child is predicted to be slower in social maturity in the five developmental areas, whereas the hearing-impaired child is expected to be comparable to peers except for those items related to communication (Myklebust, 1954).

Language development is a critical source of information for differentiating one type of handicapped child from another. The age of speech and language development and the use of language in social relationships are perhaps among the best indicators of whether a child is hearing impaired, mentally retarded, emotionally disturbed, brain damaged, or immature. Each diagnostic category presents varying patterns of speech and language development, although it must be admitted that this is more true of hearing impairment than the categories of mental retardation, brain damage, and emotional disturbance. Questions are asked about the child's awareness of sound as an infant. Was this a quiet baby? Did he make sounds when he was alone as if to entertain himself? Did he make babbling sounds and then use jargon, an imitation of speech in the absence of real words? When did the child seem to comprehend the meaning of what people said to him? Did he enjoy having stories read to him, or listening to the television? At what age did the child use his first word? When did the child start to connect words? The parent is questioned as to the degree to which the child uses age-appropriate vocabulary and sentences to communicate and the child's ability to relate a story or experience in a logical, coherent manner. Can the child remember events and relate them? Can the child remember instructions given to him? Does the child have difficulty expressing himself or does he seem to have difficulty finding the words he needs to express himself?

Clinical guidelines to making discriminations among categories of handicap, such as mental retardation, emotional disturbance, hearing impairment, and aphasia in young children who fail to develop language, were delineated in a classic study by Myklebust (1954). He described the language differences among these groups in the following way. The child who is born with a severe hearing impairment will be deficient in all phases and stages of language acquisition. Parents will report that deaf infants typically do make sounds and babble until they are about 9 or 10 months of age. There is some quantitative difference in sound making between these and nonhearing-impaired infants even at this time, as the former are described as quiet. The expressive output of the infant will mirror what he hears, so the tonal quality of the hearing-impaired child's utterances will be qualitatively different as well. As the infant ages, sounds will be excessively loud or soft and, unlike normal infants, sounds will not be used for play or imitation. The hearing-impaired child will use gestures and facial expressions for communication.

The critical period for language development in the emotionally disturbed, schizophrenic child is between eighteen and twenty-four months. According to Kanner (1944), this child develops no speech, no jargon, no characteristic tonal quality, no gesture, no use of sounds for pleasure. The child lacks affective facial expression and gesture. The autistic child has been described by Rimland as different from birth; autistic children are reported to demonstrate an early use of language, but appear to fail to associate sounds or words with meaning. Their words are described as uncommunicative, high pitched, and echolalic. Rimland has hypothesized that infantile autism is biologically caused and is the result of damage to the reticular activating system in the midbrain.

The aphasic child may have difficulty comprehending spoken language, be unable to recall words and to put words together to form a sentence. Menyuk (1964) has suggested that the language problem is not simply one of slower development, but a lack of complexity in sentence structure. The utterances of aphasic children are simpler and shorter in construction. Like the hearing-impaired child, the aphasic may use gestures and pantomime to communicate. But the aphasic child is not expected to have sounds which are qualitatively different as is the hearing-impaired child.

The child whose aphasia is related to a lack of understanding of language is easily mistaken for a deaf child, because he responds inconsistently to sounds. The difference seems to be that when the sound gets loud enough the deaf child will respond appropriately. But the aphasic child may respond to very soft sounds and not to loud sounds.

The language of the mentally retarded child develops at a rate commensurate with his mental age. This usually means a slower attainment of the developmental milestones, such as the age at which the child speaks his first word or uses a string of words to form a sentence. The degree of retardation is reflected in the attainment of language skills.

There are certain similarities in the language deficits reported by parents for children who are mentally retarded, emotionally disturbed, brain damaged, and hearing impaired. Relative to the nonimpaired same age child, these children may have a less complex language, a reduced output of language, shorter sentence construction, and an inability to control the behavior of themselves and others by using language.

There is consensus, by no means sufficiently validated, that deficits in language development are a shared characteristic among children with learning disabilities (Task Force II, 1969). This is not limited to children with severe problems brought for evaluation in the preschool years, but is descriptive of school-aged children with learning disabilities. One study which contributes significantly to this question represents an attempt to divide children with learning disabilities into distinct types (Owen et al., 1971). While there were five diagnostic categories proposed, speech and language problems were noted in three of the five categories, while the remaining two were more heavily weighted with emotional problems.

The Educational History

The child's educational history is the next area of inquiry. Did the child attend nursery school, at what age, for how long? How well did the child adjust to school? If there were any problems, what was the nature of the difficulty? If the child is of school age, the parent is asked to describe the child's academic progress in various school subjects and his adjustment to teachers and peers. Which subjects do the parents perceive to be the child's best and worst? Has the child been given special tutoring in the school or on a private basis? What kind of information about the child have teachers, principals, or other members of the school staff relayed? Do the parents believe the child has obtained a good education or do they define the school program and personnel as the source of, or contributing to, the problem?

Information available on problem behaviors of normal children (Lapouse and Monk, 1964) indicated that children in the early school years are more problematic than children at other ages. An educational history which indicates the child was a problem in nursery school, even though the child is not being evaluated until several years later, provides some evidence as to whether the problem is one that has been bothering the family for a long time or is highly specific to the time of evaluation. There is evidence to suggest that children ultimately diagnosed as learning-disabled show signs of difficulty as young children (Owen et al., 1971). More evidence on this subject should become available with the growing emphasis on preschool education for learning-disabled children.

Did he have problems early in school?

The diagnostician attempts to obtain a picture of the child as a member of the family. Parents are asked to describe the child's activities at home and his relationships with other members of the family. If there are siblings, the parents can often report on this child by comparing him with siblings. Questions are asked to determine whether this child has any responsibilities at home. Does he have chores to do? Can he take care of his own needs, handle the utensils in the kitchen or shed, manage an allowance, shop for himself or his family?

home activities

family relationship

chores, responsibility

age appropriate common sense?

Do the parents believe the child shows age-appropriate "common sense"? At the preschool level, does the child recognize dangerous situations, such as inedible substances or heavy traffic? During the school years, parents complain of such problems as lighting fires and theft. The point is to determine whether the child has some notions about the consequences of his acts, in line with expectations for his age. Does the child recognize right and wrong at the real and rhetorical levels? Rhetorical encompasses the ability to verbalize what is wrong and right, irrespective of accompanying acts, and to say the right thing at the right time. Information is sought as to the appropriateness of the child's affective responses to others and as to whether the child seems to be emotionally stable. Does the child have a sense of humor, and does this seem to be appropriate?

Does the child have any special hobbies or interests? How would the parents describe the child's motor activities? Is the child able to engage in those motor skills, such as bicycle riding or baseball, which are typical for his age group? How well does the child perform such activities as skating, swimming, or football? How well coordinated is the child at activities which require fine motor movements? Is this the child who could never have a stamp collection because he could not manipulate the stamps well enough?

hobbies, interests, motor activities

The purpose of these questions is to determine what problems the family is experiencing with this child, and what limitations learning problems are placing upon him outside of school activities. This type of information provides diagnostic information as to the nature of the child's problem, his needs for intervention, and the needs of the family for assistance in managing these problems.

If the child is enrolled in any type of school program, an interview should be conducted with the teacher and any other school personnel who work with this child. The classroom teacher has the best view of the child in terms of a concentrated time period, the comparison group of peers,

teacher interview

and the absence of vested motives in viewing the child in any paricular way. Data would suggest that teachers' ratings may be the single best diagnostic tool (Bryan and McGrady, 1972; McCarthy and Paraskevopoulos, 1969). In most instances, teachers are delighted to have an opportunity to discuss a child, especially when they have been troubled by that child's social behavior and/or lack of academic progress. Teachers not only provide information about the academic performance of the child, but they also provide accurate pictures of his ability to organize himself to do a task, the relationships he has with other children, and his attitudes toward school. The information provided by the classroom teacher and the continuing cooperation of that teacher are critical components of the diagnostic and intervention process.

NEUROLOGICAL EVALUATION

The role of medical and neurological evaluations in diagnosis and placement of learning-disabled children was investigated as part of Task Force II (Rogan and Lukens, 1969). Questionnaire data collected from 236 school districts revealed that 64 percent of the districts required a medical assessment of the child's neurological status, although only 12 percent reported that the results of the evaluation had to indicate neurological dysfunction for placement of a child in a special program. The diagnostic validity of "soft" (or ambiguous) neurological signs was accepted by 45 percent of the responding districts. More than 50 percent of the children presently enrolled in special programs were indicated to have medically established diagnoses of neurological dysfunction. This figure may, of course, be an underestimate of the true number of such children enrolled in these special programs insofar as many districts do not require a medical examination.

The rationale for referral to a neurological specialist is to either establish or rule out the presence of specific disorders of the nervous system and to establish developmental attainment of neurological integrities (Clements, 1966). The classic neurological evaluation is based upon knowledge of neurological diseases present in adults. This type of examination has been found to be inadequate in cases of children with learning problems. Thus, different methods of evaluation and different criteria for establishing the presence or absence of signs of abnormal neurological functioning have been developed for children. The procedures and findings are reported here. An examination of a child's neurological status is like the psychological evaluation in that it is not based solely on one type of measure. The data are gathered from a number of sources, the case history, observation, and examination. Often measures are included which are more psychological than neurological. The neurologist seeks to synthesize information gathered on the central and peripheral nervous systems, intellectual processes, and the behaviors of the child with information collected from the child's developmental history.

The neurological examination outlined here has been adapted from those described by Rabe (Task Force II, 1969, pp. 69–70). Rabe defines the standard neurological evaluation to include measures of *cranial nerves* I–XII; *motor system* tone and strength; *sensation* vibration, position, and touch; *cerebellar* testing; and *reflexes* stretch and cutaneous.

The examination procedures have been outlined by Rabe as:

Observation of the general appearance and behavior of the child and the means by which a child attempts tasks.

Double simultaneous stimulation of the peripheral visual field: The examiner moves fingers in the child's peripheral visual areas. In this procedure the examiner checks for signs of *nystagmus* or other abnormal behavior.

By 5 years a child should be able to follow a moving object with his eyes. A child is considered to have an abnormal response if he persists in moving his head and not using just his eyes to follow the object.

Nystagmus is a "rhythmic oscillation of the eyeballs, characterized by a slow drifting from a central gaze toward the periphery and then a sudden snap back to a central gaze position. Both eyes usually move together; it is a conjugate movement and is usually repeated many times" (Curtis, Jacobson, and Marcus, 1972, p. 318). Optokinetic nystagmus (OK nystagmus) is the normal response of this type of eye movement which occurs when a person is asked to follow a moving object. The absence of this eye movement or persistent asymmetry in the rate of this movement defines an abnormal response.

Check for *facial apraxia:* An inability to move facial muscles voluntarily in the absence of paralysis or weakness. The child is asked to blow out his cheeks, both cheeks at the same time, one cheek and then the other, and then to suck in both cheeks (make a "fish face"). An abnormal response is indicated when a child older than 9 years is unable to do these movements upon command.

Check for *hearing:* While an extensive hearing test may be conducted by an audiologist, the neurologist routinely checks out hearing, using a tuning fork or toys which have been calibrated to different sounds and intensities. In an infant the examiner watches for reflexive responses to calibrated noisemakers.

Testing the hearing of a young child is difficult, as this requires the child's cooperation. The examiner observes the child's reactions when noises of different intensities are produced near him, but out of the range of his vision. The tuning fork, watch tick, coin click, and direct whispered or spoken voice tests are gross indications of hearing acuity. If there is a question about the hearing status, the child needs further evaluation using a pure tone audiometer.

Two tests can be conducted with older children who can respond verbally to the examiner. The Rinne test (Curtis et al., 1972, p. 327) is done by holding a vibrating tuning fork against the mastoid bone. The child must indicate when the fork is no longer felt. The tuning fork is immediately placed beside the pinna. A person with normal hearing would hear the tuning fork. The Rinne test is positive when the person hears better through air conduction than through bone conduction. If the person fails to hear either placement of the tuning fork, a sensory-neural hearing loss is indicated. An abnormal Rinne test, which indicates that bone conduction is greater than air conduction, may be indicative of a problem in the middle ear or the external auditory canal. Infections in the middle ear are quite common and may interfere with hearing.

The Weber test is also used by the neurologist. In this case the stem of a vibrating tuning fork is placed on the midline of the forehead just above the glabella (between the eyebrows). The result is "Weber negative" if sound is heard as in midline and "Weber right" or "Weber left," respectively, if it is referred to the right or left ear (*Dorland's Illustrated Medical Dictionary*, 1965).

Pronunciation   By ages 3 to 4 children are expected to be able to pronounce sounds produced by lip movements (labial sounds such as *p* and *b*), by the tongue (lingual sounds such as *t* and *d*), and guttural sounds such as *k* and *g*. If the child is unable to make these sounds an apraxia is suspected.

Simultanagnosia   While the person has his eyes closed, the examiner touches him with his finger on the left-hand, right hand-left face, left hand-right face. By 5 to 6 years, the child is expected to make no more than one error of identification out of twelve stimuli.

Performance of Repetitive Motions   (a) Serial apposition of thumb and fingers (touching each of the fingers on one hand with the thumb of that hand in a sequence); alternating pronation and supination of the hands (turning the palms downward and them upward); and repetitive heel-shin tapping (touching the shin of one foot with the heel of the other). By 5 years of age a child should be able to perform these acts with smooth rhythm. An abnormal response is described as a slow and arrhythmical performance.

(b) Clumsiness, tremor, and ataxia (inability to coordinate voluntary movements) can be evaluated by having the child put marbles in a cylinder. By 3 years a child can do this task smoothly and rapidly.

(c) Synkinesiae is observed when a child mirrors a movement with one limb which is being done with the other limb on tests of repetitive motions. Up until about 9 years of age synkinesiae, or some motor overflow, will be seen in the limb. Beyond this age level, motor overflow is defined as abnormal.

Posture and Gait   The examiner observes the child's posture when he is sitting, lying down, walking, walking on his toes and on his heels. Walking is evaluated in terms of symmetrical movements of the involved body parts. Minimal hemiparesis is suspected if asymmetry of walking movements is noted. Toe walking for a minute or so will bring out sagging of one heel, while heel walking will bring out weaknesses of feet and associated movements. Clumsiness and assorted irregular arm and shoulder movements are abnormal after 5 years of age.

Visual Motor Skills   The child is asked to draw a series of geometric shapes. Developmental milestones for these shapes are:

scribble	18 to 24 months
circle	24 to 36 months
cross, vertical and horizontal straight lines	36 months
square with rounded corners	3½ to 4 years
square	5 years
triangle	5 to 6 years
diamond	7 to 8 years

visual motor

Conception of Spatial Relationships   The child is shown how three-dimensional forms of a square, circle, and triangle can be placed in corresponding places traced on heavy papers. By 21 to 28 months of age children can stack all figures on one paper following one demonstration; by 24 to 30 months can place any form on any figure; and by 30 to 36 months place all the forms on the appropriate papers.

spacial

The child is also tested on ability to place a French curve appropriately on three positions outlined on paper. In this test the child is given instructions verbally with no demonstration. Normal performance is defined as one correct out of three trials by 48 to 52 months and three correct out of three trials by 54 to 60 months.

Right-Left Orientation   By 7 to 8 years a child is expected to be able to name the left and right eye, ear, hand, and foot.

left-right orientation

Auditory and Visual Word Association and Language Usage   The child is asked to name pictures of common objects such as dog, cat, and star. By 18 months a child is expected to name or point to one picture; by 24 months name three or point to five; by 30 months name five, point to seven; by 36 months name eight; by 40 months name ten.

Finger Agnosia   (a) In-between test—following a demonstration, the child is asked to close his eyes and the examiner touches the fingertips of two fingers of one hand simultaneously. The child is to name how many fingers are in between the two which were just touched. It has been found that 50 percent of children can do this with no errors by age four and 95 percent can perform this by 7½ years.

finger agnosia

(b) Two-point test—following a demonstration the child closes his eyes and the examiner touches two points simultaneously on one finger or two fingers of one hand. The child must indicate whether one or two fingers have been touched.

reading

Reading Ability The Rabe outline indicates that reading ability is roughly assessed by use of the Gray Oral Reading or Gates Primary Reading test. The child is to be referred for psychological evaluation if the reading score is greater than one year below grade level.

Vuckovich (1968) outlined procedures which are applicable for neurological evaluation of children older than 5 years. Up through age 15 the evaluation includes an assessment of:

1. Mental state—alertness, normal shyness, cooperativeness, attention, hyperactivity, lack of shyness, or crying.
2. Language development—comprehension, expression, dyslexia, dysgraphia.
3. Visual-motor functions—performance on a Bender-Gestalt and Draw a Person tests.
4. Judgment of right and left.
5. Finger agnosia.
6. Motor functions—there are not many tests which are appropriate after the child is 5 years old. The Heath Rail Walking test is quite common and can be used to assess the child's balance. The child's gait, ability to walk on his toes, and arm swing while walking can be indicative of problems. Muscle tone, consistency, and laterality are noted. The child is asked to throw and kick a ball to establish which is the dominant hand and leg. A dynamometer is used to establish the strength of one hand relative to the other.
7. Head-size and motility of facial musculature.
8. Reflexes—abnormal signs are defined by Vuckovich as abnormal localizing signs, failure to obtain an expected response, asymmetrical responses, persistence of an initially normal response, emergence of certain signs significant to particular infections or disease states, and failure of development, which is one of the most common forms of neurological abnormality.

On the basis of extensive clinical experience, it is Vuckovich's opinion that many neurological "soft signs" are of questionable significance. There are, nonetheless, certain observations which he believes occur too frequently to be the result of chance. The kinds of characteristic problems which seem to recur with greater than expected frequency in children with learning disabilities are disturbed sleep patterns and feeding problems. These children are reportedly hyperactive and distractible and apparently develop language later than would be expected. The children are reported by kindergarten teachers to be having greater problems than other children in visual-motor tasks, such as coloring and drawing, in spite of appearing to be intellectually competent. Poor speech production is noted, although the child's vocabulary may be adequate. Polysyllabic words are difficult for these children to pronounce, and there is difficulty pronouncing consonants, or difficulty comprehending or responding appropriately to auditory requests. By first grade, these children have greater difficulty than others in learning to read,

disturbed sleep patterns

feeding problems

write, and do arithmetic, while behavior continues to be a problem. The complaints received from teachers are that they are hyperactive, unable to restrain aggressive behavior, and show poor adaptation in general.

A neurological evaluation has been a standard part of a multidisciplinary approach to diagnosis. Before discussing the research results of the utility of this examination in aiding discriminations of learning disabled from other types of children, a description of another technique often included in the multidisciplinary approach is given.

The Electroencephalogram

Until recently, one part of a multidisciplinary diagnostic evaluation was the electroencephalographic (EEG) recording of a child's brain waves. A thorough diagnosis involved the question of whether or not the child had normal brain functioning, and this was to be determined, in part, by measures obtained with an EEG. The current consensus is that this evaluation should be limited to individual cases in which there is some evidence that the EEG pattern would indicate abnormal functioning. This type of abnormality could and should be investigated in cases for drug therapy. While the EEG is no longer considered a routine part of an evaluation, there are individual cases in which it is a desirable and appropriate procedure. Teachers should be alert to when such a referral is indicated. For this reason, and to dispel the hocus-pocus often associated with the brain, this section will describe some of the procedures used and the research related to learning disabilities.

An EEG is obtained by using an internationally agreed upon system for placement of electrodes on the human scalp. Recordings are made of the signals picked up from these electrodes. The signal is detected, carried to the recording machine, and displayed on a strip of recording paper traveling at a known rate, or on an oscilloscope, magnetic tape, or computer.

The electrode is a small metal plate, covered with a salt paste on one side, sealed to the scalp and connected to the recording machine with a wire. Only the activity under the electrode should be detected (Gibbs and Gibbs, 1941). The normal EEG is a statistical concept based on empirical correlations with physiological and structurally normal nervous systems in presumably normal subjects (Glaser, 1963).

EEG records are interpreted on the basis of the organization and development of background rhythm (alpha activity), rhythmic and transient activities. Electroencephalographers have developed scaling systems which describe the quality of the various activities recorded. The scale usually describes the record as ranging from poor to excellent. For instance, alpha activity can be rated as poor, fair, moderate, or good on development and organization (rhythmicity) (Hughes, 1971). The range of frequencies includes alpha, beta, mu, lambda, vertex, theta, and delta waves. The occurrence of these frequencies varies with age and with the part of the brain to which the electrode is attached. Electroencephalographers examine the record for differences among and within individuals. The finding of an abnormal occurrence will be described in terms of where the abnormality is observed in relation to the placement of the electrodes.

EEGs are taken under different conditions and an evaluation is made of the record for each condition. In one part of the EEG the patient is awake. During this time the examination usually includes brain wake activity during hyperventilation. Hyperventilation requires the person to breathe deeply and regularly at a rate of about twenty breaths per minute for two to five minutes. There is a great deal of individual variation in the effects of such a procedure and the effects disappear within half a minute of the cessation of overbreathing. EEGs are also taken during photic stimulation. The subject is exposed to flashes of light at about fifteen-second intervals with the eyelids closed and then opened. The responses are described as: no driving (the response fails to occur), poor, good, and excellent (Hughes, 1971). Responses to photic stimulation may vary considerably, as they are affected by blood sugar level, mental activity, fatigue, and the subject's responsiveness to stimulation (Kiloh and Osselton, 1961).

EEGs are also obtained while the patient sleeps. Changes occur in the EEG pattern as the child becomes drowsy and falls into a deep sleep. Certain changes in the EEG pattern during sleep have been associated with epilepsy.

Abnormal responses are defined by the presence and absence of certain waves in certain places, by the symmetry of the two sides of the brain, and by the presence of slower and faster than expected electrical activity.

Classic work was conducted upon the developmental sequences of patterns in EEGs in young children by Gibbs and Gibbs (1941). Briefly, EEGs of newborns are found to be marked by irregular, slow waves. Each week the slow waves become faster, but not until the fourth year is there a steady frequency wave in the occipital part of the brain. When a child reaches 9 years of age, the occipital records resemble an adult's; by 14 years adultlike recordings from all electrode leads can be obtained. But it is not until about 19 years that all normal adults show adult types of records (Gibbs and Gibbs, 1941, p. 38).

Research on Brain Functioning

The historical link between brain functions and learning disabilities has led to a variety of investigations. The question is not whether brain-damaged children have learning problems, but to what degree children suffering from academic failure might be experiencing either brain damage or some neurological immaturity. As the reader will note, the characteristic research design is to compare the performances, be they on intelligence tests, reaction time measures, or on the drawing of pictures, of children already known to have a learning difficulty with the same actions of children not so diagnosed. At least four rather recent investigations have provided some support to the neurology-learning disability relationship.

Dykman, Ackerman, Clements, and Peters (1971) have reported the results of their study of eighty-two learning-disabled and thirty-four normal 8- to 12-year-old boys. While a variety of tests were administered, of interest here are the results pertaining to the neurological examination. They assessed each child on forty-one classical signs of neurological impairment. Of these forty-one items, the learning-disabled child showed greater difficulty than the normal on twenty-four items. Using an additional thirty-nine "paraclassical signs," the learning disabled showed less adequacy on twenty-one such items. While the reliability of the discrimination of any particular sign must be established in the future, the data do provide evidence for the hypothesis of neurological involvement in learning-disabled children. Of some note was the fact that the younger the child, the better the discrimination between the learning-disabled and normal child. The authors suggest then that the learning-disabled child is likely to be suffering from a developmental lag, which might be better detected at even younger ages.

The relationship of neurological examination and intellectual status was examined by Bortner, Hertzig, and Birch (1972). The learning-disabled sample was 198 children, 8- to 12-years-old, labeled by the school district as learning disabled and who had had positive neurological test results prior to their placement in special education classes. A control group of thirty-six children was included. The psychologist and neurologist on the research team were "blind" (unknowing) as to the diagnosis and status of the individual subjects. The neurological examination was that described earlier in the text (Rabe, 1969), with special attention given to the extent of distractibility, impulsivity, and meddlesomeness (i.e., hyperactivity). There were two categories of abnormality; one was the presence of classically defined hard signs and the second was the presence of soft signs. This included language and speech problems, clumsiness, motor overflow, difficulty in imitation of motor movements, unresponsiveness to double simultaneous tactile stimulation, and inadequate graphesthetic and stereognostic responsiveness.

Results were that the learning-disabled group had significantly more signs of neurological impairment than did the control group. Twenty-one percent of the learning-disabled sample demonstrated the presence of hard signs (e.g., abnormal reflexes), and 65 percent had two or more soft signs. None of the children from the control sample had any hard signs and only 5 percent had more than one soft sign. This difference is really not surprising, since the original diagnosis was based upon the presence of such signs. At least these signs showed some reliability. Perhaps of more interest was the relationship between such signs and intelligence test scores. The greater the number of soft neurological signs, the lower the intelligence test score. No soft sign was a better predictor of intelligence than another and with but one exception there was no intelligence test pattern of scores associated more with the brain-damaged than the control children. The exception was that children with one or no soft signs who were diagnosed as learning disabled were more likely to have performance IQ scores higher than their verbal IQ scores. Insofar as many comparisons between groups on the various subtests were made, it is quite possible that this last finding may have resulted from chance. Until this finding is replicated, it is best to consider it a suggestive rather than a definitive finding.

Another conclusion supportive of the neurological differences in learning-disabled children is derived from a study by Hunter, Johnson, and Keefe (1972). These investigators assessed the autonomic response patterns of twenty male nonreaders and twenty control children 8 to 11 years old. The reasoning of the authors was that if dyslexia is biological, physiological measures might discriminate between readers and nonreaders. The nonreading children had been referred for remedial reading and were tested as being more than two years retarded in reading, while the comparison children were more than one year above grade level in reading. The experimental procedures involved measurement of skin conductance potential, skin resistance level, finger, pulse, and heart rate during a habituation series; a reaction time series; and an auditory threshold series. The habituation series presented fifteen auditory stimuli of ten-second duration while the child was in a semidarkened room resting in a semisupine position on a contour bed. The reaction time series presented the child with five successive seventy-five decibel tones of ten seconds' duration. The child was to press a button, placed in his preferred hand, when he heard a tone. The auditory threshold required the child to press the button when he heard a sound and was essentially a control condition to ensure that the children did not have hearing loss. The results indicated the children were not experiencing hearing impairments. On the reaction time series the control subjects responded consistently faster across the five trials. While both groups showed habituation, the controls displayed greater anticipatory responses in heart rate than the reading-disability group. The latter group also showed they had lower basal skin conductance levels over the test trials. In line with this, the reading-disabled child demonstrated a longer reaction time responding to the auditory signal than did the comparison children.

These data are in agreement with the Dykman et al. (1970) data which suggest that learning-disabled children have slower reaction times, slower learning, slower assimilation of information, shorter attention spans, and decreased physiological activity. In effect, they do not appear to have the arousal support necessary for sustained attention.

Further evidence suggesting the presence of neurological deficit or lag in the learning-disabled children stems from a study by Owen, Adams, Forrest, Stolz, and Fisher (1971). In this investigation, a neurological examination was administered to seventy-six educationally handicapped, seventy-six of their siblings, seventy-six academically successful children and thirty-six of their siblings, of elementary and junior high school age. The neurological examination included the classical examination described earlier and assessments of the children's ability to imitate previously tapped patterns and to make visual right and left discriminations. In the latter test, "children were asked to perform tasks with their right or left hand, or to identify the examiner's right hand as he faced the child" (p. 29). Medical histories were also obtained.

Several sources of data failed to differentiate the educationally handicapped from the control groups and these included: measure of hand, foot, and eye preference, overflow movements, arm extension, walking on the balance beam, prenatal, neonatal, or postnatal complications, premature births, and birth weight differences. The medical histories, apparently derived from both hospital records and verbal reports from the mother, indicated that the mothers of educationally disabled children had more difficulty than mothers of the academically successful, with their infants being more irritable, having colic reactions, showing decreased sound production during prelingual development, and demonstrating temper tantrums.

The neurological evaluation revealed significant differences, with the educationally handicapped sample performing less adequately than either their siblings or academically successful children on imitation of tapped patterns, right-left discrimination, double simultaneous touch, and fast alternating finger and hand movements. Additionally, the educationally handicapped children demonstrated a greater frequency of speech and language problems than either their siblings or the academically successful.

The authors conclude that organic damage is not a major causative problem in learning disabilities, since there were but three children who demonstrated hard neurological signs. At the same time, however, there were many soft signs of neurological differences or immaturities in the handicapped group and to a somewhat lesser extent in their siblings. It should be noted that whatever interpretation is given to the weight of organic brain damage or maturational lag in accounting for the behavior of the educationally handicapped, it is true that the specific signs found by one investigator are not found by others. There were a number of differences between this study and others which gave greater evidence for the presence of neurological differences between learning-disabled and non-learning-disabled children. One is that the children in the study conducted by Owen et al. were considerably older than those in the earlier-mentioned studies. There is evidence that neurological facts are age specific and that some neurological signs decrease in incidence as the child ages (Ackerman et al., 1971). Since Owen et al. employed children at a more advanced age than the previous studies, it might be expected that some neurological signs would not be demonstrated.

A second difference between the Owen et al. studies and those previously cited is that Owen et al. employed children from the classrooms, while the remaining investigators employed clinic cases. It is not unlikely that children brought to a clinic, rather than managed within the classroom, may be more handicapped.

Whatever the sources of the differences in results across these studies, the absence of the usual indicators used by clinicians to point to an association between neurological factors and learning deficits led Owen et al.

to reject this hypothesis. While hard signs did not discriminate groups, they did find evidence of neurological difficulties through the presence of many soft signs. Speech and language deficits and problems in the reproduction of both auditorily and visually presented tasks did discriminate the groups.

Many questions have been raised concerning the utility of the neurological examination for understanding the learning-disabled child. Clearly it is important for school officials to detect children suffering from brain damage. But given the absence of malfunction, does the neurological examination render useful information to the learning disability specialist? While the research evidence does suggest that learning-disabled children may be suffering from some neurological deficit or lag, the evidence is not at all convincing. First, research efforts have typically compared children on very many behaviors. Of the many behaviors tested, only a few will discriminate the learning disabled from the academically successful. If enough comparisons between groups are made, then some will be statistically significant by chance. Whatever signs do discriminate, results need replication in future studies, and very few such signs have been replicated. Second, as is typically done in other areas of research, the handicapped groups are those already diagnosed. That is, known learning-disabled children are compared with academically successful ones. Thus, it is likely that the handicapped groups will consist of extreme cases, children who were easy to diagnose in the first place. Third, the neurological examination is often conducted by a neurologist who is not trained to look for the kinds of information helpful in diagnosing learning disabilities (Lerner, 1971; Vuckovich, 1968). They are more likely to focus upon the signs indicative of brain damage in adults or radical syndromes in children, not those signs correlated with the presence of a learning disability. But even if appropriate soft signs are detected, the locale of the damage cannot be specified, the nature of the problem is unknown, and there is no way to suggest a remedy for it anyway! This does not mean to say that research addressed to this issue should be discontinued. To the contrary, much more information concerning the relationship between brain and learning is needed. As yet, however, the nature of the evidence is not such as to make the neurological examination a particularly useful tool in the armamentarium of the learning disability diagnostician or teacher.

The future role of the neurologist has been explicated by Denckla (1973), a neurologist whose clinical practice and research efforts have been concerned with learning-disabled children. Denckla reports that information about the "minimal cerebral dysfunction" problem has become so widespread that many pediatricians are now competent to diagnose and prescribe medical intervention. The role of the neurologist should now shift to integrate the accumulated evidence on child development with that from adults with soft signs of brain damage in order to develop a system from which to infer the probable existence of brain damage with behavioral and learning problems. But Denckla is not stopping with inferences. The goal is to develop "neurometrics," a norm-referenced approach to neurological evaluations which are currently subjective, rather than statistically derived. Once the usual tasks included in a neurological evaluation have been standardized on normal children, much greater precision can be obtained in correlating observed deficiencies with brain functioning. The neurologist is to learn to do a "task analysis" in which the age of the child, the quality of the performance, and knowledge of brain functioning are integrated.

This chapter has provided an overview of the typical procedures in the initial steps of a child's psychological and educational assessment. We have also indicated some of the problems associated with such practices, and the data pertaining to them. It is obvious that these clinical procedures are often informally implemented; that they vary according to the parents, children, and assessor; and are likely to lead to results flawed with a variety of errors, stemming from bias, memory, and faulty traditions. But these clinical procedures do allow for the flexibility often needed when dealing with others. They have stood the test of many years of implementation, and apparently are necessary for an adequate understanding of the child. In the next chapter, we will turn our attention to the standardized tests popularly used in evaluating the learning-disabled child. Here procedures are formal, scores obtained, reliabilities available, and sources of errors and limits of applicability better known. Indeed the standardized test was originally conceived to reduce the human errors associated with informal clinical practices such as those we have described in this chapter. These tests clearly have not succeeded; but they have, on occasion, added a useful tool for the better understanding of the learning-disabled child.

REFERENCES

Ackerman, P. T., Peters, J. E., and Dykman, R. A. "Children with specific learning disabilities: Bender Gestalt test finding and other signs." *Journal of Learning Disabilities*, 1971, vol. 4, 437–444.

Bakwin, H. "Reading disability in twins." *Journal of Learning Disabilities*, 1973, 6, 439–440.

Becker, H. *Outsiders.* New York: Free Press, 1963.

Bortner, M., Hertzig, M. E., and Birch, H. "Neurological signs and intelligence in brain-damaged children." *Journal of Special Education*, 1972, 6, 325–333.

Brophy, J. E. and Good, T. L. *Teacher-student Relationships.* New York: Holt, Rinehart and Winston, Inc., 1974.

Bryan, T. "Peer popularity of learning-disabled children." *Journal of Learning Disabilities*, 1974, 7, 261–268 (a).

Bryan, T. "An observational analysis of classroom behaviors of children with learning disabilities." *Journal of Learning Disabilities*, 1974, 7, 26–34 (d).

Bryan, T. and McGrady, H. J. "Use of a teacher rating scale." *Journal of Learning Disabilities*, 1972, 5, 199–206.

Bryan, T. and Wheeler, R. "Perception of learning-disabled children: The eye of the observer." *Journal of Learning Disabilities*, 1972, 5, 484–488.

Bryan, T., Wheeler, R., Felcan, J., and Henek, T. "Come on dummy: An observational study of children's communications." *Journal of Learning Disabilities*, 1976, 9, 661–669.

Clements, S. D. "Minimal brain dysfunction in children." NINDS Monograph No. 3, Public Health Service Bulletin #1415. Washington, D.C.: U.S. Department of Health, Education, and Welfare, 1966.

Curtis, B. A., Jacobson, S., and Marcus, E. M. *An Introduction to the Neurosciences*. Philadelphia: W. B. Saunders Co., 1972.

Denckla, M. B. "Research needs in learning disabilities: A neurologist's point of view." *Journal of Learning Disabilities*, 1973, 6, 441–450.

Dion, K. K. "Physical attractiveness and evaluation of children's transgressions." *Journal of Personality and Social Psychology*, 1972, 24, 207–213.

Doll, E. A. *Vineland Social Maturity Scale*. Minneapolis: Educational Test Bureau, 1947.

Doll, E. A. *The Measurement of Social Competence*. Vineland, N.J.: Educational Test Bureau, Educational Publishers, Inc., 1953.

Dorland's Illustrated Medical Dictionary. Philadelphia: W. B. Saunders Co., 1965.

Dunn, L. M. *Exceptional Children in the Schools*. New York: Holt, Rinehart and Winston, 1973.

Dykman, R. A., Ackerman, P. T., Clements, S. D., and Peters J. E. "Specific learning disabilities: An attentional deficit syndrome." In H. R. Myklebust (ed.), *Progress in Learning Disabilities, Vol. II*. New York: Grune & Stratton, 1971, 56–93.

Farber, B. *Mental Retardation*. Boston: Houghton Mifflin, 1968.

Federal Register, 41, No. 230, November, 1976.

Flanders, N. *Analyzing Teaching Behavior*. Reading, Massachusetts: Addison-Wesley, 1970.

Gibbs, F. A. and Gibbs, E. L. *Atlas of Electroencephalography*. Mass.: Cummings Co., 1941.

Glaser, G. H. *EEG and Behavior*. New York: Basic Books, Inc., 1963.

Goffman, E. *Asylums*. New York: Anchor Books, Doubleday & Co., 1961.

Good, T. and Brophy, J. *Looking in Classrooms*. New York: Harper & Row, 1973.

Graham, F. K., Matzrazzo, R. G., and Caldwell, B. M. "Behavioral differences between normal and traumatized newborns: II, Standardization, reliability, and validity." *Psychological Monographs*, 1956, 70, 17–33.

Graham, F. K., Ernhart, C. B., Thurston, D., and Craft, M. "Development three years after perinatal anoxia and other potentially damaging newborn experiences." *Psychological Monographs*, 1962, 76 (No. 3).

Gurin, G., Veroff, J., and Feld, S. *Americans View Their Mental Health*. New York: Basic Books, 1960.

Hughes, J. R. "Electroencephalography and learning disabilities." In H. R. Myklebust (ed.), *Progressing Learning Disabilities, Vol. II*. New York: Grune & Stratton, 1971.

Hunter, E. J., Johnson, L. C., and Keefe, F. B. "Electrodermal and cardiovascular responses in nonreaders." *Journal of Learning Disabilities*, 1972, 5, 187–197.

Hyman, H. H. *Interviewing in Social Research*. Chicago: University of Chicago Press, 1954.

Kanner, L. "Early infantile autism." *Journal of Pediatrics*, 1944, 25, 211–217.

Kawi, A. and Pasamanick, B. "Prenatal and paranatal factors in the development of childhood disorders." *Monographs of the Society for Research in Child Development*, 1959, 24, #4.

Keogh, B. K., Tchir, C., and Windeguth-Behn, A. "Teachers' perceptions of educationally high risk children." *Journal of Learning Disabilities*, 1974, 7, 367–374.

Kiloh, L. G. and Osselton, J. W. *Clinical Electroencephalography*. London: Butterworths, 1961.

Knobloch, H. and Pasamanick, B. "Syndrome of minimal cerebral damage in infancy." *Journal of the American Medical Association*, 1959, 170, 1384–1387.

Kravitz, H. and Boehm, J. J. "Head banging is OK." *Northwestern Reports*, Winter/March 1973, 13–14.

Lapouse, R. and Monk, M. A. "Behavior deviations in a representative sample of children: Variation by sex, age, race, social class and family size." *American Journal of Orthopsychiatry*, 1964, 34, 436–446.

Lerner, J. W. *Children with Learning Disabilities*. Boston: Houghton Mifflin, 1971.

Lindzey, G. and Byrne, D. "Measurement of social choice and interpersonal attractiveness." In G. Lindzey and E. Aronson (eds.), *The Handbook of Social Psychology,* Second Edition. Reading, Mass.: Addison-Wesley, 1968, 452–525.

London, P. *The Modes and Morals of Psychotherapy.* New York: Holt, Rinehart & Winston, Inc., 1964.

McCandless, B. R. "Environment and intellectual functioning." In H. A. Stevens and R. Heber (eds.), *Mental Retardation: A Review of Research.* Chicago: The University of Chicago Press, 1964.

McCarthy, J. J., and Paraskevopoulos, J. "Behavior patterns of learning-disabled, emotionally disturbed, and average children." *Exceptional Children,* 1969, 35, 69–74.

Menyuk, P. "Comparison of grammar of children with functionally deviant and normal speech." *Journal of Speech and Hearing Research,* 1964, 7, 109–121.

Mercer, J. R. "Sociological perspectives on mild mental retardation." Paper presented at the Peabody-NIMH Conference on Socio-Cultural Aspects of Mental Retardation, June 1968.

Mercer, J. R. *Labeling the Mentally Retarded.* Berkeley: University of California Press, 1973.

Myklebust, H. R. *Auditory Disorders in Children: A Manual for Differential Diagnosis.* New York: Grune & Stratton, 1954.

Owen, R. W., Adams, P. A., Forrest, T., Stolz, L. M., and Fisher, S. "Learning disorders in children: Sibling studies." *Monographs of the Society for Research in Child Development,* 1971, 36, No. 144.

Rabe, E. F. Appendix A–Neurological Evaluation. In Task Force II, Minimal brain dysfunction in children. *Public Health Service Publication,* No. 2015, 1969.

Rimland, B. *Infantile Autism.* New York: Appleton-Century-Crofts, 1964.

Rogan, L. L. and Lukens, J. E. "Education, administration and classroom procedures." *Minimal Brain Dysfunction National Project on Learning Disabilities in Children Phase II, Public Health Service Publication,* 1969, No. 2015, 21–30.

Rosenhan, D. "On being sane in insane places." *Science,* 1973, 179, 250–258.

Rosenthal, R. *Experimenter Effects in Behavioral Research.* New York: Appleton-Century-Crofts, 1966.

Rowitz, L. "Socioepidemiological analysis of admissions to a state-operated outpatient clinic." *American Journal of Mental Deficiency.* 1973, 78, 300–307.

Skinner, B. F. *Beyond Freedom and Dignity.* New York: Vintage Books, 1971.

Task Force II, "Minimal brain dysfunction in children." Public Health Service Publication No. 2015, 1969.

Vuckovich, D. M. "Pediatric neurology and learning disabilities." In H. R. Myklebust (ed.), *Progress in Learning Disabilities, Vol. I.* New York: Grune & Stratton, 1968, 16–38.

Wender, H. *Minimal Brain Dysfunction in Children.* New York: Wiley-Interscience, 1971.

Yarrow, M. R., Campbell, J. D., and Barton, R. V. "Recollections of childhood–A study of the retrospective method." *Monographs of the Society of Research in Child Development,* 1970, 35, No. 5.

11 | Standardized Tests

This chapter presents brief summaries and descriptions of a number of widely employed assessment devices, and the minutiae associated with such presentations. The tests included in this chapter are not necessarily good or ones which should be employed within one's clinical practice. Rather we have selected tests primarily on the basis of their popularity, with the hope of making the reader a better critic of contemporary clinical practices so frequently encountered when dealing with learning-disabled children.

Before discussing particular tests, several considerations which affect the utility of any measure, be it an observer's ratings, standardized tests, or interviews, should be mentioned. There are three primary considerations. First is the question as to whether the test is reliable. That is, does the test measure something in such a fashion as to produce consistency in the scores obtained? For example, are the scores of one person who takes the test more than once approximately the same? If the scores vary across instances of testing, the measure is deemed to be unreliable. Irrespective of whether the cause of the variation rests in item ambiguity, confusions as to how to take the test, transient states in the test taker, or other random factors, a test which yields disparate scores across testing occasions cannot be measuring anything useful. Any particular score is meaningless if there is no stability to the score obtained. Thus, an unreliable test cannot be a valid one; that is, it cannot be measuring what it is presumed to be measuring.

The second question pertains to the validity of the instrument. Even though the test is a reliable one, it may or may not be a valid one. The test may be measuring what the constructor of the test hoped it would, but it is entirely possible that it is reliably measuring another and unrelated dimension of the person. There are a variety of ways to assess the validity of a measure. For instance, one might compare the performance of people presumed to be high on the trait or skill presumed to be assessed by the test with those presumed to be low on that skill or trait. It is important, however, for the reader to remember that a test does not necessarily measure what its constructors hope and often claim it measures; tests are not valid simply because someone says so. The claim of validity must be supported by systematically derived data, not simply personal biases. In the field of assessment, the number of tests and the pretensions of many outstrip the evidence which is available concerning their validity.

The third consideration is that a test may be reliable and valid yet fail to be clinically useful. One must consider the degree to which test scores will result in a diagnostician making errors. How many persons will be false positives, judged as possessing a skill level or personality trait which in reality they do not possess? How many will be false negatives, judged as not possessing the skill or trait when in fact they do? If there are many false judgments, the utility of the test is decreased. Finally, as Sechrest (1967) has argued, a test should yield information which is not more readily available from other less costly and time-consuming procedures. That is, tests should demonstrate *incremental validity*. Since many of these points are made in other sections of this book, they will not be belabored here. It is critical that the reader bear in mind that the merits of any particular test are in doubt without consideration of these factors.

The tests included here are not presented because their reliability, validity, and usefulness have been clearly established. Their inclusion should not be construed as an endorsement. There is no doubt that some could and should be praised on the basis of the factors we have outlined as important. No doubt some should be eliminated from the professional's test armamentarium. Unfortunately, not enough is known about many to make strong recommendations in either direction. These tests are presented simply because they are frequently used, deservedly or not, and persons concerned with learning disabilities should be familiar with, if not accepting of, them.

Assessment devices have been devised for many purposes and many children. The particular technique selected to assess a child will depend upon the reason for the evaluation, the age of the child, the professional time available, and the educational background and biases of the diagnostician. Following are examples of tests used to screen preschool, kindergarten, and school-aged children, tests used in individual studies of children and group achievement batteries.

PRESCHOOL AND KINDERGARTEN SCREENING SCALES

In the past few years concern has grown for the detection of potential learning problems in preschool and kindergarten children. Preschool and kindergarten screening tests for potential learning disabilities are predicated upon the assumption that detection and intervention at this time will prevent failure in the elementary school years. To detect and intervene requires a definition of potential failure. The assumption in this case is that failure in adequate development of certain skills or behaviors at age 3 predicts failure in school-related skills at age 8. Discrepancies in growth of critical areas, particularly language and perceptual skills, are believed to be predictive of future educational difficulties. If a child is slow for his age in the development of vocabulary and syntax at age 3, he will be retarded in vocabulary and syntax development at ages 5, 7, and later. Because of this, the child will be handicapped in the acquisition of academic skills dependent upon such knowledge. Detection of inadequacies in preschoolers is thus based upon the assumptions that a child's development proceeds in a regular and predictable fashion and that delays in defined developmental areas are linked critically to skills needed as a child progresses through the school system.

Another assumption underlying the early detection movement is that intervention provided children experiencing developmental delays will alleviate or eliminate later problems. If problems are dealt with early, the child is not expected to require special services later. These assumptions have been based in large part upon longitudinal studies of high-risk infants in which traumas related to birth were linked to conceptual and behavioral problems three years later, to post hoc analyses of parental descriptions of the developmental histories of learning-disabled children, and to studies of language development in normal and language-deviant children.

The early detection–early treatment movement is not without dangers. Developers and users of testing techniques designed for young children need to be well aware of the limitations regarding the assumptions and difficulties inherent in predicting academic performance on the basis of presumably related behaviors. As the review of infant intelligence tests in Chapter 5 indicates, there are many practical difficulties involved in the development of adequate measures. Hazards aside, many tests are being developed. Before they become used, further information concerning reliability and validity must be established.

A very serious issue in constructing techniques to detect potential learning disabilities is defining the potential learning disability. We have longstanding and continuing difficulties in defining what a learning disability is in children who are already failing in school. How, then, can we define what has not yet occurred? We need to ask how many children will be falsely labeled as disabled and how many will go undetected. In which developmental areas need a child be retarded, and how far behind need the child be, for us to say with assuredness that the child needs help? What proportion of problems would spontaneously improve with a little help from Mother Nature? We must weigh the benefits to be derived from detection against the dangers inherent in labeling children as inadequate.

Finally, there is the critical issue of providing programs for children who are labeled as potentially disabled. Assuming that we manage to define potential learning problems, what effective techniques are available for remedial programs? We do not yet know which techniques will be effective, nor whether we can prevent later school problems. In a number of instances test constructors have provided remedial programs based upon the test.

Because the test constructor recommends a test-based remedial program is no guarantee of the program's effectiveness. While the tests currently being used may not ultimately be found to have some utility for defining individual children or developing intervention techniques, their use will further our knowledge as to the adequacy of the techniques and the nature of the developing child. They are thus worth our consideration.

The *Early Detection Inventory* (McGahan and McGahan, 1967) has been designed to assess preschoolers and children in ungraded primary classes. It is not a test, but a means to organize data derived from a variety of sources: parent, dentist, speech therapist, audiologist, and "test administrator." The child is assessed in the areas of school readiness, motor performance, and social-emotional adjustment. Ratings in each area on a 1-to-3 scale are presumed to help in predicting whether or not a child will need help upon entering school. The lower the rating, the more extensive the subsequent need for help may be (McCarthy, 1972).

There are many shortcomings in the scoring procedure used, but the manual provides the information needed to set up a screening procedure and a preschool evaluation clinic. This procedure involves the setting up of stations in which the children move from professional to professional. Many children can be screened by varying professionals in an economic use of time. While we do not know whether this particular inventory captures a child's readiness for school or the need for special help, it does provide a means to organize a comprehensive case study of many children.

The *Gesell Developmental Tests* (Ilg and Ames, 1965) are based upon extensive data derived from observations of children and interviews with parents conducted at the Gesell Institute. The data base is large. Norms are available for children ages 4 weeks to 72 months for motor development, adaptive behavior, language, and personal social skills. The test is useful in detecting very deviant children; but it is questionable as to whether it will be useful in detecting learning-disabled youngsters (see Chapter 5), although some believe it may be usable (Borstelmann, 1972). It is important to note that there has been extensive research on the scales and the user can determine the usefulness and constraints in its employment. Parenthetically, the manual presents the authors' educational viewpoint that children be placed in school on the basis of developmental age rather than chronological age or IQ. Their cautionary philosophy is worth noting in a time of haste to label and place preschoolers in educational programs.

A quick screening device for children 3 to 5 years of age was developed by a Title III program in *Early Childhood Development* (Holliday, 1972). There are no norms, reliability or validity data; the purpose was simply to identify children having problems and to refer these children for more intensive study. The areas screened include vision and hearing, speech and language, social-emotional status, cognition, gross and fine motor movement, and perception.

Vision testing requires the child to place a hand in the same direction as a letter seen on the letter chart. Audition screening requires the child upon hearing a sound presented on the audiometer to respond by dropping blocks or clothes pins into a basket or by putting pegs into a pegboard. Socio-emotional status is informally judged by observing the child's response to peers.

The speech and language survey presents the child with the following items. The child is asked to tell a story about a picture shown to him, to tell what individual items are in the picture, and to point to the picture named. The child is also asked to follow instructions, such as repeating numbers and acting out short instructions (e.g., stand up, clap your hands, point to your shoes).

Cognition items require the child to remember and relate items put in a box by the examiner, to relate whether pictures seen are the same or different, to learn paired-associates, and to classify objects.

Gross motor screening assesses the child's ability to walk backwards, forwards, and sideways on a balance beam, jump on each foot and on both feet, hop on alternating feet in a rhythmic pattern, locate body parts and label them, imitate unilateral, bilateral, and contralateral movements, step over and sideways to pass a yardstick, draw a circle, connect X's in a lateral position, and draw parallel lines connecting two X's in a vertical position.

Fine motor-perceptual screening has the child replace puzzle pieces by shape and color, imitate block designs, and replicate object assembly of examiner (e.g., one apple–five birds).

Without information concerning the reliability and validity of these tests, no judgments can be made as to their usefulness in aiding the learning disability specialist, or any specialists for that matter.

THE SCREENING OF SCHOOL-AGED CHILDREN

Predictive Index

The *Predictive Index* (deHirsch, Jansky, and Langford, 1966) is the catalyst for much of the development of tests for preschool and kindergarten children. In this study deHirsch, Jansky, and Langford attempted to predict which kindergarteners might fail reading, writing, or spelling as assessed at the end of second grade. A large battery of tests was administered to a group of kindergarten children. Those tests which predicted best the children experiencing academic difficulties in second grade now comprise the Predictive Index. Trimble (1970) expanded upon the Predictive Index so that practitioners could score the items and specified the number of tests the child should fail to indicate the need for intervention. Trimble also developed an intervention program based upon the child's performance on the Predictive Index.

The Predictive Index includes the following tests:

1. Pencil use: Ability to hold and manipulate a pencil correctly.
2. Wepman Auditory Discrimination test (described in Chapter 7).
3. Categories: The child must provide category name for three stimulus items (e.g., red-green-blue, apple-hamburger-ice cream).
4. Gates Word Matching subtest: The child is shown four words and must draw a line between the two which match.
5. Bender Visual-motor Gestalt test (described in Chapter 7).
6. Horst Reversals test: The child must circle items the same as a stimulus item (e.g., to to ot ot to ot to).
7. Number of Words Used in a Story: Child is asked to tell the story of The Three Bears. Scoring is based upon the number of words, relevant details, and ability to get across the point of the story.
8. Word Recognition I, II, and III: At the beginning of the session the child is taught to read two words, "boy" and "train," and told to copy them from a model. At the end of the testing session, the child is asked to pick from a pack of cards presented successively the words "boy" and "train" and to pick the same words when the pack of cards are all exposed on the table, and then to write as much of the two words from memory as he could recall. The child is scored 3 points for the word if spelled correctly, 2 if there are two letters of the word, 1 for one letter, and 0 for no letters on "boy"; and 2 for three or four letters of "train" or 1 for one or two letters.

As yet, we know of little direct evidence pertaining to this instrument. Trimble (1970), on the basis of a study of 266 children, concluded that this test might be a useful screening device for predicting reading problems of children completing the first grade.

Devereux Elementary School Behavior Rating Scale

In the *Devereux Elementary School Behavior Rating Scale* (Spivack and Swift, 1967), the teacher is instructed to compare the child being rated to his peers with regard to classroom behavior problems. The child is rated on forty-seven scoring items related to one another in eleven categories. The categories and examples of the items within them include the following.

1. Classroom disturbance: Has to be reprimanded or controlled because of behavior in class.
2. Impatience: Starts working before getting directions straight.
3. Disrespect-defiance: Breaks classroom rules.

4. External blame: Says teacher does not help him enough.
5. Achievement anxiety: Outwardly nervous when test given.
6. External reliance: Looks to see how others are doing something before he does it.
7. Comprehension: Gets the point of what he reads or hears in class.
8. Inattentive-withdrawn: Quickly loses attention when teacher explains something to him.
9. Irrelevant-responsiveness: Tells stories which are exaggerated and untruthful.
10. Creative initiative: Brings things to class that relate to current topic.
11. Needs closeness to teacher: Seeks out teacher before or after class to talk about school or personal matters.

This scale taps many of the behaviors attributed to learning disabilities although extremes in such behaviors are supposed to be more indicative of emotional than learning problems. While there may be differences in the extremes of behaviors which result in differential labeling, many of these problems are characteristic of learning-disabled children, and the profiling of them along with comparison to peers can give the teacher or learning disability specialist one means to organize information about the child's classroom behavior.

Pupil Rating Scale

The *Pupil Rating Scale* (Myklebust, 1971) is another screening technique which attempts to tap behaviors presumably more related to learning disabilities than emotional problems. This scale was developed as part of a large study which attempted to determine the medical and psychological correlates of learning disabilities. While the intensive study of the children included medical, neurological, EEG, and complete psychometric batteries, the Pupil Rating Scale was found to be a promising measure for detecting children subsequently labeled learning-disabled. Using this instrument, the teacher rates each child on a five-point scale on five categories of behavior. These categories include the following:

1. Auditory comprehension and listening: Ability to follow direction, comprehension of class discussions, ability to retain information heard, and comprehension of word meanings.
2. Spoken language: Ability to speak in complete sentences using accurate sentence structure, vocabulary ability, ability to recall words, ability to tell stories and relate experiences, and ability to formulate ideas from isolated facts.
3. Orientation: Promptness, spatial orientation, judgment of relationships, and learning directions.

4. Behavior: Cooperation, attention, ability to organize, ability to cope with new situations, and tactfulness.
5. Motor: General coordination, balance, and ability to manipulate utensils.

Bryan and McGrady (1972) studied the factor structure and screening utility of the Pupil Rating Scale. An analysis of teacher ratings of 183 boys who had learning disabilities and 176 adequate achievers indicated that teachers consistently rate the problem learners lower on each area of the scale. While such scales no doubt have validity and reliability in detecting learning problems, the issue remains as to what behaviors of children elicit teachers' judgments.

Screening Tests for Identifying Children with Specific Language Disability

The *Screening Tests for Identifying Children with Specific Language Disability* (Slingerland, 1964) is an instrument based upon the hypothesis that deficits in information processing result in learning difficulties, particularly in those areas of learning which require language. It is one of the few tests designed to assess information processing skills in groups of children for screening and diagnostic purposes. There are three levels of the test, one for each of the following grade levels: mid-grade one to mid-grade two; mid-grade two to mid-grade three; mid-grade three to mid-grade four. There are eight subtests at each level which assess various means of visual and auditory processing in the context of school like activities. For instance, the visual tests require the child to copy a paragraph from a distance and at a near point, to remember a stimulus presented in a multiple choice and to reproduce the answer in writing. The auditory tests require the child to repeat words and a short story dictated to him, and to indicate sounds heard at the beginning and end of words.

The adequacy of this test is unknown insofar as insufficient information on validity, reliability, and standardization samples is available (Deno, 1972). It should be noted also that the test lacks sufficient measures of language usage and comprehension—critical skills for adequate academic performance.

DIAGNOSTIC TESTS AND THE SCHOOL-AGED CHILD

Up to this point the focus of this chapter has been upon screening techniques for the detection of present and potential learning problems. In the remainder of this section we shall describe some of the tests used to assess intelligence, specific diagnostic tests, and achievement tests. There are many more and better tests available for the assessment of older children, no doubt as a result of the generally higher reliability or stability of older children's performance on tests.

Intelligence tests have had a long and generally useful role in education. They were devised to aid in school placement decisions and have been heavily utilized since their inception. Here we will discuss some of the instruments designed to assess intelligence, but the reader is referred to a more detailed discussion of the concept of intelligence and the utility of these tests in Chapter 5.

Wechsler Intelligence Scale for Children

The *Wechsler Intelligence Scale for Children* (Wechsler, 1946), the WISC, is widely used for the assessment of intelligence in children ages 5 to 15. (There is also a form available for testing adults, the Wechsler Adult Intelligence Scale [WAIS], and one for children ages 4 to 6, the Wechsler Preschool and Primary Scale of Intelligence [WPPSI].) The scale consists of twelve subtests, two of which are optional. Five of these form the basis for the verbal intelligence score and five comprise a performance intelligence score; the two groups combined provide a full scale IQ.

Most of the verbal tests correlate with each other to a higher degree than with tests on the performance scale and vice-versa. The tests labeled verbal and performance differ in the skills they measure, but both tap factors which cut across the delineation of categories.

The IQ score obtained is a *deviation* IQ. It indicates the amount by which a person deviates from the average performance of individuals of his own age group. The 100 IQ is set to equal the average score for each age. The highest 1 percent of individuals at any age level will have IQs over 135 and the lowest 1 percent will have IQs of 65 or below. Fifty percent of children will have IQs from 90 to 110 at each age level. The various subtests which constitute the verbal scale of the test, along with example items, include the following.

1. General information: From what animal do we get milk?
2. Comprehension: What is the thing to do if you cut your finger?
3. Arithmetic: The child is presented with arithmetic problems.
4. Similarities: The child is asked to explain in what manner various items are alike, for example, a peach and a plum.
5. Vocabulary: Definitions of common words are required of the child.
6. Digit span (optional): Children are required to repeat after the examiner sets of digits as presented and in reverse sequence.

It should be noted that the arithmetic and the digit span subtests show the least correlation with verbal IQ scores, and other studies have suggested that these tests may be tapping mathematical rather than purely verbal skills (Freides, 1974). Also noteworthy is that the digit span subtest is the only assessment of immediate or short-term memory in the WISC and is often employed as a test of such a function. However, this subtest is not a highly reliable one and should not be used to draw general inferences about an individual's memory.

The various subtests which constitute the performance scale of the WISC, along with example items, were discussed more fully in Chapter 5.

Patterns of subtest scores have often been used for clinical assessments, following Wechsler's (1958) suggestions. We believe such a use is unwarranted. The subtests are not reliable and empirical justifications for this practice are not available.

Other investigators have suggested that WISC subtest scores be combined in other than the verbal-performance scales to better describe certain types of learning problems. Keogh, Wetter, McGinty, and Donlon (1973) subdivide the WISC into a three-factor test. The factors are (a) verbal-comprehension, comprised of information, vocabulary, and comprehension; (b) analytic-field-approach of object assembly, block design, and picture completion; and (c) attention-concentration of arithmetic, digit span, and coding. A comparison of learning and behavior problems, hyperactive learning-disabled, and mentally retarded boys on these three WISC factors revealed that both learning-disabled groups, in contrast to the mentally retarded, were adequate on the verbal and analytic factors and lowest on the attention-concentration factor. This suggests that low subtest scores on this combination of subtests may typify learning-disabled children.

Studies of WISC scores in disabled readers have led Bannatyne (1968) and Rugel (1974) to suggest that the verbal and performance scales of the WISC be reclassified as spatial, conceptual, and sequential (Rugel, 1974) or spatial, verbal conceptualizing, sequencing, and acquired knowledge. This is recommended because the traditional split of verbal/performance appears to be invalid; tests classified as performance ones, or arithmetic for instance, require both verbal comprehension and verbal response from the child. Bannatyne (1974, p. 273) regroups the subtests in this way.

verbal/performance may be invalid

Spatial ability: picture completion, block design, object assembly.
Verbal comprehension ability: comprehension, similarities, vocabulary.
Sequencing ability: digit span, arithmetic, coding.
Acquired knowledge: information, arithmetic, vocabulary.

Studying the test scores of twenty-two disabled readers, Rugel reported that the disabled readers perform best on the spatial category, second best on the conceptual category, and poorest on the sequential category.

Subtest scores have also been utilized to plan remediation programs (Ferinden, 1969, 1970). Children low in a particular area are given exercises which are believed to reflect the same skill. There is great similarity between the item and the remedial technique suggested, so this may be helpful. Since there has been no empirical study of such implementation of test results, one cannot say whether or not this is an advisable practice.

Stanford-Binet Intelligence Scale

The *Stanford-Binet Intelligence Scale* (Terman and Merrill, 1960) is an individually administered test of intelligence appropriate for children ages 2 to 18. It is widely used, and is probably the preferred test of intelligence for children ages 2 to 6. The analyses of the Stanford-Binet made by Anastasi (1961) and Freeman (1962) are adapted here.

> *Years 2–5:* At this age level the subtests involve manipulation of objects (placement of pieces in a simple formboard block building), recognition of body parts, the recognition of objects referred to by name and by function. Rote memory, the use of words in combination, verbal comprehension, and word knowledge are also assessed.
> *Years 6–12:* The child is tested for form perception, visual motor skills, rote memory, word knowledge, number concepts, and arithmetical reasoning.
> *Years 13–Superior Adult III:* At this level, visual analysis and imagery, visual motor skills, rote memory for digits, words and sentences, work knowledge, and problem solving are assessed.

Memory, spatial orientation, numerical concepts, and language skills are tapped at scattered age levels using increasingly difficult items. For example, tests of memory may require the child to recall objects or the content of passages; numerical tests start with simple counting and proceed to complex reasoning problems.

This test is heavily weighted toward verbal abilities. Anastasi (1961) reports correlations between scores on the vocabulary test and the mental age based on the entire test as ranging from .71 to .83 for children 8 through 14 years. She further indicates that this test is more reliable for older than for younger children and more reliable for lower than higher IQ scores. The Stanford-Binet test is quite useful in predicting future school achievement. Being heavily weighted to tap verbal skills, it is not surprising that the test can yield useful prediction in activities which weight such skills. As Anastasi points out, the test is an achievement test.

Peabody Picture Vocabulary Test

The *Peabody Picture Vocabulary Test* (Dunn, 1959), the PPVT, is an individually or group administered test of verbal intelligence. The test was designed for use with handicapped children who might have unusual difficulties responding verbally to test items. Thus, the test is designed for children suffering from mental retardation and cerebral palsy, who have speech problems, are brain damaged, or emotionally disturbed. The test contains 150 test plates, each with four pictures (see Figure 11-1). The examiner says a word and the child must point to the correct picture. The test

FIGURE 11-1: Examples from the Peabody Picture Vocabulary test

SOURCE: Dunn, L. M. *Peabody Picture Vocabulary Test.* Minneapolis, Minn.: American Guidance Service, 1959.

is appropriate for children ages 2½ through 18 years and provides scores in the form of deviation IQs, mental age, and percentiles. It is popular because it is quick, easy to administer and score, and can be given by untrained persons. While it does correlate in the 70s to 80s with the WISC and the Stanford-Binet, there is some concern for what the test actually measures (Lyman, 1965); and this concern is increased if nonprofessional persons use the information to make judgments, predictions, and pronouncements about children. The learning disability professional is cautioned against using scores on this test as a substitute for standardized intelligence tests, because it samples a restricted range of human behavior. It is recommended solely as a measure of verbal comprehension of single words.

Goodenough-Harris Drawing Test

The *Goodenough-Harris Drawing Test* (Harris, 1963), previously referred to as the Draw a Person Test (Goodenough, 1926), is a quick and reliable measure of intelligence for children 3.3 years to 13 years of age (Harris, 1963). The child is instructed to make a drawing of a man as best he can. An 8½ × 11 sheet of white paper is used and the child must complete the drawing using a pencil. The test is not timed.

The child is scored one point for each detail of the human body which is represented and additional points for the correctness of the proportions of the body. Norms and scoring procedure are also available for drawings of the self and a woman.

The child's score, like the IQ, is expressed with an average of 100 and a standard deviation of 15. The child's score is standardized by age and sex groups. The IQ from the DAP is not identical with the IQ derived from an individual intelligence test, although the correlation is quite high. The score on the Goodenough-Harris test, as an indicator of intelligence, is quite reliable between the ages of 5 and 10 years.

This test can be subclassified as an assessment of visual-motor skills and compared to other visual-motor and visual-perceptual tests which require the child to remember, reconstruct, compare, and discriminate visual stimuli. One further note: while the test is often employed by clinical psychologists and other specialists as a device for making inferences concerning the child's personality dynamics and content, there is reason to doubt the validity of such procedures. The test yields a good quick assessment of intelligence scores obtained on other measures, but it is unlikely that it can be used as a personality assessment device.

SPECIFIC DIAGNOSTIC TESTS

Diagnostic tests are designed to measure performance on tasks which are believed to be essential to academic achievement. While general measures of intelligence define children according to some classification scheme, the purpose of diagnostic tests is to specify educational or remedial programs (Kirk and Kirk, 1972). By assessing presumed impediments to later achievement, the diagnostician can map out the specifics of an intervention program.

Illinois Test of Psycholinguistic Abilities

The test which has had the greatest influence in diagnosing learning disabilities is the *Illinois Test of Psycholinguistic Abilities* (Kirk, McCarthy, and

Kirk, 1968). The development of this tool has had an enormous influence upon the conceptualization, diagnosis, and treatment of learning-disabled children.

The ITPA attempts to assess three dimensions of communication skills: the channels of communication, levels of organization, and psycholinguistic processes. Channels of communication refers to the sensory modality which is being used for the reception or comprehension of the stimulus and which is being employed for expression. In this case, the modalities being evaluated at the receptive level are audition and vision; the modes of expression include speech and gesture.

The two *levels* of language organization are the *automatic-sequential,* activities which require retention and expression of automatic chains, and the *representational,* communication which requires meaning attached to symbols. The automatic-sequential level involves memory and imitation of spoken utterances, whereas the representational level indicates the thought processes operating behind the signal.

Psycholinguistic processes refers to the acquisition and use of all the learned abilities necessary for language usage. Three main abilities are presumed to be assessed: decoding, association, and encoding. Decoding refers to abilities necessary to obtain meaning from auditorily and visually presented material (e.g., receptive language, comprehension of what is seen and heard). Association, which denotes manipulation of linguistic symbols internally, is a central process elicited by decoding, which elicits, in turn, encoding (e.g., thought). Encoding is comprised of all the abilities which are required for expressive language.

There are twelve subtests in the 1968 revision of the ITPA. The test is appropriate for use with children ages 2.4 to 10.3. The test is standardized so that a number of scores can be obtained. A psycholinguistic composite age, which is a composite of the combined subtests, can be computed. Like mental age, it is an overall index of psycholinguistic abilities. A psycholinguistic age is available for each of the subtests. Scaled scores are used to plot a profile of psycholinguistic ages, which permits a direct comparison of the child's performance from one subtest to another. Tests at the representational level of language organization and examples of items follow.

1. Auditory reception: The child is presented with a short question to which he must respond "yes" or "no." An example of such an item is, "Do scouts signal?"
2. Visual reception: The child is presented with a stimulus picture which is then removed from his visual field. The child must then identify the same item from a set of four pictures. The catch is that the correct choice is semantically, but not visually, identical. Examples are a baby cup and a coffee cup, a saddle shoe and a tennis shoe.
3. Auditory association: The child's ability to relate concepts orally is presumed to be measured on this test. The test is similar to a sentence

completion exercise, in which the items are presented and answered orally. An example is the item, "A kitty says meow, a doggie says ____?"

4. Visual association: The child's ability to relate concepts presented visually is assessed. The stimulus input is visual, the response is verbal. The child is presented with a single stimulus picture surrounded by four optional pictures, one of which must be associated with the stimulus. The child is asked to indicate which of the four goes with the stimulus picture. Examples include man's hat with man, pocketknife, hammer, or watch; high heel shoes with woman, man, girl, or boy.

5. Expression, verbal: This subtest refers to the child's ability to express himself verbally. The child is given a series of common objects (e.g., a ball, a block, an envelope) and asked to describe and tell about each object.

6. Expression, manual: Here the child's skill in communicating nonverbally is measured. The child is shown an object, then a series of pictures of objects and is asked to show, through gestures, how such objects are employed. Examples of the objects used in the subtest are a guitar and a clarinet.

In addition to those subtests designed to assess representational processes, there are those which purportedly measure language organization at the automatic-sequential level. These subtests are listed following, with examples of their items.

1. Automatic, grammatic closure: These items are designed to measure the child's use of grammatical forms and rules which are acquired in other than formal classroom contexts (i.e., automatically acquired). In this subtest, the child is presented with a picture. Then the examiner starts a sentence and the child is to complete it with the appropriate form of the stimulus word. For instance, the examiner says, "Here is a dog; here are two ____. This horse is not big, this horse is big, this horse is even ____. These children all fell down, he hurt himself, she hurt herself, they all hurt ____."

2. Automatic, visual closure: This subtest is employed to assess the child's recognition of objects when only a part of the object is visible. The stimulus picture is given to the child and he is then required to discover that stimulus in the remaining parts of the picture. Thus, he may be presented with a shoe as the stimulus and then be asked to discover shoes depicted in a picture of a cluttered room where the shoes are only partially displayed.

3. Sequential, auditory memory: The child is asked to repeat a series of digits given him orally by the examiner.

4. Sequential, visual memory: Here the child is asked to reproduce a sequence of nonmeaningful forms from memory. The child is shown

a set of geometric designs, the stimuli are then removed from his visual field, and the child must then duplicate the demonstrated series.

Two supplementary tests were added to the 1968 revision of the ITPA. These were the auditory closure test and the sound blending subtest. In the auditory closure test, the child is asked to recognize a word when only part of the word is orally presented to him. In the sound blending subtest, the child is required to synthesize sounds into a meaningful word.

An extensive review of the ITPA by Carroll (1972) reveals the following insights. A review of factor analytic studies suggests that the test taps three or four (not nine) factors. These include vocabulary, immediate memory span, and auditory processing. Differences in the scores on these factors have been found for middle-, upper-, and lower-class children. The standardization sample used to construct the test scores were average middle-class children; thus, care must be taken in applying the test to children who are from different socioeconomic and cultural backgrounds and to children who have severe handicaps. Auditory handicaps, for instance, might reflect differences in ability to understand different dialects, not intellectual defects or defects in information processing. While the reliability of the test is apparently good, there is high variance in the subtest scores among the average children for whom the test was intended.

A serious question is raised regarding the use of ITPA test scores to program intervention (Newcomer and Hammill, 1975). This is particularly serious, because the practice has become so widespread and popular. Furthermore, there are no studies showing that remedial programs chosen on the basis of ITPA test subscores are effective. Finally, Carroll raises some questions regarding the utility of the ITPA to discriminate between good and poor readers; the data are inconclusive in this regard. The ITPA thus has fairly good reliability with a fairly stable profile of scores. There are some questions about the validity of the test, and the standardization sample is middle class, thus limiting the generalization and interpretation of test scores to other groups of children. For middle-class children, it is a widely used test of verbal comprehension and general information, immediate memory, visual and auditory perception, and one kind of expressive verbal fluency (Carroll, 1972).

Detroit Tests of Learning Aptitudes

The *Detroit Tests of Learning Aptitudes* (Baker and Leland, 1935) was designed to assess auditory and visual information processing and is a battery of nineteen tests applicable to individuals from age 4 to adulthood. The examiner selects those subtests suitable to the age of the person being tested; from nine to thirteen subtests are usually recommended for different age groups. It appears to be the only diagnostic test available for children over 10 years of age. Like the ITPA, it has specific subtests to measure auditory and visual processing of information. It has, in addition, tests of social adjustment and orientation. The test was constructed in the 1930s and the standardization is not up to more modern standards, nor are many of the pictures used as stimuli contemporary ones. The test results must be interpreted with a grain of salt.

Here are examples of subtests appropriate for children above age 10.

Verbal absurdities (9 years and older): Consists of twenty questions in which the child must indicate what is foolish about a situation described by the examiner. An example is, "If I am in a hurry, I get a horse because automobiles are too slow."

Verbal opposites (9 years and older): This subtest requires the child to respond with the opposite of a stimulus word spoken by the examiner. Examples are: boy . . . cooked . . . raw . . . victory . . . ecstasy.

Speed and precision (3 to 14 years and older): The child must put an X in each of a large number of circles presented on one page. A check is made at the point a child has reached at the end of each minute.

Auditory attention span for unrelated words (3 to 14 years and older): The examiner says a sequence of words and the child responds by imitating the sequence. The child is scored for each word he recalls correctly. Examples: cat . . . ice; fish . . . clock . . . heart . . . sun . . . box . . . frog; ear . . . boat . . . key . . . pig . . . south . . . knob . . . ink . . . rope.

Social perception (3 to 12 years): The child is asked what to do in a variety of situations. Example: What is the thing to do if: Someone wants you to throw stones at the windows of another person's house? You have some partly worn-out clothes which you do not need? You have to sit next to someone you do not like at a party?

Visual attention span for objects (3 to 14 years and older): On this subtest, the child is shown a card with pictures on it and must recall from memory the items on the card.

Spatial and time orientation (3 to 12 years): There is a series of twelve questions such as: Are you taller than I am? Can you touch the moon? What season is it now?

Free association (3 to 14 years and older): The child is asked to say all the words he can think of, any words at all. Time limits are suggested for various age levels.

Memory for designs (3 to 14 years and older): This test has three parts. In the first, the child is asked to copy a design; the second part requires the child to finish from memory a partially complete geometric figure, while in the third part the child is asked to reproduce from memory the total geometric figure.

Auditory attention span for related syllables (2 to 14 years and older): Sentences of increasing length are presented to the child. The child is credited with the parts of the sentence he repeats correctly. Examples are: My doll has pretty hair. Green leaves come on the trees in early spring. Each four years voting takes place which results in many men being placed in office for. . . .

Social adjustment (3 to 14 years and older): Child answers questions such as, "What is a jail?" "What is a school nurse?"

Visual attention span for letters (3 to 14 years and older): The child is shown a sheet with letters on it. The child must indicate which letters he has just seen.

Visual discrimination and sequencing (9 to 14 years and older): The child is shown a picture of a disarranged figure, the parts of which have been numbered. On a separate sheet of paper the child must indicate where the pieces should go by placing the number in the appropriate place. There are ten pictures and the child is scored for correctly placed pieces.

Oral directions (9 to 14 years and older): The child is to follow a series of instructions. Examples are: Put a one in the circle and a cross in the square box. See the three circles: put a number two in the first circle, a cross in the second circle, and draw a line under the third circle. Cross out the even number in a square, the odd number in the second triangle, the number in the third circle, the biggest number that is in a square, and the number in a circle below twelve.

Likenesses and differences (9 to 14 years or older): The child is to specify in what ways things are alike and different. Examples are: morning/afternoon; telescope/microscope; mentia/dementia.

Bender Visual Motor Gestalt Test

The *Bender Visual Motor Gestalt test* (Bender, 1938) is a rather popular test with professionals. More commonly called the Bender Gestalt, this test is used for a variety of purposes, which range from personality assessment to measuring the presence of brain damage. The test consists of nine simple designs, one of which is shown in Figure 11-2, which are presented

FIGURE 11-2: An example of a design from the Bender Visual Motor Gestalt test

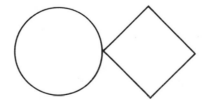

SOURCE: Bender, L. "A Visual Motor Gestalt test and Its Clinical Use." *American Orthopsychiatry Assoc. Res. Monograph,* 1938, No. 3.

one at a time to the respondent. His task is to copy the design shown to him. The test performance is evaluated in terms of the adequacy of the copy. For example, rotations of the figures are noted, as well as general failures to connect components of the design. The test was originally designed to assess brain damage in adults, but now is also commonly used in clinical assessments of children.

Koppitz (1964) has provided scoring procedures and normative information for the use of this test with children between the ages of 5 and 11. Norms for evaluating the child's test performance are based upon 1,104 children from public schools located in rural, urban, and suburban settings in the Midwest and East. While this sample size is seemingly large, it should be remembered that for some age categories, such as the 10 to 10½ and 10½ to 11 years, the number of children used in developing the norms was quite small, twenty-seven and thirty-one respectively. Koppitz presents data pertaining to the correlation of children's scores on the test with performances on the WISC, readiness and achievement tests, teacher judgments, reading and arithmetic performances, and various states of psychopathology. In general, the test appears to correlate with about everything.

In spite of Koppitz's recommendations, however, the data she presents regarding the use of the test to assess emotional problems would rule out such use. The number of false positives and negatives is too great to rely on the test for such purposes. Koppitz has provided a valuable empirical start in conducting and reporting the results of the studies on reliability and validity.

Developmental Test of Visual Motor Integration

The _Developmental Test of Visual Motor Integration_ (Beery and Buktenica, 1967) is quite similar to the Bender Gestalt insofar as the child is required to copy geometric shapes. In this test, however, the geometric shapes are varied in difficulty and are suitable for children from ages 2 to almost 16. The score obtained from the test is a developmental quotient, which is similar to a mental age and is expressed in years and months. The Beery test consists of twenty-four geometric forms presented in a test booklet with a space underneath each form in which to copy the form. For each form the manual presents scoring criteria to determine if the child's reproduction passes or fails. Techniques for determining specific areas of difficulty in the visual-motor spectrum are also provided. A shorter test booklet with just the first fifteen forms is available for testing children ages 2 to 8. According to Chissom (1972), there are a number of advantages to this test which may make it preferable to the Bender Gestalt. The format of the test is likely to yield greater reliability in scoring. Moreover, there is some data suggesting that the test might be useful in predicting first-grade reading achievement (see Figure 11-3).

FIGURE 11-3: An example of an item from the Developmental Test of Visual Motor Integration

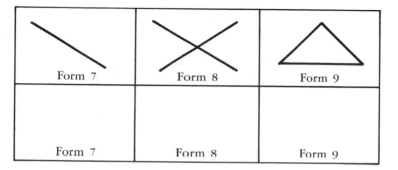

SOURCE: Beery, K. E. and Buktenica, N. A., *Developmental Test of Visual Motor Integration.* Chicago, Ill.: Follett Educational Corp., 1967.

Frostig Developmental Tests of Visual Perception

The *Frostig Developmental Tests of Visual Perception* (1961), like the ITPA, has been used for diagnosis of specific visual information processing problems and has been accompanied by specific remedial programs to alleviate the deficit skill. The test is appropriate for children ages 3 to 8, but it has been used with older children evidencing difficulty in visual perception. The areas tested include: eye-motor coordination, figure-ground, consistency of shape, position in space, and spatial relationships. The score is standardized to yield a perceptual age equivalent. The median score is 100, upper and lower quartiles 110 and 90. The test is designed for use as a screening device with younger children of nursery school, kindergarten, and first-grade ages, or as a clinical tool with older children manifesting learning problems. The test can be administered to children individually or in groups. The subtests and some example items follow.

1. Eye-motor coordination: The child is required to draw a line between two specified boundaries.
2. Figure ground: The child is shown figures which overlap, in one case a rectangle and triangle. The child must outline the "box" only.

3. Constancy of shape: The child's task is to recognize various shapes (circles, squares, rectangles, ellipses, and parallelograms) when they appear in a variety of sizes, shadings, textures, and positions in space and outline the shape specified by the examiner.

4. Position in space: The child must make discriminations among reversals and rotated drawings. This is similar to reading readiness tests. The child is presented with a series and must find which of the items is different or the same as a stimulus item.

5. Spatial relationships: The child sees a dot pattern on one side of the page and must reproduce it by drawing appropriate connecting lines between dots on the other side.

Chissom (1972) has provided a review of the research relevant to this test which leads to the following observations. Studies find that the administration and procedures for scoring the test are clear. The test-retest reliability is good when the test is used for first- and second-graders. There does appear to be some relationship between scores on this test and reading achievement, but this should not be interpreted to mean that the test is useful in diagnosing *specific* reading difficulties.

It should be noted that the children on whom the test was developed did not include minority culture children and thus this test should not be employed with them. Additionally, studies have indicated that the test does not measure five distinct factors of perception, as implied in the format of five subtests, but rather performance on all subtests is related to each other. Thus, apparently one visual motor function, rather than five, is being assessed, at least when the test is applied to young children.

Purdue Perceptual-Motor Survey

The *Purdue Perceptual-Motor Survey* (Roach and Kephart, 1966) is an informal survey appropriate for testing perceptual-motor development of children in grades two through four. The child receives oral instructions on what to do while performing each of the tests. The activities evaluated are laterality, directionality, and skills of perceptual-motor matching. The activities include the walking board or balance beam, jumping and hopping, identification of body parts, imitation of movement, ability to move through an obstacle course, movements of arms and legs (angels in the snow), stepping stones, chalkboard drawing, ocular pursuit, and visual achievement forms (copying geometric shapes). All of the items of the Purdue Perceptual-Motor Survey are arranged from easiest to hardest.

The teacher scores the child's performance informally, rating it as *1* if the child cannot perform the task, *2* if the child hesitates or is markedly inaccurate, *3* if the child shows slight hesitancy and slight inaccuracy, and *4* if the performance is adequate. As with the Frostig test, the results on this survey are said to be related to various forms of remediation.

Jamison (1972) has provided a critical review of the test. She questions whether the subtests can be reliably scored on the basis of instructions in the manual. In addition, she argues that the items are not appropriately grouped to measure various abilities and that the conditions for the testing of the child are not sufficiently detailed to allow standardized testing procedures. In conclusion, she writes, "It is recommended that the PPMS not be used" (p. 875). Another reviewer, Landis (1972), while commending the test for its theoretical basis, does suggest that basic information concerning the scoring of the test is lacking so as to make its use by all but the very experienced impossible.

TESTS OF AUDITORY SKILLS, LANGUAGE, AND READING

Auditory Discrimination Test

The *Auditory Discrimination test* (Wepman, 1958) is designed to assess the ability of children 5 to 8 years of age to discriminate between sounds by indicating whether pairs of words sound the same or different. The test consists of forty word pairs which are read aloud to the child. Test norms have been established. The child must be able to understand the concept of same/different or same/not the same. Examples of the words are:

gear–bear	led–lad	rub–rug
fret–threat	bar–bar	cart–tart

The child's score is based upon the number of errors he commits on items which are the same and on those which are different. The number of X responses (responses to word pairs which are different) which are considered diagnostically significant at various ages is:

> 5 year olds . . . greater than six errors
> 6 year olds . . . greater than five errors
> 7 year olds . . . greater than four errors
> 8 year olds . . . greater than three errors

The test is very easy to administer and takes but a few minutes. The user is cautioned to be sensitive to cultural differences, as children from a non–English-speaking background may pronounce and discriminate sounds tapped in this test in a different manner than would English-speaking children. The test reliability appears to be good. It is quickly administered and easy to score (DiCarlo, 1965) and does assess one skill without confounding performance with other skills. The technique is a limited assessment of auditory discrimination insofar as it measures auditory discrimination on one single type of task.

Northwestern Syntax Screening Test

The *Northwestern Syntax Screening test* (Lee, 1970) is a screening instrument to identify children, ages 3.0 to 7.11, who are delayed in the use of syntactical forms. Receptive and expressive use of grammatical features such as prepositions, personal pronouns, nouns, negatives, plurals, and possessives are tested at a receptive and expressive level.

To test the child's comprehension of spoken stimuli (i.e., receptive functions), the child is presented with a page containing four pictures; two are decoys and two are to be identified on the basis of a grammatical contrast spoken by the examiner. For instance, the examiner would say, "This is the Mother's cat," and "This is a mother cat." The child is to point to the pictures named as the examiner repeats the sentences. To assess the child's language output (i.e., expressive functions), the child is presented with two pictures on a page which are labeled by the examiner, but which are not pointed to. The examiner than asks the child to identify the appropriate picture by talking about it. Information is available indicating receptive and expressive age norms at 90th, 75th, 50th, 25th, and 19th percentiles for each 6-month age group.

Several features of the test should be noted. First, it is designed to assess but one language area, syntax. No attempt is made to measure phonology (speech sounds) or semantics (vocabulary). While this is a narrow focus, it is ultimately to the administrator's advantage to assess adequately one function rather than to try to assess many functions and do so inadequately.

Second, as has been typically the case, the sample upon which the norms have been developed is small. Thus, for the age groups 3 to 3½ only thirteen children were tested; for the ages 5 to 5½, fourteen children were employed; for the ages 7½ to 8, only sixteen served as the normative sample. Moreover, the children used in the development of the norms were drawn from middle-class homes. The representativeness of the sample and the adequacy of the norms presented are open to serious question.

Utah Test of Language Development

In addition to the assessment of the child's comprehension of grammatical forms and production of speech sounds, it is important to note how adequately the child speaks. In the *Utah Test of Language Development* (Mecham, Jex, and Jones, 1967), the authors have developed a simple test of language development for children ranging from 1 to 15 years of age. Additionally, Mecham et al. have provided a means to evaluate the child's performance by grouping items into grammatical classifications. The child's score on the test can be transformed into a language-age equivalent. The test consists of fifty-one items in which the child is asked to repeat digits and sentences, to name the days of the week, and to perform certain motor tasks. The authors suggest that this instrument is of particular value in assessing brain-damaged children.

Butler (1972), in reviewing the test, indicates some of its rather severe limitations. First, the sample upon which the test was developed consisted of but 273 white children residing in Utah. Only thirty of these children serve as the normative population for the 12½- to 14½-year-old population. Clearly, and particularly for the upper age ranges, the small number of children used precludes much confidence in the norms for this age group. Additionally, norms are based upon white children and thus should not be employed for assessing children of minority groups. Second, the number of items within the age ranges tapped are often few in number. At age 7, four items tap language skills, while there are twenty items for children ages 1 to 3. Insofar as the reliability of a score is associated with the number of items used to compute the score, the reliability of the test is likely to be greater at some ages than at others. Finally, there is little evidence concerning the validity of the test. What the test score predicts is as yet unknown. Butler suggests that the test

is particularly useful at the preschool level due to the preponderance of items at this level and the absence of time limits. If an examiner is interested in a language screening device and keeps in mind the small normative population and its geographical bias, he may wish to use the . . . [test] (p. 1367).

Developmental Sentence Scoring

In *Developmental Sentence Scoring* (Lee, 1970, 1974), the author has proposed a method for measuring syntactic language development in children's spontaneous speech. In this method the child's mastery of syntactic rules is assessed by his verbal use of them. The examiner is instructed to spend one hour in conversation with the child. Using any stimulus materials to facilitate conversation, the child's language is tape recorded. The examiner then selects fifty complete sentences to score. Sentences must have a noun and verb, be different from one another, be intelligible and nonecholalic. Eight linguistic features are scored: indefinite pronoun or noun modifiers, personal pronouns, main verbs, secondary verbs, negatives, conjunctions, interrogative reversals, and who-questions. The child is awarded points for use of these parts of language plus an additional point if the sentence is grammatically correct. Percentiles are provided for 6-month age groups between the ages of 3.0 and 6.1 years so that the individual child can be compared to his peer group. This is clearly a time-consuming test, which should be applied for children experiencing real deficits in language development. Analysis of those parts of language with which the child is experiencing difficulty can be helpful in developing a remedial language program.

This test has been shown to have adequate reliability, particularly for older children, and does appear to have validity in measuring the linguistic development of the child. At least this is so when employed with white children from middle-class homes, those children most approximating the sample used in the development of the test (Lee, 1974).

Reading Miscue Inventory

The growth of psycholinguistics has had great impact on the conceptualizations of the reading process, as well as on methods of assessment and instruction in reading. A popular example of this impact can be seen in the Reading Miscue Inventory (RMI; Goodman and Burke, 1972), a test of reading comprehension based on miscues made during oral reading. Basically, the child's reading level is determined by having the child read a list of words. Then the child is asked to read orally paragraphs which are somewhat difficult; paragraphs on which he is sure to make errors. In the RMI, errors are called "miscues." The miscues are seen as indicators of the child's linguistic competency and skills in interpreting written material. These miscues provide the basis for analysis of the child's oral reading abilities. While oral reading may not be the same as silent reading and while linguistic applications to comprehension may not enlighten us about all reading problems, the RMI offers a new and promising approach to reading assessment and remedial intervention planning.

An RMI kit is available which contains the rationale for this approach. It is a self-instructional package with audio tapes and protocols for learning to record relevant behaviors, student inventories, record forms for formal assessments, and written material suggesting teaching techniques to help students.

Before administering the RMI, it is necessary to ascertain the student's current reading level. This is necessary so as to ensure that the material to be read as part of the analysis is sufficiently difficult to ensure that the child makes miscues but not so difficult that the child cannot read independently and with reasonable comfort. Thus, the idea is to have enough miscues during the test so as to permit an analysis of the child's linguistic skills; an analysis of what he knows and what cues he neglects.

The RMI is administered by using any graded reading materials. Goodman and Burke suggest that if a story is used, it should have a plot; if information is used, it should be clearly stated. The content of the material should be unfamiliar to the reader but contain ideas the reader can comprehend. The length of the oral reading materials should be such as to allow children to complete the reading in about fifteen to twenty minutes.

The oral reading of the child is done while the teacher/diagnostician records the types of miscues made by the child. Responses such as omissions, substitutions, repetitions, insertions, and punctuation changes are recorded. Note is made as to whether the child corrects the miscue, uses a word correctly and then erroneously changes his response, tries but fails to correct his miscue, and/or anticipates difficulty with subsequent words. Each miscue is further analyzed by considering nine categories which include dialect, intonation, graphic similarity (does the miscue word look like the word that was presented to the child?), sound similarity (does the miscue sound like the word presented?), grammatical function (does the miscue reflect the same case grammar as the presented word?), correction of miscue (as specified above), grammatical acceptability (is the miscue in a form which is grammatically acceptable?), semantic acceptability (even with the miscue, is the sentence meaningful?), meaning change (does the miscue result in a major or minor change in the meaning of the sentence?). Each of these categories is coded as to whether the response was extensive, minor, or not present.

The miscue analysis has the teacher judge the reader's departures from the text in accordance with these various categories. Rather than providing the traditional and usual grade equivalent score, the RMI yields descriptive information about the reader's comprehension and types of errors. It is believed that a miscue which fails to alter the meaning of the sentence reflects a less significant reading problem than one which does alter the meaning, and therefore the comprehension, of the material.

Following the reading of the material, the child is asked to recall what has just been read. This retelling is analyzed and judged relative to the miscues of the child. The notion behind this is to determine how much information the child comprehends and recalls relative to the types and frequencies of miscues by the child during reading.

While this technique appears promising, there are some limitations concerning it. First, the scoring procedures are very cumbersome, the categories are not well defined, and they appear to overlap. Moreover, the manual does not present data pertaining to the reliability of the categories nor to their validity in predicting behaviors. Until these problems are resolved, the test will have limited application in either individual diagnosis or research programs.

DIAGNOSTIC AND ACHIEVEMENT TESTS

Wide Range Achievement Test

The *Wide Range Achievement test,* Revised Edition (Jastic and Jastic, 1965), provides scores in three subtests: reading, spelling, and arithmetic for children divided into two age levels, 5–11 and over 12 years. The reading subtest assesses the child's ability to recognize and name letters and read words, while the spelling subtest incorporates items which have the child copy geometric shapes, write his name, and spell in written form words dictated orally by the examiner. The arithmetic subtest involves counting, naming, and solving addition and subtraction problems orally at the younger age level and solving written computation problems of addition, subtraction, multiplication, and division at the older level.

The test's authors claim that it is useful to diagnose reading, spelling, and arithmetic disabilities, to assign children to instructional groups, to compare school achievement with other characteristics of the person (namely intelligence and personality traits), and to study the degree of loss of skills which might result from brain damage or other physical disabilities. Some have suggested that the test might be appropriate as a quick estimate of an individual's general level of ability and educational background (Thorndike, 1972). However, the test has been severely criticized by Merwin (1972). The sample upon which the norms for the test are based is not sufficiently described so that a child's score can be meaningfully compared to other children of his age and social status. Merwin also raises questions concerning the adequacy of the reliability and validity data presented by the test constructors.

Gates-McKillop Reading Diagnostic Tests

The *Gates-McKillop Reading Diagnostic tests* (Gates and McKillop, 1962) consists of a variety of techniques designed to discover the deficiencies in reading of children 7 to 12 years of age. The particular value of this set of tests is that it guides the examiner's interpretation of the errors made by the child in oral reading and instructs on how to compare these errors with the child's performance on other subtests. The tests lack clear or usable scores, but provide clinical advice on interpretation of reading problems (Della-Piana, 1965). There is no measure of reading comprehension, but the subtests and the manual's instructions make this a popular instrument for both informal and formal assessments of reading difficulties.

Following is a list of some of the tests and some examples of the items used within them.

1. Oral reading: Grade and age norms are available for this subtest, which consists of seven paragraphs increasing in difficulty. The child is instructed to read aloud until making a specified number of errors. An example of a test paragraph is: "After the rat got into his hole, he began to peek at the dog. This drove the dog nearly mad. He said: 'I like raw meat to eat. If you do not stop, I will eat you.' Then he left the rat alone."

2. Words—flash presentation: Here the examiner quickly presents and removes words. The child's task is to say the word. Such words as "so, perhaps, affectionate" are used as stimuli.

3. Words—untimed presentation: On this task, the child reads the words aloud at his own speed. Examples of the words used are: "so, king, window, irregular."
4. Phrases—flash presentation: Various phrases are rapidly presented and the child's task is to repeat the phrases. An example phrase is: "Go to the store."
5. Recognizing and blending common word parts: The child is to say aloud twenty-three nonsense words. When he errs, he is shown the sound parts and encouraged to blend the parts. An example is: tright . . . tr . . . ight . . . tright.
6. Giving letter sounds: Here the child tells sounds associated with letters.

Other tests are included in the battery but will not be presented here. The reader is referred to Gates and McKillop (1962) for further details.

Unfortunately, the test manual fails to provide information concerning the number and type of children tested as the basis for establishing normative or usual performances. As such information is lacking, the usefulness of the test as a precise measure is highly questionable. It may be useful clinically, as suggested by Bryant (1965), but comparison of performances of children with those of unknown origin can be quite misleading as well.

Peabody Individual Achievement Test

The *Peabody Individual Achievement test* (Dunn and Markwardt, 1970) is designed to survey achievement in mathematics, reading recognition, reading comprehension, spelling, and general information. The test is applicable to individuals from the preschool years to adulthood. Scores can be converted to grade and age equivalents, percentile ranks, and standard scores. The advantage of this test is that it requires no written work by the test taker. The child can respond by pointing or speaking; it is quickly administered and easily scored.

The test was standardized on close to 3,000 children in kindergarten through twelfth grade with urban, suburban, and rural children represented. The test-retest reliability of the subtests is good, although the total score is more reliable than the subtest scores. Validity has been established by correlation with the Peabody Picture Vocabulary test. As such, the validity and test-retest reliability do not seem as strong as on other achievement tests (French, 1972). The test manual is well written, as it provides the reader with cautionary statements about use of this test. French recommends that the PIAT be used as a test which a trained paraprofessional could administer, that it could be used as a screening device to obtain both a rough estimate of educational level and indications of where more intensive testing might be needed.

Metropolitan Achievement Tests

The *Metropolitan Achievement tests* (Durost, 1961) is a series of tests designed to measure achievement in content areas in school curricula. Of particular relevance to the learning disability specialist are the various reading tests. Three scores are yielded at the primary level: word knowledge, word discrimination, and reading. Two scores are obtained for children at the upper levels, grades 7 through 9: word knowledge and reading. The word knowledge test consists of asking the child to identify the functions, consequences associated with, or the synonyms for the stimulus word or picture from one of several alternatives. The reading test is a comprehension test. The word discrimination task requires the child to select from a list of words that word which was dictated to him by the examiner.

According to the review by Robinson (1965), the subtests show good reliability and various measures of validity have been obtained. Standardization of the test was exceptional insofar as the number of children used to develop norms numbered over 100,000. Directions for administration and interpretation are clear. Robinson concludes this reading test is

> one of the best survey tests of reading achievement on the market today for the elementary grades. It has been carefully planned, carefully tested, and well produced. It serves its purpose as a rough measure of reading achievement for comparative purposes and as a tool of identification upon which further evaluation may be based (p. 797).

Vineland Social Maturity Scale

The *Vineland Social Maturity scale* (Doll, 1947) represents one of the few scales designed to assess the development of social and personal competence in the conduct of everyday activities by individuals from infancy to 30 years of age. The learning disability specialist might well employ this scale as a means to determine the degree to which the child of concern demonstrated behavioral problems and incompetencies around the home. The scale is designed to tap, through 177 items, eight areas of function: general self-help, self-help in eating, self-help in dressing, self-direction, occupation, communication, locomotion, and socialization. Unlike other tests, scores yielded are not based upon the child's response to some stimulus items, but rather are based upon data obtained by the interviewer from the child, parents, friends, or whoever might be knowledgeable concerning the individual's performance. The scale directs the examiner to conduct a guided interview. The subtests and sample items follow.

1. Self-help general: Cares for self at toilet (ages 4 to 5); tells time to the quarter hour (ages 7 to 8).
2. Self-help eating: Eats with fork (ages 2 to 3); uses table knife for cutting (ages 7 to 8).

3. Self-help dressing: Washes hands unaided (ages 3 to 4); goes to bed unassisted (ages 6 to 7).
4. Self-direction: Makes minor purchase (ages 9 to 10).
5. Occupation: Helps at little household tasks (ages 3 to 4); uses tools or utensils (ages 8 to 9).
6. Communication: Relates experience (ages 2 to 3); uses pencil for writing (ages 6 to 7).
7. Locomotion: Walks downstairs one step per tread (ages 3 to 4); goes to school unattended (ages 5 to 6).
8. Socialization: Plays cooperatively at kindergarten level (ages 3 to 4); disavows literal Santa Claus (ages 7 to 8).

The child's performance is scored so that a comparison can be made of his performance in each of the eight areas and a total score has been constructed to provide a Social Quotient. Normative information is based upon a sample of 620 subjects, composed of ten normal persons of each sex to age 30. Additional normative data have been gathered.

Several reviewers have suggested that the items are sufficiently vaguely worded and the examiners sufficiently free to impose their unique interpretations of the responses given, so that the reliability of the test might be much lower than necessary (Kinder, 1938; Rothney, 1949; Teagarden, 1953). In spite of this possibility, the test has been judged useful in aiding the examiner to make discriminations among the mentally defective and in the evaluation of the physically handicapped (Cruickshank, 1953; Loutt, 1949). There appear to be no data to indicate the utility of this test in aiding predictions about the learning-disabled child, so the test appears to be of limited validity. It would seem to these authors that many of the distinctions that are required in dealing with the learning-disabled child are sufficiently subtle so that this test would not be sufficiently sensitive to help the examiner.

THE INDIVIDUAL EDUCATIONAL PROGRAM

The Education for All Handicapped Children Act of 1975 specifies that the assessment of each handicapped child by those receiving federal funds result in an Individualized Education Program (IEP). An IEP is defined as a written statement of the child's present level of educational performance, and the teacher's annual goals, including short-term instructional objectives of the specific educational services to be provided the child, and the extent to which the child will be able to participate in regular educational programs. The law demands that written statements be provided as to what stage the handicapped child is educationally, the goals of the teacher for that child, the means by which these goals will be accomplished, and a guess as to the child's subsequent integration into regular classroom programs.

To devise an IEP, several questions must be answered. First, what are the current educational demands facing the child and how are his competencies assessed in regard to these demands? A recent investigation by a university graduate student, Rosemary Verché, illustrates the importance of going beyond simple test scores in constructing an IEP. This student attempted to establish an IEP for a seventh-grade learning-disabled student involving the mathematics curriculum. Children within this school district were administered a district-wide mathematics achievement test. Mrs. Verché found that the most frequent type of item on the test involved knowledge of whole numbers, while the second most frequently occurring items concerned geometry. However, in this school, geometry was among the very last units presented to the seventh-graders. Thus, all students were at a disadvantage. Additionally, data presented by the test constructors indicated that the standard error of measurement for the mathematics test was almost three years. This combination then raises the specter of a child being defined as learning-disabled for being two years behind grade level in mathematics achievement, while being statistically within the normal range of seventh-graders on assessed mathematics. It is important when involved in individual diagnoses to assess both the constraints of the test and the curriculum in affecting the performance of an individual student. One must consider both the test and the student's accomplishments relative to his classmates, because the peer group may reflect the strengths or limits of the curriculum.

Given poor performance on an adequate test, the law requires that if you desire federal monies, you must specify short- and long-range goals of classroom curriculum in the appropriate subject areas. No doubt goals will vary from student to student, teacher to teacher, school district to school district. It is important that careful monitoring of progress toward achieving these goals is initiated. The frequent use of tests to assess progress is necessary. If progress is not being made, then improved teaching strategies will be necessary, which in turn must be assessed. Assessment procedures should not rely exclusively upon infrequently given standardized commercial tests but rather should also scrutinize the classroom's current academic content.

There is no doubt that the IEP involves considerably more effort by the teacher and diagnostic team than the old-fashioned psychoeducational assessment procedures which simply employed psychological tests. No longer will it suffice that the teacher simply generate an auditory memory excercise on the basis of a psychologist's opinion that the learning-disabled child suffers from auditory memory difficulties. The IEP really can provide an educational plan which matches the child's skills and deficits to the demands of the school curriculum.

CONCLUSION

We have presented many tests and many details about them. Because of the popularity of these tests as well as the controversy often surrounding them, we thought it wise to go into great detail. As you have probably noted, many of the tests discussed are not very efficient. The questions raised in their evaluation are basic ones which can be addressed to all published tests. The publication of and the author's claim about the test are not sufficient to justify its use. Questions concerning reliabilities, the sample upon which the test was developed, the predictive value of their scores, and their ease of administration are legitimate and relevant to all standardized procedures. These basic questions serve to winnow, from the thousands of published tests, those which can serve useful educational and research purposes from those which cannot. They are part of scientific inquiry.

Finally, while we have been somewhat critical concerning many of the tests presented in this chapter, it is important to realize that they may be better than the alternatives available.

REFERENCES

Anastasi, A. *Psychological Testing.* New York: The Macmillan Co., 1961.

Baker, H. J. and Leland, B. *Detroit Tests of Learning Aptitudes.* Indianapolis, Ind.: Bobbs-Merrill, 1935.

Bannatyne, A. "Diagnosing learning disabilities and writing remedial prescriptions." *Journal of Learning Disabilities,* 1968, 1, 242–249.

Beery, K. and Buktencia, N. *Developmental Test of Visual-Motor Integration.* Chicago, Ill.: Follett, 1967.

Bender, L. "A visual motor Gestalt test and its clinical use." *American Orthopsychiatry Assoc. Res. Monograph,* 1938, No. 3.

Borstelmann, L. J. "Review of Gesell Developmental Tests," in O. K. Buros, ed., *The Seventh Mental Measurements Yearbook.* N.J.: The Gryphon Press, 1972.

Bryan, T. and McGrady, H. J. "Use of a teacher rating scale." *Journal of Learning Disabilities,* 1972, 5, 199–206.

Bryant, N. D. "Some principles of remedial instruction for dyslexia." *The Reading Teacher,* 1965, 18, 567–572.

Butler, K. G. "Review of the Utah Test of Language Development." In O. K. Buros (ed.), *The Seventh Mental Measurements Yearbook, Vol. II.* New Jersey: The Gryphon Press, 1972, 1366–1367.

Carroll, J. B. "Review of the Illinois Test of Psycholinguistics." In O. K. Buros (ed.), *The Seventh Mental Measurements Yearbook, Vol. II.* New Jersey: The Gryphon Press, 1972, 7, 819–823.

Chissom, B. S. "Review of Frostig DTVP." In O. K. Buros (ed.), *The Seventh Mental Measurements Yearbook, Vol. II.* New Jersey: The Gryphon Press, 1972.

Cruickshank, W. M. "Review of the Vineland Social Maturity Scale." In O. K. Buros (ed.), *The Fourth Mental Measurements Yearbook.* New Jersey: The Gryphon Press, 1953.

de Hirsch, K., Jansky, J., and Langford, Q. *Predicting Reading Failure.* New York: Harper and Row, 1966.

Della-Piana, G. M. "Review of Gates-McKillop Reading Diagnostic Tests." In O. K. Buros (ed.), *The Sixth Mental Measurements Yearbook.* New Jersey: The Gryphon Press, 1965.

Deno, E. "Review of Slingerland's Screening Tests for Identifying Children with Specific Language Disability." In O. K. Buros (ed.), *The Seventh Mental Measurements Yearbook, Vol. II.* New Jersey: The Gryphon Press, 1972.

DiCarlo, L. M. "Auditory discrimination test." In O. K. Buros (ed.), *The Sixth Mental Measurements Yearbook.* New Jersey: The Gryphon Press, 1965.

Doll, E. A. *Vineland Social Maturity Scale.* Minneapolis: Educational Test Bureau, 1947.

Dunn, L. M. *Peabody Picture Vocabulary Test.* Minneapolis, Minn.: American Guidance Services, Inc., 1959.

Dunn, L. M. and Markwardt, F. C. *Peabody Individual Achievement Test.* Circle Pines, Minn.: American Guidance Service, 1970.

Durost, W. M. (ed.). *Metropolitan Achievement Tests.* New York: Harcourt, Brace & World, Inc., 1961.

Ferinden, W. E., Jr. *Educational Interpretation of the Wechsler Intelligence Scale for Children (WISC).* Linden, N.J.: Remediation Associates, 1969.

Ferinden, W. E., Jr. *Educational Interpretation of the Stanford-Binet Intelligence Scale Form LM and the Illinois Test of Psycholinguistic Abilities.* Linden, N.J.: Remediation Associates, 1970.

Freeman, F. S. *Theory and Practice of Psychological Testing.* New York: Holt, Rinehart and Winston, 1962.

Freides, D. "Human information processing and sensory modality: Cross-modal functions, information complexity, memory and deficit." *Psychological Bulletin,* 1974, 81, 284–310.

French, J. L. "Review of Peabody Individual Achievement Test." In O. K. Buros (ed.), *The Seventh Mental Measurements Yearbook.* N.J.: The Gryphon Press, 1972.

Frostig, M. *Frostig Developmental Tests of Visual Perception.* Palo Alto, Calif.: Consulting Psychologists Press, 1964.

Gates, A. I. and McKillop, A. S. *Gates-McKillop Reading Diagnostic Tests: Manual of Directions.* New York: Teachers College Press, 1962.

Goodenough, F. L. *Measurement of Intelligence by Drawings.* Tarrytown-on-Hudson, N.Y.: World Book Co., 1926.

Goodman, Y. M. and Burke, C. L. *Reading Miscue Inventory Manual: Procedure for Diagnosis and Evaluation.* New York: Macmillan Publishing Co., Inc., 1972.

Harris, D. B. *Children's Drawings as Measures of Intellectual Maturity: A Revision and Extension of the Goodenough Draw-a-Man Test.* New York: Harcourt, Brace & World, 1963.

Holliday, F. B. "Title III Program in Early Childhood Development" (Evanston Screening Program), Timber Ridge School, Skokie, Ill., 1972.

Ilg, F. L. and Ames, L. B. *School Readiness: Behavior Tests Used at the Gesell Institute.* New York: Harper and Row, 1965.

Jamison, C. B. "Review of The Purdue Perceptual-Motor Survey." In O. K. Buros (ed.), *The Seventh Mental Measurements Yearbook.* New Jersey: The Gryphon Press, 1972.

Jastic, J. F. and Jastic, S. R. *The Wide Range Achievement Test.* Wilmington, Del.: Guidance Associates, 1965.

Keogh, B. K., Wetter, J., McGinty, A., and Donlon, G. "Functional analysis of WISC performance of learning disordered, hyperactive, and mentally retarded boys." *Psychology in the Schools,* 1973, 10, 178–181.

Kinder, E. F. "Review of the Vineland Social Maturity Scale." In O. K. Buros (ed.), *Mental Measurements Yearbook, Vol. 1.* N.J.: The Gryphon Press, 1938.

Kirk, S. A. and Kirk, W. R. *Psycholinguistic Learning Disabilities: Diagnosis and Remediation.* Urbana: University of Illinois Press, 1972.

Kirk, S. A., McCarthy, J. J., and Kirk, W. D. *Illinois Test of Psycholinguistics Abilities* (rev. ed.). Urbana, Ill.: University of Illinois Press, 1968.

Koppitz, E. M. *The Bender Gestalt Test for Young Children.* New York: Grune & Stratton, Inc., 1964.

Landis, D. "Review of The Purdue Perceptual-Motor Survey." In O. K. Buros (ed.), *The Seventh Mental Measurements Yearbook, Vol. II.* New Jersey: The Gryphon Press, 1972.

Lee, L. L. "A screening test for syntax development." *Journal of Speech and Hearing Disorders,* 1970, 35, 103–112.

Lee, L. L. *Developmental Sentence Analysis.* Evanston, Ill.: Northwestern University Press, 1974.

Loutt, C. M. "Review of the Vineland Social Maturity Scale." In O. K. Buros (ed.), *The Third Mental Measurements Yearbook.* N.J.: The Gryphon Press, 1949.

Lyman, H. B. "Review of Peabody Picture Test." In O. K. Buros (ed.), *The Sixth Mental Measurements Yearbook*. N.J.: The Gryphon Press, 1965.

McCarthy, J. J. "Review of the Early Detection Inventory." In O. K. Buros (ed.), *The Seventh Mental Measurements Yearbook*. New Jersey: The Gryphon Press, 1972.

McGahan, F. E. and McGahan, C. *Early Detection Inventory*. Chicago: Follett Educational Corporation, 1967.

Mecham, M., Jex, J., and Jones, J. *Manual of Instructions: Utah Test of Language Development* (rev. ed.). Salt Lake City: Communication Research Associates, 1967.

Merwin, J. C. "Review of Wide Range Achievement Test." In O. K. Buros (ed.), *The Seventh Mental Measurements Yearbook, Vol. 1.* New Jersey: The Gryphon Press, 1972.

Myklebust, H. R. *Pupil Rating Scale*. New York: Grune & Stratton, 1971.

Newcomer, P. L. and Hammill, D. D. "ITPA and academic achievement: A survey." *The Reading Teacher*, 1975, 28, 731–741.

Roach, E. and Kephart, N. C. *Purdue Perceptual-Motor Survey*. Columbus, Ohio: Charles E. Merrill, 1966.

Robinson, N. A. "Review of Metropolitan Achievement Tests." in O. K. Buros (ed.), *The Sixth Mental Measurements Yearbook*. New Jersey: The Gryphon Press, 1965.

Rothney, J. W. M. *Review of the Vineland Social Maturity Measurements Yearbook*. New Jersey: The Gryphon Press, 1949.

Rugel, R. Q. "WISC subtest scores of disabled readers: A review with respect to Bannatyne's recategorization." *Journal of Learning Disabilities*, 1974, 7, 48–61.

Sechrest, L. "Incremental validity." In D. N. Jackson and S. Messick (eds.), *Problems in Human Assessment*. New York: McGraw-Hill Book Co., 1967.

Slingerland, B. H. *Screening Tests for Identifying Children with Specific Language Disabilities*. Cambridge, Mass.: Educators Publishing Service, 1964.

Spivack, G. and Swift, M. *Devereux Elementary School Behavior Rating Scale*. Devon, Pa.: The Devereux Foundation, 1967.

Teagarden, F. M., "Review of the Vineland Social Maturity Scale." In O. K. Buros (ed.), *The Fourth Mental Measurement Yearbook*. N.J.: The Gryphon Press, 1953.

Terman, L. M. and Merrill, M. A. *Measuring Intelligence*. Boston: Houghton-Mifflin, 1937.

Thorndike, L. "Review of Wide Range Achievement Tests." In O. K. Buros (ed.), *The Seventh Mental Measurement Yearbook*. N.J.: The Gryphon Press, 1972.

Trimble, A. C. "Can Remedial Be Eliminated?" *Academic Therapy Quarterly*, 1970, 5, 207–213.

Wechsler, D. *Wechsler Intelligence Scale for Children: Manual*. New York: The Psychological Corporation, 1949.

Wechsler, D. *The Measurement and Appraisal of Adult Intelligence* (4th ed.). Baltimore, Md.: Williams & Wilkins, 1958.

Wepman, J. *Auditory Discrimination Test*. Chicago: Language Research Associates, 1958.

12 | Remediation

HISTORY OF INDIVIDUALIZED INSTRUCTION

Remediation techniques developed in the field of learning disabilities have been based upon the belief that children differ greatly in how they learn and the rate at which they learn. Such techniques assume that children vary considerably in their styles of learning, their abilities to master skills, and their motivations. These assumptions led to the individual tailoring of particular techniques to particular children to facilitate learning.

Implicit is the faith or hope that professionals know enough about children and teaching techniques so that this tailoring will produce an effective fit. This goal is very persuasive; after all, who could deny that the goal of greater efficiency is a worthwhile one? But the emphasis upon individualized instruction is a relatively recent one. Whether it is because we have become more sophisticated about how people vary, or because of the complex demands of society, educational institutions are increasingly attempting to match child and teaching method.

It was not long ago that a fixed curriculum for all students was the modus operandi. Children who failed to learn within this highly restricted course content dropped from the system, and had the choice of becoming, among other things, farmers, businessmen, servants, or crooks. With time, however, the skills necessary to be a farmer, businessman, or perhaps a crook increased until the public realized it was more expedient to maintain potential dropouts within the school system. School systems then devised curriculum materials more suitable to students who were more heterogeneous in their talents and abilities than had been acknowledged.

The psychological testing boom, a product of the World War I national emergency, produced the apparatus which made possible an increasingly complex assessment and perspective of the individual. The development of intelligence and specialized aptitude tests, particularly those administered to groups, served as precursors of the present concern with individualized assessment and instruction. If adults and children evidenced wide ranges of differences in mechanical, mathematical, or clerical aptitudes, then greater precision in matching child and curriculum might result in closer alignment of potential and achievement. Thus, the testing movement became the vehicle and rationale for sorting "bright" from "dull" students for placement into "slow" and "accelerated" classrooms. The road to sorting, then as now, has not been a smooth one. Intelligence tests and, for adults, aptitude tests are not powerful predictors of achievement in skill areas. While they may be among the best predictors, the competition is not very keen.

One assumption of the early users of such tests was that achievement tests could be helpful in predicting the rate of learning on tasks presumed to require the same array of skills. If a child showed achievement in mastering arithmetic, it was expected he would excel in algebra. As early as 1946, however, Woodrow challenged this position. After twenty years of research in this area, Woodrow concluded that the rate of learning is inconsistent from one task to another. If this is the case, an achievement test score might be useful in predicting the child's performance on a particular task but useless and perhaps misleading in predicting the same child's score on a variety of related tasks. We know little about what such tests assess, what is demanded of the child in terms of successful mastery of any particular content area, or the interactions of those unknown skills with the task demands. As yet, there is little justification for identifying mental test scores with the ability to learn (Cronbach, 1971).

The attempts to study learning processes within the field of educational research were and are based upon two schools of thought (Walberg, 1971). Since both are reflected within the efforts of learning disability experts, Walberg's definitions are included here. The first is the experimental approach, springing from the traditions of experimental psychology with its origins in the work of Wundt and Pavlov. This approach focuses upon how conditions and processes of instruction can be employed to optimize learning. The emphasis is upon the immediate stimulus, with the hope of determining those processes which will increase the learning of most, or "average," children. The tendency is to ignore how children differ and to concentrate upon the discovery of processes likely to maximize the learning experiences of many children. The essence of the procedure is to randomly assign some children to one form of instruction, a second group to a variant form of instruction, and then to assess the differences between these two groups of children on a common test criterion.

The second approach used was, and is, correlational and has its origins in the work of Galton and Spearman. The focus in this case is upon individual differences and their interrelationships (Walberg, 1971). The question posed in this approach is how children might differ among themselves and how these differences might be related to yet other differences. Are all slender children athletic? Are all chubby children good-natured? Is the child with eyeglasses smarter than those without them? Is the child who cannot learn to read, write, or compute arithmetic problems really more motorically active than the child who can master these skills?

We do not have a great deal of research involving remediation techniques with learning-disabled children. But what we do have can be divided into these two frameworks. Examples of the first or experimental approach would be those studies which investigate the efficacy of different remedial approaches or studies of the effects of distractions, such as music, upon learning and performance. The second approach can be seen both in efforts to establish how learning-disabled children differ from nonlearning-disabled children and efforts to group and educate children in accordance with test profiles. The bulk of research appears to have been conducted within the framework of determining individual differences, in particular how the learning disabled differ from their normal counterparts and how such differences might be related to one another.

The greatest impetus within special education in the study of individual differences was derived from the work of Strauss (Cruickshank and Holloran, 1973). Strauss made a major contribution to special education, and ultimately to the development of the field of learning disabilities, by examining individual differences in brain-injured mentally retarded children. While the assessment of individual differences in intellectual skills had been achieved initially by Binet in his development of the intelligence test, it was Strauss who took the next step by further defining differences within a group of specified handicapped children. It was not sufficient to say that children were bright or dull, but rather, he argued, clinicians should look further at how children who were dull differed among themselves. Descriptions of the child thus underwent further refinements, permitting the growth of a taxonomy of individual differences among children. Strauss continued to develop his taxonomy by further defining procedures of instruction for children based upon the individual differences he carefully observed.

The next major step in developing approaches to individualizing instruction came during World War II. Modern educational technology in programmed instruction and the techniques of behavior modification stemmed from the war efforts of Glaser, Lumsdaine, and Skinner, among others, who generated significant contributions. Glaser and Lumsdaine were assigned the difficult task of developing rapid, effective methods of teaching complex motor tasks to men. Skinner was apparently assigned very little to do, and thus spent his time developing a technique to teach very complex motor behaviors to pigeons (Skinner, 1960). The common element among these men was their focus upon task analysis rather than person analysis.

More than their predecessors, these contributors carefully analyzed the movements and skills necessary to learn to perform a complex task. Skinner did not consider the ability of the individual pigeon, but analyzed the task at hand and trained the bird to perform these movements. The primary focus was upon the analysis of the job to be accomplished by the pupil, be it person or pigeon, and how best to teach him to perform this task.

Concurrently, Grace Fernald (1943) was training illiterate adults to become competent in reading so that they could be inducted into the armed forces. These adults had skills which were needed during that time of national crisis; and Fernald set about helping them to become useful citizens. Like Glaser, Lumsdaine, and Skinner, Fernald addressed herself to the analysis of the task. She argued that individual differences, at least within the wide range of talents called "normal," were irrelevant to the acquisition of basic school subjects: reading, writing, and arithmetic. To be an effective teacher, one must understand the requirements of the task, or one could adopt the Fernald technique to teaching basic subjects, as discussed later in this chapter, under the heading of *The Multisensory Approach*. This technique and the school at which Fernald taught adults and educationally handicapped children are still in use today.

Since World War II, efforts in regular elementary education and separate special education have gradually moved toward both greater considerations of individual differences in learning and increased emphasis upon task analysis. As the technology developed, tasks have been analyzed into their discrete elements. The materials for evaluation of necessary skills and their remediation of deficits have also become available. Thus, more subtle individual differences can be reliably determined.

While mentally retarded children could be reliably labeled for grouping into three major categories, different educational treatments had to await the development of task analysis and the related educational materials to better educate the handicapped child. In terms of children subsequently labeled learning disabled, a giant step had been taken. It carried the educator beyond the narrow perspective of viewing learning-disabled children as being unintelligent, insane, or apathetic; and toward helping the learning-handicapped child who had a particular difficulty on a particular task with a particular technique for solution.

Such was the background for the development of much of the faith, hope, and goals of the learning disability specialist today. Yet, hard questions must be asked, not about faith, good intentions, or bright hopes but about our knowledge concerning the efficacy of educational techniques. At this point we can ask the following questions. Which variables affect learning? Which variables affect the learning-disabled child, and are these different from those affecting the academically successful child? Which remedial programs used in the field of learning disabilities have been studied in a systematic way which permits evaluation of the effectiveness of the approach? Which methods should learning disability specialists incorporate into their teaching in order to more effectively serve the learning-disabled child?

FACTORS AFFECTING SCHOOL LEARNING

There are three major all-inclusive components which can be construed as affecting school learning. These include 1) the student's aptitudes or intelligence, general intelligence, and specific skills, be they derived from genes, experiences, or both; 2) methods of instruction; and 3) the classroom environment (teacher warmth, organization, reinforcement properties, classroom size, school philosophy and architecture, peer relationships, and what have you).

According to one prominent investigator's review of research on school learning, the single most important variable affecting school achievement is the child's intelligence. The least important is the method of instruction, the factor to which educators, and particularly learning disability specialists, have addressed the greatest portion of their energies. To quote Walberg (1971), methods of instruction have been found to "typically make little differences in learning" (p. 18). This is not to say that children do not learn but rather that the particular method which is used to teach children makes little difference. Many methods seem equally effective in helping children to learn. In spite of all the technological innovations surrounding instructional methods, the teacher's belief system and the child's intelligence still account for the bulk of the learning which occurs. Apparently, the same conclusion was reached by Stephens (1970) as he reviewed many years of research on teaching methods. Stephens apparently concluded that what we think should make a difference in reality makes very little difference. This is not to say that some instructional techniques are not better than others, at least for some people some of the time and in some environments. As yet, however, no one can claim with much assurance that any particular method is more efficient than another method for most children, or even that a particular method will work with a particular child some of the time in most environments. In sum, there is much to be learned about learning and much to be humble about.

Within the field of learning disabilities, data suggest that intelligence contributes 40 percent to 60 percent of the variance in school achievement, and that instructional methods account for very little. These conclusions may be discouraging but they are also enlightening. The major thrust of the remediation of the deficits in learning-disabled children has been in the attempts to develop instructional techniques better suited to such children. Yet, according to Walberg's (1971) summary of the factors influencing learning in the regular elementary classroom, it is just this factor which seems to be the most elusive in terms of development and the least potent in terms of effects. Of course continued efforts should be made to develop more refined instructional methods. But to have a more effective impact on remediation of problems, it may be necessary to direct efforts to the study of other variables, such as teacher actions, instead of limiting the path of our efforts to development of ever more instructional materials.

As it now stands, two of the important correlates and perhaps determinants of learning, intelligence and classroom atmosphere, are either established before the intervention is initiated or are of such a nature that they are outside the influence of the learning disability teacher. This specialist cannot systematically or wittingly alter by much the child's intelligence. Nor is it likely that the elementary school teacher has the time or inclination to undergo an extensive diagnosis of her performance, be it by means of classroom observations or tests. It is likely, though by no means certain, that if alterations could be effected on these variables, in the direction and with the magnitude desired, the learning disabled child would benefit. As yet, such changes are technically impossible in the case of intelligence and difficult to achieve in the case of classroom atmosphere. Ironically, those factors which appear to be most helpful to both learning and remediation of learning deficits are those which also appear to be the least accessible to manipulation and control by the learning disability teacher.

Thus far we have discussed the lack of evidence indicating that one instructional method is superior to another when employed in regular classrooms. The question must then be raised as to whether the specialized instructional methods developed for use with learning-disabled children are more effective than those developed within the mainstream of elementary education. As far as can be determined, there are no systematically gathered data which would provide such an answer. Efforts have been concentrated on delivering services to these children. The generation and proliferation of instructional techniques have far outstripped the accumulation of data relevant to the value and efficacy of these methods. Few data have been made available in which the pertinent comparisons have been made with the appropriate comparison groups included.

Over the past twenty-five years we have seen the development of certain ideas about what types of programs will facilitate learning in disabled children, as well as the production of methods and materials to implement these ideas. The question is whether we suffer the same problem in learning disabilities which Stephens (1970) raised about regular elementary education: do those things which we now commonly believe promote learning in disabled children actually make any difference at all? The next question would be, what shall we do to try to improve the status of knowledge and remedial efforts in this field?

ORGANIZATION OF SERVICES

Learning disability specialists work in a variety of educational settings. When special education services were first introduced, the primary site for rendering aid was self-contained classrooms, modeled after classes for educable mentally retarded children. In this type of setting the child spends all of his school time in isolated classrooms, with a limited number of classmates, often regulated by the school district or state as no more than ten to fifteen children. It was presumed that by providing self-contained classrooms children would receive special benefits by having specially trained teachers and individualized instruction. These presumptions apparently were not warranted. Hammill and Bartel (1975) claim that while there were fewer children in self-contained classrooms, the teachers were not necessarily adequately trained, and the child did not receive individualized instruction. Moreover, their academic achievement was not superior to children who remained within a regular classroom setting. Additionally, the rapid growth of the learning disability field, with the accompanying increase in the number of children found in need of special services, made self-contained classrooms economically infeasible. It is probable that most school districts currently prefer other forms of providing special services to learning-disabled children.

A second, more popular form of service delivery is the resource room. In rendering service through resource rooms, children receive specialized instruction for limited daily periods, spending the remainder of their school day within the regular classroom. There are several advantages of the resource room as compared to the self-contained classroom approach. These advantages include providing services for more children, as well as greater flexibility in the time, groups, and duration of services.

A third method of providing services to the learning-disabled child is through an itinerant program. In such instances, the special education teacher is assigned to more than one school and travels between them. This type of program is probably less desirable than the resource room program, because it prohibits the special education teacher from establishing good relations with regular teachers, requires considerable travel time on the part of the teacher, and the transportation of the materials is a chronic problem (Hammill and Bartel, 1975).

A fourth form that delivery of services may take is that of casting the special education teacher in the role of consultant. With this form of operation, the teacher serves exclusively as a consultant to classroom teachers. Individuals who serve in this capacity must have considerable skill in devising programs across a variety of academic topics, and also in supervision and administration. The teacher-consultant should be an expert in diagnostics and educational intervention and should provide expertise to regular teachers as to how to provide help to individual children within a regular classroom. This technique for rendering services remains to be evaluated.

Development of both the more flexible resource room itinerant teacher and the teacher-consultant models for service delivery have supplanted, but not displaced, the use of segregated classrooms. These alternate models developed because of the lack of demonstrated effectiveness of the self-contained classroom, because of economic advantages, and from the hope of

avoiding stigmatizing children by virtue of diagnostic labels and segregation. It remains to be seen if these models can live up to their promise
of service.

REMEDIATION TECHNIQUES

Perceptual-motor Training

Among the better-known types of remedial programs in learning disabilities
are those which involve training of perceptual-motor skills. Most studies
concerning program effectiveness have been addressed to the impact of
various perceptual-motor training programs upon the subsequent acquisition
of those skills believed necessary to academic achievement.

Outstanding in this area is the work of Kephart (1963) and Frostig
and Horne (1964). The programs developed by these professionals are based
upon the assumptions that visual perception is a primary skill in the acquisition of reading skills and that perceptual-motor training will facilitate both
perceptual-motor skills and reading competence. According to Kephart,
the processing of visual information is critically dependent upon the child's
previous experiences in the development of motor skills. "Behavior develops
out of muscular activity, and so-called higher forms of behavior are dependent upon lower forms of behavior, thus making even these higher activities
dependent upon the basic structure of the muscular activity upon which
they are built" (Kephart, 1971, p. 79).

The remediation program is based upon observations and ratings of the
child's perceptual motor skills. Five areas of perceptual motor skills are
assessed: balance and posture (ratings of the child's walking and jumping);
body image and differentiation (identification of body parts); perceptual-motor match (such as rhythmic writing on a chalkboard); ocular control (essentially visual tracking of a moving object); and form perception
(the child is requested to copy geometric forms). If a child is rated as
developmentally retarded in any of these areas, he then receives exercises
specific to that area. It is believed that such exercises serve to increase
the child's motor competencies and his reading, writing, and arithmetic
achievement as well.

Frostig, less concerned with gross motor abilities than Kephart, focuses
upon the visual-perceptual skills of the child. Again, it is suggested that
such skills are necessary precursors of academic achievement and that deficits
in such activities have generalized effects on retarding their acquisition.
Remedial efforts in the Frostig program are based primarily upon the child's
performance on a test she developed, the Developmental Test of Visual
Perception (Frostig and Horne, 1964). The test is purported to assess five
aspects of visual motor functioning: eye-motor coordination; figure-ground
capability; form constancy; position in space; and the ability to assess spatial
relationships. The child is asked to do such tasks as draw a straight line

between two parallel lines (eye-hand coordination), discover hidden figures within a picture (figure-ground skills), or recognize and trace a square or circle (form constancy). If the child performs poorly, relative to peers, on any one of the five areas, there are work sheets available which have content parallel to that tested. The assumption is made that such exercises will increase the child's ability to acquire academic skills.

Assumptions and exercises notwithstanding, what are the available research data concerning the impact of perceptual-motor training upon the academic performance of children?

Several investigators have reported results which suggest that such training can be corrective with respect to reading. Thus Kephart (1971) and Frostig and Horne (1964) reported that children exposed to some form of perceptual-motor training excelled, relative to children who did not receive this training, in their reading achievement. However, most investigators have had less success in producing these significant differences. Falik (1969) provided a perceptual-motor training program for kindergarten children and did not find differences in reading readiness or in reading achievement two years later between children who did and did not receive this training. Similarly, Sullivan (1972) studied 113 elementary, junior, and senior high school students and found no evidence to support the contention that perceptual-motor training increased the reading performance of children.

Hammill (1972) reviewed twenty-five intervention studies. He concluded that it is not at all apparent that visual perception, as currently defined, can even be trained! While the data might be disheartening to the proponents of such training programs, one might find solace in the reports of other investigators that visual perception may not even be related to the acquisition of academic skills. Cohen (1969) was unable to demonstrate a correlation between perceptual-motor abilities and reading achievement. Goodman and Wiederholt (1972) studied the correlations between visual perception, readiness at kindergarten, first-grade achievement, and intelligence to reading performance fourteen months later. Only first-grade achievement was an adequate predictor of reading performance. Perhaps the most widely known study of the correlates of reading and initial school performance was that of deHirsch, Jansky, and Langford (1966). On only one of thirty-seven tests, the Bender Gestalt, was the correlation between test score and reading achievement at second grade higher than .35.

As of now, there is little evidence to support the faith that the perceptual-motor abilities of the child, at least within the broad range of talents measured in learning-disabled children, are critical to the development of traditional academic skills. And, even if such evidence did exist, there is none to demonstrate that the training programs based upon these theoretical assumptions affect school performance. At the outset, any intervention program should be assessed in terms of the cost of the program and also the possible deprivations for the child as a consequence of being involved in this program. It was this issue which gives import to a study by Rosen

(1966). In this case, children in twelve classrooms received perceptual-motor training for a period of twenty-nine days in an adaptation of the program outlined by Frostig. Reading achievement of these children was subsequently compared to that of children in thirteen classrooms who were not given a Frostig type perceptual-motor training experience. These control classes had spent equivalent periods of time on reading instruction, in this instance listening to and talking about stories. The results might have been predicted. Children who received perceptual-motor training improved on perceptual-motor skills, while children who had activities more closely related to reading gained most in reading.

It is probably quite fair to say that perceptual-motor programs help some children sometimes. Unfortunately, it is not likely that the current state of knowledge is such as to permit prediction of which child will be helped at which time. The use of these training programs may serve an important function as a welcome novelty for the child and teacher, providing for both a time out from orthodox methods of reading, writing, and arithmetic instruction. As such they can be justified on this basis alone. At the same time, it does seem apparent that the utilization of these programs cannot be justified on the basis of their impact on progress in the acquisition of traditional academic skills. Whatever value such training programs may provide, be it in producing novelty, creating a more pleasant day for the participating child, more intellectual stimulation for the teacher, or some sort of technology which serves to reassure the learning disability expert of his expertise, these programs do not have any apparent value in facilitation of school achievement in participating children.

Physical Fitness

One of the characteristics often associated with the learning-disabled child is awkwardness or clumsiness (Clements, 1966). Observations have been made that such children trip more, fall more, stumble more, spill more, and generally have a difficult time maneuvering body and objects in space (Lewis, Strauss, and Lehtinen, 1960). Why this occurs, if indeed it does, is a moot point. Perhaps stumbling, slipping, and spilling reflect minor brain damage, or a lack of attention, or poor and limited experiences in motor activities. Whatever the reason for this description of learning-disabled children, at least one well-known albeit controversial program has been developed to treat these symptoms. Doman and Delecato developed the Institutes for the Achievement of Human Potential (Delecato, 1963, 1966), a neurologically based program in which diagnosis and training are directly related to the authors' conceptualizations of the dynamics of the brain, brain structure, and motor skills. Diagnosis and remediation reflect the idea that learning problems are directly related to a failure on the part of the child to have sequentially experienced and developed certain movements. When these motor activities are not sufficiently experienced or developed in the proper order, the brain is unable to develop properly. It is assumed that the brain can and will develop if certain motor activities and child-rearing practices are put into effect.

Diagnosis is based on an evaluation of the child's handedness, eyedness, footedness, creeping and walking patterns, and body positions while sleeping. Insofar as learning difficulties are reflections of neurological disorganization reflected by performance on these activities, the remediation program requires that the child retrace the sequence the brain needs to follow to develop. Appropriate motor activities then become the vehicle for the development of more effective brain organization. For a particular child, therapy might include creeping, crawling, and walking exercises, changes in body position while sleeping, eating with both hands without utensils, and facilitation of a variety of primitive body movements.

Virtually every aspect of the Doman and Delecato approach has been criticized, from their theories about the structure, development, and dynamics of the brain to the research statistics cited to support these theories (Gearheart, 1973).

What evidence exists regarding the effectiveness of the Doman and Delecato training procedures? Few studies have been addressed to this method, and those which have been conducted focused primarily upon mentally retarded rather than learning-disabled children. Kershner, reported by Masland (1969), investigated the impact of this approach upon mentally retarded children, ages 8 to 18. A highly complicated program was administered which involved training movements, exercises in creeping and crawling, alterations of resting and sleeping posture, and the use of eye patches to establish consistency of cerebral dominance. The control group was exposed to games and activities solely designed to "give reason for the teacher to direct individual and group praise and encouragement" (Masland, 1969, p. 82). It was reported that the treated group became more efficient creepers and crawlers, and showed some gains in their intelligence test scores as measured by the Peabody Picture Vocabulary Test. Unfortunately, insufficient data were presented to evaluate whether these gains, be they in creeping or in intelligence levels, were statistically significant. Insofar as the experimental group had lower intelligence test scores than the control group on the pretest, any differential increment, even if significant, might reflect a statistical artifact. The results of this study must be taken as suggestive, at best, rather than as definitive.

O'Donnell and Eisenson (1969) studied the effects of the Delecato training program upon reading achievement and visual-motor integration. Second-, third-, and fourth-grade children were selected on the bases of low scores on a reading achievement test and also the presence of visual-motor integration difficulties, as defined by performance on the Harris Test of Lateral Dominance. These children were randomly assigned to one of three treatment conditions. One group had exercises in cross pattern creeping and walking, visual pursuit, and filtered reading tasks. The second group received the visual pursuit task, filtered reading, and selected physical education activities. The third group was a control group which received selected physical education activities. There were no significant differences found between these three groups when they were retested for reading achievement and visual-motor integration.

Other studies cited by Masland (1969) were not directly related to the Doman and Delecato approach, but are of related interest. Corder (1966) studied the effects of a physical education program on the intellectual and physical development of mentally retarded children. The program lasted for three weeks. During this time, one group of boys engaged in physical education training; a second group served as observers of the first; a third group remained in the classroom. The results indicated that the children who received the physical education program improved in physical and intellectual prowess. The catch in this finding, however, is that the observers also demonstrated intellectual benefits. This suggests that the motor training itself was not the critical variable producing the desired changes. Finally, Masland (1969) reported a study conducted by Solomon and Pangle which resulted in the conclusion that physical education training may improve physical fitness, but not intelligence or self-concepts.

Like perceptual-motor training, the physical fitness approach has not been shown to facilitate those cognitive processes correlated with or necessary for academic achievement. The studies which have sought to link these variables have often been flawed by poor methodology (Gruber, 1969). Perhaps with better research methods such effects will be found. Gruber believes that because of a correlation between intelligence and complex play activity the play activity stimulates the growth of intellectual skills. We take a more pessimistic view. It seems more likely that the causal linkage, if there is any, in the correlation between intelligence and play activity is that intelligent children learn more readily a variety of skills, and this includes complex play activity. While athletic skills, muscle size, speed, or sex appeal may be enhanced through physical education programs, it seems unlikely that reading, writing, or arithmetic proficiency will be similarly affected. Whatever values these programs have, they do not appear to include the facilitation of academic skills.

Multisensory Approach

The underlying assumption in the multisensory approach is that learning can be facilitated and maximized if the relevant information is presented through many sensory modalities (Fernald, 1943; Gillingham and Stillman, 1960). The therapeutic emphasis is upon the stimulus presentation, not upon the motor activities demanded of the child. Those motor activities which are included in the training procedures are directly related to the academic task at hand and not to any presumed precursors of these skills.

Grace Fernald's method is discussed as one example of a multisensory approach. In the Fernald approach the child's acquisition of reading, writing, and arithmetic is believed to be facilitated by visual, auditory, and kinesthetic cues becoming conditioned to one another. To aid him in the acquisition of each word, the child follows a series of steps to learn that word. He is requested to trace and then copy the presented word while pronouncing it aloud. Then the child writes the word in the absence of the stimulus word. The child thus receives visual, auditory, tactile, and kinesthetic cues to guide him in learning each word.

In a similar vein, Gillingham and Stillman (1960) employ multiple sensory inputs to the child in the training program they developed. There are significant differences between the Fernald and Gillingham and Stillman approaches. Fernald presents whole words to be learned, and cursive writing is taught from the beginning of the program. Gillingham and Stillman use a highly structured phonics approach in which isolated phonemes are initially taught. Nonetheless, the two methods revolve around the differential use of sensory modalities to enhance the likelihood of learning.

The Gillingham and Stillman approach presents the child with a card which has a letter written on it. The child is taught the name and sound of the letter in conjunction with the presentation of the stimulus card. The visual symbol is removed, and the child is taught to associate the sound of the letter with its name. A series of steps follow in which the child traces, copies, writes from memory, and writes without looking at the card. The child learns to recognize and reproduce each phoneme using these visual-auditory-kinesthetic steps, referred to as the "language triangle" by its authors.

Fernald and Gillingham and Stillman have enjoyed fine reputations within special education. It is somewhat surprising that there has been a dearth of research activity related to a comparison of the use of the multiple sensory input approach with other methods. The only reference which can be brought to bear on this topic is but tangentially related. Travers (1964) reviewed the effects of multimedia presentation on learning and reported that there was no support for the position that multisensory presentation of information is a more effective teaching method than unimodal presentations.

It is clear that these teachers and intervention programs enjoy great respect among fellow teachers and clinicians. Unfortunately, the source of their success is still in doubt. One cannot yet determine whether their success was related to the use of multisensory inputs, the individual attention, warmth, skill, or some other personality characteristic of the teacher, the selective sampling of children who were most likely to respond to these particular methods, or some other accidental or conscious variable. The source of success remains an enigma.

Language-based Programs

The previously outlined remediation programs focus upon visual and perceptual training as a therapeutic approach to correcting reading deficits. Other professionals have recommended a remedial approach which emphasizes language training. One of the best-known language-based programs is that developed by Doris Johnson and Helmer Myklebust (1967). Myklebust's extensive experience with deaf and aphasic children resulted in his development of a paradigm based upon the relationship of the brain to human functioning, particularly to language-related activities. In this paradigm the brain is viewed as being organized into semiautonomous systems which allow parts of the brain to work independently or together, depending upon the task to be accomplished. In addition, the brain is viewed as having the left side responsible for verbal types of material, while the right side of the brain is responsible for nonverbal types of information. Differential performance on tasks can be used to make inferences about the presence or absence of brain damage and the possible location of such damage.

Myklebust also postulated five levels of learning. The lowest level involves the ability to receive sensations. The second level is perception, the ability to recognize and differentiate between sensory inputs received. Imagery, the third level, refers to the capacity to remember or recall a sensation. The fourth level is symbolization, the ability to verbally label sensations, perceptions, and images. Conceptualization, the fifth and highest level of learning, involves making abstractions and categorizations of material. Each level of the learning hierarchy requires the development and integrity of the preceding levels.

Diagnosis and remediation are based upon a task analysis of the semiautonomous systems of the brain, the right and left or verbal and nonverbal nature of the material, the level of learning involved and the child's skills or deficits in each of these areas. To devise a remedial program requires the teacher to make a task analysis in which the material to be learned and the child are evaluated in terms of the intra- and intersensory natures implicit in the tasks, and present or deficit in the child. For example, a child might be asked to discriminate whether two sounds are alike or whether two pictures are alike. This typifies an intrasensory task. If a child is to specify whether a sound he hears is the same as a picture he sees, intersensory functioning is being assessed. The verbal or nonverbal nature of the material is also considered. The child's recognition of environmental sounds or of geometric patterns as alike become part of the diagnostic appraisal, and if need be, part of the remedial program. Attention is directed to the modes of response required by the task. A distinction is made between the child's ability to receive the information or comprehend at the steps of learning and his ability to express the information he has received.

A child may have little or no difficulty in comprehending the information presented, but great difficulty in expressing that information. A problem at the comprehension level is seen as having more serious implications for learning, as it reciprocally affects expression. A problem at the expressive level may be circumvented by utilization of a more intact type of expressive mode for that child. A number of types of responses are encouraged, to see if a child totally incapable of demonstrating learning in one modality may be able to succeed quite well with another means of expression. Thus, a child unable to pass a dictated spelling test by writing responses may be able to pass the test if allowed to respond by orally spelling the words, or if the test is presented in a multiple-choice format (Johnson, 1967).

Remedial efforts are based upon these diagnostic evaluations of the child's intact and deficit modes of comprehension and expression. In this teaching method, it is advocated that children be taught new material through their intact modalities. If the child learns well visually, present unfamiliar material in a visual format. If he learns well auditorily, then he should be allowed to learn unfamiliar tasks by listening. If a child has difficulty in writing, let him take tests auditorily or tape-record written assignments. In addition, the child is given specific exercises to remediate the deficit areas. While he may not be able to take written exams initially, the goal of the remedial program is to assist him with this problem so that the child ultimately can function using the deficit areas.

A number of language-based programs have been developed to facilitate language development in preschool-aged children, both normal and handicapped. An example of this type of program is that which was developed by Tina Bangs (1968). The goal of this program is to increase the language skills and conceptual abilities of children ages 3 to 6. The activities are designed to facilitate the acquisition and use of language. For instance, to develop comprehension of language, Bangs recommends a variety of exercises. The child is exposed to activities which involve recognizing objects by their names and functions, categorizing objects, serial directions, and spatial orientation. To facilitate the development of expressive language, the child is asked to name, describe, or dramatize objects, scenes, and themes. This program provides a rather complete prekindergarten program with a particular emphasis upon language-related activities.

The more widely known language-based programs, such as those developed by Johnson and Myklebust (1967) and Bangs (1968), have not received empirical attention. It is not clear why this is so. The efficiency or efficacy of these techniques remains unknown. Whether they work is not known. If they work, it is not known why. If they work and if they work better than some other approach is also not known. It appears that Myklebust's research efforts have been devoted to testing hypotheses about brain functioning and correlates of brain damage. Johnson's research has also not been addressed to problems of training children. Bangs came to this field as a speech therapist and her program appears to be service rather than research oriented. It is possible that these programs are being placed within clinical settings which traditionally emphasize trying to help children with problems rather than concern for the effectiveness of such help. Like many critically important human problems, there is the difficulty of convincing others that some children should be denied the presumed assistance of a remedial program in order to evaluate the effectiveness of such a program. Even though we do not know just how worthwhile such remedial programs are, we are loath to create a group of untreated children with whom to compare the treated group. While provocative hypotheses can be advanced concerning the remedial programs, little systematically gathered data can be brought to bear upon the efficacy of these programs.

Although there have been no tests of the effectiveness of a particular remedial training program or of the efficiency of one program compared to another, there has been some research regarding the skills which might facilitate language competency in young children, particularly as related to the acquisition of reading. Two separate perspectives have dominated this research. One has been the application of theories or ideas concerning the relationship of sensory modality functions to the acquisition of reading; the second is based upon a behavior modification approach.

An outgrowth of all the concern about the parts of the brain and learning has been an interest in the relationship between sensory competence and instructional technique. Theorists have hypothesized that differential reading treatments should be accorded to individual children based on profiles of sensory functioning. It was assumed that if a child were diagnosed as having visual rather than auditory strengths, or was a visual learner, he should be trained to read using a visual approach. If a child were assessed an "auditory learner," he should receive an auditory approach to reading (Bateman, 1969; Johnson and Myklebust, 1967; Smith, 1971). In this approach, there is general agreement that children strong in learning by the visual modality be given an analytic or whole-word introduction to reading, whereas children who are strong in learning auditorily be given a phonics reading program. There is evidence directly related to this hypothesis.

Bliesmer and Yarborough (1965) compared ten beginning reading programs used in the first grade. Five of the programs were based on phonetic presentation, while five were presented by the whole-word approach. Reading achievement was evaluated by performance on five subtests from the Stanford Achievement Test. The results suggested the overwhelming efficiency of the phonetic method. If there were individual differences among the children in terms of their being either auditory or visual learners, these differences were not so great as to make any difference. Another attempt failed to find any significant association between the specific teaching method used and the presumed aptitude for this method (Harris, 1965).

Bateman (1969) studied the efficacy of dividing children into auditory and visual types for the purpose of receiving phonetic or whole-word reading methods of instruction. Eight kindergarten classes were included in the study. Four of the classes were divided so that two received a phonetic approach and two received a whole-word approach to beginning reading instruction. Children from the remaining four classrooms were divided into auditory or visual types on the basis of their scores on the auditory and visual memory subtests from the Illinois Test of Psycholinguistic Abilities. If the child's auditory score exceeded the visual score by more than 9 months, the child was labeled "auditory"; if the difference between the auditory and visual scores was less than 9 months, the child was labeled "visual." The children defined as "auditory" types received the Lippincott beginning reading program, while the "visual" types received the Scott Foresman series. At the end of the first grade a reading score was obtained from scores on the Gates Primary Word Recognition and Paragraph Reading tests and a spelling score was obtained from a list of twelve words and six nonsense words.

The results were that the auditory method proved to be significantly superior to the visual method. The auditorily trained group had scores on the reading achievement and spelling tests which were significantly higher than those of the children trained by the visual method. The children labeled as "auditory" types performed significantly better than children who had been labeled as "visual" types. Of sixteen good readers, fourteen had had the auditory approach; of eighteen poor readers, sixteen were visual types and twelve had had the visual approach. The visual types who fared well were children who had IQs considerably above the average for this group, while the auditory types who were poor readers were below the average IQ for the group. It should be noted that the IQs among these children ranged from 121.6 to 126.0 and that the "poor reader" in this context was a first-grader scoring at a 2.9 grade level.

There are a number of problems in interpreting these data. The high IQs of the group in general make generalizations to other populations tenuous. In addition, the definition of poor reading in a child reading above grade level is also questionable. On the other hand, it is equally defensible to say that this study represents a good demonstration for the use of a structured phonics approach to beginning reading as superior to a visual method, especially because the results were not confounded by subjects having had low intelligence or differences among groups in intelligence; nor was it confounded by low socioeconomic status of subjects. Since the study did not suffer from effects of these other variables which are known to affect reading acquisition, we believe it makes a fairly strong statement in favor of phonetic approaches to reading, irrespective of subject types.

Carolyn Smith (1971) also investigated the efficacy of matching subject type to reading approach, but using a different sample of children. As in the Bateman study, the focus was upon the relationship of reading method and reading achievement with auditory and visual modality preferences in children. In this case children were divided into auditory and visual types by averaging their test scores on the Illinois Test of Psycholinguistic Abilities. The auditory score was an average of results on the subtests Auditory Reception, Auditory Association, Grammatic Closure, and Sequential Memory. The visual score was an average of results on the subtests Visual Reception, Visual Association, and Visual Sequential Memory. Children with discrepancies greater than twelve months between their auditory and visual scores were labeled according to their higher score. There were a small number of children who fit this definition of auditory types; thus five children with ten- or eleven-month discrepancies were included in the auditory group. The control group was comprised of children with auditory-visual differences of less than one month. There were seventy-two children divided so that eight received each treatment.

The treatments were such that each group of children was taught by the same teacher for two years using one of three reading programs. The programs included: (a) the Initial Teaching Alphabet (ITA) *Early-to-Read Series* followed by the Lippincott series; (b) the *Words in Color* (WIC) Program (Gattegno, 1963) followed by the Lippincott series; and (c) the Supplemental Conventional Reading Program (SCRP), which included the *Reading for Meaning Series* (McKee, Harrison, McCowan, and Lehr, 1963) and supplemented by *Reading with Phonics* (Hay and Wingo, 1960).

At the end of the first and second grades the Metropolitan Achievement test was administered. There were no significant differences between the auditory, visual, and control groups on the Metropolitan Achievement test scores. With respect to individual treatments, the means were ranked. For the ITA treatment the highest performers were the visual types, followed by control and auditory. For the WIC program, the means were auditory highest, then visual and control. For the SCRP program, the means were visual highest, then control and auditory. There was no significant interaction between type of program and type of child.

These results are contradictory to the results of the Bateman study, which indicated that auditory types with auditory methods learn to read more effectively than visual types receiving visual methods. But there were differences in IQ, socioeconomic status, and definitions of auditory and visual types in these two studies. Smith suggests that the percentages of children who can be labeled as auditory or visual learners seems to vary with IQ and/or socioeconomic status, and that age and race may also play a role.

Bruinincks (1970) investigated the relationship of auditory and visual competence in the child and the effectiveness of teaching through one or the other modality. In this case subjects were selected from a sample of disadvantaged boys. One group was identified as having auditory strengths and visual deficits, while the second group was to have auditory weakness and visual strengths. Each child was taught thirty words he did not know. Fifteen of the words were taught using a phonetic method and fifteen using a whole-word approach. The results failed to confirm the notion that learning can be made more effective by matching the auditory and visual strengths of the child to an auditory or visual method of instruction.

Finally, Sabatino and Streissguth (1972) tested the hypothesis that training children who demonstrated visual strength relative to auditory deficits on a visual training program would result in their making greater gains than children with visual deficits and auditory strengths who also received this training on a number of tests: specifically the Bender Visual Motor Gestalt, the Wide Range Achievement, the Gates-McGinitie Reading Comprehension, and the Word Form Configuration. In a rather well-controlled study, these two types of children were either exposed or not exposed to a visual training technique. The results failed to support the hypothesis that "visiles" (children with visual strengths) benefited more from perceptual training than "audiles" (children with auditory strengths).

The link between sensory modality skills and learning to read has not been established. It is clearly advantageous to analyze the subskills and processes required in the act of reading so that deficits can be understood and programs devised to help a child. But it is not apparent that either the correct skills or the analysis of the task of reading have been adequately identified or defined. As of now, we think individual variations in auditory or visual processing seem to make very little difference in learning to read.

To this point, our discussion of psycholinguistically oriented remediation has been focused upon intervention models based on the ITPA. We now turn to those based upon psycholinguistic models which are derivatives of Chomsky and his friends' views of language.

To develop an intervention program, several important recommendations have been made. Gruenewald and Pollack (1975) suggest that first one must analyze the classroom context; that is, the teacher's language. These authors point out that the syntactic and semantic complexity of the teacher's instructions to the students can inadvertently complicate what may appear to the adult to be simple exercises. Teachers' instructions, they suggest, should be assessed for length, rate, and the number and types of concepts presented relative to the child's linguistic development. When a detailed account of such an analysis will not be given, an example will be. Gruenewald and Pollack point out that the concept *before* in the instruction "wash your hands *before* dinner" is quite different from the use of *before* in mathematics, and that "on top of the table" is quite different in meaning from "on top of the paper." Children having delays or difficulties understanding concepts of time and space may have considerable difficulty with teacher instructions based on such concepts as "more, less, before, after, all, and same." In effect, concepts derive meaning from context.

Gruenewald and Pollack also suggest that student language, particularly spontaneous speech, be recorded as a means of assessing the student's linguistic development in order to aid the teacher in using more appropriate instructional language. They suggest that one important piece of information is the child's use, or lack of use, of the word *and*. A child not yet using *and* may not be ready for addition problems. What would the child know about "3 *and* 5"? Likewise, the child's use of *wh* questions *(who, what, when, where, why)*, plurals, possessives, correct word endings, and prepositions may be critical for his understanding of classroom events. The teacher's monitoring of the spoken language within the classroom does seem an appropriate place to start planning a program of language intervention.

A second suggestion regarding a language intervention program is that such programs employ meaningful words, in a format which makes syntactic and semantic sense. For example, in a sequencing exercise the teacher should *not* employ nonmeaningful chains of words such as "ball push truck." Lasky, Jay, and Hanz-Ehrman (1975) examined the effectiveness of several auditory training programs which used nonlinguistic, nonmeaningful stimuli, such as animal sounds, noises from a vacuum cleaner, and rings of a telephone, as compared with those employing linguistically meaningful stimuli. They found that meaningful stimuli are easier to learn than nonmeaningful stimuli. Additionally, the authors felt that meaningful stimuli appeared to increase attending behaviors during the nonmeaningful presentations.

A number of methods and related materials to facilitate language development skills in learning-disabled children have recently been developed. One program is noteworthy, that developed by Lee, Koenigsknecht, and Mulhern (1975).

Lee and her colleagues have developed a language development teaching method, The Interactive Language Development Program. This program can be used with children in their early elementary school years who have delayed language development, and can be employed with either small groups or on an individual basis. There are programs specified for helping the child either acquire basic sentence structures, or more advanced grammatical structures. The Interactive Language Development Program is administered by a teacher storytelling technique, followed by the children responding to specified questions from the teacher about the story. The stories deal with everyday affairs which are likely to be familiar to the child rather than being fantasy-based. The teacher is guided in implementing the program because each lesson's concepts and vocabulary, necessary materials, and the specific grammatical structures to be emphasized are specified. The program also outlines instructional techniques which the authors feel will facilitate the children's performances. For example, in responding to a child's errors, it is recommended that the teachers both repeat the sentence correctly and then repeat for the child those parts of the sentence which he omitted. Other techniques include asking the child to expand an incomplete response, having the child correct an incorrect response without the teacher presenting the right response, and repeating the incorrect response by the child in order to elicit a correction from him. Besides the explicitness of this program, an additional feature is that the program includes methods by which to monitor the effectiveness of the intervention. That is done by means of the Developmental Sentence Score, described in Chapter 10.

Lee, Koenigsknecht, and Mulhern (1975) have attempted to empirically demonstrate the effectiveness of this program in facilitating language development. They report that twenty-five language-delayed children, ages 3 to 5, who had received approximately eight months of intervention, showed significant gains on a variety of language tests. The fact that this intervention program is being systematically assessed is encouraging. No doubt further research will show both its merits and limitations. Of course much more research is needed on many intervention programs, but at least further data should be forthcoming concerning this intervention program.

The study of psycholinguistics has not only spawned programs for language intervention but has also affected both the nature of research on reading and the intervention programs generated to aid the disabled reader. Researchers and educators alike have become more sensitive to the idea that there is a relationship between reading and language development (Blanton, 1972).

Apparently two different psycholinguistically inspired intervention strategies have been evidenced, one which emphasizes *decoding,* the other *comprehending.*

The *decoding* strategy, probably the more familiar of the two strategies, can be seen in the perspectives of Bloomfield and Fries (Fries, 1963). In this perspective, learning to read is seen as a matter of breaking the linguistic code. Learning to read is a function of figuring out the relationship between one's own oral sounds and the written letter. The phoneme-grapheme relationship is the key to mastery, while morphology, syntax, and semantics are relatively unimportant. Teaching children to read involves initially presenting only words which have a sound consistent with letter symbol spelling, using initially consonant-vowel-consonant spellings (e.g., can-nan-tan), which then may be strung together to make sentences (e.g., Nan can tan). This perspective on reading appears to be reflected in Bateman's position that ". . . all evidence supports the currently unpopular notion that reading can and should be taught as a formation of a series of rote, nonmeaningful, conditioned bonds between visual stimuli (letters) and vocal responses (sounds) . . . reading should be viewed as a rote, non-meaningful process" (1964, p. 291).

The other psycholinguistic approach to reading emphasizes the importance of *comprehension* in facilitating reading. It is believed that reading is facilitated by exploiting the child's "natural" sense of the sentence. Initial reading instruction in this perspective uses the child's oral language as the instructional material. Reading is taught by having the child read his own language productions. The work of Goodman and Burke (1972) is an example of this perspective. In their intervention techniques children are presented with written words which they have produced in their telling of stories. The reader is then encouraged to ask himself questions when reading; for example, whether the material makes sense to him. During the lesson the teacher aids the child to discriminate between significant and trivial information, and thus presumably helps the child decide which words are important in which contexts.

According to Pflaum (1976) there is evidence that when the language used for reading material is at the oral language level of the reader, comprehension is increased. Pflaum thus offers some guidance for teaching reading. Her basic idea is that it is essential to help students who do not comprehend the material by dealing directly with the syntactic structures within the written stimuli. For example, she recommends teaching connectives directly by having the teacher start with easy common connectives and moving toward the more complex ones, thus paralleling the child's own linguistic development. The progression of teaching proceeds as follows: "connectives of addition (and, also, in addition); connectives of contrast (but, yet, however, except); connectives of result (therefore, such as, notably, that is); connectives of clarification (for example, such as, notably, that is); connectives of consequence and exception (even though, although, in spite of)"; connectives of condition (if, unless); connectives of cause (because, since, as)" (p. 11).

Pflaum recommends that teachers may aid children who are troubled by passive constructions by having those children detect the agent, or doer, of the verb within the sentence. Another suggestion is related to reading of multi-embedded sentences, that is, sentences in which there are many kernal sentences. An example of such a sentence would be "Her grandfather, a retired sea captain who carved wooden figures for a living, suggested letting Jessica, a hen that had been trying to hatch a doorknob, sit on the egg" (p. 11). To aid children's comprehension of such complex presentations, given that one must make them at all, Pflaum suggests taking the complex sentences apart and putting the simple sentences together in different ways. Finally, like Goodman and Burke (1972), Pflaum also recommends helping children by teaching the reading strategies. This means teaching students to ask the right questions and to focus on possible areas of difficulty; to make sentences from the *wh* words, making statements into questions and vice versa; and discussing the meaning of the written material already covered.

Another approach to assisting the acquisition of language skills and reading has been based upon operant conditioning. According to this perspective, behavior can be influenced through the use of reinforcements or rewards administered contingent upon the occurrence of a desired behavior. The technology surrounding operant conditioning is fairly sophisticated in terms of the timing and amount of the rewards which will result in optimum gains, but the underlying assumption is simple. Children will learn to do whatever leads them to get what they want.

A number of remedial programs has been developed which combine behavior modification with a program of instruction based upon linguistic analyses of language production or reading. Gray, Baker, and Stancyk (1969) developed a program for remedial reading instruction; Gray and Fygetakis (1968) applied this approach to dysphasic children (children unable to speak), and Fygetakis and Ingram (1973) reported a case study of a 5-year-old dysphasic child. This method is described in some detail because it incorporates a number of practices which may be valuable in the improvement of educational approaches for children with learning disabilities. It is important to note that any behavior modification approach requires that the educator maintain a continuous record of the child's behavior. This record permits the teacher to make adjustments immediately and continuously in the rate of introduction of new material, the speed with which the child learns, the appropriateness of the level of task difficulty, and the evaluation of a program over time. This approach can be easily adapted to a wide variety of learning problems, from behavior disturbances to difficulties in written language. This is the approach being promoted in "prescriptive teaching," but it provides a more exact description of the steps to be followed in evaluating the results of the learning sessions.

Gray, Baker, and Stancyk (1969) based their approach on the Bond and Dykstra (1967) summary of reading research. Bond and Dykstra indicated that: (a) the best single predictor of first-grade reading achievement is the ability to recognize the letters of the alphabet; (b) there is no methodological advantage for any single approach; (c) class size, teacher experience, and teacher efficiency do not correlate significantly with pupil success; and (d) the emphasis should be placed upon the learning situations and procedures rather than upon methods and materials. As a result of these findings, Gray, Baker, and Stancyk base their reading program upon conditioning or learning principles. In this case the assumptions made are that: (a) reading is responsive to laws of learning; (b) decoding is antecedent to comprehension and should be taught first; (c) success should be abundant and result in immediate rewards; and (d) characteristics such as visual perception, IQ, sequencing ability, etc., do not affect reading acquisition unless a very severe deficit exists (1969, p. 256).

The remedial reading training procedure, Performance Determined Instruction, or PDI, was developed. Children need to know the alphabet and most sound-symbol relationships to be put into this program. Children who have not mastered the alphabet are first provided with an alternate training procedure. Once the child is placed on the PDI, the following program is used. Two children receive biweekly, thirty-minute training programs. The first fifteen minutes involves training in word attack skills, which requires the child to read the words on a list. The words are presented in a sequential way based upon their phonetic complexity and length. The teacher's job is to keep track of the correct and reinforced answers and response errors on a tally sheet. The teacher dispenses poker-chip tokens when the child reads the word correctly. When the child makes a mistake, it becomes the second child's turn to read. An error response results in the child not getting a poker chip and losing his turn to perform. The second fifteen minutes are devoted to reading contextual material. Each child is started just below his grade level in a graded reading series. One child reads and obtains a token for each correctly read sentence. An error results in losing his turn to the second child and not obtaining a token for that sentence. Again the teacher keeps track of correct responses, errors made, and the transferring of turns from one to the other child. When a child responds correctly for three minutes, he is stopped and given a bonus token. The second child is then given an opportunity to perform. At the end of the thirty-minute session the tokens can be exchanged for M&M candies, five tokens to one piece of candy.

The authors emphasize that the teacher activity is more critical than the materials employed. The material is selected to follow a sequential order in which the complexity is increased in a meaningful manner. The materials used in the instance reported here included word lists from Bloomfield and Flesch and graded reading material from Harper and Row, Harr and Wagner, Sullivan and Heath for reading comprehension. Materials for contextual reading can be selected to suit the mood and interests of the child, as this program does not specify that there need be a relationship between the word lists and the contextual reading materials.

The program is arranged so that the child performs with correct responses

92 percent of the time. This was chosen as ideal because children who fail in reading require a great deal of success, but less than 92 percent correct results in less adequate reading performance, while greater than 92 percent correct performance results in boredom without any appreciable increase in reading skills. Also manipulated is the amount of reinforcement administered when the child responds correctly. The child receives either continuous reinforcement, one token to one correct response, or partial reinforcement, one token for each series of five successive correct responses, or one token for each ten successive correct responses, or one token for each series of fifteen successive words per token and three word lists per difficulty level. Each page of the word lists contains five word lists of eighteen words apiece. The amount of work at each level of difficulty and the rate of reinforcement were manipulated by the instructor. The child is started at continuous reinforcement, one correct response resulting in a token, and with five word lists. After three instructional sessions, the child is shifted to receiving three word lists per difficulty level and reinforcement for fifteen successive correct responses.

The authors reported that the system was tested on nine 9-year-old boys enrolled in the Monterey Institute for Speech and Hearing for remedial reading problems. After twelve hours on the PDI, the boys improved one year on the Gray Oral Reading Passage. This approach thus appears to be quite effective, at least with respect to quickly improving the decoding skills of remedial readers. At this time, comprehension skills had not been tested.

The behavior modifiers have taken a radical approach relative to the views of more orthodox theorists. They abstain from preoccupations with the perceptual, auditory, visual, and/or brain process of the learning-disabled child. Instead, the diagnosis of the child is focused upon what the child likes, what he will work for, and ultimately what he will learn for. Their radicalness takes another turn when they ignore the materials to be used beyond a simple placement of the child on some graded series and when they ignore the traditional role of the teacher to instruct the child. The focus is upon careful documentation of the effects of individualized instruction upon the individual child. Careful observations are made and impact is assessed. The role of the teacher then shifts to becoming a data collector and reinforcer. Irrespective of whether the success of this approach is due to this careful documentation, or to these techniques being superior to those produced under differing perspectives of disability, it appears that this approach has yielded the most fruitful remedial techniques, if not the most elaborate diagnostic ones.

Miscellaneous Remediation Techniques

Thus far, the discussion of remedial techniques has been addressed to specific theories and well-defined remedial programs based upon these theories. Evidence about the effectiveness of these programs has been sparse and the results often disappointing. But perhaps we should not be surprised. As indicated earlier, Walberg (1971) did suggest that specific instructional techniques do not seem to be particularly powerful in affecting the child's academic progress. Other variables related to dimensions of classroom activity have more impact upon the child's learning success. Based upon information derived from research efforts in other fields as well as efforts in learning disabilities, it appears to us that many ideas about remediating learning disabilities may reflect more "fancy" than "fact."

We believe that many of the problems faced by learning-disabled children are not at all academic, but rather are of a social nature. Many children who have difficulty learning in school are not labeled learning disabled although they meet the legal definitions set up by their respective school districts. We suggest that the label "learning disabled" does not depend entirely upon the inability to experience academic success, but is at least equally related to social behaviors. It is not simply a learning disability which marks this child (as noted by the Clements, 1966, list of characteristics); it is the inability to perform, plus additional negative behavioral characteristics which result in this label being applied. It should be noted that the limitation of remedial techniques, as noted in the literature, may be related to the fact that these techniques ignore the behaviors of the child which resulted in his being labeled in the first place, and concentrate all efforts on remediating the learning problems. Only the behavior modification approach included an accounting of the child's responses, and this may be the secret of success of such an approach.

One prevalent view of children with learning disabilities is that they often have memory deficiencies. It is a common belief that individuals vary in their capacity to retain information, some people believing that they have a "terrible" memory while others claim some affiliation with elephants, which are noted for "exceptional" memories. Memory deficits are indexed by a person's performance on subtests of the Wechsler Intelligence Scale for Children, such as digit span or coding, and by auditory and visual sequential memory tests on the Illinois Test of Psycholinguistic Ability. Remedial programs to improve memory are then based upon these test scores when a child performs poorly.

There are several sources of difficulty with the assumption that children have memory deficits and that remedial programs can alleviate and improve such problems. First, digit span and coding subtests on the WISC are not related to memory on other tasks, at least not yet. The statistical and empirical difficulties inherent in this procedure have been well documented (McNemar, 1957). A second point is that such tests are not simply a matter of memory, as memory is related to learning, and in these tests the degree of learning is not controlled. For a child to repeat five digits, frontward and backward, requires that he learn the list, not just that he remember the list. A large body of research in verbal learning has consistently failed to demonstrate any individual differences in memory. Individual differences are evident in terms of the original learning of the material, not in their recall (Underwood, 1945; 1964). This is the source for different scores on memory tests—not memory! If the amount of learning is the same for any two people, their recall of that material will be the same. If efforts to improve the initial stage of learning are not provided, all of the efforts to improve memory are a waste of time and will not yield the desired results. When children score poorly on tests of memory, we should address ourselves to the child's technique of learning new material and an improved approach for that child in his ability to make such acquisitions.

Another assumption frequently made about the learning-disabled child is that he is distractible. Remedial programs have been designed to decrease this distractibility, with some demanding that teachers wear only plain black dresses with no jewelry and that the classroom be similarly stark. Perhaps every child who causes trouble within the schools is labeled distractible. This has been the case with the brain-injured child (Browning, 1967). Obviously, if a child is distractible when he is supposed to be learning academic materials, his performance will suffer. There have been a number of studies conducted relevant to the belief that distractibility in children will affect their performance on learning. Browning (1967) tested brain-injured and nonbrain-injured children on a discrimination learning task. During the learning trials, the child was to note the contingency between the discrimination of a triangle, from a circle or square, and the receipt of a candy reward. Some children from each group were to perform this task with multicolored lights flashing to distract them. Other children from the brain-damaged and nonbrain-damaged groups were not presented with this visual distraction. There were no differences in learning between the brain-injured and nonbrain-injured children under conditions of visual distraction. The results indicated that distraction is no more devastating to the performance of brain-injured children than it is for nonbrain-injured children.

A second study addressed to the effects of distraction upon learning in learning-disabled children was completed by Vernetti and Jacobs (1972). In this, the distraction was noise and the task was the completion of math problems in the classroom. Fifty-three children, eleven girls and forty-two boys enrolled in a self-contained learning disabilities classroom, were instructed to complete pages of math problems. During this time they were exposed to regular background noise or to taped music. When the child completed the page, the teacher recorded the time to completion. Each child was tested eight times under each condition (noisy and not noisy). There were no differences reported in the performance of learning-disabled children under the noisy and not noisy conditions.

Contradictory results were reported by Hartman and Richards (1969). In this study it was hypothesized that a very quiet and sensory isolated room (no visual or auditory distractions) would enhance the ability of brain-damaged children with severe reading difficulties to learn the association between labels and pictures. Half of the subjects were presented the learning task in the ordinary classroom. The remaining children were placed in a very nondistracting environment. Children learned more within the sensory isolated condition than those who remained in the classroom. Unfortunately, the results of this study are subject to an alternative explanation. Subjects in the sensory isolated room were presented the stimulus materials through a rather elaborate apparatus, while those in the classroom had to make do with a Language Master presentation. The differential learning of children in these two environments may be related to the presentation of the material and not to the potentially distracting or nondistracting environment.

As yet, there is little support for the idea that children with learning disabilities are more distractible than other academically successful children or that eliminating sources of distractibility will enhance the results of an educational program.

It is commonly believed that children who are slower to achieve need more time, be it to apply their learning strategies to the task at hand or to assimilate the lessons proposed by the teacher. Within learning disabilities, we realize, "more" is not enough and the "more" must also be different. To express this we reject the notion of "tutoring," which is associated with simply providing "more" without taking into account how the presentation should differ from that under which the child has already failed. The term *clinical teaching* was substituted. Nonetheless, it is believed that an increased time allotment for instruction is going to raise the performance of slow students (those with less than average aptitudes) to a given criterion level, while fast students will finish the same material more quickly. There is, however, little research from classroom settings to support the idea that time is curative. There appears to be little relation between the amount of time spent in instruction and the achievement level reached by the student, given at least some exposure to the material (Walberg, 1971). In this case we have only anecdotal data to make inferences about how the time factor might affect learning-disabled children. One child with a delayed speech and language history, on drugs to control potential epileptic attacks, with very slow motor responses and questionable ability to use language in any abstract sense, was reading above grade level. The teacher complained that the child spent most of the day daydreaming and engaging in "nervous mannerisms," like playing with paper clips and shreds of paper. It is suggested that time in itself was not relevant to the academic performance of this clearly handicapped girl. Once she had the idea it stuck with her, and the usual exercises in which children overlearn school material may not have any more effect for successful learners than it was having for this child, who was not engaging in these repetitive tasks.

What are the factors which might affect learning? In a discussion of programmed instruction, Gagne and Paradise (1961) suggest the following variables: (1) the skills the learner has when he starts; (2) the skills he has specific to the task at hand; (3) the ability to be acquired; (4) the general level of intelligence of the student. Insofar as little seems to be known about the interactions of variables associated with numbers 1, 2, and 3, these recommendations provide but a framework and starting point for attacking any learning task.

There appears to be consensus that the differences in rates of learning cannot be altered by having the child repeat a task or simply spend more time on the task. To determine the ideal amount of time a child spends on an activity, the desired repetition of responses and amount of reinforcements which will facilitate learning, it is suggested that a learning curve be drawn for the child. A recent study of learning curves in retarded readers was reported by Camp (1973). In this study, forty-two retarded readers were accepted for a remedial reading program. The materials used included the SRA Reading Laboratories, 1a, 1b, and 1c. The children received one to five tutoring sessions per week using the Staats Motivation Activation Reading Technique (SMART). Each half-hour reading lesson included the introduction of new vocabulary, paragraph reading, total story reading, and answering comprehension questions. Token rewards were given which could be exchanged for money. The lesson was not complete until the child had one unprompted complete trial with each word on the new vocabulary list and one trial with each paragraph in which all the words were read correctly without prompting. Children were then exposed to the next level of difficulty. The tutor's job was to keep track of each response given on the lesson. The words on which the child made one or more errors during the lesson were used to make up the vocabulary test given at the end of each block of twenty lessons. The data used to plot the learning curve came from the daily records made by the tutor of the daily lessons and the vocabulary review tests. The daily record required the tutor to count the total number of errors produced on the vocabulary and paragraph reading parts of the lesson. Acquisition curves could then be plotted by listing the cumulative scores against the cumulative total number of lessons completed and total number of words presented. The ratio of total errors to total words presented became the measure of learning rate.

The author had presupposed that retarded readers would have more heterogeneous learning curves. But, indeed, the retarded readers' scores resulted in the same curves which are seen in nonretarded or normal readers on a variety of learning tasks. This is marked by a general pattern of initial acceleration followed by a gradual slackening of the rate of learning.

Camp suggested that this type of learning curve can be used by the teacher to regulate the flow of information presented to the child. The curve can be used to measure whether the child's learning acquisition is increased by repetition of materials or by more trials with different material. Differing curves should be used to differentiate ways of presenting material in terms of length of word lists or paragraphs and repetitiveness. In essence, Camp tried to do this. Children with error rates above 20 percent repeated a set of lessons. Children who had shown normally shaped curves showed decreased error rates with repetition. The children who did not demonstrate this change either had a curve with continuous acceleration or a high error rate with minimal deceleration late in the set of lessons. Camp concluded that "individual differences in learning rate may account for a large share of individual differences in reading achievement, even among a group of severely retarded readers" (1973, p. 71).

The above studies suggest that children with learning disabilities have the same general learning curves as academically successful peers. Little has yet been said about those factors which might affect learning and/or performance. Theories of learning, as studied by psychologists, are controversial in terms of their details. Some believe that children can learn simply by observation of adults and peers (Aronfreed, 1969; Bandura, 1969). Others argue that learning is linked to reinforcements, either in the child's history or in the situation at hand (Gewirtz, 1969). There is some consensus that children will perform that which has been learned because there is the possibility they will receive some material or social reward (Bandura, 1969). Whatever the truth of these conflicting theories, remedial techniques have taken segments of these varying positions to facilitate learning-disabled children's performance. These individual studies do not present a guide book of procedures designed to increase the child's capacity to read, write, and compute, but they do suggest some ideas as to the processes which might be followed and explored to facilitate the acquisition of such skills. The remainder of this chapter will be devoted to a discussion of those theories and research efforts which appear to have important implications for classroom and special education teachers.

BEHAVIOR MODIFICATION

Boredom has led people to drink, to sex, and to "busy" work. It led B. F. Skinner to some of the most profound and influential studies in modern psychology (Skinner, 1960). Skinner (1971) argued that behavior is controlled through the appropriate use of reinforcements. By giving a child a reward of candy, praise, or hugs and kisses, the behavior of the child which immediately preceded the reward will be very likely to recur. Skinner and colleagues developed extensive knowledge as to how such rewards might be utilized in optimal ways. These rewards came to include all the old tricks teachers have been using for centuries: stars, displays of classroom work, and verbal praise.

Skinner's refinement of knowledge about human behavior can be divided into four areas. First, he and his students were not content to simply administer a pellet to the pigeon or an M&M to the child. They went much further and specified how many pellets or M&Ms need to be given, when they should be given, and how often they need to be given to effect the desired behavior. The contribution of specification of the conditions under which reinforcements should be administered to obtain particular goals cannot be underestimated.

Second, a very empirical orientation was brought to education. It became necessary to note the change in a child's behavior which resulted from the actions of clinicians, teachers, and parents. Third, their work involved a denial of much of the popular psychological rhetoric concerning the child. The motto might be: focus not upon nonobservable motives, thoughts, and needs; let concepts of the id, ego, and superego die of disuse. Think not in the abstract terms proposed by psychodynamic theorists Freud, Jung, Adler, and Horney. Rather, study the behavior of the child. Let the conceptualizations of children be specified in behavioral terms.

Finally, the Skinnerian, or behavior modification, perspective demands that attention not be limited to the child's behavior (or symptoms) but to the interaction of the child's behavior with his environment. The focus was shifted to the effects of environment, particularly the people in the child's environment, and to what factors were eliciting and maintaining undesirable and maladaptive behaviors by means of reinforcements. Now it is no longer adequate to diagnose what is right or wrong about a child; one must analyze the interaction which occurs between variables in the environment and the child. This is a critically important emphasis, as there are many sources and types of reinforcers capable of affecting any particular child. Children, strange beasts that they are, often have strange tastes in incentives. The analysis of the individual child and his surroundings will often lead to the discovery that there is a reinforcer more potent than that which is assumed on an a priori basis. One student teacher, for example, reported that a child participating in a learning project selected for a reinforcement to have a parakeet sit in her hair.

While Skinner and his followers have continued to emphasize the import of reinforcement in governing behavior, the term *behavior modification* has been extended to include a variety of influence processes other than reinforcements. Any approach that produces change and which apparently is based upon contemporary principles of learning theory is presumed to be a reflection of the behavior modification approach. While such a definition can legitimately be challenged (cf. London, 1972), there are some common characteristics of perspectives shared by those who call themselves behavior modifiers.

The emphasis of the behavior modifier still continues to be upon systematic empirical efforts toward evaluating his intervention strategy, a careful analysis of the environmental events which may affect behavior, and caution regarding the use of intervention procedures against hypothesized problems which are not being evidenced in current behaviors. In effect, they attempt to treat that which is ailing the client, not that which is presumably producing the ailment; and they do so by manipulating certain features of the environment under circumstances where the outcome of such treatment will be systematically assessed. Furthermore, there are two areas of influence which most concern the behavior modifier. One concern is the role of models upon children. Essentially, what are the effects upon children of observing others' behaviors? Second, there is the concern for reinforcements.

What reinforcements, in what magnitude, with what frequency, and under what circumstances, affect children?

The implications of behavior modification are profound for the remediation of learning problems. There are implications for the direct improvement of academic achievement as seen in the Camp (1973) study and for the correction of the many behaviors defined as undesirable in children. This approach thus has direct value for altering inattentive, hyperactive, disruptive behaviors and also for increasing the degree to which a child learns to read.

While most of the direct applications of the behavior modification approach to the classroom have been concerned with the importance of reinforcements, and particularly the use of token economies, studies involving modeling have appeared which have at least indirect relevance to the remediation of the learning-disabled child. The remaining discussion of behavior modification will focus upon the importance of models and token economies in the remediation of difficulties experienced by the learning-disabled child.

BEHAVIORAL MODELS

One of the most commonly stated justifications for mainstreaming handicapped children into regular school classrooms is that such children will imitate, and learn from, their nonhandicapped peers (Snyder, Appolloni, and Cooke, 1977). Unfortunately special educators have not really examined whether handicapped children imitate the nonhandicapped, or indeed, whether the nonhandicapped don't imitate the handicapped, or those circumstances in which imitation might be facilitated or retarded. Moreover, there apparently has not been an attempt to employ modeling as an educational strategy within classroom settings. While the evidence concerning classroom modeling by the learning-disabled child is nonexistent, there are a number of studies which suggest that modeling may play an important role in the life of such children and that remediation techniques might be developed through the use of models.

Models have been used to change maladaptive behavior and to produce prosocial activities. A child who observes a film in which the actor shows courage in dealing with a frightening object (at least to the observing child) will himself show more courage when presented with the aversive object. Weissbrod and Bryan (1973) were able to reduce children's fears of snakes, and Bandura, Blanchard, and Ritter (1968) alleviated their fear of dogs, by presenting them with films of courageous models. In a more extensive modeling training program, Sarason (1968) was able to develop more appropriate social behaviors in institutionalized adolescent juvenile delinquents. Bryan (1975) has reviewed a number of experiments which have demonstrated that an altruistic model will increase the child's altruistic behavior, even when the child is unobserved and tested at a later date and in a different locale. There is little question, as the Puritans well knew when instructing their teachers, that models can play a powerful role in affecting the social and emotional behaviors of the observing children. This happens to be the case whether the model is live or televised, a peer or an adult, a male or female. As the Puritans maintained, teachers do have to pay particular attention to their own behavior since the children do; moreover, they might deliberately use their behavior to affect the child's behavior.

Before reviewing research concerning modeling and its effects on learning-disabled children, it is worthwhile to indicate some of the conditions and facilitators of children's imitation. According to Bandura (1969), imitative behavior will occur when the following circumstances are met. First, the child must be attentive to the model's behaviors. Attention might be increased by making the behaviors novel, increasing their salience through intensity of action or instructions, or by decreasing the frequency of competing and distracting stimuli. In other words, attention can be increased by the usual methods employed by teachers to gain their students' attention.

A second condition involves the child's ability to remember what he has seen. If the modeled behavior is too complex, or the child cannot code it in some manner, then imitation is not likely to occur. To aid the child, the teacher might wish to attach verbal labels to the demonstrated behavior, or to repeat frequently that behavior. Perhaps the teacher might instruct the child to verbalize to himself the behavior that he is witnessing. Additionally, the child must have the motor skills necessary for the imitation of the model's actions. As Bandura has pointed out, no matter how frequently you view a famous and gifted athlete, for example a Chris Evert hitting a tennis ball, you are unlikely to reach the same level of mastery. Finally, to elicit a motor demonstration of the learned skill, it is frequently important for the child to be motivated to demonstrate it. Without a reinforcement, why should he do it? According to Bandura, reinforcements primarily govern the performance of the behavior, not its learning. Learning can occur by looking.

Given that these conditions exist, certain kinds of situations seem to increase the likelihood of a child's imitation. One factor appears to be whether the child views the model as having some power over him, that is, as someone who can affect the child's receipt of reinforcements. If the model is a powerful one, imitation is more likely to occur (Bandura, 1969; Bryan, 1975). There is no question that the teacher is likely to be construed as a very powerful person to the observing child, and is likely to be an influential model. In addition, it appears that children are more likely to imitate individuals who are similar rather than dissimilar to themselves. Boys will probably be more likely to imitate male models while girls are more likely to imitate female models. Finally, a very important factor in affecting imitation is the consequences to the model as a result of his behavior. If the model is punished, imitation is unlikely to occur. If, on the other hand, the model is praised, imitation is incremented. While it is probably unlikely that teachers are frequently praised or punished within their classroom, it is probably quite likely that children are. Thus, children observing other children who receive praise are likely to imitate that peer; those observing one that is punished are unlikely to follow his lead. Finally, there is recent evidence (Bryan, 1971; Lerner and Weiss, 1972; Midlarsky and Bryan, 1972; Roberts, Santogrossi, and Thelan, 1977) that the model's own affective responses to his behavior will affect imitation. If the model shows pleasure in conjunction with the action, the child is more likely to imitate the model than if the model shows no affect. The model who is trying it and liking it will be more influential than a model who is trying it and not liking it.

Insofar as the learning-disabled child is deficient in so many ways, it is reasonable to ask whether such children are immune from the influences of models. Happily, they also are affected by the behavior of those around them. Schwartz and Bryan (1971) found that learning-disabled and non-disabled boys were equally likely to imitate a model's altruistic behaviors, although the disabled children had a more difficult time remembering what the model had said and enacted. Likewise, studies by Mercer, Cullinan, Hallahan, and LaFleur (1975) and Mercer, Hallahan, and Ball (1977) suggest that learning-disabled children do imitate others.

Given that learning-disabled children do imitate others, what can be said concerning classroom applications and the limitations of the modeling method of intervention? Unfortunately, not too much, for research is just beginning. It should be noted, however, that at least one investigator has attempted to influence classroom behaviors of emotionally disturbed children through the use of peer models. Csapo (1972) enlisted socially mature peer models to demonstrate appropriate behaviors to six emotionally disturbed children. The goal was to evoke better, less disruptive, classroom behavior from these disturbed children. To do this, Csapo asked a peer model to sit next to the emotionally disturbed peer throughout the school day for a period of fifteen days. The model's job was to demonstrate appropriate classroom behavior. The emotionally disturbed child was informed that the peer model wanted to help him in the classroom and that he should try to act similarly to the peer model. The disturbed child was told that the peer would let him know when he was responding correctly by giving him a token (with no exchange value) which would indicate his progress. The results indicated that the number of inappropriate behaviors of the disturbed children decreased. Csapo also reports that the effects of the treatment seemed to generalize to other situations, and that the attitudes of the peer models were extremely positive. Indeed, the models became concerned and protective of their "charges." Because of the lack of certain control groups, one cannot tell whether the results of the treatment were due to the models, to peers suddenly becoming concerned about the disturbed child, increased status and/or attention from the teacher, the model's behaviors plus the instructions and/or tokens from the teachers and models, or a combination of all of these factors. However, the results do suggest that peer modeling might have beneficial effects for the observing emotionally disturbed child, and for the model as well.

What may be the possible limiting factors in the use of modeling as an intervention technique? Most of the studies reviewed have dealt with the imitation of rather gross motor actions, actions easily learned and often rewarding in their performance. What are influences of models upon effecting more complex or subtle behaviors? There is evidence that children will imitate the model's speech patterns, even the syntax of such patterns, after very little exposure (Bandura, 1969). There is some hope then. However, studies of modeling effects upon children's impulsivity have generally failed to obtain important effects. If a child is shown a "deliberate" model, that is, one who is slow in making decisions concerning choices which are difficult, the child will also tend toward greater reluctance in his decision making. Unfortunately, however, the number of correct responses by the child does not increase. In effect, the child becomes deliberate but equally incorrect (Messer, 1976). Moreover, studies by Mercer, Cullinan, Hallahan, and LaFleur (1975) and Mercer, Hallahan, and Ball (1977) have found that modeling by learning-disabled children is positively correlated with their ability to attend to stimuli, a finding expected on the basis of Bandura's theory. This would suggest learning-disabled children with severe attentional deficits would be less susceptible to modeling effects than would those with longer attention spans.

While the applications of modeling theory to the treatment of learning disabilities is in its infancy, we feel that it holds great promise. Several considerations prompt this bias. First, models have been shown to affect a wide variety of conduct by children, normal or abnormal (Bandura, 1969). There seems little reason to assume a priori that the learning-disabled child is of a species so far removed from the normal, the emotionally disturbed, the deaf, or the retarded that he would be impervious to influences which affect these groups. Secondly, this method of treatment can be implemented with little cost. If children learn violence from television, if they learn about nature from nature films, they certainly can and do learn social and perhaps cognitive behaviors from films about people. Moreover, unlike such individualized remediation techniques as counseling, and one-to-one tutorials, films can be presented to large numbers of children simultaneously. As Bryan and Schwartz (1971) have indicated, canned television therapy may be on the horizon.

TOKEN ECONOMIES

The greatest extension of behavior modification principles into the classroom has been through the introduction of the token economy. Many of the children displaying learning problems in the classroom are those who have not responded to the usual techniques employed by teachers to control classroom behavior. Some children have not been affected by praise or reproof, stars or grades, peer or parent pressures. To meet this challenge, investigators instituted the now prevalent token economy program. These programs exploit the fact that children will behave in a manner which will get them something they want. If teachers provide desirable rewards, most children will literally "shape up" and perform in accordance with the teacher's desires. In token economy programs, teachers give children a token contingent upon the commission or approximation of a desired behavior. When the child accumulates a sufficient number of tokens, he may select to exchange his tokens for one of many valued objects.

The hallmark of the token economist, or the operant conditioner, is sensitivity to the effects of reinforcements upon behavior. It is not just the institution of the token that marks these programs, but the preoccupation with the impact of all reinforcements, positive and negative, upon children. These workers have focused not only upon the effects of the token, but the degree and nature of many forms of reinforcements which might maintain a child's behavior or misbehavior. Thus, the types of reinforcements given a child might be altered in light of the influences of the peer groups supporting the child. Teacher attention which is elicited by a child when he misbehaves is eschewed, and most forms of punishment are discouraged, particularly when teacher-child interactions are involved (Kazdin and Bootzin, 1972; O'Leary and Drabman, 1971).

Can the judicious use of a token economy program ameliorate problems associated with learning-disabled children? The answer seems to be yes. For example, the reinforcement of nondisruptive behaviors has been demonstrated to greatly reduce the occurrence of the disruptive behavior and increase the occurrence of studious behavior and academic achievement (Kazdin and Bootzin, 1972; O'Leary and Drabman, 1971). It might be predicted that academic skills would be immune to alteration by tokens because of the new learning demanded; nonetheless, gains have been reported to result through the use of token economy systems. Wolf, Giles, and Hall (1968) introduced a token economy into a remedial program for elementary school children who had low academic achievement. Tokens were given to the children contingent upon correct academic performance in reading, language, and arithmetic. Gains were made in all areas of performance associated with the reinforcement procedures. Hewett, Taylor, and Artuso (1969) found that 8–11-year-old emotionally disturbed children's academic performance in arithmetic, but not reading, could be improved when they were exposed to a token economy program. The effects of token economy programs have been positive in controlling aversive behaviors and in improving academic performances.

There is reason to be optimistic regarding remediation efforts which are based upon principles of behavior modification, at least those using token economies. Children do have to sit in their seats or at least attend in order to learn, and they are, by and large, well motivated to do so by means of incentives. Numerous studies reviewed by O'Leary and Drabman (1971) and Kazdin and Bootzin (1972) amply documented the utility and power of the appropriate use of reinforcements within the classroom setting. Of course, teachers, adults, and even children have long recognized the power of a carrot, and yet their use of the carrot often appears to be less than optimal. The token economists have given us many useful suggestions as to how to implement the power of the carrot. Relying on the above-cited reviews, the following procedures should be considered.

A target behavior must be determined. Without a clear understanding of the behavior to be changed, it is likely that reinforcements for that behavior or its approximations will be sporadic and elicited for nontarget responses. In addition, without a careful specification of the behavior to be changed, it would be impossible to assess the effectiveness of the program.

Appropriate reinforcements must be determined and the "purchasing power" of the token reinforcements must be made clear to the children. The children must know that the token can purchase something they desire, a so-called backup reinforcer. In setting up a token economy, care should be taken to provide a sufficient number and variety of backup reinforcers so that all the participating children will have an incentive worthy of effort. Reinforcers may be chosen on the basis of the most frequently engaged-in activity of the child. If he likes it a lot, he will probably work to do it more often. Hence, backup reinforcers may include excuses from the class, watching television, helping the teacher, running errands, and obtaining candies or toys. The selection of reinforcing reinforcers can be accomplished by asking the children what they want.

Care should be taken in determining the type of token to be employed. Tokens have included activities and objects like teacher ratings, plastic chips, and stars. The nature of the token is critical only in the sense that suggestions are particularly helpful. These authors indicate that the following characteristics of tokens be considered. The value of the token should be easily understood by the child. The exchange rate and the contingency of obtaining tokens should be understood. It is probably better to dispense rating marks than plastic tokens. The token should be easy for the child to manage and yet not distract him from his usual academic routine. Tokens should not be toys, but symbols. Finally, they should be easy for the teacher to dispense.

The critical feature of the token economy is that the token be administered contingent on the the occurrence of the desired behavior. No desired behavior—no token. Programs are generally set up so that reinforcements are contingent upon an individual's performance, not the performance of the group. This differs from procedures currently used in the U.S.S.R. in which children are rewarded on the basis of the group's allegiance to standards (Bronfenbrenner, 1970). The current practice in the United States is to reward individuals for their own rather than the group's appropriate behavior. There have been few studies of the impact of token economies on a collective and no studies which have compared a group-oriented procedure to those currently in vogue in the United States (O'Leary and Drabman, 1971).

Typically, when a child performs the target behavior, he receives a token. What other events might mitigate or facilitate the effectiveness of a token economy? It is now generally believed that teacher attention, whatever its nature, might serve to increase the very behavior the teacher wants to eliminate. It is generally recommended that teachers ignore disruptive behavior, while reinforcing appropriate behaviors through rewards. This is not always easy; sometimes it is not possible. In order to inhibit disruptive behaviors, programs have included time-out procedures (i.e., absence from the room and from the token economy), quiet verbal scoldings and deductions or fines in the form of removal of already earned tokens (O'Leary and Drabman, 1971). It has been claimed that each procedure has some success in altering disruptive classroom behavior.

Techniques aside, attention must be paid to the characteristics of the teacher and child which may facilitate or inhibit the impact of the token economy. If the teacher fails, the program fails. But relatively little work has been done on training teachers in the use of token economies or molding teacher attitudes toward such systems. There is some evidence that teachers who believe that the program does not work find that the program does not work. There is little evidence to indicate what type of training would be best for teachers, although one investigator indicated that having program operators rehearse the behaviors in training led to better performance than the usual lecture training method (Gardner, 1972). Kazdin and Bootzin (1972) reviewed investigations which suggest that even if the initial training of the teacher is adequate, repeated training sessions may be necessary to maintain the original level.

Young lower-class children who may have had below-average intelligence have been the subjects for most token economy programs. It is likely that the effectiveness of the behavior modification program will depend on the academic level of the children. No amount of tokens, no matter how skillfully administered, can teach a child who cannot count to understand set theory. If the child does not have the necessary skills within his repertoire, no amount of reinforcement will elicit more complex skills. The success of the token economy is thus dependent upon a careful diagnosis of the child's achievements and a careful task analysis of the behavior to be required of him. It would seem that within this context the learning disability specialist will be particularly able to make a significant and unique contribution to the child with problems.

Although the token economy strategy has been very successful for classroom management, the problems and limitations of this method should be recognized. One obvious issue is the durability of the effects of such programs. As things stand today, the use of token economies is short term and children are withdrawn from them. What happens when the token economy program is discontinued? The bulk of the literature suggests that the reinforced behavior will decrease in frequency unless it gets some occasional reinforcement. As long as the token economy is in operation, the teacher can expect to maintain rather good control of classroom behavior. When the program is discontinued the desired behavior diminishes: "good behavior is under environmental control as long as there is a token in it for [the student]" (O'Leary and Drabman, 1971).

A major concern is the degree to which behaviors learned in the token economy room will generalize or be evidenced in other situations, with other teachers, or some other time. If a child will sit still for tokens in one room, will he sit still in another classroom or in the same class with a substitute teacher? O'Leary and Drabman sum up the situation at present:

> Those investigators who have assessed the generalization of behaviors reinforced in the token programs to those same behaviors when the token program is not in effect, in different situations and at different times, have not found generalization (1971, p. 394).

Aside from the problems associated with the generalization of the reinforced behaviors across time and space, there is an additional and troublesome problem, and that is whether reinforcement programs might attenuate rather than increase the target behavior. Regrettably, the answer does appear affirmative. Under some conditions, procedures which would appear, a priori, to be reinforcers might decrease rather than increase the "reinforced" behavior. Two circumstances appear to produce such effects, one revolving around the use of token economy programs, the other around the personal or social characteristics of the reinforcer. First let us look at token economies. Within the past several years, there have been increasing recognition and demonstrations that the use of token economy programs may decrease an individual's interest in the task required for obtaining the reinforcement. Levine and Fasnacht (1974) have cited several investigations which have demonstrated that if individuals, even children, are given token rewards for engaging in tasks which have some intrinsic interest to them, subsequent interest in the task will diminish once the tokens are removed. These authors suggest several explanations of this diminution effect. One hypothesis is based upon attribution theory, a theory which suggests that "how we attribute the causality of our behavior will in turn determine future behavior" (p. 816). In effect, they suggest that children who receive token rewards for performance on a task will attribute their interest in the task to the token, not the task. Subsequently when tokens are absent, children will attribute less interesting features to the task than if they had not received the token in the first place.

A second explanation offered by Levine and Fasnacht is that the introduction of token rewards focuses the child's attention away from task features to token properties, presumably depriving the child of the opportunity to explore the potentially interesting components of the task. Levine and Fasnacht then caution against implementing token economies unless there is no real alternative to their use. Indeed, they urge that "teachers should look at the interest level of the curriculum before looking to reinforce learning of material that kids just do not like" (p. 820).

It should also be noted that some forms of social approval may become aversive rather than pleasing to the child, serving to inhibit rather than increment the behavior targeted for contingent reinforcement. In a recent study, Midlarsky, Bryan, and Brickman (1973) reported that when an adult praised an act which she herself would not commit (donating money to the March of Dimes), the praise served as an inhibitor to the child. That is, the praise decreased the occurrence of the behavior of concern. In an unwritten study, Bryan, Slater, and Bertelson, while failing to find such an inhibition effect, did find that children were less happy with, and tended to avoid, the individual giving social approval when that individual would not engage in the actions which she was approving. The technical message of these latter two studies is that if one wants from a child behavior which one is not also willing to commit, it is better not to praise than it is to praise.

Other problems have been noted if not systematically studied. One common concern of the public regarding the instruction of token economies has been the issue of bribery. Some people argue that by having a token economy one is bribing the child to behave. Although this concern is not usually explicated further, the concern reflects an interest in the impact of tokens upon the attitudes and expectancies of the child. It would be naïve to assume that such programs do not have effects upon attitudes and expectancies; surprisingly these effects have not been subject to systematic study. On the basis of anecdotal evidence, it has been suggested that children will model the "if-then" position of the token economist. Bushell, Wrobel, and Michaelis (1968) reported that children negotiated contracts with peers in which pay-offs would accompany requested behavior. These behaviors might have occurred on a nonreciprocating basis prior to the initiation of the token economy program. Meichenbaum, Bowers, and Ross (1969) reported that adolescent female delinquents turned the tables on the investigators. The girls were on a part-time token economy and blackmailed the investigators to extend the token periods. They were not going to work unless there was a pay-off.

It is our opinion that the judicious use of behavior modification programs offers considerable power of control to the teacher over a child's classroom behavior. The child with learning disabilities demonstrates many behaviors which have been shown amenable to the effects of token economies (Bryan and Wheeler, 1972; Bryan, 1974d). On-task behavior has certainly been shown to be influenced by token economy programs. Moreover, there is evidence that academic skills can be improved through the use of proper incentives (Hewett, Taylor, and Artuso, 1969; Drass and Jones, 1971). The fact that such programs lead to little generalization of good behavior to other teachers, classrooms, or similar behaviors should not be of great concern. Most studies concerned with generalization have focused upon social or deportment behaviors. They have not evaluated the durability of academic skills produced by behavior modification procedures. Social behaviors are most likely to be affected by the power of reinforcement contingencies available within the environment.

It is quite another matter to think that academic skills would be lost under the condition in which reinforcement is terminated. The motivation to continue to achieve may cease, but it is highly unlikely that past learning somehow disappears from the child's repertoire (Underwood, 1964). It would be desirable if behavior modification procedures could be developed so that their application would result in a generalization of their effects to other situations. But to criticize these attempts and the success of these programs on these grounds would seem quite unjust. Parents and educators attempt to train children's "character," to develop a child who will show a desirable behavior across a variety of situations for a lengthy period of time. But those factors which facilitate this development are not well known. To criticize these techniques on the basis of this particular limitation is to condemn all known techniques used to influence children. It is an achievement of considerable magnitude and importance that control of behavior can be obtained on a predictable basis within the classroom. As to the attitudinal and expectancy effects of such programs, little can now be said concerning their nature or desirability. Perhaps the direction taken in research on token economies in the future will be to systematically study and evaluate such effects. In the meantime, anecdotal reports do not indicate that such effects would warrant the discontinuation of token economies. Even if token economies produced a reciprocal orientation toward interpersonal and academic relations, one must ask whether these effects are worse than those produced by continuing school failure and side effects of low self-esteem, social rejection, and parental anxiety.

It does seem clear, however, that employing token economies to increment performance on tasks which have intrinsic interest to the child, or which might become interesting to that child given other forms of presentations, is probably unwarranted. The teacher should be sensitive to the boomerang effects of the token economies upon behaviors which are interesting to the child, and take care to discriminate the interesting from intrinsically dull tasks. Moreover, the teacher must also remember that her behavior interacts with the influence of her words of praise; and to reinforce the child for behavior which she herself will not commit may produce results opposite from that which is desired.

All students interested in the remediation of learning disabilities, either within the context of classroom, resource room, or clinic, must be concerned with developments in the field of behavior modification.

MODELS AND TOKENS

As previously noted, psychologists' theoretical interests have generally focused on either the role of models or on the impact of reinforcements. There is no reason why these two important influencers cannot be combined for purposes of remediation. This section will outline one particularly promising approach to remediation, a method which employs both models and reinforcements as well as tutorials.

The credit for this approach, called "cognitive-behavior modification" (CBM), belongs to Professor Donald Meichenbaum. The basic assumption underlying this method is that maladaptive behavior can be changed by teaching the child how to think; that is, by direct training in the processes we use for problem solving. The learner is also taught how to manage his own behavior. To train the child, frequently models will be employed along with verbal instructions and reinforcements. Basically, the child observes a teacher go through the steps of solving a problem, practices the solving of the problem with the teacher, hears the teacher explain his thoughts during problem-solving activities, and then is rewarded for imitating the cognitive processes of the teacher (Meichenbaum, 1976). Such procedures have been effective in reducing impulsivity, both in terms of quickness and correctness of response. Thus this problem-solving approach to the learning-disabled child's difficulties seems promising (Messer, 1976).

One example of how this program has been applied to help hyperactive and aggressive young males is the Think Aloud program developed by Bash and Camp (1975). While the method is used to guide children in various kinds of conceptual learning, the authors have also attempted to teach social perception by giving a number of lessons on understanding emotions. Because difficulties in understanding other people are considerable for the learning-disabled child, this program is of particular importance.

Initially in the program, children were guided in learning how to discriminate happy and sad emotions presented in pictures. During this period children were led in discussing techniques for determining emotions. For example, children were asked how they might determine another's emotional condition, even with their eyes closed.

In the second lesson, children are presented with a series of pictures which depict a child falling from a bicycle and crying. The object of this presentation is to help the children generate notions about antecedent and consequent actions; the why's and because's of affective displays.

The third part of the instruction encourages the children to think of what they can do and say when encountering a person in distress; in this instance it was a girl who had fallen from a bicycle. There is thus an attempt to teach the children to recognize emotions, to discriminate among them, to understand the ways (the channels) by which we recognize emotions, to generate ideas concerning the determinants of emotions, and then how to respond appropriately to other children's distress.

From this problem-solving perspective in remediating social difficulties, other technqiues have also been offered. Jabichuk and Smeriglio (1975) have studied the remediation effects of providing children with models of vicarious self-reinforcement and direct tutorials concerning social behavior. One group of preschool-age children who were characterized as displaying low levels of social responsiveness to others were shown films of an isolated child. Initially, the actor was shown playing alone. The scenario then depicts the child approaching peers, and finally playing happily with his peers in a variety of situations. Accompanying this visual display was a soundtrack which expresses the child's feelings of isolation, coping responses to the stressful events, and then giving himself praise for his actions. When comparing the group of preschool children who viewed this scenario with control groups, it was found that the former group showed more social responsiveness to others and that these improvements were maintained for at least a three-week period.

ATTRIBUTIONS

For many decades, many people's preferred treatments for solving problems experienced by exceptional children have involved trying to change what these children think about themselves. Sometimes the popular treatment has focused upon altering unconscious forces, and sometimes upon conscious thoughts. Whatever the focus, the theory has been that changing the way the child thinks about himself and the world will yield not only a happier child but one that thinks and acts appropriately. Of particular consequence to the learning disability expert has been the notion that the children with whom they work have poor self-concepts. Apparently it is believed that such children do not like themselves, do not think they are competent, or as good as others. The method usually prescribed for improving self-concepts is counseling, either within a group or individual context. The theoretical underpinning of such counseling has traditionally been based upon Freudian or neo-Freudian, and Rogerian orientations.

It is our belief that such counseling procedures are unlikely to be very effective for easing the multitude of difficulties experienced by learning-disabled children. Given the high incidence of their linguistic deficits (Wiig and Semel, 1976) and their difficulties in perceiving and interpreting emotional states (Bachara, 1975; Bryan, 1974e), it seems unlikely that learning-disabled children could benefit from a procedure which focuses upon talking about emotional states of oneself and others. Such procedures have not been found to be generally effective with normal children, and it is unlikely that they will be any more effective with learning-disabled ones (Prout, 1977).

Recently, however, there has been an increased awareness of the importance of the child's interpretations of the events surrounding him, particularly his attributions concerning the causes of his and others' behaviors. What may be especially important is the degree to which the learning-disabled child attributes his successes and failures either to himself or to other external events. That is, does he attribute an *internal* or *external* determinant of his behavior? Another important consideration is whether the child's attributions carry the connotations of a permanent or temporary state of affairs (Whalen and Henker, 1976).

Let us speculate as to the attributions of the learning-disabled child. First, it is likely that most children have some idea of the concept of intelligence, and that their notions parallel those of adult laymen. That is, it is likely that most children think of intelligence as being reflected by their academic achievement, and also believe that intelligence is a fixed ability. Given these assumptions in combination with the learning-disabled child's continual school and social failures, it is reasonable to assume that such children define themselves as currently stupid, and likely to remain so forevermore. Thus the learning-disabled child is unlikely to exert much effort, in the absence of any hope, to alter his current difficulties.

A similar line of reasoning can be applied to those children who are receiving medication for hyperactivity, as Whalen and Henker (1976) have so aptly demonstrated. They report results from an interview with a 10-year-old boy which indicates he thinks his own hyperactivity is out of his control and is also semipermanent.

Interviewer: I've been hearing a lot about the word *hyperactive.* What does it mean, really?
Child: Well, it's a—it's a—well, you're just born with it.
Interviewer: You're born with it.
Child: And some people can—some people get rid of it. Some people it just goes away when they're about 12 or 13.
Interviewer: And what about the other people?
Child: They just have it.
Interviewer: Is it like a habit that people pick up?
Child: No.
Interviewer: Do you think people can get over it if they work on it?
Child: No.
Interviewer: Do you think people just outgrow it sooner or later?
Child: Yeah—some people.
Interviewer: And others?
Child: Half of them outgrow it, and half of them just keep—just stay on it. They're still hyperactive (p. 1125).

While we know of no specific studies of learning disability children's attributions, or their change, the current work of Dweck and her colleagues in their work of "learned helplessness" carries important implications for the learning disability specialist. Dweck and Reppucci (1973) reported that some children, after a failure experience, do not subsequently perform the response required to succeed even though they have the capability and are motivated to do so. They found that children who persevere in the face of failure differ from children who give up. They have referred to the latter group of children as those who have "learned helplessness." They found that the children who learn helplessness attribute failure to their lack of ability.

Dweck (1975) followed this lead and conducted an experiment in retraining children who had learned helplessness toward greater self-sufficiency.

For children receiving attribution retraining, the experimenter suggested that each failure on the task (a mathematic test) was attributable to a lack of motivation and that they should "try harder." The comparison children who had also learned helplessness were given tasks in which they always experienced success. Whenever the children from either group experienced successes they were reinforced by receiving a token. In effect, the comparison children were in a program analogous to those used in token economies. The results indicated that children who were trained to attribute their failures to motivational factors, which could be changed by their efforts, were more likely to show continual improvement in the face of failure than those children not exposed to attribution retraining.

Attributional analysis of the learning disability population is sorely needed. It is our guess that learning-disabled children frequently learn helplessness. If our guess is correct, then remediation programs can and should be designed to aid the child to mobilize his energies in coping with his failures. Certainly the learning disability specialist should be aware of the power of attributions and his role in their creation and maintenance.

DRUGS

Perhaps there is no issue more controversial and emotionally loaded in the field of learning disabilities than that concerning the employment of drugs to control hyperactive children. At least it seems an important issue to experts who deal with such children. While the use of such drugs is frequent, there are probably many who feel like Walker when he writes that "History will record another disastrous fad from our own times—the use of Ritalin and amphetamines to subdue children who are hyperactive" (1974, p. 43). This author further writes, "In my medical practice I see many hyperactive children. I have never prescribed stimulants for these patients, and I never will" (1974, p. 43).

Walker's protest may represent a minority view, at least if we look at the estimates of the number of children receiving drug treatment for hyperactivity. Offir (1974) has estimated that between 500,000 and two million children are taking drugs like Ritalin (methylphenidate) or Dexedrine (dextroamphetamine). Whalen and Henker (1976) indicate that between 3 percent and 20 percent of the school-age population of the United States are defined as hyperactive, and many of these children receive drug treatments. Ayllon, Layman, and Kandel (1975) have reported estimates of approximately 200,000 children in the United States receiving amphetamines to control their hyperactivity. Whatever the true figures are regarding drug use and hyperactivity, one can be sure that many, many children are taking drugs.

The literature concerning drugs and hyperactivity is vast. The following paragraphs rely heavily upon the report by Whalen and Henker (1976), and readers interested in the original sources will find this article listed in the references. Whalen and Henker have concluded that Ritalin appears to help 60 percent to 90 percent of the children who receive it. The help rate of Dexedrine is somewhat lower than that of Ritalin but still substantial numbers do seem to improve with its implementation. There is a catch, however, and Whalen and Henker explicate it when they write, "We know that the drugs can and often do have powerful, positive effects; we do not know when, why, how, or with whom. It is also becoming apparent that many of the children who show marked improvement while taking medication fail to maintain these gains once medication is discontinued, . . . " (p. 1114). Whalen and Henker, after reviewing the literature, have reached the following conclusions.

1. Drugs are not likely to reduce motor activity of hyperactive children when they are in an unstructured situation, for example on the playground. In such contexts, drugs might even increase activity. However, drugs appear to reduce the motor activity of children when they are confronted with a structured task, as in most school work.

2. Stimulants, such as Ritalin and Dexedrine, appear to reduce children's impulsivity (response speed and incorrect responding) in their attempts to solve difficult problems, such as those presented on the Matching Familiar Figures Tests. When correctness of a response is uncertain, the stimulants appear to help the child inhibit his answer and to subsequently perform more competently. When the responses are easy, that is, when the correct answer is obvious, such as in a vigilance task, the stimulant drugs appear to increase response speeds. Sometimes the tasks require fast responding, at other times, slowness in responding. Apparently drugs help many children in both situations. In effect, the drugs appear to allow the child to better integrate and to better control his motor responses, so as to more competently cope with the task.

3. Stimulants appear to aid the hyperactive child to maintain his attention. They increase his vigilance to the task. But on the other hand, reasoning, problem solving, reading achievement, and intelligence test scores do not show improvement soon after the administration of the drug.

4. Drugs affect some forms of social-emotional behavior, at least when such behavior is assessed by means of rating scales. Stimulants have been found to reduce aggressive conduct and hyperactivity (i.e., the child's physical activity, concentration, impulsiveness, irritability, temper outburst, and school work). The meanings of such changes are not clear because the rating scales are not consistently correlated with the child's observed behavior. Apparently drugs do not affect ratings of the child's sociability or anxiety.

5. Children who used to receive medication do not fare any better in social or academic pursuits than those who had never received medication. Moreover, the effects of medication do not appear to persist in its absence.

6. While a number of attempts have been made to determine which child is likely to benefit from the drugs, predicting responses to medication is not yet possible. There is no strong evidence to indicate which child is most or least likely to derive benefits from the administration of such stimulants.

In general, Whalen and Henker suggest that while medication has some positive consequences for the child, there is much yet to be determined as to the hows and whys of these effects. Meantime, warnings concerning its use have been voiced by many, including Whalen and Henker. Offir (1974) has suggested that the use of such drugs may well be associated with the suppression of normal growth, irritability, depression, nausea, and insomnia. Greenberg (1976) also cites authorities expressing many of the same concerns, including the possibility of addiction to the drugs, and its use as a "cop-out" for poor teachers and techniques.

In addition, Greenberg cites others who are concerned with the possible problems associated with "state-dependent learning." State-dependent learning refers to the possibility that some learnings acquired under the influence of drugs are not demonstrated when the child is in a condition without the drug.

Whalen and Henker cast their warnings within the context of attributional theory. They suggest that the administration of the drug allows the child to attribute his difficulties to physiological problems, problems beyond his control. If such attributions are made, the child's belief that he can, through his own efforts, remediate his condition is severely reduced. Moreover, they argue, the successes experienced by the child may be attributed, by the child, parents, physicians, and teachers, to the impact of the drug rather than to the efforts of the child. In effect a situation is created so that the child becomes convinced he can't control his problems. His achievement is attributed to an external source, the drug, rather than to the child. Whalen and Henker suggest that such an arrangement may well lead to demoralization of the child.

REFERENCES

Allyon, T., Layman, D., and Kandel, H. J. "A behavioral-educational alternative to drug control of hyperactive children." *Journal of Applied Behavior Analysis,* 1975, 8, 137–146.

Aronfreed, J. "The concept of internalization." In D. A. Goslin (ed.), *Handbook of Socialization Theory and Research.* Chicago: Rand McNally, 1969, 263–323.

Bachara, G. H. "Empathy in learning-disabled children." *Perceptual and Motor Skills,* 1976, 43, 541–542.

Bandura, A. *Principles of Behavior Modification.* New York: Holt, Rinehart & Winston, 1969.

Bandura, A, Blanchard, G. B., and Ritter, B. "The relative efficacy of desensitization and modeling approaches for inducing behavioral, affective, and attitudinal changes." *Journal of Personality and Social Psychology,* 1969, 13, 173–179.

Bash, M. and Camp, B. "Think aloud program." Unpublished manuscript. Boulder, Colorado: University of Colorado, School of Medicine, 1975.

Bateman, B. "Reading: A controversial view." In L. Tarnopol (ed.), *Learning Disabilities.* Springfield, Ill.: Charles C. Thomas, 1969.

Blanton, B. "The acquisition of language: Implications for reading." *Reading Teacher,* 1972, 25, 579-585.

Bliesmer, E. P. and Yarborough, B. H. "A comparison of ten different beginning reading programs in first grade." *Phi Delta Kappan,* 1965, 500-504.

Bond, G. L. and Dykstra, R. "The cooperative research program in first-grade reading instruction." *Reading Research Quarterly,* 2 (Summer 1967).

Bronfenbrenner, U. *Two Worlds of Childhood: U.S. and U.S.S.R.* New York: Russell Sage Foundation, 1970.

Browning, R. M. "Effect of irrelevant peripheral visual stimuli on discrimination learning in minimally brain-damaged children." *Journal of Consulting Psychology,* 1967, 31, 371-376.

Bruininks, R. "Teaching word recognition to disadvantaged boys." *Journal of Learning Disabilities,* 1970, 3, 28-35.

Bryan, J. H. "Model affect and children's imitative behavior." *Child Development,* 1971, 42, 2061-2065.

Bryan, J. H. "Children's cooperation ahd helping behaviors." In E. Mavis Heatherington (ed.), *Review of Child Development Research.* Chicago: University of Chicago Press, 1975. Vol. 5.

Bryan, J. H. and Schwartz, T. "The effects of film material upon children's behavior." *Psychological Bulletin,* 1971, 75, 50-59.

Bryan, J. H., Slater, J. E., and Bertelson, K. Unpublished study. Evanston, Ill.; Northwestern University, 1975

Bryan, T. "An observational analysis of classroom behaviors of children with learning disabilities." *Journal of Learning Disabilities,* 1974, 7, 26-34 (d).

Bryan, T. "Stranger's Judgments of Children's Social and Academic Adequacy: Instant Diagnosis." Unpublished manuscript, 1974 (e).

Bryan, T. and Wheeler, R. "Perception of learning-disabled children: The eye of the observer." *Journal of Learning Disabilities,* 1972, 5, 484-488.

Bushell, D., Wrobel, P. A., and Michaelis, M. "Applying 'group' contingencies to the classroom behavior of preschool children." *Journal of Applied Behavior Analysis,* 1968, 1, 55-63.

Camp, B. W. "Psychometric tests and learning in severely disabled readers." *Journal of Learning Disabilities,* 1973, 6, 512-517.

Clements, S. D. "Minimal brain dysfunction in children." NINDS Monograph No. 3, Public Health Service Bulletin #1415. Washington, D.C.: U.S. Department of Health, Education, and Welfare, 1966.

Cohen, S. A. "Studies of visual perception and reading in disadvantaged children." *Journal of Learning Disabilities,* 1969, 2, 498-507.

Corder, W. O., "Affects of Physical Education on the Intellectual, Physical and Social Development of Educational Mentally Retarded Boys." *Exceptional Children,* 1966, 32, 357-360.

Chronbach, L. J. "Individualization of instruction." In M. D. Merrill (ed.), *Instructional Design: Readings.* Englewood Cliffs, N.J.: Prentice-Hall, 1971.

Cruickshank, W. M. and Halloran, D. P. "Alfred A. Strauss: Pioneer in learning disabilities." *Exceptional Children,* 1973, 39, 321-327.

Csapo, M. "Peer models reverse the 'one bad apple spoils the barrel' theory." *Teaching Exceptional Children,* 1972, 5, 20-24.

de Hirsch, K., Jansky, J., and Langford, Q. *Predicting Reading Failure.* New York: Harper and Row, 1966.

Delecato, C. H. *The Diagnosis and Treatment of Speech and Reading Problems.* Springfield, Ill.: Charles C. Thomas, 1963.

Delecato, C. H. *Neurological Organization and Reading.* Springfield, Ill.: Charles C. Thomas, 1966.

Drass, S. D. and Jones, R. L. "Learning-disabled children as behavior modifiers." *Journal of Learning Disabilities,* 1971, 4, 418, 425.

Dweck, C. S. "The role of expectations and attributions in the alleviation of learned helplessness." *Journal of Personality and Social Psychology,* 1975, 31, 674–685.

Dweck, C. S. and Reppucci, N. D. "Learned helplessness and reinforcement responsibility in children." *Journal of Personality and Social Psychology,* 1973, 25, 109–116.

Falik, L. H. "The effects of special perceptual-motor training in kindergarten on second grade reading." *Journal of Learning Disabilities,* 1969, 2, 325–329.

Fernald, G. M. *Remedial Techniques in School Subject.* New York: McGraw-Hill, 1943.

Fries, C. C. *Linguistics and Reading.* New York: Holt, Rinehart & Winston, 1963.

Frostig, M. "Visual perception, integrative functions and academic learning." *Journal of Learning Disabilities,* 1972, 5, 1–15.

Frostig, M. and Horne, D. *The Frostig Program for the Development of Visual Perception.* Chicago, Ill.: Follett, 1964.

Fygetakis, L. J. and Ingram, D. "Language rehabilitation and programmed conditioning: A case study." *Journal of Learning Disabilities,* 1973, 6, 60–64.

Gagne, R. M. and Paradise, N. E. "Abilities and learning sets in knowledge acquisition." *Psychological Monographs,* 1961, 75, No. 14.

Gardner, J. M. "Teaching behavior modification to nonprofessionals." *Journal of Applied Behavior Analysis,* 1972, 5, 517–522.

Gattegno, C. *Teacher's Guide: Words in Color.* Chicago: Encyclopaedia Britannica Press, 1963.

Gewirtz, J. L. "Mechanisms of social learning: Some roles of stimulation and behavior in early human development." In D. A. Goslin (ed.), *Handbook of Socialization Theory and Research.* Chicago: Rand McNally, 1969.

Gillingham, A. and Stillman, B. *Remedial Training for Children with Specific Disability in Reading, Spelling, Penmanship.* Cambridge, Mass.: Educators Publishing Service, 1960.

Goodman, L. and Wiederholt, J. L. "Predicting reading achievement in disadvantaged children." Unpublished manuscript. Dept. of Special Education, Temple University, Philadelphia, Pa., 1972.

Goodman, Y. M. and Burke, C. L. *Reading Miscue Inventory Manual: Procedure for Diagnosis and Evaluation.* New York: Macmillan Publishing Co., Inc. 1972.

Gray, B. B. and Fygetakis, L. "Mediated language acquisition for dysphasic children." *Behavior Research & Therapy,* 1968, 6, 263–280.

Gray, B. B., Baker, R. D., and Stancyk, S. E. "Performance determined instruction for training in remedial reading." *Journal of Applied Behavior Analysis,* 1969, 2, 255–263.

Greenberg, J. S. "Hyperkinesis and the schools." *Journal of School Health,* 1976, 46, 91–97.

Gruber, J. J. "Implications of physical education programs for children with learning disabilities." *Journal of Learning Disabilities,* 1969, 2, 593–599.

Gruenewald, L. and Pollack, S. "Analyzing language interactions in academics." *Journal of Learning Disabilities,* 1975, 8, 544–550.

Hammill, D. "Training visual perceptual processes." *Journal of Learning Disabilities,* 1972, 5, 552–559.

Hammill, D. and Bartel, N. R. *Teaching Children with Learning and Behavior Problems.* Boston, Mass: Allyn & Bacon, 1975.

Harris, A. J. "Individualizing first grade reading according to specific learning aptitudes." Office of Research and Evaluation, Division of Teacher Education, City University of New York, 1965.

Hartman, R. T. and Richards, G. B. "The effect of using a black light apparatus to reduce attention scatter in brain-injured children." *Journal of Learning Disabilities,* 1969, 2, 391–394.

Hay, J. and Wingo, C. *Reading with Phonics, Teacher's Edition.* Philadelphia: Lippincott, 1960.

Jabichuk, Z. and Smeriglio, U. "The influence of symbolic modeling on the social behavior of preschool children with low levels of social responsiveness." Unpublished manuscript, University of Western Ontario, 1975.

Johnson, D. J. "Educational principles for children with learning disabilities." *Rehabilitation Literature*, 1967, 28, 317–322.

Johnson, D. J. and Myklebust, H. *Learning Disabilities: Educational Principles and Practices.* New York: Grune & Stratton, 1967.

Kazdin, A. E. and Bootzin, R. R. "The token economy: An evaluative review." *Journal of Applied Behavior Analysis,* 1972, 5, 343–372.

Kephart, N. C. *The Brain-Injured Child in the Classroom.* Chicago: National Society for Crippled Children and Adults, 1963.

Kephart, N. C. *The Slow Learner in the Classroom.* Columbus, Ohio: Merrill, 1971.

Kershner, J. R. "An investigation of the Doman-Delecato theory of neuropsychology as it applies to trainable mentally retarded children in public schools." Bureau of Research Administration and Coordination, Area of Research and Development, Department of Public Instruction, Commonwealth of Pennsylvania, May 1967, p. 105 (mimeo.). Cited in Richard L. Masland, "Children with minimal brain dysfunction–A national problem." In Lester Tamopol (ed.), *Learning Disabilities,* Springfield, Ill.: Charles C. Thomas, 1969.

Lasky, E. Z., Jay, B., and Hanz-Ehrman, M. "Meaningful and linguistic variables auditory processing." *Journal of Learning Disabilities,* 1975, 8, 570–577.

Lee, L. L., Koenigsknecht, R. A., and Mulhern, S. T. *Interactive Language Development Teaching.* Evanston, Ill.: Northwestern University Press, 1975.

Lerner, L., and Weiss, R. L. "Role of value of reward and model affective response in vicarious reinforcement." *Journal of Personality and Social Psychology,* 1972, 21, 93–100.

Levine, F. and Fasnacht, G. "Tokens may lead to token learning." *American Psychologist,* 1974, 29, 816–820.

Lewis, R. S., Strauss, A., and Lehtinen, L. *The Other Child.* New York: Grune & Stratton, 1960.

London, P. "The end of ideology in behavior modification." *American Psychologist,* 1972, 27, 913–920.

McKee, P., Harrison, L., McCowen, A., and Lehr, E. *Reading for Meaning Series.* Boston: Houghton Mifflin, 1963.

McNemar, Q. "On WAIS difference scores." *Journal of Consulting Psychology,* 1957, 21, 239–240.

Masland, R. L. "Children with minimal brain dysfunction–A national problem." In L. Tarnopol (ed.), *Learning Disabilities.* Springfield, Ill.: Charles C. Thomas, 1969.

Meichenbaum, D. *Cognitive-behavior Modification Newsletter,* 1976, #2.

Meichenbaum, D., Bowers, K. S., and Ross, R. R. "A behavioral analysis of teacher expectancy effect." *Journal of Personality and Social Psychology,* 1969, 13, 306–316.

Mercer, C. D., Cullinan, D., Hallahan, D. P., and LaFleur, N. K. "Modeling and attention-retention in learning-disabled children." *Journal of Learning Disabilities,* 1975, 8, 444–450.

Mercer, C. D., Hallahan, D. P., and Ball, D. W. "Modeling and attention of mentally retarded, learning-disabled, and normal boys." Unpublished manuscript. Gainesville, Fla.: University of Florida, 1977.

Messer, S. B. "Reflection-impulsivity: A review." *Psychological Bulletin,* 1976, 83, 1026–1052.

Midlarsky, E. and Bryan, J. H. "Affect expressions and children's imitative altruism." *Journal of Experimental Research in Personality,* 1972, 6, 195–203.

Midlarsky, E., Bryan, J. H., and Brickman, P. "Aversive approval: Interactive effects of modeling and reinforcement on altruistic behavior." *Child Development,* 1973, 44, 321–328.

O'Donnell, P. A. and Eisenson, J. "Delecato training for reading achievement and visual motor integration." *Journal of Learning Disabilities,* 1969, 2, 10–15.

Offir, C. W. "Are we pushers for our own children?" *Psychology Today,* December 1974, 49.

O'Leary, K. D. and Drabman, R. "Token reinforcement programs in the classroom: A review." *Psychological Bulletin,* 1971, 75, 379-398.

Pflaum, S. W. "Application of linguistic concepts to instruction in reading comprehension." Unpublished manuscript, University of Illinois at Chicago Circle, 1976.

Prout, H. T. "Behavioral intervention with hyperactive children: A review." *Journal of Learning Disabilities,* 1977, 10, 141-146.

Roberts, M. C., Santogrossi, D. A., and Thelan, M. H. "The effects of model affect on imitation." *Personality and Social Psychology Bulletin,* 1977, 3, 75-78.

Sabatino, D. and Streissguth, W. "Word form configuration training of visual perceptual strengths with learning-disabled children." *Journal of Learning Disabilities,* 1972, 5, 435-441.

Sarason, I. G. "Verbal learning, modeling, and juvenile delinquency." *American Psychologist,* 1968, 23, 254-266.

Schwartz, T. and Bryan, J. H. "Imitation and judgments of children with learning disabilities." *Exceptional Children,* 1971, 38, 157-158.

Skinner, B. F. "Pigeons in a pelican." *American Psychologist,* 1960, 15, 28-37.

Skinner, B. F. *Beyond Freedom and Dignity.* New York: Vintage Books, 1971.

Smith, C. M. "The relationship of reading method and reading achievement to ITPA sensory modalities." *Journal of Special Education,* 1971, 5, 143-149.

Snyder, L., Apolloni, T., and Cooke, T. P. "Integrated settings at the early childhood level: The role of nonretarded peers." *Exceptional Children,* 1977, 43, 262-269.

Stephens, T. M. *Directive Teaching of Children with Learning and Behavioral Handicaps.* Columbus, Ohio: Charles E. Merrill, 1970.

Sullivan, J. "The effects of Kephart's perceptual-motor training on a reading clinic sample." *Journal of Learning Disabilities,* 1972, 5, 32-38.

Travers, R. M. W., ed. "Research and Theory Related to Audio-Visual Information Transmission." *U.S. Office of Education Interim Report Contract,* No. 3-20-003: Salt Lake City: Bureau of Educational Research, University of Utah, July, 1964.

Underwood, B. J., "Speed of Learning and Amount Retained: A Consideration of Methodology." *Psychological Bulletin,* 1945, 51, 276-282.

Underwood, B. J. "Degree of Learning and the Measurement of Forgetting." *Journal of Verbal Learning and Verbal Behavior,* 1964, 3, 112-119.

Vernetti, C. J. and Jacobs, J. F. "Effects of music used to mask noise in learning disability classes." *Journal of Learning Disabilities,* 1972, 5, 21-24.

Walberg, H. "Models for optimizing and individualizing school learning." Ontario Institute for Studies in Education, University of Toronto, Canada, *Interchange,* 2, 1971.

Walker, S., III. "We're too cavalier about hyperactivity." *Psychology Today,* December, 1974, 43-48.

Weissbrod, C. and Bryan, J. H. "Film treatment as an effective fear reduction technique." *Journal of Abnormal Child Psychology,* 1973, 1, 196-201.

Whalen, C. K. and Henker, B. "Psychostimulants and children: A review and analysis." *Psychological Bulletin,* 1976, 83, 1113-1130.

Wolf, M. M., Giles, D. K., and Hall, R. V. "Experiments with token reinforcement in a remedial classroom." *Behaviour Research and Therapy,* 1968, 8, 51-84.

13 | To the Teacher of Learning-disabled Children

There are currently a number of popular alternative intervention programs for learning-disabled children. The self-contained classroom is a segregated setting in which the learning-disabled child is programmed with a small number of other similarly handicapped youngsters. Many children are serviced through itinerate or resource-room arrangements in which they obtain remedial help on a part-time basis while remaining in their regular elementary school setting. Some children attend private schools and others are served through university or hospital clinic programs. The mainstreaming concept of intervention is the most recent approach. This involves retaining the learning-disabled youngster in the regular classroom, with the learning disability teacher either working directly with that child in that room or helping the classroom teacher to provide appropriate materials for that child. Needless to say, we do not yet know which of these many programs the child should receive, nor which program is most effective for which child. We can say, happily, that a study of tutoring vs. classroom instruction (Bausell, Moody, and Walzl, 1972) as well as other studies of the effectiveness of intervention (Balow, 1965) have shown that special help does make a positive difference.

While teacher training and experience have not been found to be related to achievement of children, we think that teachers of learning-disabled children need a number of unique qualities. There are no empirical data of which we are aware, so this represents an indulgence in espousing our personal feelings.

The success of any type of educational program for learning-disabled children rests on the success of integrating this child into regular settings. A single major goal is maintenance of children in home and school settings or reintegration of the child into these settings. To maintain a child with severe academic and behavioral problems in his home environment is not easy. Data have been cited on the rejection of learning-disabled children by teachers and peers, and on the differences in feelings of parents of such children toward them and their siblings. Maintaining problem children in the elementary school system, or reintegrating them, requires financial and institutional support from school administrators; it often requires special help from secretaries, lunchroom attendants, and building engineers. Their support is critical. To obtain acceptance and help requires great skills in interpersonal relations on the part of the learning disability specialist.

Ombudsman

The learning-disabled child needs his own lobbyist. The learning disability specialist needs to interpret for others the learning and behavioral problems of the child. These problems are often misunderstood if not ignored. The absence of a physical defect or obvious mental retardation often results in the child's problems being misinterpreted. We have seen instances where a child has developed his own way of compensating for his learning problem (speaking aloud in order to work through a visual motor problem) only to have school personnel interpret his "talking out loud all the time" as crazy; or a teacher saying the family should not keep the child so drugged, when it was that treatment which allowed the child to attend school. The learning disability teacher has to explain to others and interpret for others the learning problems the children have, as well as be available when the teacher or parents are having problems dealing with the child.

The learning disability specialist should also be responsible for coordinating all the special and not-so-special services rendered the child. Parents are too often subjected to fragmented services from many professionals. Someone needs to integrate findings from various professional sources for the parents as well as for the school personnel.

Courage Part of being the learning-disabled child's representative involves obtaining the needed resources from the school system. When resources are in short supply, or when there is resistance to developing a learning disability program, the learning disability specialist needs to represent (vigorously) the institutional needs of the disabled children. Enlisting community/parent help is an honorable means of dealing with this problem. This is probably the most difficult kind of role for learning disability specialists to play, because they are basically sympathetic, agreeable, nice people. Fighting is antithetical to such characteristics. But sometimes it is necessary to keep uppermost the needs of the children and make a stand for the resources they deserve.

There are no guidebooks for solving the problems of learning-disabled youngsters. The answers are not there; some of the questions haven't even been asked yet. The children make progress, but it is often slow, and some children do not seem to make lasting progress. The learning problems are severe and require sustained assistance. The learning disability specialist operates in a field which requires great flexibility, the ability to work when progress is slow and maybe limited, and in a situation of great ambiguity. Are we doing the right thing? Is there another way? To work with a limited technology, to experience the consequences and the frustrations by so doing, requires courage as well.

More Courage   We are well trained to be accepting and understanding of the learning and behavioral problems of children. But learning disabilities are associated with many aversive behavioral characteristics, and it is the responsibility of the learning disability specialist to help the child to stop engaging in obnoxious behaviors. Sometimes this can be done through a loving approach, but sometimes it is much more effective to directly and actively inhibit such behaviors. For instance, learning-disabled children sometimes engage in insulting others ("You're fat, not fat like him but fat"). Training in "making friends, not enemies" is in order, and this may require toughness.

Data Collecting

Keeping records is not one of the joys of teaching, but good record-keeping has a number of important benefits. It is suggested that lesson plans be developed so that the teacher collects daily records on the specific material covered, the child's daily progress, and the test and retest data. This provides a continuous record of specifically what the child has achieved. One incentive is that carefully kept records of learning permit a continual analysis of the effectiveness of the educational program. In addition, this material provides the means to defend the program should it be challenged. The teacher is all too often "one down" on multidisciplinary team approaches to child assessment; having the data should increase the teacher's status by making the critical information he or she offers more specific for others.

No Hardening of the Categories

This field is young and the problems difficult to solve. "Keeping an open mind" and "not throwing the baby out with the bath water" are two clichés to keep in mind. It may not be easy to live with ambiguity as to the "rightness" of selected educational programs, but in this field we cannot promise the teacher a rose garden.

Finally, some comment is in order on the future of the field of learning disabilities. A major problem facing this field is the boundaries or definition of learning disabilities. On the one hand we have turned our back on the specification of brain damage as a criterion for labeling a child as having minimal cerebral dysfunction; on the other hand we may dissolve our identity as a field entirely by taking in every child with very minimal learning problems. Will we swallow general education or will general education swallow us? That is the question. It is our opinion that we must confine our concerns to children who demonstrate moderate to severe learning problems, and advise and consult on lesser difficulties. While the brain-damage approach was sufficiently limited so that we cannot return to this, we can specify the learning disability on the basis of demonstrated severe retardation in critical growth areas.

The definitional problem has yet another unfortunate consequence, one shared and sometimes neglected by other professionals. Specifically, this problem is the lack of a definition of "cures." It is not enough to devise criteria to include children or adults within a diagnostic category. On a humanitarian basis alone, it is also necessary to specify the criteria by which the individual can leave that diagnostic group when he is defined as "cured." Fields which are addressed to mental health and learning problems have traditionally failed to provide the basis by which one can be pronounced as "cured," and thereby shed some of the stigma and anguish associated with the original diagnosis. If the definition of a "pathological" condition is based upon ambiguous terms, it will render the generation of specific standards of "cures" difficult. But however difficult it may be, there should be attempts to specify exactly what conditions determine both an individual's entrance and *exit* from a diagnostic category.

Anyone who has had experience within the field of learning disabilities has probably had more than one contact with an adult who was diagnosed, at one time or another, as perceptually handicapped or learning disabled. Unfortunately, these individuals often view themselves as continuing to be disabled, in spite of their achievements in the home, business, or community. This designation is buttressed by the common experiences of being occasionally inattentive to a dull book or lecture, forgetting this or that, or committing some other action which demonstrates the fallibility of the human condition. The anguish of such people is genuine, and our failure to provide standards which allow for "cures" contributes to and sustains it. Perhaps there ought to be a law which dictates that categories should not be generated until standards are developed to allow one to escape from them.

To make progress in defining learning disabilities requires more labels, not fewer; labels which describe behaviors in very specific terms. Rather than saying a child has a perceptual motor problem, let us describe that problem (e.g., the child has difficulty writing cursive letters, or the size and shape of letters are correct but the child cannot sustain writing efforts for more than a few minutes). To get beyond overused, meaningless, generic terms (e.g., hyperactivity) requires that we collect a great deal of specific information on learning-disabled children. Ultimately, we should have the clinical knowledge base, buttressed by empirical studies, to categorize learning problems and to trace effective interventions.

Meanwhile, it is necessary not to fall prey to fads in our ideas either as to what causes or what will resolve learning problems. Careful consideration of new ideas and methods, retention of what seems to work, and evaluation of both will in time help us sort out this thing called learning disabilities.

We have been highly critical of the ideas, methods, and practices of the field of learning disabilities. We hope this critical stance will not be interpreted as a lack of sympathy. If we lacked sympathy with the goals, efforts, and concerns of the fraternity of learning disability specialists, we would not have bothered writing this text. But for a field to grow scientifically and conceptually, judicious evaluations are needed, and practitioners free of dogma need to be encouraged.

Our objective for this text was to provide information and challenges so as to prepare you to be discriminating and thereby more effective in this professional field. In the last analysis, an unthinking and uncritical practitioner is more dangerous to the field and the clients that he will serve than one who challenges dogma and is ultimately proven wrong. This is how technology grows.

Glossary

Ablation   Surgical removal.

Agnosia   Lack of sensory ability to recognize objects; associated with abnormality of the central nervous system.

Aniseikonia   A visual defect in which the image of an object seen by one eye differs in size and shape from that seen by the other eye.

Anoxia   A severe or prolonged deficiency of oxygen in the body's arterial blood, inspired gasses, or tissues, which may result in permanent damage.

Aphasia   The absence of development, or the loss or impairment of the power to use words in reading, writing, speaking, or understanding. This condition is usually the result of a brain injury.

Apraxia   A disorder of voluntary movement which causes loss or impairment of the ability to perform complex coordinated movements, and inability to make use of objects. This condition is the result of a deficiency or disorder of the central nervous system.

Astigmatism   An eye lens defect which causes a person to see blurred, imperfect images.

Ataxia   Loss of the power to coordinate voluntary muscle movements; symptomatic of some nervous disorders.

Attention   Defined as having four components; alertness, stimulus selection, focusing, and vigilance. Deficits in attention are believed to be caused by malfunction of the reticular activating system.

Auditory dyslexia   Inability to comprehend information one hears.

Autism   Absorption in self-centered mental activity such as day-dreams, fantasies, delusions, and hallucinations, especially when accompanied by a marked withdrawal from reality.

Behavior modification The technique of changing human behavior by applying the theory of operant conditioning; that is, teaching desirable behavior which operates on the environment to produce rewarding and reinforcing effects.

Brain stem Connects the spinal cord with the forebrain and cerebrum. Its parts are the medulla oblongata, the pons, the diencephalon, and the midbrain. It controls certain visceral functions and motor reflexes.

Broca's aphasia Loss of the power to express oneself by speech, writing, or signs. Also known as *expressive, motor,* or *ataxic* aphasia.

Broca's area A part of the frontal cortex associated with the production of speech.

Central aphasia A condition in which the patient has difficulty or is unable to use language for cognitive purposes such as thinking or dealing with abstract ideas.

Cerebellum A large dorsally projecting part of the brain lying below the cerebrum and above the pons and medulla oblongata. It is primarily concerned with the coordination of muscles and maintenance of bodily equilibrium.

Cerebrum The forebrain and midbrain with their derivatives. It controls the conscious mental process. The cerebrum is divided into right and left hemispheres, and four major regions or lobes: frontal, temporal, parietal, and occipital.

Cognitive-behavior modification (CBM) A remediation approach which combines a number of principles from learning theory, in particular reinforcement, modeling, and verbal rehearsal.

Conduction aphasia With this affliction the patient can speak or write in a way, but skips or repeats words or substitutes one word for another. The defect results from a lesion in the association tracts connecting the various language centers.

Conceptualization Making abstractions and categories; considered by some educators the highest level of learning.

Corpus callosum The major fiber tract which connects the right and left sides of the brain.

Cross-modality perception Neurological process of transferring information received through one sense or input modality to another system within the brain.

Decoding In relation to learning to read, decoding is determining the relationship between oral language sounds and written letters.

Dichotic Affecting or relating to the two ears differently in regard to a conscious aspect (such as pitch or loudness) or a physical aspect (such as frequency or energy) of sound.

Disinhibition The revival of an extinguished conditioned response by an unconditioned stimulus; the inhibition of an inhibition.

Distractibility Being abnormally affected by external stimuli; easily diverted or confused by inconsequential occurrences.

Dysarthria   Disturbance of articulation due to emotional stress or to paralysis, incoordination, or spasticity of the muscles used for speaking.

Dyscalculia   A deficit in the ability to manipulate mathematical symbols, usually as a result of neurological dysfunction.

Dyseidetic dyslexia   In this condition the patient has difficulty remembering the appearance of letters or words; but can read phonetically, by sounding out combinations of letters.

Dysgraphia   Difficulty in performing the motor movements needed for handwriting; often attributed to neurological dysfunction.

Dyslexia   A disorder in which a person fails to learn to read in spite of adequate intelligence and proper instruction; implies neurological dysfunction.

Dysphasia   The inability to speak; loss of or deficiency in the ability to use or understand language as a result of injury to or disease of the brain.

Dysphonetic dyslexia   A condition in which the patient has a limited sight vocabulary; can read only a small number of words, and has great difficulty deciphering new words.

Echolalia   Imitative repetition of words spoken by another person; echoing them without understanding their meaning.

Electroencephalograph (EEG)   Instrument for graphically recording and measuring electrical energy generated by the cerebral cortex during brain functioning; produces a tracing of brain waves called an electroencephalogram.

EMR   The educable mentally retarded.

Etiology   All of the causes of a disease or abnormal condition; a branch of knowledge dealing with causes.

Expressive dyslexia   Difficulty in writing.

Facial apraxia   The inability to move facial muscles voluntarily in the absence of weakness or paralysis.

False negative   Inaccurately low scores on a poorly prepared test which misdiagnoses a person as *not* having disabilities or personality problems, when in fact he *does* have them.

False positive   High test score on a poorly prepared test which incorrectly measures a person's characteristics, implying that he *has* attributes which he does *not* have.

Field dependence   Inability to organize what one sees because of being strongly affected by irrelevant features in the perceptual field. This problem is characteristic of persons who are unable to be attentive.

FLK (funny-looking kid) syndrome   Children with physiognomic abnormalities of a type also associated with schizophrenia and mental retardation.

Frontal lobe   The anterior division of each cerebral hemisphere.

Gene   The functional unit of heredity; an element of the germ plasm, capable of self-reproduction, that transmits hereditary characteristics by specifying the structure of a particular protein or by controlling the function of other genetic material.

Gerstmann syndrome An hypothesized complex disorder of cerebral function due to brain damage which is presumed to be associated with difficulty in reading, space-form disability, left-to-right disorientation, dyscalculia, dysgraphia, and finger agnosia.

Grapheme Unit or symbol (as a letter) of a writing system.

Graphical dyscalculia A condition in which the patient has difficulty writing mathematical symbols.

Gyrus A convolution on the surface of the cerebral hemisphere.

Heuristic Providing aid or direction in solving a problem, but otherwise unjustified; related to exploratory problem-solving techniques.

Holophrastic Expressing a complex of ideas in a single word or a fixed phrase. The term "holophrastic speech" is used to describe the idea that very young children may express complex ideas in their first single words.

Hyperactivity Motor behavior which is unnecessary to the situation or task at hand, and disruptive to others.

Hyperkinesia Abnormally increased and usually purposeless, uncontrollable muscular movement.

Hyperopia Farsightedness, caused by an eye lens defect in which the visual image comes to a focus behind the retina instead of on it.

Hypoglycemia Abnormal decrease of sugar in the blood, characterized by hunger, nervousness, profuse sweating, faintness, and sometimes convulsions.

Hypokinesis Diminished or slow movement.

Ideognostical dyscalculia The patient with this problem has trouble understanding mathematical ideas and doing mental calculations.

Imagery The capacity to remember or recall a sensation.

Impulsivity Behavior which appears to reflect little thinking concerning its consequences; making quick and often erroneous judgements.

Inadequate fusion A defect in which, during a single perception, the two eyes see an object at different distances away instead of at the same distance.

Increment Increase in quantity or value; a minute increase in quantity; a positive or negative change in value of one or more of a set of variables.

Lesion An abnormal change in structure of an organ or part due to injury or disease.

Lexical dyscalculia This condition is characterized by problems in reading mathematical symbols; for example, numbers or operation signs.

Mainstreaming Placing of learning-disabled children in the regular school system, particularly in the regular classroom.

Maturational lag A time lag in the development of some skills relative to others.

Minimal brain dysfunction A mild neurological abnormality causing learning difficulties in a person with near-average intelligence.

Mixed aphasia   A condition in which the patient has problems in both the comprehension and expression of language; a combination of motor and sensory aphasia.

Mixed dysphonetic-dyseidetic dyslexia   The patient with this condition, referred to as a "hard-core dyslexic," lacks both visual and auditory abilities to understand the written word. Without intensive help he will remain a nonreader.

Mnemonic   Assisting or intended to assist memory; of or relating to memory.

Modality   Pathways through which a person receives information and learns; thus, various forms of sensation such as touch, hearing, or vision.

Model   An example to imitate or emulate; something set before one for guidance, as a pattern or ideal.

Morpheme   Any of the smallest meaningful linguistic units in a language.

Morphology   The linguistic system of meaningful units in a language.

Movigenics   A theory developed by Raymond Barsch concerned with the maturation of movement, and particularly children's motor development.

Myelination, myelinization   The bodily process by which an outer sheath develops to cover and protect the nerves.

Myopia   Nearsightedness, caused by an eye lens defect in which the visual image comes to a focus in front of rather than on the retina.

Number blindness   Failure to recognize a number.

Nystagmus   A conjugate rhythmic oscillation of the eyeballs, either horizontal, vertical, or rotary.

Occipital lobe   The posterior lobe of the cerebrum that processes visual information.

Open class words   One of two classes of words used by very young children, about eighteen months old. Examples of such words are "daddy" or "mama," which may be used alone, or either preceded or followed by a pivot class word, such as "my."

Operant conditioning   The theory that desirable human behavior can be taught by a system of rewarding and reinforcing good behavior and ignoring or punishing undesirable responses.

Operational dyscalculia   A condition in which the patient has difficulty carrying out mathematical operations.

Paradigm   An outstandingly clear or typical example or archetype; a pattern.

Parietal lobe   The middle division of each cerebral hemisphere, which processes information from sensory receptors.

Perception   The brain's process of interpreting the raw data received through the various senses.

Perceptual-motor impairment   A condition in which a person has difficulty coordinating his perceptions with his motor activities.

Perseveration   Behavior in which a person is unable to change the focus of his attention or stop an activity once it is started, even when he wants to do so.

Phoneme   Any of the smallest units of speech in a language.

Phonics   Technique in teaching reading in which the sounds (letters, letter groups, and syllables) of a language are associated with the equivalent written symbols.

Phonology   The study of speech sounds, how they are produced and combined.

Phrenology   The study of the conformation of the skull based on the the belief that this indicates mental faculties and character.

Pivot class words   One of two classes of words used by very young children, and always accompanied by an open class word. An example of a pivot class word is "my."

Population   A body of persons or individuals having a certain known quality or characteristic in common.

Practognostic dyscalculia   This problem renders the patient unable to manipulate symbols or objects for mathematical purposes.

Psycholinguistics   The study of linguistic behavior as conditioning and conditioned by psychological factors.

Psychometrics   The psychological theory or technique of mental measurement.

Receptive dyslexia   Difficulty in understanding what one reads.

Reticular activating system   A diffuse network of fibers which begins in the spinal cord, enlarges in the brain stem, and connects with many other parts of the brain.

Scatter   Variability in an individual's test scores.

Semantics   The study of word meanings.

Sensorimotor   Relating to both the input of sensations and the output of motor activities.

Simultagnosia   A form of visual agnosia in which the patient is able to perceive parts of a pattern or picture but fails to recognize the meaning of the whole.

Sociolinguistic   Of or relating to the social aspects of language.

Special education services   Educational and/or remedial teaching designed for learning-disabled children and taught by especially trained instructors; may be tailor-made for the individual child.

Stereognosis   The faculty of recognizing the size and shape of objects by the sense of touch.

Strabismus   A "squint" caused by imbalance of the eyeball muscles. In this condition one eye cannot, at the same time, look at the same object which the other eye is looking at.

Strauss syndrome   A group of behavioral characteristics; namely, hyperactivity, distractibility, or disinhibition.

Strephosymbolia   Mirror vision; reversal in direction of reading; failure to distinguish between similar letters such as p and q, or n and u.

Sulcus   A shallow furrow on the surface of the brain, separating the adjacent convolutions or gyri.

Symbolization   The ability to verbally label sensations, perceptions, and images; man's capacity to develop a system of meaningful symbols.

Synchrony   Execution of simultaneous movements.

Synkinesis   Involuntary movement accompanying a voluntary one, such as the movement of a closed eye following that of the open eye, or swinging of the arms while walking.

Syntactical   Relating to or according to the rules of syntax; the way in which words are put together to form phrases, clauses, and sentences.

Tachistoscope   An apparatus for the brief exposure of visual stimuli that is used in the study of learning, attention, and perception.

Taxonomy   Orderly scientific classification, according to presumed natural relationships.

Telegraphic speech   The first multiple word combinations a very young child uses, in which some words are omitted, as in a telegram. For example, the child might say "doggie ball" instead of "the dog has the ball."

Temporal lobe   A part of the cerebral cortex associated with processing of auditory stimuli.

Token economy   A behavior modification program in which the teacher gives the child a token as a reward for desired behavior. When the child accumulates enough tokens he may exchange them for one of several valued objects.

Verbal dyscalculia   Those afflicted have difficulty both in understanding oral presentation of mathematics and in giving oral responses to mathematical questions.

Vigilance   Ability to sustain one's efforts to complete a task; alert watchfulness.

Visual agnosia   A loss of spatial organization and visual discrimination.

Visual aphasia   The inability to name objects even though they are perceived.

Visual dyslexia   Inability to understand stimuli presented visually.

Wernicke's aphasia   Loss of the ability to comprehend speech; a combination of word deafness and visual aphasia.

Test Index

DIAGNOSTIC AND ACHIEVEMENT TESTS

AUDITORY SKILLS, LANGUAGE, READING, AND MATHEMATICS TESTS

Index